RELATED KAPLAN BOOKS

College Admissions and Financial Aid

Parent's Guide to College Admissions
Scholarships
The Unofficial, Unbiased Guide to the 328 Most Interesting Colleges

Test Preparation

ACT
SAT 1600
AP Biology
AP Calculus AB
AP Chemistry
AP English Language & Composition
AP English Literature & Composition
AP Macroeconomics/Microeconomics
AP Physics B
AP Statistics
AP U.S. Government & Politics
AP U.S. History
Ring of McAllister
SAT & PSAT
SAT Math Mania
SAT Math Workbook
SAT II: Biology
SAT II: Chemistry
SATII: Literature
SAT II: Mathematics Levels IC and IIC
SAT II: Physics
SAT II: Spanish
SAT II: U.S. History
SAT II: World History
SAT II: Writing
SAT Verbal Velocity
SAT Verbal Workbook
SAT Vocabulary Flashcards: Flip-O-Matic
Smart Girl's Guide to the SAT

STRAIGHT TALK ON PAYING FOR COLLEGE:
Lowering the Cost of Higher Education

by Trent Anderson and Seppy Basili
with Allen Plummer

Simon & Schuster

NEW YORK · LONDON · SINGAPORE · SYDNEY · TORONTO

Kaplan Publishing
Published by Simon & Schuster
1230 Avenue of the Americas
New York, NY 10020

For bulk sales to schools, colleges, and universities, please contact Order Department, Simon & Schuster, 100 Front Street, Riverside, NJ 08075. Phone: 1-800-223-2336. Fax: 1-800-943-9831.

Kaplan® is a registered trademark of Kaplan, Inc.

Editor: Larissa Shmailo
Educational Research Manager: Jessica Shapiro
Cover Design: Cheung Tai
Interior Page Design and Production: Hugh Haggerty
Production Editor: Jessica Shapiro
Production Manager: Michael Shevlin
Managing Editor: Déa Alessandro
Executive Editor: Del Franz

Special thanks to Angela Cress, Laurel Douglas, and Rudy Robles

Manufactured in the United States of America
Published simultaneously in Canada

September 2003
10 9 8 7 6 5 4 3 2 1

ISBN: 0-7432-4109-6

TABLE OF CONTENTS

TRENT & SEPPY SAY...

Hi, we're Trent and Seppy, and we're here to offer you some straight talk about (gulp!) paying for college. Let's face it: To make smart decisions about how to pay for your student's (or plural, students'!) education, you need more than just wishful thinking. And you don't need to face what may look like an overwhelming maze of forms, loans, tax information, and ever-growing college costs alone. So we created *Straight Talk on Paying for College:* financial aid and money management strategies you can use written in plain language and presented in simple, step-by-step terms. And we threw in some laughs (yes, it's not all bad news!) to help you through this process. You deserve it!

Want to figure out what the real cost of college will be for your family? We broke down the costs, direct and indirect, including all those "miscellaneous" items you may not have thought of, and asked parents of college-age students—real people like you—how they paid them. Want to know how to apply for financial aid and get the best package? We asked financial aid officers at some of the nation's top colleges to tell us. Want tips on saving for college and what tax breaks may be out there for you? We've given you the latest on 529 plans, Education Savings plans, and tuition tax credits. Want to know how to pay the bills that financial aid won't cover? We show you your options for meeting your share—without going broke.

And of course, we've also included our own personal advice and insights throughout this book. Why should you listen to us? During our careers, we've worked with thousands of families, helping them with financial aid advice, test prep, and college admissions. Our comments are based on our own experience and what we've learned by speaking to students, their parents, and college personnel throughout the years.

So relax (it's okay!). We'll take you through the steps, with checklists at the end of each chapter to keep you on your way. We'll point out the mistakes that others have made, and help you avoid them. And we'll save you some money, too. Now, that's not bad!

Trent Anderson is the Vice President for Education at Cablevision, Inc., where he oversees the "Power to Learn" initiative. Before joining Cablevision, Trent was the Vice President of Publishing for Kaplan, Inc., where he developed book projects for the education market. During his 10 years with Kaplan, Trent was a test prep instructor, admissions advisor, financial aid expert, and author and contributing editor of several books, including *Once Upon a Campus, The Unofficial, Unbiased Guide to the 328 Most Interesting Colleges,* and Kaplan's precollege and pregrad school test prep titles. Trent spent his college years in Southern California, where he earned his bachelor's degree at UCLA and his J.D. and M.B.A. at the University of Southern California. Prior to working at Kaplan, Inc., Trent taught undergraduate business law at the University of Southern California.

Seppy Basili, Kaplan's resident "College Guru," has been analyzing college trends for more than 15 years. During his Kaplan career, Seppy has overseen Kaplan's test preparation programs and publications for the SAT, ACT, and PSAT exams as well as college admissions services. Along with Trent Anderson, he is the co-author of *Once Upon a Campus* and *The Unofficial, Unbiased Guide to the 328 Most Interesting Colleges.* He also founded the Kaplan-Newsweek imprint publications, which include the annual How to Get Into College guide. Seppy has spent many years on college campuses, receiving his B.A. from Kenyon College, M.Ed. from the University of California—Berkeley, and J.D. from Emory University.

As a financial journalist, co-author **Allen Plummer** has written for Bloomberg, Morningstar, AOL/Time Warner, The Bureau of National Affairs, and Thomson Media. He regularly contributes to several financial trade publications. A graduate of Virginia Commonwealth University, he plans to return to school for his MBA in the near future. Allen lives in Richmond, Virginia with his wife, Sara.

This book was reviewed by **Jade Kolb**, financial aid manager for New York University, who served as a consultant in its production.

PART ONE

THE
FINANCIAL AID CHALLENGE

CHAPTER ONE

Getting Started

"One of the most important contacts you can make at your student's college is the financial aid office."
—*Connie Gores, vice president for enrollment, Randolph-Macon Woman's College*

Odds are, you've picked up this book because you have a child who's getting ready to go to college. You've probably looked at some schools, flipped through a few college catalogs and viewbooks, and tried to get a sense of what this grand, life-changing experience for your student is going to cost.

Then again, maybe you've been afraid to find out. (If so, we can't say we blame you.) The truth is, there's good news and bad news. Since most people prefer to get the bad news over with, we might as well get that out of the way.

Unfortunately, the cost of a higher education is rising every year and will almost certainly continue to do so in the future. Just as the costs of cars and homes have increased over the past decades, so has the cost of attending college.

(Our apologies if that last sentence was difficult to read, but we promise it gets better.)

> **Starting Early**
>
> "I suggest students and families visit a financial aid office as early as eighth grade, or when the student is a freshman in high school," offers Jack Toney, director of financial aid at Marshall University. "It gives families a chance to get an overview of what to expect to pay for college, and they'll have a few years to prepare."

THERE IS HELP

The good news is that there's help all over the place if you know where to look. The government, businesses, foundations, and even universities offer ways to help manage and reduce the cost of getting a higher education. Despite the price, there are people who can and want to help you and your student afford college. After all, getting a college degree not only benefits your student, but the rest of society as well.

And lucky you—you've already found one source of help. This book was created solely to help you and your son or daughter understand and get through the process of finding and applying for financial aid. But before we dive in, there are a few things you should know up front.

Look at Financial Aid

"Families should look at financial aid offices when comparing universities," says Jade Kolb, manager of financial aid at New York University. "They should ask questions such as, how long are lines for requests, and is it easy to speak with someone on the phone? These kinds of inquiries give you a good idea of how helpful a financial aid office can be."

GETTING A GAME PLAN

First, this isn't a weekend project. There's a reason we compared college to buying a home or car, and that's because it takes the same amount of time, effort, and planning. Most people wouldn't buy a car without some shopping around and number crunching, and you certainly wouldn't buy a house without doing research. The same should be true for college. Since your student's education will likely cost as much as a new car (or even a house!), doesn't it make sense to put as much time and energy into the process as you would for those decisions?

Also, you'll be glad to know that your student will need to become involved in this process. Although you may claim them as dependents on your income taxes, you can't do this alone. There are going to be plenty of discussions and decisions that will involve talking (gasp!) to your son or daughter. Affording college is about things like budgets, living expenses, and spending money. Getting your student involved will help them realize the financial burden of college. And if you're lucky, they may take their education more seriously as a result.

After the Fact

"People think they can get money later in the process, so often a student gets in, then the family asks for financial aid after the fact," says Ellen Frishberg, director of Student Financial Services, Johns Hopkins University. "It happens all the time."

Finally, this book will encourage you to be proactive. Not only will we explain the process and use the real life experience of other parents to help you understand how it works, but we've created a number of things to nudge you along the way. At the end of this chapter, you'll find a calendar to help pace yourself for going through the financial aid process. While we don't live in a perfect world, it represents an ideal timeline for getting things done. We've also included short checklists at the end of each chapter to suggest things you and your student should be doing along the way. They're by no means comprehensive, but it's a good place to start. A handful of worksheets and tables will help make life easier than guessing and estimating costs in your head. We've also done a lot of legwork to find other resources so you don't have to. Websites, phone numbers, and contacts are plentiful throughout this book, so you'll always have places to find additional information.

YOU ARE NOT ALONE

Remember you're not alone in this process; millions of other American families are going through the same steps and facing the same problems. Even financial aid officers send their kids to college. "My daughter is a senior in high school, and I've been helping her friends' families compare their aid packages," says Connie Gores, vice president for enrollment at Randolph-Macon Woman's College and parent of a high school senior. "There's a lot of confusion and incorrect assumptions out there. A lot of parents also don't understand the differences between a public and private college. Also, I'm learning that a lot of families don't understand the financial aid process, so there really are a lot of people out there that need help and guidance." She adds, "The one thing that surprised me, even being in this field, is the anxiety this process can create. There's an immense amount of pressure on students and families during the whole process, and I never realized it until I went through it myself."

There may be times when dealing with financial aid feels like balancing your checkbook, doing your taxes, and taking a test all at once. Understanding the process is half the battle. When it comes to financial aid, knowledge is power, and this book will give you the information and guidance you need to make the best decisions to help you pay for the best possible education your son or daughter can have—without going to the poorhouse.

> ## TRENT & SEPPY SAY...
>
> **Trent:**
>
> *Depending on where you live, some college financial aid officers come to speak at high schools and educate parents.*
>
> **Seppy:**
>
> *West Virginia, for example, has a state program to do just that. In fact, Marshall University, in Huntington, WV, encourages students as young as high school freshmen to come in with their parents and learn how to prepare for college!*

MOVING ON

In the next chapter, we'll tackle the reality of financial aid, and separate the myths from the facts (and it's not all bad news!). We'll also discuss some misconceptions to help you learn the truth about financial aid.

✓ CHECKLIST:

1. Review the following financial aid calendar. The information in this book will guide you through this process, so set up a schedule for working through it chapter by chapter that works for you.

2. Attend "College Nights." The majority of high schools in this country hold evenings when representatives and alumni from various universities come to your high school. These events give you an opportunity not only to learn about the colleges, but possibly get some preliminary financial aid information.

FINANCIAL AID CALENDAR

August
- Begin looking and applying for scholarships and grants.
- Begin talking about the types of colleges you might be interested in.
- Create or narrow your list of prospective schools, including dream and safety colleges.
- Request applications and catalogs from prospective colleges.
- Create folders for prospective colleges.
- If necessary, take the SAT again.

September
- Begin asking for letters of recommendation for college applications.
- Compare the costs of colleges in your state, as well as other states your student is interested in.
- Begin looking at your family's budget, and find ways to save money or cut expenses in light of upcoming college costs.
- Find out which financial aid applications your prospective colleges require, and request them.

October
- Continue looking and applying for scholarships and grants.
- Attend College Night at your high school.
- Visit prospective colleges and financial aid offices.
- Complete a Cost of Attending worksheet for each school you are considering.
- Register for the CSS Profile (if necessary).
- Contact your state's higher education agency to find out what state grants and loans are available.
- Request paperwork for any programs you are interested in.

November
- Send in Early Decision application, if applicable.
- Contact your employer to determine if your student will continue to be covered under your insurance.
- Review your investments to find ways to help pay for college. If you have a financial advisor, meet with them to begin planning for college costs.

December
- Continue looking and applying for scholarships and grants.
- Begin educating yourself about various types of student loans.
- Fill out and file CSS Profile form, if necessary.

January
- Complete and file federal income taxes.
- Submit your FAFSA as soon as possible.
- Complete admissions applications.
- Complete any state, institutional, and other financial aid forms necessary.

February
- Continue looking and applying for scholarships and grants.
- Call each potential college to verify that your applications and financial aid information are complete.
- Begin contacting lenders about various types of student loans. Compare rates and terms for later use.

March
- Review your SAR, and make corrections if necessary.
- Provide verification information to colleges, if necessary.
- If you're interested, request and complete the necessary forms for calculating Federal Methodology and Institutional Methodology, either in paper or online.

April
- Continue looking and applying for scholarships and grants.
- Begin receiving award letters and financial aid packages from colleges. (Be sure to note deadlines for acceptance.)
- Compare packages, and negotiate offers if necessary.
- If your student has received any outside or private aid, notify your colleges and find out if it will impact aid packages.
- Accept award package from the college you'll be attending.
- Notify other colleges you will not be attending.

May
- Watch for housing information from your college, as well as other financial aid paperwork.
- Contact the college your student is attending to find out key dates in the payment cycle.
- Request information about your college's tuition payment plan.

June
- Continue looking and applying for scholarships and grants.
- Make sure final high school transcript is sent to your college (if necessary).
- Research various types of loans to determine which is best for you and your student.
- Complete loan paperwork and prepare to pay tuition bill in near future.

July
- Receive and pay tuition bill from college.

CHAPTER TWO

Financial Aid— Myth Versus Fact

When was the last time you bought something at full price? If you're like most people, the answer may take a little bit of thought. As Americans, we are a nation of bargain seekers and coupon clippers, and as such, companies know that with all the options out there, they'd better give us a good reason to put down our hard earned cash for their product.

It's not surprising, then, that we live in a society of discounts. Televisions and radios bombard us with ads proclaiming "no money down," "no payments for twelve months," or "get 50 percent off." To make things even more interesting, the Internet has become a great tool in increasing people's buying power. Comparison websites and online services mean that hardly anyone need pay full price these days.

And although colleges don't always advertise, a wonderful similarity exists.

Almost no one pays the full cost of a college education, which is a good thing since the skyrocketing cost of a higher education may cost as much as your home. Of course, if you've already seen the figures for your prospective colleges, you're well aware of this. Let's take a look at what drives these rising costs.

WHY IS COLLEGE SO EXPENSIVE?

Over the past few years, our economy has faced increases in unemployment, large drops in the stock market, significant international policy issues, and just about any other type of money problem you could name. As 2003 started, almost every state in the nation faced budget cuts from the federal government. As you're probably aware, this has impacted the amount of money states passed on to colleges. In turn, these colleges were forced to make do with less money by cutting expenditures and raising the cost of tuition and expenses. To make a long story short, college is more expensive than ever before.

But what you may not know is that it's not necessarily that simple. The cost of going to college continues to rise because of a number of factors:

- Just as higher energy prices means a higher electric bill for you, colleges are also paying more for utilities. As campuses grow in size and student populations increase, more money is needed for maintenance, food, and housing. And of course, colleges compete for students by offering high quality educations, so any cost that will keep a school competitive is a priority.

- As our economy takes a hit, alumni are less likely to donate to their alma mater. Foundations that support universities through regular donations have found themselves with less money to give. Corporations that may support college programs or pay for new buildings have found they can't afford to make such gestures when their business is suffering.

Public Problems

College tuition and fees at public universities increased as much as 24 percent from 2001–2002 to 2002–2003.

Source: National Center for Public Policy and Higher Education

THE BARGAINS

- San Diego State University's in-state tuition is $2,014 and out-of-state tuition is $8,902 (2002–3).
- CUNY John Jay School of Criminal Justice is $3,309 in-state and $6,509 out-of state (2002–3).
- University of California schools have no in-state tuition–but look out for fees that hike them up to numbers like $4,200 (Berkeley) and $4,378 (Los Angeles).
- Berea College is a Christian college in Appalachia which requires all students to work on campus but gives everyone a full scholarship for tuition.
- The College of the Ozarks provides mandatory student work and private/federal scholarships to make it "free" for everyone.
- Cooper Union students get full tuition scholarships.
- At military academies like West Point and Annapolis your degree is "free"–except for service commitments of five years or more.

YES, THIS IS ONLY FOR ONE YEAR . . .

- Kenyon University $30,330 (2003–04).
- Sarah Lawrence $29,360 (2002–3), (George Washington University $29,350, (2003–4).
- MIT $29,130 (2002–3).
- Washington University in St. Louis $29,053 (2003–4).

Universities need to offer salaries that attract well-established researchers and professors with terminal degrees (Ph.D.s, M.B.A.s, and J.D.s). Just as businesses today need I.T. professionals, improvements in college technology require a knowledgeable workforce to maintain and fix it. Administrative and legal needs continue to grow as colleges must comply with the ever-changing and complex state and federal regulatory requirements. Any addition, change, or improvement to a college results in some kind of increased expense.

And perhaps most importantly, the growing expectations of a higher education push colleges to continue spending. No longer is it acceptable for a college's library to be open until 10 or 11 P.M. Instead, libraries are often open 24 hours a day. Likewise, it's not enough to have each dorm room wired for telephones and dial-up Internet access; when it comes to a college's technology, things like DSL connections are rapidly becoming the norm. "As a college, if you don't offer those things, then you're not able to compete with other schools," explains Karen Krause, director of financial aid at the University of Texas at Arlington. "The expectations are already there. Unfortunately, none of these costs are included in financial aid."

These expectations for improved libraries, athletic facilities worthy of a pro football team, cutting-edge technology, sophisticated laboratories, and top-notch student centers all are causing schools to spend more money each year, as funding from both public and private sources continues to drop. "It's going to get very interesting," continues Krause, "Texas is facing budget shortfalls at the same time colleges here are experiencing growth in enrollment. If things continue, at some point it will have to reflect service." It has already been reflected in tuition.

While all these factors aren't going to affect the process of applying for financial aid, it will be to your benefit to stay informed about them. As someone with a son or daughter in college, things like state education cuts, college programs, and teacher salaries will affect how much you pay for your student's education. And as someone who pays for these things, your opinion matters.

THE MYTHS OF FINANCIAL AID

Have you ever started your car and thought, "I've got plenty of gas," only to have the engine cut off minutes later? How about writing a check as you tell yourself, "There's probably enough in the account to cover it," only to have the check bounce days later?

At one time or another, we've all made assumptions that turn out be wrong, and although you may not realize it, people make assumptions about financial aid that are incorrect as well. Just as bouncing a check can cause frustration and headaches, so can believing these myths. So to save yourself trouble and worry down the road, let's clarify these assumptions.

Do you expect financial aid to pay for everything?

Financial aid is just what it claims to be—assistance. By assuming that government and state financial aid programs will pay 100 percent of your son's or daughter's education, you're making a dangerous error. The purpose of these programs is to help people afford college, which is completely different from saying, "I can't afford college, so the government will have to pay for it." Parents and students who think this way are in for a harsh wake-up call.

Do you rely on financial aid to afford college?

This is a common assumption, even though most families qualify for some sort of financial aid. The problem is, right now you don't know how much financial aid you'll receive. If you're fortunate, your son or daughter may have a significant amount of their education paid for through scholarships, loans, and/or grants. Other families find that financial aid covers only half, if not less, of the cost of college. So while expecting financial aid is one thing, relying on it to cover the majority of expenses associated with your student's college experience is risky.

"Many families I've talked to don't think about financial aid until after they receive their aid packages," explains Connie Gores, vice president for enrollment for Randolph-Macon Woman's College. "Once they get them, then they want to know how they can get additional assistance. They didn't consider aid as part of the application process."

Do you expect to make a financial sacrifice for your student's education?

Financial aid is based upon your family's ability to pay for school, not how much you're willing to pay. As you'll soon find out, state and federal programs use your income tax to determine how much financial aid you qualify for. To do this, they determine your Expected Family Contribution (EFC) using these numbers. The EFC is your responsibility for your student's education, and financial aid provides assistance in covering part, most, or all of the difference. So even though you may disagree with your EFC, it's non-negotiable. Just as you can't change your tax rate because you need the extra money, you can't change your EFC because you don't have the money handy.

"A big misconception is that your EFC is what you'll pay for college, and that's really not true," says Jade Kolb, manager of financial aid for New York University. "It's a government analysis, and it may be the same as the amount you'll pay, or it could be more or less depending on the school."

The Department of Education is planning to change federal EFC calculation in fall of 2004. Not surprisingly, the change is going to cost you and your student money. See chapter eight for more information on this important development.

Do you assume your financial status doesn't matter to colleges?

The good news is that to some, it does. Currently, federal and state financial aid programs are not able to keep up with the rising cost of education. An increasing number of colleges recognize the impact this has on lower-income families and consider a family's financial status before awarding financial aid. This practice is called "need aware," while colleges that do not use a family's financial status are considered "need blind." Also, many schools that are need blind offer merit-based aid as a way of providing financial aid to top students regardless of their families' income.

The main reason for clarifying these myths is so you won't make any costly and frustrating decisions down the road. The bottom line is, instead of making assumptions about financial aid, you should prepare to contribute as much as you can to your student's education. (We'll help you figure out how to do this later on, so don't worry.)

> ## TRENT & SEPPY SAY...
>
> **Trent:**
>
> *Your Expected Family Contribution (EFC) is going to be one of the most important parts of the financial aid process, so you'll hear the term often throughout the book. Remember that "EFC" simply means the amount you're expected to pay for college.*
>
> **Seppy:**
>
> *I always thought EFC meant "Every Final Cent."*

STICKER SHOCK

Colleges are like cars...sort of. Coming to this realization is a lot like going car shopping. You see something you like, you look inside, kick the tires, and maybe take it for a test drive. But once you take a glance at the price sticker on the side window, your heart almost stops beating, you gasp, and begin to wonder just how long it would take to bicycle to work.

It's called sticker shock, and once you see the cost of tuition and board at your student's favorite university, you'll probably feel the same way. It used to be that the most expensive purchases a family could make would be a house and a car. Today, it's a house and college, with a car just behind them. In fact, according to the College Board, which administers the SAT exams, the annual cost of attending a four-year public university in 2002 was $9,663 for a student who lived on campus. Students who lived on campus at a private college averaged $18,273. Multiply that times fours years of school, and you could spend $73,092 on your student's education.

But don't panic. When sticker shock happens to car shoppers, they almost immediately remember their trade-in, which reduces the price of a new car significantly. They also begin deciding what options they can do without—leather interior, air conditioning, that computer voice telling you that your car door is open. Factor in special rates, discounts, and dealer reductions, and the difference between a car's sticker price and what you'd actually pay can be quite different.

The same is going to be true for college, without the salesmen, balloons, or haggling. Instead of having a trade-in, you and your son or daughter will have financial aid to reduce the cost you're quoted. Just as you may do without leather seats, your son or daughter might be able to do without things like the most expensive meal plan or a telephone in his or her dorm room. Also, discounts and reductions are available to some students in the form of grants or scholarships. So take a closer look at all your prospective colleges, and don't dismiss any one on the sticker price alone.

Tuition Guesstimates

Many parents misjudge tuition costs by as much as 50 percent in either direction, according to a 2003 Harris Poll.

The Flip Side of the Coin

However, the unfortunate reality for most families is that cost is a very real factor in college decisions. "Wait a minute," you're probably thinking. "Didn't I just read that I shouldn't dismiss a college based on cost?" Yes, you did, but it's important to understand that these two statements don't contradict each other.

Samuel Ellison, a student employment manager and financial aid adviser at Morehouse College notes that it's financial aid that plays a factor in affording college, not cost. If you toss out a prospective school based on cost alone, you'll never find out if your student will be offered scholarships, receive a significant amount of financial aid, or what financial aid doors may open to her. In other words, a college that's much more expensive than your other prospective schools may offer more financial aid to make themselves competitive. But you'll never find out if your student doesn't apply there.

The bottom line is, don't let cost alone keep your student from applying to that expensive school. But once the acceptance letters arrive and you start getting financial aid offers, then you'll have to look at the reality of what your family can afford. We'll go into more detail about this later, but for now, remember to keep your options open.

MOVING ON

To wrap up, we began by looking at the current financial state of colleges, so that you'll have a better understanding of why college seems to be so expensive, and why it may keep getting more costly. We debunked a few myths about financial aid, but also looked at how almost no one pays the full price of college. To explain this, we compared colleges to cars, discussing the difference between a "sticker price" and what students and families actually pay. And although cost alone should not keep a student from applying to a school, we acknowledged that it's a very real and important factor for almost everyone when going through this process.

In the next chapter, we'll look at the different college options open to your son and daughter, and discuss the decisions involved and how to factor costs and aid into the equation. We'll look at the different types of schools, including "dream schools" and financial safety schools. We'll discuss how to get your son or daughter involved in all aspects of the decision-making process, including the financial ones. But before you move on, take a look at the checklist for this chapter.

✓ CHECKLIST:

1. Begin educating yourself about the financial issues facing universities. For example
   - Is your state planning on cutting back university funding?
   - Are tuitions expected to increase drastically in the next few years?

   Changes taking place now may affect your son's or daughter's education as early as next year, and it helps to be informed.

2. Begin looking at your family's budget, and find ways to save money or cut expenses in light of upcoming college costs. For example
   - Can you put money aside each month to help with college?
   - Are there expenses that can be reduced or cut to help out?

3. Contact all your potential colleges to determine if their financial aid is need aware or need blind. If they are need aware, ask for information or request any additional forms that might be necessary. Keep notes of your findings.

WEBSITES

FinAid
www.finaid.org

U.S. Department of Education—Student Guide to Financial Aid
www.ed.gov

EdFund
www.edfund.org

SallieMae
www.salliemae.com

NellieMae
www.nelliemae.com

National Association of Student Financial Aid Administrators
www.nasfaa.org

Financial Aid/Admission Awareness Month
www.faam.org

KAPLAN

## CHAPTER THREE

Finding the Best Value

Although you may not realize it, there are many different kinds of colleges, each creating a different financial picture for your family. The first decision your son or daughter will have to make is what kind of college he or she wants to go to. We'll look at the options, including the best values for your student's goals and your bank account.

TYPES OF COLLEGES

In the broadest sense, college is simply where your student will go after high school to continue his or her education. From this view, there are three basic kinds of schools your student could attend: a traditional four-year college, a career college (or trade school), or a community college.

Four-Year Schools

The traditional American college is a four-year institution accredited by a recognized accrediting agency (this means the school has passed a review and meets certain standards of educational quality). These schools offer a bachelor of arts (B.A.) or bachelor of science (B.S.) degree.

Public versus Private

Four-year schools are either public or private, and the two are very similar with one exception. Public colleges and universities receive substantial financial support from state and federal governments through tax dollars. Private colleges and universities may or may not; when they do, they usually receive less than public institutions. With some notable exceptions, you'll find few basic differences between public and private colleges, except for the cost. Private colleges are usually much more expensive than public ones, with higher student fees and tuition making up for the loss in government aid. However, with states facing budget shortfalls, public schools are now raising tuitions at a higher rate than private schools.

Public and Private College Tuitions— 2002–2003 versus 2001–2002

- At 4-year private institutions, tuition and fees averaged $18,273, up from $17,272 (a 5.8% increase).
- At 4-year public institutions, tuition and fees averaged $4,081, up from $3,725 (a 9.6% increase).

Source: Trends in College Pricing 2002, Collegeboard.com

Ellen Frishberg, director of Student Financial Services at Johns Hopkins University points out one of the biggest differences between public and private colleges. "I see a lot of people who don't understand the different costs of public and private schools, and explaining these differences is really necessary. As taxpayers, people pay subsidies to public schools through their taxes, which reduces their costs to students. So really, when you take those taxes into account, public colleges cost about the same as private schools. It's just that you've already paid some money through your taxes."

Most of the time, private schools tend to be thought of as more prestigious than public colleges. After all, Harvard, Stanford, and Yale are all private universities, as are other Ivy League schools. But it's important to note that not all private universities are the same. Research has suggested that mediocre private schools may not offer a better education than a good public college. Also, depending on your student's future plans, even a top-notch private school may not make a difference. For example, a Yale degree won't make much difference if your son or daughter plans on becoming a minister, elementary school teacher, or social worker. So while you shouldn't rule out private colleges because of their cost, you also shouldn't assume that private schools always provide a better education.

That's Why They Make the Big Bucks

A 1998 study found that in most cases, graduates of elite universities made higher incomes not because of where they went to college, but because of the individual's intelligence and attributes.

— *Researchers: Alan B. Krueger and Stacy B. Dale, the Andrew W. Mellon Foundation*

In addition, a private college, when aid and loans are factored in, may be less expensive than a state school, especially an out-of-state school. "A friend of my daughter lives in North Carolina," says Connie Gores, vice president for enrollment at Randolph-Macon Woman's College, "and she applied to both in-state and out-of-state schools. The out-of-state schools accepted her, while the in-states didn't. So now, she's having to choose between options that really may not be the best fit for her, and because the family assumed that private college would be too expensive, she didn't apply to any."

So despite that churning in your stomach, don't automatically assume a particular college shouldn't be considered because of cost. Regardless of sticker shock, you should compare state schools to private schools to see what you can afford. This early in the process, don't let price stand in your way. Several factors will influence your final decision, and cost is just one of them.

In-State versus Out-of-State

This may seem obvious, but an in-state school simply means it is in the same state as where you live. If your son or daughter leaves their home state to go to college, it is considered out-of-state. These terms are used to refer to both students and colleges. These terms exist because most colleges charge out-of-state students a higher tuition than in-state students. This is based on the idea that in-state students already give the college some money by paying state taxes that are passed on to the college. Some schools, however, offer a "good neighbor" tuition break to students from nearby states, sometimes charging only in-state tuition, especially for students with high grade point averages or SAT scores.

> **Room and Board—Food for Thought**
>
> At 4-year private colleges, 2002-2003 room and board averaged $6,779, up from $6,479 (a 4.6% increase).
>
> At 4-year public colleges, room and board averaged $5,582, up from $5,266 (a 6.0% increase).
>
> *Source: Trends in College Pricing 2002,*
> *Collegeboard.com*

It's important to note that any combination of these four terms can be applied to a college. Your student could go to an in-state private school, or an out-of-state public school. The important thing to realize is that while these words describe a type of college, no one type is better than another.

Community Colleges

For students who cannot attend a four-year college for any number of reasons, community colleges provide an extremely affordable option. Designed for students living at home (and saving fees for room and board), they offer a two-year degree (called an Associate's degree) that can mirror the first two years of education a student would get at a four-year college; alternatively, students can enroll in career-oriented programs, studying for professions that are in high demand in technology, allied health, and other fields. Community colleges also offer remedial study in preparation for college work.

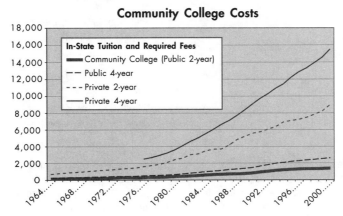

Community College Costs

In-State Tuition and Required Fees
- Community College (Public 2-year)
- Public 4-year
- Private 2-year
- Private 4-year

Source: National Center for Educational Statistics

BEST VALUES

Guidance counselors from across the nation call the following schools the best values for quality of education versus price:

Arizona State University	AZ	University of South Carolina	SC
University of Michigan–Ann Arbor	MI	Truman State University	MO
University of Virginia	VA	University of Colorado–Boulder	CO
University of Minnesota–Twin Cities	MN	University of Idaho	ID
Grove City College	PA	Eastern Michigan University	MI
Rice University	TX	Louisiana State University and A&M College	LA
University of Maryland–College Park	MD	York College of Pennsylvania	PA
Georgia Institute of Technology	GA	Murray State University	KY
Penn State University–University Park	PA	Duke University	NC
University of Delaware	DE	Purdue University–West Lafayette	IN
University of Arizona	AZ	Winona State University	MN
University of North Carolina–Chapel Hill	NC	University of Missouri–Columbia	MO
Indiana University–Bloomington	IN	Washington State University	WA
University of Oklahoma	OK	Florida A&M University	FL
University of Wisconsin–Madison	WI	Roanoke College	VA
University of Pittsburgh	PA	Penn State University–Erie	PA
Rutgers University–New Brunswick	NJ	University of Washington	WA
University of Iowa	IA	Clark Atlanta University	GA
University of Alabama	AL	Concordia College	MN
University of Georgia	GA	Northwest Missouri State University	MO
Spelman College	GA	State University of New York–Geneseo	NY
Miami University	OH	Keene State College	NH
Oklahoma State University	OK	South Dakota State University	SD
Auburn University	AL	University of North Dakota	ND
Baylor University	TX	University of Wyoming	WY
University of Texas–Austin	TX	Albertson College of Idaho	ID
Mississippi State University	MS	University of Connecticut	CT
Hampton University	VA	University of New Mexico	NM
West Virginia University	WV	University of New Hampshire	NH
Florida State University	FL		

Results from Kaplan's *2003 National Guidance Counselor Survey* (a scientific survey conducted by Market Measurement, Inc.) from *The Unofficial, (Un)Biased Guide to the 328 Most Interesting Colleges, 2004 Edition*. "Best Values" is one of 15 guidance counselor lists including "Hidden Treasures," "Hot and Trendy," "Overrated," "Underrated," and "Peter Pan" (low four-year graduation rate schools).

Many students who finish a two-year community college program—usually in the lowest price range for any higher education—are able to move on and receive their Bachelor's degree after two more years at a traditional college, saving thousands of dollars.

Career Colleges

Career colleges (also known as technical institutes) are postsecondary institutions that provide training for skill-based careers in law, business, information technology, health care, criminal justice, and more than 200 other fields. In contrast to community colleges, which are usually funded by state or local governments, career schools are independent, privately-owned institutions. Career schools account for 47 percent of all postsecondary educational institutions in the United States. At many career schools, the majority of programs are related to one career field, such as health care (Maric College in San Diego), business (Nebraska School of Business in Omaha), or automotive (Wyoming Technical Institute in Laramie). Other career colleges offer training in multiple fields, with online study options. Programs in allied health, arts and sciences, criminal justice, design and graphic arts, information technology, paralegal studies, and travel and tourism are among those available.

Career colleges primarily offer occupational degrees, rather than the academic degrees offered by colleges and universities. The training is much more focused on the practical skills and knowledge needed for a specific career. If what your son or daughter wants is practical training for a specific career, a program at a career school might save him or her time: Depending on the profession and college, a student may attend for as little as eighteen months. And a student who attends a program on radiation therapy, for example, can earn as much as a graduate of a traditional college.

Tuition for career colleges can vary widely, so before you commit to a loan, find out how long the program takes to finish and how much it will cost. Look into whether the school offers scholarships, and what other types of financial assistance are available. Check the school's accreditation: Accreditation by a reputable national or regional accrediting body means the school has passed a thorough examination of its educational quality. Besides ensuring quality, accreditation by one of the accrediting bodies recognized by the Department of Education means that students can qualify for federal financial grant and loan programs.

OTHER OPTIONS

College Abroad

While study abroad doesn't describe a certain type of college, it refers to students who continue their education outside the United States. In fact, study abroad can refer to almost any type of college we've mentioned. More and more students are attending colleges in Canada after realizing they can get a similar education to schools in this country while paying significantly less money.

> **Canadian Bargains**
>
> In 2003, prestigious McGill University charged international students (that includes Americans!) $6,900–$7,300 tuition for most programs.

Adventurous future chefs may become expert in creating pastries by studying in Paris, while a future translator for the United Nations may become fluent in German by attending a college in Berlin. Also, many United States schools offer a semester or year of study abroad at a cooperating institution in the host country. Such a semester can prove to be an added expense to be factored into your college cost equation if your son or daughter has his or her heart set on it, but bargains are available for those who plan ahead. Check if the tuition you will pay for study abroad will be that of your son's or daughter's primary school or the host school abroad. It's possible to save money if the foreign institution charges a lower tuition.

Online Programs

Online programs have become increasingly popular in recent years because they break many of the barriers people confront when trying to enroll in traditional college programs. Online students can study anytime, anywhere. Tuition for online schools is competitive when compared to traditional colleges and universities. Many online institutions also offer scholarships, payment plans, and other methods of making tuition payment more convenient. However, while online degrees are gaining in acceptability and even status, they may not be as attractive in the job market as a "regular" degree.

If you're looking at an online school, investigate its accreditation: Just like traditional on-ground schools, some online schools are accredited and some aren't, or only specific programs have received accreditation. Accreditation is a sign that the school is serious about education and ensures that high academic standards are maintained. Some types of accreditation allow the school to take advantage of federal financial aid programs, so check with the institution you're considering to see if it offers such aid.

> **Check Out the Financial Aid Office**
>
> "You really need to see how you're treated by the financial aid office before you apply, because that's a good indicator of how much help you'll receive," remarks financial aid officer Connie Gores, parent of a college-aged daughter. "If a financial aid office isn't helpful and treats you like just another number before your student even goes there, you can bet it'll be worse if your student attends."

Since the majority of students attend traditional four-year and community colleges each year, the government forms and requirements we will discuss later on will be applicable to them. But if your son or daughter is attending one of these other types of colleges, this book will still be helpful. We're also going to discuss everything from private loans to grants and scholarships than can help you no matter where your student is going to get his or her education.

GETTING YOUR STUDENT INVOLVED

Very few students know for certain what they want to do with their lives after graduating from college, and odds are, yours may feel the same way. (If not, great! Your problems aren't completely solved, but you're off to a good start.) So before we even get into financial aid, budgets, and loans, it's essential to make sure you and your son or daughter are on the same page to avoid future headaches and wasted time.

As mentioned in the introduction, this book is based on the idea that affording college is the responsibility of both you and your student. After all, the decisions you're making affect them as much as you. So if you haven't already talked about college with your son and daughter, it's time to get started. We're not starting with anything that's too difficult or that may cause an argument, but with basic ideas your student needs to understand.

Does Your Student Know What He or She Wants from College?

This doesn't mean they have to choose a major right now, of course, but do they have any idea of what they want to study? Is your son torn between acting and writing? Maybe your daughter wants to go into science, but loves both chemistry and math.

> ## TRENT & SEPPY SAY...
>
> **Trent:**
>
> *If you and your son or daughter talk about finances before college applications go out, chances are you'll both be happier in the long run.*
>
> **Seppy:**
>
> *There's no problem with applying to a dream school if you have a safety school just in case*

What about sports or activities? Does your student want to play tennis for his college? Maybe she's thinking about moving on from playing around with your home video camera into learning filmmaking.

Then again, some students have a better sense of what they don't want, rather than what they do. It's not uncommon for a student to insist that he attend an out-of-state college because he wants to become independent from his family. Still others may have a certain area of the country in mind, or even a city where they want to go. An actor may want to attend college in New York or California, or a future politician may want to get an education near Washington, D.C.

The point is, your student probably has some idea of what she wants from college, even if she hasn't told you about it. A desire to go into a certain field or live in a certain place will impact not only the cost you two will pay for college, but also the types of financial aid you'll qualify for. So be open to what your student may say.

Unfortunately, money is going to be a significant factor in this decision. So while you and your son or daughter should by all means consider prestigious, more costly universities, it's also necessary to develop a game plan to ensure your student attends college no matter what happens. To that end, here are four things you need to look at if you intend to cover all your bases.

Local Colleges and Universities

Odds are you have at least one, if not a few, colleges in your area. They may be in your town, a few miles down the road, or within walking distance of your home. Regardless, you and your son or daughter should consider these local schools as you look at colleges. Granted, most students dream of leaving home and going away to college, but local universities often mean significant savings for the student and parent.

Living at Home

One of the main reasons local colleges are appealing for many families is that the student can continue to live at home. Rather than pay for room and board, not to mention things like travel, phone calls, and food, your family doesn't incur any increase in living expenses from this option. In fact, the expenses you'll face if your student remains at home may be significantly less than those same expenses if he were to go away. Naturally, this shouldn't be a deciding factor in your selection of schools, but it is one advantage to attending a local school.

Part-Time Work for Students

Another aspect to this game plan is that awful four-letter word: work. Ideally, most people agree that a student should focus her time on studies, not babysitting, working the counter at a video store, or spending her weekends waiting tables. But just a few hours working each week can make a significant impact in college-related expenses. Textbooks can be paid for, gas and car insurance can be bought, and other such incidentals can be handled without you handing over money. Most importantly, disciplined students all over the country work part-time while going to school, with little impact on their grades.

> ### Work Ethic
> According to some schools, working can actually be good for your student. "Research has shown higher satisfaction ratings and a better percent of matriculation when a college student is working," says Ellen Frishberg, director of Student Financial Services for Johns Hopkins University.

The Financial "Safety" School

Finally, there's the idea of a "safety" school. Traditionally, this has meant applying to a college that the student feels fairly certain will accept them. Yet, a safety school should also be one that you know your family can afford. After all, a college that's completely out of your price range isn't very "safe," is it? In most cases, safety schools are public, located in the family's area (within driving distance), and offer financial aid to the majority of their students. Students who attend their safety school often live at home for the first few years to save on costs.

The bottom line is you'll need to discuss each of these options with your son or daughter and develop a safety school as part of your overall plan. Some students attend their safety school (be it a local university or community college) for a few years, then transfer to their dream school to receive their degree. So remember that attending a safety school does not necessarily mean settling, since it's often a temporary compromise on the way to getting a degree.

Does Your Student Understand the Costs Involved in Going to College?

While your student may hold a part-time job, file his own taxes, or make his own car payments, he probably doesn't have experience dealing with loans for large sums of money, creating a budget meant to last a year, or stretching money by reducing expenses. Because of this, the high cost of going to college may not be a reality to him. It doesn't take new drivers long to learn that car expenses are costly and gas isn't free. By bringing your student into the financial aid process, there's a good chance he'll quickly learn just how large a sum of money is involved.

"There are parents who give their kids a free ride to college," offers Karon Ray, who has put two children through college (one has finished and one has completed two years), with another one about to start. "The problem is that they graduate from college having never done a budget." Karon and her husband, an Army officer, set aside for their three children a lump sum of money before they started college, but didn't tell them how to use it. "So really, our kids faced the sticker shock before they started classes. They had to decide if they really needed that high-end computer, or should be saving money for the next semester. Basically, it's about teaching them that things cost money."

Explain to Your Student That Loans Are Going to Be Their Responsibility

Nothing is more frightening to a free-wheeling college student than seeing how much she owes in student loans. We'll get into loans in more detail later in the book, but for now, it's important for both you and your student to realize that federal loans are going to be in the student's name. The most important reason your student should want to be involved in this process is because the debt she's creating is going to be her responsibility in a few short years.

Do They Have Realistic Expectations of College?

This is probably the hardest thing for students to realize. In high school, college represents freedom, choices, independence, and a lot of fun. And while we're not suggesting you become a stick in the mud and lecture them on the consequences of slacking off, don't let them forget that every once in a while they will have to study, papers will have to be written eventually, and exams are going to be difficult.

Although it may not seem obvious, each of these points should lead into the next one. A student who has an idea of what she wants from college is going to be more willing to take part in the financial aid process. A student who's involved in the process is going learn (very quickly) that much of the cost will be her responsibility, and a student who's aware of her financial obligations will have a more balanced expectation of what college is about.

MOVING ON

To wrap up, in this chapter we reviewed the types of colleges out there with a look at their comparative costs. We discussed the traditional four-year schools, community colleges, and the nontraditional study options such as career colleges, online study, and attending college in a foreign country. We discussed how the type of college might affect the cost of higher education, and recommended having a serious discussion with your son or daughter to get them involved in the financial side of a college decision. We introduced the concept of a financial safety school, and how students can help ease the economic burden by living at home, working, and understanding that loans will be their responsibility.

In the next chapter, we'll talk more in-depth about the difference between a college's sticker price and the actual amount you can expect to pay. You'll begin breaking down different costs and comparing how these can differ from college to college, as we teach you how to determine the actual cost of college for you and your student.

✓ CHECKLIST:

1. Begin talking with your son or daughter about the types of college he or she might be interested in.
   - Do they want to go in-state, or out-of-state?
   - Attend a public school or private?

2. Begin comparing the costs of colleges in your state, as well as other states your student is interested in. For example,
   - Are universities in your state cheaper than neighboring states?
   - How do out-of-state tuitions in other states compare to in-state tuitions in your state? Are "good neighbor" or regional tuitions available?

3. Determine and select a safety school with your student. As you do so, discuss the following:
   - Is there a nearby college they could attend?
   - Will they be willing to live at home if need be?
   - Are they willing to work part-time if they stay home?

4. Perhaps your student is interested in a visual art school, an acting school, or a career school.
   - Discuss the pros and cons of each, and begin a list of possible schools.

5. Talk with your son or daughter about the financial side of attending college. Discuss his or her expectations for college, as well as the possibility that most of the loans and financial burden involved will become his or her responsibility after graduating. Encourage him or her to take an active part in this process, and help him or her understand why it is worth his or her time.

WEBSITES

National Center for Public Policy and Higher Education
www.highereducation.org/

American Association of Community Colleges
www.aacc.nche.edu/

Association of Universities and Colleges of Canada
www.aucc.ca/

Study Overseas
www.studyoverseas.com/

The International Education Site
www.intstudy.com/

CollegeLink
www.collegelink.com/

Office of Postsecondary Education Accreditation Information
www.ed.gov/offices/OPE/accreditation/

## CHAPTER FOUR

Calculate the Real Cost of College

OVERCOMING STICKER SHOCK

So far, we've looked at the big picture when it comes to financial aid, and you should have a good idea of what to expect, as well as what your options are. In this chapter we'll start on the nuts and bolts of the process, which means numbers. Fortunately, if you can balance a checkbook, you can do the calculations necessary to get through this process. Having said that, grab a pencil and some paper, a calculator if you've got one, and read on.

TRENT & SEPPY SAY...

Trent:

Lots of parents panic when it comes to creating a budget or filling out financial aid forms. The truth is, the math on your student's SAT was harder than what you'll be doing, so don't worry!

Seppy:

And if you believe two heads are better than one, ask your student to double-check your math. Compared to the SAT, this stuff should be a piece of cake!

In chapter two, we compared the price of college to that of a car, explaining that both have "sticker prices" which usually vary greatly from the actual cost itself. But in order to compare the sticker price quoted by a university to the actual cost of your college, you're going to have to break it into separate parts (just as the sticker price of a car is broken down into parts).

While you may not be looking forward to doing this, it's essential for making an informed choice of which college is best for you and your son or daughter. Sometimes costs change, estimates may not include additional fees that impact you, and housing expenses can vary greatly depending upon the selections chosen by a student. In fact, most housing costs you see are based on an average which means you may end up paying more or less than that amount depending upon your choices. You wouldn't sign a car loan if you had only an estimate of what you'd be paying, so why do it for a college?

This chapter will open your eyes in determining what's needed and what's not when it comes to your student's college education (leather seats, anyone?). You'll be creating worksheets that list all these costs, so you can do a side-by-side comparison of each school you're considering. But before you actually start crunching numbers, let's take a look at the different types of expenses you'll need to know.

DIRECT VERSUS INDIRECT

When it comes to college, the terms "direct" and "indirect" are used by financial aid administrators to define costs. Essentially, every cost associated with college falls into one of these two categories, and they're easy to understand.

Direct Costs

Direct costs are directly related to your student's education and are usually paid to the school itself. There are four types of direct costs.

Tuition

This is the amount that a college requires from all students in order to attend class. At some colleges it's a flat rate, while others charge depending on how many credit hours (classes) your son or daughter takes. Tuition also varies depending on whether or not the school is public or private, and whether or not your student is in-state or out-of-state. (For definitions of these terms, see chapter three.)

> **Get Credit**
>
> Every class is broken down into credit hours, which reflect how long the class is and how much time it takes out of the student's schedule. Most classes are 3 credit hours, and most students take an average of 4–5 classes each semester.

Be sure to determine the exact amount of tuition for each college you're considering, since they vary greatly. If a school bases tuition on the student's number of credit hours, assume 15 credit hours per semester.

Fees

For every college, there are some fees that must be paid simply because your child will be a student there. They may be named differently from school to school, but most provide funding for general expenses a college incurs. Other fees can vary depending on a student's major or their activities.

Student service fees are related to activities that your student may choose to participate in, such as sports, performing groups, or clubs. These fees may be optional depending upon the college. Class-related fees are most commonly found in the arts and sciences. For example, chemistry majors may pay additional fees to cover laboratory and chemical costs. Likewise, a photography major will likely pay a fee to cover costs associated with developing pictures.

Textbooks

Often underestimated, textbooks can cost hundreds of dollars a semester. English and literature majors may have to buy dozens of novels, while history majors can expect thick books that would give a weightlifter a workout. Most colleges provide an estimate, but it's almost always too low. An accurate expectation is $1,500–$2,000 per year, but this can increase by as much as 30 percent with the addition of just a few books! To be safe, assume $800 for your student's first semester, and adjust accordingly.

> **Cost It Out**
>
> "Some schools do a really good job of mapping all their costs out," says financial aid officer Connie Gores. "Those kinds of costs should always be in the catalog, or easily available from the school. If a college isn't able to share prices for fees or other costs beyond tuition and room and board, then you should think strongly about that school. This is a good indicator of how helpful a financial aid office can be."

"When you visit colleges, visit the bookstore on campus," suggests parent Joe Sanseverino. "That was a real eye opener of us! You'll be shocked the first time you see a book cost $150."

Supplies

These costs usually impact art and science majors, and reflect equipment that the university does not provide for the student. For example, art majors usually must provide their own paints, sketch pads, pencils, and erasers, while chemistry majors usually provide their own safety glasses and calculators.

Indirect Costs

Indirect costs are all the other expenses related to attending college, such as room and board, travel, and personal expenses.

There are seven types of indirect costs:

Room

Simply put, this is where your student will live. Most colleges refer to this as housing, and there

> **TRENT & SEPPY SAY...**
>
> **Trent:**
>
> Never underestimate the advantages of buying used textbooks, which can significantly reduce your costs. Also, search the Web for online textbook stores, which offer competitive pricing (but watch out for shipping!). Even Barnes & Noble and eBay usually have textbooks available.
>
> **Seppy:**
>
> Borrowing a friend's book and photocopying it, however, is not recommended. Not only is it illegal, but imagine the time you'd spend on a 500 page book about Chinese history!

are two types: on-campus and off-campus. On-campus means your student lives in a college residence hall ("dorm" for short), and you pay a lump sum to the college each semester. In turn, the college pays all the bills associated with the housing—heat, hot water, electricity, etc. Most often, your student will share a room with one or more students. Off-campus means your student lives in an apartment or house literally off the college's campus. Students living off-campus can expect increased responsibilities such as monthly bills, grocery shopping, and rent.

> ### How Much Does *Animal House* Cost?
>
> Many colleges require that freshmen live on-campus, so be sure to check with each school you're considering. Also, on-campus housing costs for a college can vary depending on residence hall. Some dorms may cost more because they're newer or more convenient to campus, so be sure to ask!

It may be easier and more convenient for your student to live on campus, especially if they are about to start their first year of college. But don't assume living on campus is always cheaper. Especially at urban colleges in large cities, campus housing can be limited and expensive compared to local apartments. Also, find out if close friends of your student are attending the same college. If so, would it be cheaper for them to share an apartment? In rare instances, some parents actually buy a small house or apartment near campus. The student then lives there, and the other rooms are rented out to help make mortgage payments. Parents with experience in real estate can actually make money from such an investment.

Board

You've probably heard the term "room and board" before, and while room is self-explanatory, board refers to food. Meal plans are offered by colleges, allowing students to eat at campus dining halls without paying out of pocket. Some colleges charge a flat rate for meal plans, while others offer a few varieties depending on how often the student expects to eat there.

"Many people don't understand that tuition and room and board are two different things," says Connie Gores of Randolph-Macon Women's College. "One of my daughter's friends received a scholarship covering half her tuition, and her family thought that it would pay for half of the cost of the college. They didn't realize room and board was in addition to tuition costs."

> ### It Pays to Itemize
>
> Some colleges combine room and board into one cost on their literature, so check your brochures to see if your prospective colleges have done this. If so, request a breakdown of these two items.

It's important to realize that meal plans only cover food your student will eat at the dining hall, so you'll also need to account for snacks, dining out, and the occasional pizza delivery.

Transportation

This covers the costs associated with your son or daughter getting around campus and the area where the college is located. Often, this is minimal, since many students living on-campus simply walk everywhere. However, this could include a bicycle, public transportation, or a car. If your student intends to have a car while in college, you'll need to also factor in the cost of gas and insurance in this amount.

> **Car Culture**
>
> Some colleges do not allow freshmen who live on campus to have cars. So if your student plans on having one, be sure to check with your prospective schools.

Travel

The cost of travel can vary greatly depending on how far away your student's college is, as well as how often they plan to come home. If your student is attending a college in your state, you may choose to drive to campus and pick him or her up for a holiday or long weekend with the family. But if your student is attending a university on the other side of the country, he or she will likely be flying home for visits. Only you and your son or daughter know how often he or she will travel, and how he or she will chose to do so. Unlike other costs, you'll find that travel expenses can vary greatly from school to school.

Personal

This area is usually one of the most flexible when it comes to determining how much college will cost. Personal expenses can cover everything from long distance phone calls to entertainment, laundry, shopping, and gifts. Most parents look at the student's spending money, and chose a set amount designed to last the semester.

To best determine how much you and your student will need to allocate for personal expenses for a semester of college, look at how much your student currently spends per month and multiply by four (since there are just under four months in a semester). You'll probably want to increase this number slightly to cover "non-fun" things like laundry, phone calls, and toiletries.

Medical and Dental

Although it's often overlooked, you'll need to determine how much your student's medical and dental insurance will be. If your student is currently covered by your employer's insurance, you'll need to find out if they are still eligible once they go to college. Depending upon your insurance, you may have to pay an extra fee, or your student may not be covered at all.

Most colleges offer health insurance, so if your current health plan will no longer cover your son or daughter, check with prospective colleges to find out what your options are.

Miscellaneous

While it sounds vague, miscellaneous expenses are everything else that goes beyond the basic costs of attending college. This can include fraternity or sorority dues, athletic expenses associated with playing a sport, clubs, tutoring, and costs associated with summer programs. Students with disabilities would add any additional expenses in this category.

Miscellaneous expenses usually are not as flexible as personal expenses, since reducing this amount means the student must give up sports, clubs, or activities. But while this number can vary from school to school, you'll likely include the same things for each college. (In other words, if your student plans to try out for the tennis team, they'll likely do so regardless of which college they attend.)

TRENT & SEPPY SAY...

Trent:

Many airlines, bus lines, and trains offer student discounts with a college ID, so consider several options when planning your student's travel. Advance tickets can also save money, especially when planning for the holidays.

Seppy:

Actually, college students get discounts on just about anything if they have their ID—theater tickets, hotels, stores. In fact, Hollywood director Kevin Smith supposedly stayed in film school just because of the discounts he got when buying film to make his first movie!

CALCULATING INFLATION

If your son or daughter is in his or her senior year of high school, inflation won't impact your worksheets. But if your student has a few years until he or she starts college, you'll need to factor this in.

Inflation is an estimate of how much the cost of something will increase over time. We all know that a pack of gum costs more today than it did twenty years ago. That's inflation, and it affects everything. So if your student won't be starting college in the immediate future, you'll want an idea of how much her education will cost once she starts.

The national average increase for the cost of college is 6 percent every year, so if your student is planning to start college in two years, you can expect to pay 12 percent more than what college currently costs. Take a look at the following chart that gives an inflation factor, which you'll be using at the end of this chapter (unless your student starts college next year).

YEARS BEFORE STUDENT STARTS COLLEGE	INFLATION FACTOR
1	1.06
2	1.12
3	1.19
4	1.26
5	1.34
6	1.42
7	1.50
8	1.59
9	1.69
10	1.79
11	1.90
12	2.01
13	2.13
14	2.26
15	2.40
16	2.54
17	2.69
18	2.85

To use this chart, you'll simply find the inflation factor for the number of years your son or daughter has until he or she starts college, and multiply that inflation factor by the total cost of his or her education. (Not only will the cost of tuition, room, and board go up, but so will everything else.)

For example, if a student has three years until they start college, and the cost of attending a particular college is currently $25,000 a year (including indirect costs such as travel, personal expenses, etc.), then the costs associated with attending that same college would be $29,750 in three years. The chart above shows the inflation factor for three years is 1.19, so

$$\$25,000 \times 1.19 = \$29,750$$

Remember that this provides an estimate, so the actual cost may be more or less than this number (but you'll likely be close).

THE ACTUAL COST OF COLLEGE

At the end of this chapter you'll find a worksheet created to help you keep track of all these expenses. It's called the Cost of Attending (COA) worksheet, and you'll need to do it for each college you and your student are considering. You may want to photocopy the worksheet, or create your own on your computer, or maybe you prefer to write everything out on a legal pad or notebook. It really doesn't matter, as long as you have everything written down and accounted for.

As you fill out these worksheets, be sure to keep your notes and calculations that so that you'll remember how you got each number. For example, if personal expenses include the cost of a cell phone, or transportation expenses include the costs associated with your student's car, write that down with the amount you expect to spend for each. As you'll find out in a minute, these notes will come in handy.

TRENT & SEPPY SAY...

Trent:

By keeping your calculations for these worksheets, you'll be able to go back later and make adjustments to certain expenses without trying to remember how you came up with your numbers.

Seppy:

Don't feel like you have to go overboard, though. These are estimations, so you don't need 8 pages of numbers about how much fast food your student eats a month.

According to Karen Krause, director of financial aid at the University of Texas at Arlington, schools should offer average numbers to help you calculate your COA worksheet. "Most schools should be able to give you ballpark figures," she explains. "For example, we recently did a bookstore survey that looked at textbooks for six different majors at different years in college. We then used these to get an average cost for our students."

Since you're going to fill out these worksheets for your colleges, this might be a good time to organize everything you have so far. You've probably got brochures, letters, forms, and notes from each college you and your student are considering. Since these Cost of Attending worksheets will be compared side-by-side, we recommend taking a few minutes to organize the bulk of information and papers you've got. Use whatever works best for you; regular folders, big legal-sized envelopes, one of those accordion folders with different sections. But whatever you use, it's a good idea to separate these papers by college so that you'll be able to easily find things later.

STUDENT INVOLVEMENT

Finally, if you haven't already realized it, this is where you really need to make sure your son or daughter is involved. The numbers you come up with on the Cost of Attending worksheets are going to be largely impacted by the choices your student makes. Without their involvement and input, you might as well be guessing, which will make the process of affording college much more difficult. For example, will your student want to join the Greek system? How often does he plan to eat out? If she wants to attend a college in a major city, will she use public transportation to go exploring off campus? What about phone calls? How often will he call home?

The bottom line is, by having your student help calculate these expenses for each potential college, you'll have the most accurate worksheets possible. Getting your student involved will also help iron out differences in opinion about what's a necessity and what's not. After all, your student may assume that having a cell phone is an absolute must, while you may believe that a long-distance phone card is enough to keep in touch.

COMPARING THE WORKSHEETS

Once you and your student have finished the Cost of Attending worksheets for your prospective schools, you'll be able to accurately compare all these colleges and see what your student's education is going to cost. You'll realize that all the hard work was worth it as soon as you sit down and are able to compare colleges with just a few sheets of paper and a handful of numbers. You'll probably also realize that not only does tuition vary greatly from college to college, but those indirect expenses you spent so much time on vary greatly as well. If anything, these comparisons will give you an idea about how much your student's higher education will cost. In most cases, you can look at the difference between your safety school and your most expensive private, out-of-state college to get this range. Don't be surprised if it's a big difference. For most families it usually is.

MAKING ADJUSTMENTS

As you compare the Cost of Attending worksheets for your colleges, you'll find that some schools are much more appealing to your checkbook than others. Rather than count out a college at this point, sit down with your student and see if there are any expenses that can be trimmed or reduced. (This is where your notes will come in handy, since you can use them as the basis for your changes.)

Naturally, tuition can't be changed, but what about personal and miscellaneous expenses, as well as things like travel? Is your student willing to come home only for major holidays if it means she can afford going to college in New York City? Would he consider not joining a fraternity if doing so means he could go out-of-state? Does she want to attend her dream college so much that she would give up her car to do it?

TRENT & SEPPY SAY...

Trent:

Your student may not be happy having to pick and choose which luxuries to do without while in college, but even if there are some arguments, it's better to deal with them now. Otherwise, your student may call one day and ask for an extra few hundred dollars for her cell phone bill.

Seppy:

Just make sure your student doesn't get the wrong idea. One parent said his student is willing to cut back on expenses, but thinks Mom and Dad are going to set her up with a furnished apartment with all the money they're saving once she graduates!

MOVING ON

To wrap up, we began by explaining why it's important to break down the cost of college. We then looked at direct versus indirect costs, and learned the four types of direct costs, as well as the seven types of indirect costs. We discussed how inflation can impact the cost of college for students who aren't starting in the near future, and then introduced the Cost of Attending worksheet. We then looked at why it's important that your student be involved in these worksheets and what to do once they are completed. Finally, we touched on how you can compare and adjust COA worksheets to better determine what you can afford.

In the next chapter, we'll talk about just where all this money is going to come from. You'll learn about different types of income and how each can be used to help meet your share of your student's college education. But before you move on, take a look at the checklist for this chapter.

✔ CHECKLIST:

1. Organize the information you have from prospective colleges.
   - Create a folder for each school.
   - Make sure you have all the information necessary to complete a COA.
   - Contact colleges to request any information you need.

2. Contact your employer to determine if your son or daughter will continue to be covered under your insurance.
   - Will you pay an additional cost?
   - What if your student attends an out-of-state school?

3. Photocopy the Cost of Attending worksheet at the end of this chapter, or create your own, and add it to your folders for each college.

4. Complete a Cost of Attending worksheet for each prospective school you are considering.
   - Go step-by-step and refer to this chapter if you have questions.
   - Keep your notes and calculations for changes later on.

5. If necessary, calculate the inflation for each prospective school based on how long it will be before your student attends college.

6. Once your Cost of Attending worksheets are completed, compare and review their results. If necessary, make adjustments based on your notes and calculations.

WEBSITES

VarsityBooks.com
www.varsitybooks.com

efollett.com
www.efollett.com

Travelocity.com
www.travelocity.com

Amtrak
www.amtrak.com

Greyhound
www.greyhound.com

KAPLAN

Cost of Attending Worksheet

College: _____

Telephone: _____

Website: _____

Direct Costs:

Tuition $_____

Fees $_____

Books $_____

Supplies $_____

Indirect Costs:

Room $_____

Board $_____

Transportation $_____

Travel $_____

Personal $_____

Medical & Dental $_____

Miscellaneous $_____

Total Cost of Attending This College: $_____
(*Total of above items*)

Inflation (If necessary):

Number of Years Before Student Attends College: ____

Inflation Factor (see chart in chapter 4):   ____

Cost of Attending This College: $_____

Multiplied by Inflation Factor: ✕____

Cost of Attending this College in __ Years: $_____

## CHAPTER FIVE

Making the Most of Your Money

WHERE WILL IT ALL COME FROM?

By now, you should have an accurate estimate of how much college is going to cost. And while knowing this is better than closing your eyes and hoping everything will work out, there's a new issue now. Now that you know how much college is going to cost, you've got to find a way to come up with enough money for it.

To help you, this chapter is going to look at various ways you can pay your EFC. There's no one-answer-fits-all solution, so while everything we'll look at can be of help to families, some approaches may not be right for your situation. In the last chapter we discussed the difference between a student who is going to college in the near future and a student who has a few years before she starts her higher education. This difference is also going to impact which options are best suited for you.

College is a life-changing expense, similar to buying a house, getting your first car, or starting your own business. And just as each of those situations require planning and preparation, so does planning for college. In a perfect world, every parent would start saving for their student's college education while he's still in diapers. But of course, life isn't perfect, and unless you're incredibly rich, there seldom seems to be enough money to go around. We've all heard that you should start saving early for your child's education, but rather than focus on the past, let's focus on what can be done now.

PLANNING IS ESSENTIAL

If you have a few years until your son or daughter starts college, take advantage of this time. With each year that passes by, the amount of money you'll be able to provide for your student's education becomes less and less. Just as people plan to have money for retirement, they should also plan to have money for college.

By the way, it's a common misconception that if you save for college, you won't qualify for as much financial aid. Since you've already learned that financial aid is primarily based on your income tax, not the amount of money you have, you should understand why this isn't true.* Financial aid programs won't care if you have $300,000 in the bank or $300. Instead, they'll care that your family makes $45,000 each year. As far as they're concerned, what you do with your income is your choice.

One of the best ways to explain this is what Barry Simmons, director of financial aid at Virginia Tech, calls his "K-Mart™ theory":

"Everybody wears clothes; everyone owns a pair of blue jeans. Now, you can go to K-Mart™ and get a pair of jeans for $20, or you can go to an expensive store and shell out $80 or more for a pair of jeans. If someone wants to spend $80 on a pair of jeans, that's their business, but there's really no difference between the two. The way I see it, that's $60 you should be putting away for education. Those kinds of purchases take away the money you have for college, and schools shouldn't have to give someone more financial aid because they decide to spend $80 on a pair of jeans rather than $20."

So keep in mind the cost of inflation, and try to make sure that the money you're putting away at least matches the inflation factor you used in the last chapter. This shouldn't be hard, as you'll soon see.

USING SAVINGS TO PAY FOR COLLEGE

You may have heard the saying, "Make your money work for you, instead of working for your money!" It means that if you invest or save your money, it makes more money for you.

---

*FAFSA does take into consideration a small percentage of assets if you filed form 1040 (long form) and made over $50,000, or if you filed 1040A. See chapter eight for all the details.

MONTHLY INVESTMENT REQUIRED TO SAVE $10,000 FOR YOUR CHILD'S EDUCATION				
Investment Period	Monthly Contribution	Total Contributions	Interest Earned*	Total Saved
18 years	$32	$6,912	$3,187	$10,099
14 years	$45	$7,560	$2,552	$10,112
10 years	$68	$8,160	$1,853	$10,013
6 years	$124	$8,928	$1,144	$10,072
2 years	$401	$9,624	$378	$10,002

*Based on an interest rate of 4%.

"Whatever you do, plan to save," advises Ellen Frishberg, director of Student Financial Services at Johns Hopkins University. "There's this myth that people shouldn't save because they think it'll keep them from qualifying for financial aid. Yet the odds are, if they make enough money to save for college, they won't qualify anyway because of their income. If you have a significant income, you're not going to get much aid, so you need to save for college."

Savings 101

Traditional Savings Accounts

The most common type of past income, saving usually means keeping money in a bank account for use later. A minimal amount of interest is paid, and although you won't make much in savings, there is less risk involved than with investments.

Stocks

Stocks are a way you can invest in companies, and when you buy a stock you actually own a tiny piece of that company. Most often, people buy stocks, keep them until the company is more successful, and then sell the stock at a higher price to make money. All stocks work the same way, but depending on the company, some are more risky than others. Although they charge a fee, stockbrokers and financial advisers can help pick stocks and other investments to suit your needs.

TRENT & SEPPY SAY...

Trent:

Interest is the amount that your money earns when kept in a saving account. It's usually a percentage, and works like the opposite of inflation. If you save $100, and your interest rate is 3% per year, then you'll make an additional $3.

Seppy:

And any interest is better none. The only thing you'll get by keeping money under your mattress is a lumpy bed.

TRENT & SEPPY SAY...

Trent:

The more risky an investment is, the more you'll stand to gain in return. This is called the risk/return ratio, and it means that the greater the possibility you'll lose money on an investment, the more you stand to make if it is successful.

Seppy:

Generally, savings accounts are considered one of the least risky ways to save and invest, while some stock market investments such as options, futures, and derivatives are much riskier. Some people even invest on what they think the weather is going to be like in some places!

Bonds

When you borrow money from the bank, it's called a loan. When companies or the government borrow money from people like you, it's called a bond. There are basically two types, government bonds and corporate bonds. In both cases, you loan money to the government or business, and they agree to pay you back in the future with interest. Government bonds can be bought from the bank, and corporate bonds are available through stockbrokers.

Mutual Funds

Imagine that you want to buy a bunch of stocks, but that you only have enough money for one or two of them. That's where mutual funds come in. They are bought and sold like stocks, but instead of investing in one company, you are investing in several similar companies at once. These companies may all be in the same business, they may be the same size, or share other traits in common. Mutual funds can also represent the entire stock market, and these are called index funds. A fund manager is paid by investors in the mutual fund to select stocks to buy and sell, and it's their responsibility to make sure the index fund makes money.

"If a family plans to use some of their investments to pay for college," advises parent Clark Ray, "I'd suggest moving that money into a good U.S. index fund three or four years before they'll need it. It's a good way to stay in the market and still be conservative. At that point, you should be looking to preserve what you've got invested, not trying to beat the market."

CDs

These aren't silver disks that play music, but Certificates of Deposit (hence the term "CD") usually offered by banks. When you get a CD, you give the bank money, which they agree to return to you on a set date in the future (called a maturity date), with interest. CDs, like savings accounts, are not investments, yet the two differ in one important way. When you have a savings account, you can take the money out of the bank whenever you need it. With a CD, you agree that you won't need the money back until the maturity date. CDs are offered for anywhere from a few months to a few years, and if you take your money out of a CD before the maturity date, you are penalized and lose money. The longer the CD, the more you'll make in interest.

Treasury Notes

Often called "T-bills" or "treasuries," treasury notes are a way of investing money with the United States government. Treasury notes usually mature in anywhere from two to ten years, while some shorter treasury bills mature in under a year. One advantage of treasuries is that they're exempt from both state and local taxes. But like CDs, if you need the funds back before they mature, you can expect to lose money.

529 Savings Plans

In 1997, Section 529 plans were created for the sole purpose of giving families a way to save for college. All fifty states offer these investment plans, and contributions to a 529 savings plan are made with after-tax dollars. Since 2002, earnings on these plans have been granted federal tax exemption when used to pay for qualified higher education expenses. This means that earnings are no longer just tax-deferred, but tax free. And when the plan makes a distribution to pay for the beneficiary's college costs, the distribution is free from federal taxes as well (this tax break lasts until 2010, when Congress has the option of extending it). With a 529 savings plan, families invest money as they would through other investment plans. But unlike a brokerage account or mutual fund, these state-supported plans remain tax free as long as their funds are used for approved college expenses such as tuition, room and board, books and fees, and other expenses that students are required to pay to attend any accredited college or university in the United States. Most are administered through an outside firm.

Section 529 savings plans often offer several investment options. Because some states welcome out-of-state investors, you should shop around. But be sure not to overlook your own state, since it may offer the best tax advantages to residents. Most plans permit lump-sum contributions of over $100,000; unlike other tax breaks, high earners are not excluded and benefits are available to all taxpayers. In addition, 529 plans can now be transferred to a first cousin as a beneficiary, meaning that if your child chooses not to go to college, the money can go to someone outside the immediate family (until this change, 529 plan beneficiaries could only be transferred to a sibling). In a 529 savings plan, the parent remains in control of the account, and decides when withdrawals are made. Most plans allow funds to be withdrawn for non-college purposes, although there are penalties and tax consequences.

Your 529 savings account is treated as an asset in determining eligibility for federal financial aid. This means that your expected contribution (more about that in chapters seven and eight) to the cost of college will include 5.6 percent, or less, of the value of your account. Compare that to the 35 percent assessment against assets in your student's name or a custodial account, and you have a deal.

While this sounds great, we should add a note of caution. In recent years, 529 plans have come to face difficult times. With the struggling economy forcing cutbacks in many areas, states are feeling pressure to reduce the amount of money in 529 plans. Likewise, the stock market in the United States has taken a serious hit because of the drastic changes in our country over the past few years, which means that 529 plans aren't doing as well as they were in the 1990s. Remember that 529 plans are investments, and investments mean risk.

Another disadvantage is the possible confusion associated with these plans. Because of the many choices available to parents and investors, understanding and selecting the best 529 plan isn't easy, and when combined with the new tax law, there's lots of room for mistakes. That's why these plans work best when incorporated into your financial planning. For example, 529 plans affect tax planning by changing how investors treat earnings and withdrawals from accounts. It can also affect estate planning for everyone involved. Situations differ from state to state, so be sure you're informed before you select a 529 plan for your student.

529 Prepaid Tuition Plans

With a 529 prepaid tuition plan, families buy tuition credits for colleges at current prices. This means that if you buy five credits through a plan, it doesn't matter how much they cost when your son or daughter actually attends college, because you'll have already paid for them. The state agrees to pay the difference, as long as your son or daughter attends an in-state public college. States offering prepaid tuition contracts covering in-state tuition will also often allow you to transfer the value of your contract to private and out-of-state schools (although you may not get full value depending on the particular state). Tax law now allows colleges to offer their own 529 prepaid programs, a new development that permits families to target their financing to a certain school or group of schools (see the websites in the sidebar to monitor breaking news in this area).

> **529 Links**
> Two of the best websites to learn about 529 plans are *www.savingforcollege.com* and *www.collegesavings.org*. These sites also provide links to state-supported websites for 529 plans.

A 529 prepaid tuition plan works differently than a 529 savings plan in the federal financial aid formula. Here your investment doesn't show up at all on the FAFSA (the form for federal aid, which we'll go through in depth in chapter seven). But the benefits paid out will be considered by colleges as a resource that reduces your student's overall financial "need," which means less aid eligibility. For example, if your prepaid tuition contract pays out $10,000 in tuition benefits this year, you will be considered as having $10,000 less need for aid. "Right now, the two types of 529 plans are treated differently," explains Karen Krause, director of financial aid at the University of Texas at Arlington. "529 tuition plans are considered financial aid, while 529 savings plans are considered assets. Hopefully, that'll change in the future."

Prepaid tuition lets you lock in the cost to attend certain colleges, but if your account earns more than the rate of inflation of the cost of attending your colleges, you don't come out ahead. In contrast, in a 529 savings plan, you benefit when your investments earn more than the rate of inflation. However, if the cost of college continues to rise as dramatically as it has been, above the rate of earnings for most investments, a prepaid tuition plan holder is a big winner.

Education Savings Accounts

These saving accounts are specifically designed to help parents plan for college. As of 2002, they allow contributions of up to $2,000 each year per student, and withdrawals for qualified educational expenses are federal tax free. Your account grows federal-income tax free, and annual investments are allowed until a college-bound beneficiary turns 18.

Contributions aren't deductible, but there are no tax penalties on earnings or withdrawals. And even better news: you can now take tax-free withdrawals to cover your student's grade school to high school (K-12) costs. Eligible expenses include private school tuition, room and board, and even transportation. Public school students can use withdrawals for books, tutoring, computer equipment and software, and even Internet fees.

This is an investment, because parents decide how the money in their account will be invested and how much risk they will assume. But remember that an education savings account is considered an asset of the student, not the parent, which can be a disadvantage in applying for financial aid. Withdrawals while in college can also bring a negative financial impact on the following year's aid eligibility because they are counted as your student's income. Coordinating withdrawals with other tax benefits, especially the Hope or Lifetime Learning credits, can be challenging.

TAX CREDITS FOR EDUCATION

In the late 1990's, the federal government created two tax cuts specifically for parents who are sending their students to college. One of these may apply to you.

The "HOPE Scholarship" Tax Credit

Parents can receive up to $1,500 of a tax break on tuition and other required fees. It allows for a 100 percent tax credit on the first $1,000 of college fees, as well as a 50 percent tax credit on the second $1,000 of college fees. This means that parents who pay $2,000 out-of-pocket for their student's education are eligible for a $1,500 tax credit. To qualify, parents must meet certain income requirements, and the student must be in their first two years of college.

Lifetime Earning Tax Credit

This tax credit gives a 20 percent federal income tax credit for the first $10,000 in tuition and related expenses. This means parents who pay $10,000 out-of-pocket for college are eligible for a $2,000 tax break. If you are claiming a Hope Scholarship Credit, you can't apply for a Lifetime Learning credit. To qualify, parents must meet certain income requirements.

To learn more about these tax credits, and to find out if you qualify, visit the IRS website at *www.irs.gov*. Do a search for the names of these two tax credits, and you'll find up-to-date information.

USING PRESENT INCOME TO PAY FOR COLLEGE

Present income refers to money you're earning now. Depending upon your financial situation, this may be coming from more than one source.

Wages

The most common source of income, wages are the money you make from your job. Your employer pays your wages by paycheck. For most people, this is their major, if not only, source of present income.

ROI

When you sell stocks or other investments and you make a profit, that amount is considered your Return on Investment (ROI). Parents who own stock sometimes sell some or all of their shares to help pay for their student's college. While stocks themselves reflect past income because they were bought in the past, the money someone gets when they sell investments is considered present income.

Dividends

Another source of investment income is dividends. Some companies choose to pass along the money they make to people who own stock in the company (called shareholders). Not all companies pay dividends, but those that do send checks to their shareholders four times a year (unless the company did not make a profit). A set dividend is paid to each share of stock, so those who own more shares of stock in that company receive more dividends. Dividends are usually a few cents per share.

Other Income

Any other way you receive money on a regular basis would count as other income. Child support is an additional source of income for single parents that receive it, as are payments from the military received by retired members of the armed forces. A family may rent out an apartment above their garage, or receive rent from

---

TRENT & SEPPY SAY...

Trent:

Many families want to avoid loans altogether. It's a great goal to have, but seldom practical. Unless you're wealthy, refusing to take out loans for college means your student will have few options when selecting a school.

Seppy:

It's understandable that a parent wouldn't take a loan out to buy their sixteen year old a brand new luxury car, but college is a different story. The type of car you buy today won't matter in twenty years, but your student's education will.

people living in a second home they own. Anything that you claim on your taxes as additional income could be very helpful in affording college.

BORROWING TO PAY FOR COLLEGE

Student loans, credit cards, and mortgages are all examples of borrowing, or using future income for needs in the present. Getting a loan to afford college may seem risky, but unlike loans for some other purchases, it's actually a good idea. Loans are a way of deferring payment on something you're getting now, and if what you're getting is going to increase in value, like an education, then this is referred to as "good" debt. When you use loans to buy something that is going to decrease in value, such as most credit card purchases for things like clothes and electronics, it's referred to as "bad" debt.

> **New College Grad Hiring: Ups and Downs**
>
> Employers projecting the highest increases in college hiring are:
>
> | | |
> |---|---|
> | Construction companies | 35.7% |
> | Consulting services organizations | 14.3% |
> | Public accounting firms | 14% |
>
> Those looking at the steepest cuts in college hiring include:
>
> | | |
> |---|---|
> | Utilities companies | 31% |
> | Engineering/surveying firms | 29.1% |
> | Chemical manufacturers | 22.8% |
>
> *Source: National Association of Colleges and Employers (NACE), 2003.*

When it comes to the increased cost of private schools, parents should plan on borrowing. "You can buy a Saturn with cash," says Ellen Frishberg, director of Student Financial Services at Johns Hopkins University, "but not a Mercedes. So be prepared to borrow for a private school."

Consider a home mortgage. When buying a house, you borrow from a lender to afford a costly house, and then agree to spread out repayments of this amount over a number of years. You pay interest, but often the value of the house increases beyond the interest you are paying. With college, it's a similar situation. College graduates will also pay interest on student loans, but they can expect their earnings to increase in the future far beyond the interest they are paying.

> **The Student Loan Low-Down**
>
> Students borrow an average of $27,600 in educational debt, according to a 2003 Nellie Mae survey. That's three and a half times the amount from a decade ago.

Also, college loans are truly an investment in your student's future. Compare the difference in income between high school graduates and college graduates, and you'll see why student loans aren't only "good" debt—they're the best debt you can have.

AVERAGE STARTING SALARIES BY MAJOR	
Accounting	$41,360
Business administration	$36,515
Computer science	$46,536
Chemical engineering	$52,169
Civil engineering	$41,067
Economics/finance	$40,764
Electrical engineering	$50,566
Liberal arts	$29,543
Marketing	$35,822
Management information systems (MIS)	$41,543
Mechanical engineering	$48,659

Source: National Association of Colleges and Employers Spring 2003 Salary Survey

MOVING ON

To wrap up, we began by explaining how planning for your student's education is just as important as planning for retirement. We then learned about the three different types of income: past, present, and future, and learned of several sources for each of these incomes. We reviewed the difference between "good" and "bad" debt, and learned why student loans are considered good debt to have.

In the next chapter, we'll look at the role financial aid will play in your student's education. You'll learn about the three basic types of financial aid and the various financial aid programs available, as well as your rights and responsibilities when applying for financial aid. But before you move on, take a look at the checklist for this chapter.

✓ CHECKLIST:

1. Decide if there are sources of income you can use to help pay for college. To get the best results, begin by looking at savings, then present income, then at borrowing options.

    - Do you have savings or investments that could be used for college?
    - Do you receive dividends or other sources of current income that can be saved or invested for college?

2. Review your household budget to look for ways you can set money aside for your student's college.

3. Depending on your student's age and income, consider if investments would help college expenses down the road. Stocks and bonds can help long-term, while short-term CDs may provide a better return than a savings account.

4. Consider opening a separate account for your student's college fund, if you don't already have one. Doing so helps keep track of how much you have for these expenses. Look at 529 plans and education savings accounts to see if they are right for you.

5. Begin educating yourself about various types of student loans. You won't need to apply for them until after completing the financial aid paperwork, but the more you learn now, the easier the process the will be later.

WEBSITES

The Motley Fool
www.fool.com

Savingforcollege.com
www.savingforcollege.com

College Savings Plan Network
www.collegesavings.org

Upromise
www.upromise.com

## CHAPTER SIX

Get Your Share of Student Aid

Once you've reviewed your income and know how much you can afford to contribute to your student's education, you're ready to begin navigating your financial aid options. But before addressing the specifics of applying for financial aid, it's helpful to have an understanding of the types of aid available, as well as the differences between them. By understanding both the basics of financial aid and the programs out there, you and your son or daughter will be able to find assistance that best suits your needs and budget.

THE BASICS OF FINANCIAL AID

As you learn about various types of financial aid, you'll see that there are two primary categories of assistance: need-based aid and merit-based aid.

Need-Based Aid

As the term suggests, need-based aid looks at a family's financial resources to determine how much money the student needs to attend college. Examples are government-supported student loans and grants offered to low-income families.

Financial aid offices at colleges and universities look at your income and financial situation to determine how much you should be able to contribute to your student's education (your EFC). This involves a mathematical calculation referred to as need analysis. This need analysis will be done both by the federal government and the financial aid offices at each school to which your student is applying. Usually, the government calculates its need analysis for your student, then informs each of your potential colleges of its decision. This in turn, may influence the need analysis calculated by those schools. For those that are interested, we'll look at this calculation in depth in chapter eight. Otherwise, you just need to be aware that this process exists.

TRENT & SEPPY SAY...

Trent:

The need analysis process basically subtracts your expected family contribution (EFC) from the cost of college. The difference that's left is how much your student will need to afford his or her education. Cost – EFC = Need

Seppy:

Your need will be different from school to school. But no matter what it turns out to be, well... hey, we all need help sometimes.

"Every parent should ask prospective schools if they meet students' full financial need, and what formula they use to determine need," says Ellen Frishberg, director of Student Financial Services at Johns Hopkins University. "Schools can use liberal calculations to determine need, but those results are useless if they don't have the money to back them up."

Merit-Based Aid

Merit-based financial aid is not based on financial need but upon a student's achievements, ability, contributions, or potential and is awarded regardless of the recipient's financial status. For example, athletic scholarships are merit-based aid, as are grants awarded to top academic students for their grades. Merit-based aid is usually awarded by colleges, organizations, or businesses and corporations.

The factors involved in awarding merit-based aid depend upon the school itself, as well as the type of aid given. If an academic scholarship pays for the tuition of a student who majors in biology and is a minority, qualifying students must not only have good grades, but must obviously major in biology and be a minority. Not all merit-based aid is so narrow in scope. Corporations may offer scholarships to students based solely on grade point average, or a local organization may provide a grant to an exceptional student in the area. Scholarships and grants are also available based upon artistic talents and other abilities beyond academics and athletics.

Because of the nature of merit-based aid, colleges use these types of assistance to remain competitive with other schools. For example, a well-known state school with a good academic reputation may try to compete with Ivy League schools for top students. In this situation, the public school may offer a top student a free education in hopes of luring the student away from an Ivy League school. Likewise, schools that are trying to become more diverse may award scholarships to minorities in hopes of creating a more diverse student body.

Although this book focuses primarily on need-based aid, you and your son or daughter should actively look for merit-based aid regardless of academic grades, SAT scores, or your financial situation. You should ask prospective schools about merit-based aid, as well as your employer, local businesses, and organizations to which you belong.

It's also important to note that some financial aid can be a combination of both need and merit-based aid. For example, a college may offer a scholarship to a student with high grades and an excellent G.P.A., but may also require the recipient to come from a low-income household.

Non-Need-Based/Non-Merit-Based Aid

The good news is that it exists. The bad news is that it is primarily granted in the form of loans. This aid is offered without any special stipulation regarding achievement or potential, and is granted irrespective of the family's financial status. Unsubsidized Stafford Loans (we'll talk more about them later in this chapter) are not need or merit based, so any student is eligible for them. Similarly, any parent is eligible to apply for Parental Loans for Undergraduate Students (PLUS Loans) (good credit here is important—more on these loans later).

TRENT & SEPPY SAY...

Trent:

The Internet can be a valuable resource in finding sources for merit-based aid, but stay away from websites offering assistance for a fee. Many of these are scams, and what they don't tell you is that the information they provide can be found free of charge in libraries, guidance offices, financial aid offices, and on the Web.

Seppy:

So don't pay a website for a list of scholarships that you can find on your own. It's one thing to like convenience, but no one likes to throw their money away.

THE THREE TYPES OF AID

While need and merit-based aid define the two categories of assistance, there are three basic types of financial aid; grants and schlarships (gift aid), loans (self-help aid), and work-study programs (work aid).

Grants, Scholarships, and Tuition Discounts (Gift Aid)

Any financial aid that does not need to be repaid is gift aid. Grants, scholarships, and tuition discounts are financial gifts that do not need to be given back or returned at a later date. Some gift aid is given to students for one time only, while some is renewed each year.

Loans (Self-Help Aid)

Financial aid that must be repaid to a lender is considered self-help aid. The vast majority of this type of aid is in the form of loans borrowed by either a student or parent.

Work-Study Programs (Work Aid)

Often called work-study programs, work aid is money earned by the student to help afford college. Most colleges offer work-study programs, where students work on campus part-time. Depending upon the school or program, students may receive paychecks, or the money may be subtracted from their tuition and fees. Most work-study programs require students to work ten to fifteen hours a week during the semester.

> **Not Just Loans**
>
> "There's a myth that student aid just means loans," offers Jack Toney, director of financial aid for Marshall University in West Virginia. "People think loans are the only thing available to them, and it often discourages them from getting involved."

Not surprisingly, there are pros and cons to each of these types of aid. Gift aid is obviously the most desired type of financial aid, but scholarships and grants may require a student to maintain a certain grade point average, attend a particular college, or major in a particular discipline. Self-help aid, unlike gifts and work aid, will have to be repaid at a later date. And while helpful, work aid requires the student to add the responsibility of part-time work to their schedule, which may prove difficult for some.

Most families use a combination of these three types of aid to afford college, although loans and self-help aid are increasingly making up the majority of financial aid for students. Work aid can be of great help to disciplined students, but can create additional stress for a student who must maintain a high G.P.A. to keep their scholarship. Academic scholarships are extremely helpful, but student athletes can expect to devote a great deal of time to their sport. Once your son or daughter is offered these various types of financial aid, the two of you will be able to decide what is best for him or her.

FINANCIAL AID PROGRAMS

"Financial aid programs at public and private colleges aren't all that different," says Karen Krause, who has worked in financial aid offices at both public and private schools. "The key difference for students is that private colleges may require an insitutional aid form. Sometimes funding sources are different, especially in the area of grants, but that's the major difference."

In order to find the best financial aid options for you and your son or daughter, you will need to understand the different types available and which you qualify for. To help, the chart below separates various programs by comparing need and merit-based aid. In a moment, we'll look at each of these programs in more depth.

KAPLAN

NON-NEED-BASED AID	NEED-BASED AID
Federal Aid	**Federal Aid**
	Federal Pell Grant
	Federal SEO Grant (FSEOG)
Student Employment Program	Federal Work Study
	Federal Perkins Loan
Unsubsidized Federal Stafford Loan	Subsidized Federal Stafford Loan
Federal Parent PLUS Loan	Federal Parent PLUS Loan
	Federal Direct Student Loan
State Aid*	**State Aid***
State Grant Program	State Grant Program
State Loan Program	State Loan Program
Institutional Aid	**Institutional Aid**
Academic Incentive Awards	Need-Based Grants
Merit-Based Scholarships	Tuition Discounts/Waivers
Combination Merit & Need-Based Awards	Combination Merit & Need-Based Awards
Other	**Other**
Private Scholarships	Private Scholarships
Alternative Private Loans	Alternative Private Loans

* Since state aid programs vary from state to state, not all options may be available in your state. You'll need to contact the agencies in your state to determine what is available to you. See the Financial Aid Resources section for a listing of state aid agencies.

You'll notice that every option listed in the chart above is a grant or scholarship (gift aid), a loan (self-help aid), or a work study program (work aid). In order to better understand the options within each of these three types of aid, let's look at each type separately.

GRANTS, SCHOLARSHIPS, AND TUITION DISCOUNTS (GIFT AID PROGRAMS)

When looking at grants and scholarships, you will see that there are six types of gift aid programs.

Institutional Grants and Scholarships

Institutional aid is the term used to describe money offered to students from the institution's own funds. The criteria and policies for these types of awards vary from college to college, but if your student is eligible for federal financial aid, these institutional funds are linked to the federal financial aid they will receive. As mentioned earlier, this area can be very competitive, since it allows colleges to vie for students. These awards may require additional application forms which must be turned in by a set deadline, often with the application to attend the school. The majority of institutional aid is awarded to full time students. While academics aren't always the only criterion, they are important. "Good academics are essential to getting scholarships," Samuel Ellison of Morehouse College comments. "To be considered for our academic scholarships, a student needs a minimum SAT score of 1150 and a G.P.A. of 3.5."

An increasingly popular form of gift aid, tuition discounting began to soar about a decade ago as government grants decreased. They are typically offered to recruit the brightest students, and high SAT scores or a solid G.P.A. can lead to thousands of dollars off the price of tuition. On the DePauw University website, for example, you can enter an SAT score, grade point average, and class rank, and receive your discount amount online. Public colleges are now also beginning to offer discounts.

Full tuition waivers are also available from some institutions, notably the military academies like West Point and Annapolis. While tuition and other expenses are free, there is a catch: a military service requirement of five or more years. If that doesn't seem like much of a gift, consider New York's Cooper Union, which is tuition-free. (See the "Bargains" sidebar in chapter two.)

Government Grants

State Grants

Every state offers a grant program, and to be eligible for these awards, a student usually must be a resident of the state. Most state grants also require the student to go to school in-state, as well, although a handful do not. While the bulk of state grants are geared toward need-based students, some are merit-based and awarded regardless of financial need or a family's income. To learn more about grants offered by your state, you'll need to contact your state's higher education agency. The Financial Aid Resources section in the back of the book lists these agencies in each state and how to contact them.

FREE MONEY! NON-NEED-BASED GIFT AID		

Admit it: You dream of someone handing your student a big scholarship or award, not because she needs it but because she deserves it. Your dream could come true! Here are some schools that give non-need-based gift aid to a large percentage of their students:

School	% Full Time Undergrads Receiving Free Money	Avg. Award Per Student
Cooper Union	100%	$25,000
Manhattanville College	92%	$8,334
Morehouse College	64%	$4,482
Denison University	52%	$9,759
University of Georgia	50%	$4,255
Birmingham-Southern College	49%	$9,285
Kalamazoo College	49%	$9,450
New College of Florida	48%	$4,992
Berry College	46%	$10,129
Hendrix College	44%	$12,623
Truman State University	43%	$4,021
Whitman College	43%	$8,000
Hampden-Sydney College	42%	$13,044
DePauw University	42%	$10,337

Federal Pell Grant

The largest grant program offered by the federal government, Pell Grants are need-based. The amount a student receives is based upon their need analysis and whether the student will attend college full or part time. Millions of students from low-income families receive Pell Grants each year, but the vast majority of middle-income families do not qualify for this aid. When filing financial aid forms with the federal government, you will be considered for a Pell Grant.

Federal Supplemental Educational Opportunity Grant (FSEOG)

The FSEOG is a federal grant awarded by colleges to the neediest students who will be attending the school. Because of this, FSEOGs are often given to Pell Grant recipients.

Other Federal Grants

A handful of merit-based grants and scholarships are awarded by the federal government each year. The majority of these awards are specific to a field or major, such as science, nursing, or earmarked for honors students. Some are designed to be given to graduate students. Although these grants are funded by the federal government, they are awarded by state scholarship agencies.

Private Grants and Scholarships

Many corporations and organizations offer financial aid to students all over the country, and these types of gift aid exist outside the federal and institutional types of aid offered. For example, high schools may offer small grants to exceptional seniors, corporations may offer scholarships to children of employees, minority groups may offer assistance to minority students, or college alumni associations may offer grants to exceptional students attending their university. There are many kinds of aid offered by private organizations and corporations, so don't assume it's not worth the effort—some are need-based, some are merit-based, and some are a combination of both. These types of aid require a bit of legwork and research, but are worth the time and energy.

> **Check With Your Employer**
>
> Be sure you check with your employer about tuition benefits, as well as grants or scholarships. Most Fortune 1000 companies have funds set aside for this, and finding out is as easy as calling human resources.

"The ideal time to start looking for these kinds of grants and scholarships is early in the student's junior year," says Jack Toney, director of financial aid for Marshall University. "The student won't be able to apply then, but they'll learn which scholarships they're interested in, and when the deadline is for the following year when they'll apply."

Connie Gore, vice president for enrollment for Randolph-Macon Woman's College notes, "Some scholarships are very specific in their requirements, but I also know that a lot of aid out there goes unclaimed. Local scholarships are really a good option if your family is involved in a group or organization within the community or if you are part of a small group or community."

"When it comes to scholarships," says Clark Ray, an Army officer with three children, "there are a lot of scholarships in the $500 to $1,000 range on bases. Actually, if a student is the child of an enlisted member of the armed forces, there seem to be more available than if their parent is an officer."

Still, make sure you and your student remain realistic when applying. "Lots of people oversell themselves in this area," says Barry Simmons, director of financial aid at Virginia Tech. "Many believe that a solid B student is going to receive a significant amount of scholarships. Some scholarships can be competitive," he acknowledges, "and parents need to be realistic about competition for them."

LOANS (SELF-HELP)

Loans 101

Before we discuss the various types of loans available to you and your student, you'll first need to know some basic terms and ideas behind loans.

Interest Rate

Just as banks pay interest when you put money into a savings account or CD, you have to pay lenders interest when you borrow money from them. Interest on loans can be a fixed rate or a variable rate. A fixed rate means that you pay the same percentage of interest throughout the length of your loan. A variable rate means that the amount of interest you pay will change at certain times during the length of the loan. A fixed rate gives you the security of knowing exactly how much you'll have to pay each month, but if the interest rate drops in a few years, you'll be paying higher than that amount. With a variable rate, there is some uncertainty regarding just how much your interest will be, but when interest rates drop, so will the amount of interest you'll pay.

Repayment Terms

This refers to how long you will be required to pay back the loan, as well as when you will be expected to start making payments. Just as car loans can be five or seven years long, repayment on student loans can be anywhere from ten to thirty years. Also, some student loans may indicate that the student or parent make payments once the student graduates from college, while others may indicate that repayment start while the student is still attending college. The terms of repayment, along with the interest rate, are the two most important things you should know when considering a loan, since they will impact how much you will pay each month.

Fees

You've learned that colleges charge fees in addition to tuition, room, and board. So do banks and lenders. These can charge administration fees, application fees, and other kinds of charges. These fees are not included in the amount you borrow, but are subtracted from the amount you actually receive. This means that the more a lender charges in fees, the less of the loan you actually get to use for college. Because of this, families often borrow more than the actual amount they need, so that there will be enough to pay for school once fees are taken out. Before applying for any loan, make sure you ask about any fees associated with the loan so you won't be surprised later.

Net versus Gross

Gross refers to the total amount you are requesting when applying for a loan, while net refers to the amount you will receive after fees are taken out. If you ask for a $10,000 gross loan, and the bank lending you the money charges $850 in fees, your net would be $9,150.

Monthly Payment

Your monthly payment simply means the amount you will owe the lender each month, and educational lenders will offer examples of various monthly payments to help you estimate your monthly payment.

Deferment Options

Deferment means the borrower may postpone making payments on the loan during certain situations. For example, many educational lenders allow borrowers to defer monthly payments while their student is in college. Other options allow borrowers to make payments on their interest only, meaning the principal (amount borrowed) is deferred. Deferment options vary from loan to loan, and you'll need to know what these are.

Prepayment Penalty

Some lenders charge a fee if the loan is repaid early, and this is called a prepayment penalty. Try to avoid this penalty, since it will give you and your student the option of paying your loan off early. If you can afford to do this, you'll save money because you'll pay less interest.

Consolidation

This is simply combining several loans into one lump sum. If you and your student take out a loan for each year he or she is in college, you'll find yourself with several different loan payments due each month. By consolidating those loans, you'll then only have to make one payment. In addition, consolidating often reduces the amount you'll pay each month, since the final monthly payment you'll owe will probably be less than the separate checks you write otherwise. If you expect to take out loans each year, it may be a good idea to try and use the same lender for each loan, since that will make consolidation more convenient in the future.

To make consolidation easier, the federal government has created the Federal Consolidation Loan Program, which lets Federal Stafford and Federal Perkins loans be consolidated under one lender and interest rate. It also offers extended repayments, although this will increase the interest you owe.

SELF-HELP PROGRAMS

When reviewing self-help programs, there are basically six types of loans available.

Federal Perkins Loan

Perkins Loans are need-based loans offered to students at five percent interest. Colleges have set funds designated for Perkins Loans and select recipients to receive them. Interest on a Perkins Loan does not accrue while the student is in college, and repayment doesn't begin until nine months after the student graduates.

Subsidized Federal Stafford Loan

Subsidized Stafford Loans are need-based federal loans made by a bank or similar lender. Your student's college must certify their eligibility on the loan application, so you can expect to turn the bank's form over to your college for their verification. Like the Perkins Loan, interest does not accrue while your student is in school and repayment begins six months after graduation. There are fees associated with Subsidized Stafford Loans, and the remaining balance is paid directly to your student's college.

Unsubsidized Federal Stafford Loan

Unsubsidized Stafford Loans are similar to Subsidized Stafford Loans with two exceptions. First, Unsubsidized Stafford Loans are not need-based, so any student is eligible for them. Also, interest accrues on these loans while the student is in college. These loans are also made by a bank or similar lender, although the amount a student may borrow is slightly higher than the Subsidized Stafford Loan. There are fees associated with Unsubsidized Stafford Loans, and the remaining balance is paid directly to your student's college.

Federal PLUS Loan

Parental Loans for Undergraduate Students (PLUS) are federal loans for the parents of undergraduate students only. These unsubsidized loans are not need based, so any parent is eligible. Repayment begins 60 days after the money is loaned, and parents can borrow up to the cost of the college (minus any financial aid). Fees are charged, and because lenders check the parent's credit history, a cosigner may be required or the loan may be denied if there are credit problems.

Federal Direct Student Loan

The Federal Direct Student Loan program is similar to the Stafford Loan program, and most colleges participate in one or the other. The major difference between the two is that while Stafford Loans are provided by a bank, credit union, or other lender, the Federal Direct Loan is provided by the U.S. Department of Education. So while students with Stafford loans make payments to a bank, students with a Direct Loan will make payments directly to the federal government.

State Loans

As with state grants, the types of state loans available vary from state to state, so you'll need to find out what is available. To learn about the loans offered by your state, you'll need to contact your state's higher education agency. The Financial Aid Resources section in the back of this book lists these agencies in each state and how to contact them.

DEEP IN DEBT: AVERAGE LOAN DEBT PER STUDENT	
You'd better be sure that the school you choose is worth every single penny, or you'll regret it when it's time to start paying back your loans. The average loan debt carried by undergrads at these schools is a bit intimidating:	
Embry-Riddle Aeronautical University	$34,546
Pepperdine University	$31,179
Tuskegee University	$30,000
Kettering University	$29,281
Villanova University	$28,217
Rose-Hulman Institute of Technology	$27,000
Elon University	$26,663
University of Notre Dame	$25,595
Wake Forest University	$24,769
Rensselaer Polytechnic Institute	$24,590
University of Puget Sound	$24,272
Vanderbilt University	$24,023

LOAN FORGIVENESS

There are certain situations where government loans can be forgiven, and these strict guidelines usually deal with certain employment situations or government service. To qualify, you must perform volunteer work in specified organizations, perform military service, teach or practice medicine in certain types of communities, or meet other criteria specified by the forgiveness program. For example, the government's Child Care Provider Loan Forgiveness Program, which is designed to attract college-educated individuals into the early child care profession, offers an incentive for college-educated individuals to stay in the field. The Peace Corps and the National Guard are also among the organizations offering loan forgiveness.

Debt Forgiveness Link

To learn more about loan forgiveness, go to *www.finaid.org*. The website provides an extensive list of organizations offering loan forgiveness, as well as links to sites offering other information on these programs.

"I always joke with my kids that the Marine Corps is always hiring," laughs Clark Ray, an Army officer stationed at West Point, NY. "When it comes to paying for their share of college, there's lot of financial support in the armed forces. That's not for everyone, but there are other loan forgiveness programs out there that can also make a big difference."

LOAN FORGIVENESS

These volunteer organizations offer loan forgiveness:

- **AmeriCorps.**
  Serve for 12 months and receive up to $7,400 in stipends plus $4,725 to be used towards your loan. Call 800-942-2677.

- **Peace Corps.**
  Volunteers may apply for deferment of Stafford, Perkins, and Consolidation loans, and partial cancellation of Perkins Loans (15 percent for each year of service). Contact the Peace Corps at 1111 20th St., NW, Washington, DC 20526 or call 800-424-8580 or (202)692-1845.

- **Volunteers in Service to America (VISTA).**
  Provide 1,700 hours of service and receive $4,725. Call 800-942-2677 or (202)606-5000.

- **Military**
  Students who are in the Army National Guard may be eligible for their Student Loan Repayment Program, which offers up to $10,000.

- **Teaching**
  Students who become full-time teachers in an elementary or secondary school that serves students from low-income families can have a portion of their Perkins Loan forgiven. Contact your school district's administration to see which schools are eligible.

  Perkins loans can be cancelled for full-time service as a teacher in a designated school serving students from low-income families, as a special education teacher, or as teacher of math, science, foreign languages, bilingual education in designated teacher shortage areas. See the U.S. Department of Education's pages on Cancellation/Deferment Options for Teachers and Cancellation for Childcare Providers for a complete list of forgiveness programs.

WORK-STUDY PROGRAMS (WORK AID)

There are basically two types of part-time employment programs available to college students: work study programs supported by the federal government, and those supported by the state government.

TRENT & SEPPY SAY...

Trent:

Many schools offer part-time jobs, which means the student works on campus instead of at a local business. Usually, these jobs offer more flexibility and convenience than working somewhere else.

Seppy:

And since these jobs aren't need-based, any student is eligible. Workers receive their paychecks, so they're not required to apply them to their education. (This may be good news, or bad, depending on your student.)

Federal Work-Study Program

Need-based, the Federal Work-Study Program awards college students money for use towards their education through part-time employment. Most of these jobs are on campus, with students often working in cafeterias, libraries, or other light administrative desk work. Most colleges will ask if your student wishes to be considered for work-study when you apply for financial aid, and positions are awarded based on your need analysis.

State Work-Study Programs

A small number of states offer work-study programs that are similar to the federal program, except that state programs are funded with state rather than federal funds. To learn if your state offers a work-study program, you'll need to contact your state's higher education agency. The Financial Aid Resources section in the back of the book lists these agencies in each state and how to contact them.

STRATEGIES TO MAXIMIZE FINANCIAL AID

Student versus Parent Assets

We'll return to this point later, but it's important to stress it here: The more assets and investments your student has, the less financial aid he or she may qualify for. When schools determine a family's expected contribution (EFC) for college, they expect 35 percent of a student's assets to be used for college, while as little as six percent is expected to come from the parent's assets. Because of this huge difference, it's wise to transfer assets in your son's or daughter's name to yours. This tip alone can mean a significant difference in the amount of financial aid your student receives. And we'll repeat it in upcoming chapters.

Should Students Take Out Loans?

Many families wonder if student loans should be in the student's name or the parents'. In reality, every family is different. Often, this burden is split between parent and student, although some parents shoulder their student's entire loan debt and some students have all their student loans in their name. Opinion regarding this is divided, with some parents insisting that their student pay for as much of his or her education as possible, while others believe it's best to keep their student's debt at a minimum.

Regardless, student borrowing differs from other loans. When you apply for a loan, lenders use your monthly income to estimate your loan payments. Students, on the other hand, must rely on estimates of their future income in order to determine their potential to pay back a loan for college. Unfortunately, you can't predict your son's or daughter's income after graduation, but you might be able to estimate their average salary based on entry-level incomes in that field.

TRENT & SEPPY SAY...

Trent:

When considering loans, the amount you and your student are able to borrow may differ depending on whose name the loans are under. Be sure to ask about these differences as you consider various types of loans and lenders.

Seppy:

The more information you get from lenders, the easier it'll be to decide how much you'll want to borrow and what's best for you.

RIGHTS AND RESPONSIBILITIES

Now that you've learned about the numerous types of financial aid programs available to you and your student, you'll also need to know what your rights and responsibilities are when applying for financial aid. Refer to the list below as you begin considering financial aid programs.

Your Rights

You have the right to:

- Privacy—all records and data you submit with financial aid applications should be treated as confidential information.
- Accept or decline any offer of financial aid.
- Be notified before any financial aid is cancelled, as well as the reason for the cancellation.

You have the right to know:

- What financial aid is available from federal, state, and institutional resources.
- Procedures and deadlines for submitting financial aid.

- How financial aid recipients are selected.
- How your financial aid eligibility is determined, including all resources considered, with this information made available to you by the financial aid office.
- How and when your financial aid funds are going to be dispersed.
- The full details of each financial aid award you receive.
- The criteria used to determine satisfactory academic progress for keeping financial aid awards.
- How to appeal a decision by the financial aid office concerning a financial aid award.

For student loans, you have the right to know:
- The interest rate.
- The total amount you must repay.
- When repayment begins.
- The length of repayment period.
- Cancellation or deferment options.

For Work-Study programs, you have the right to know:
- A description of the job.
- The hours the student must work.
- The rate of pay.
- How and when the student will be paid.

Your Responsibilities

You are responsible for:
- Reading and understanding all financial aid documents.
- Filling out all applications completely.
- Complying with any deadlines.
- Keeping copies of any form you are required to sign.
- Providing correct information on all financial aid applications and forms (misrepresentation can be considered a criminal offense).
- Providing documentation to support your application.
- Repaying any student loans you receive.

- Reporting any change in the student's enrollment, housing, or financial status (including scholarships or grants from outside sources), as well as changes in personal status (including address, name, and marital changes).
- Reporting any personal or enrollment changes to your lender.
- Completing an entrance and exit interview if you receive a student loan.
- Using financial aid funds for educational-related expenses only.

MOVING ON

To wrap up, we began by comparing need-based and merit-based kinds of financial aid. Building upon that, we then discussed the three types of financial aid; gift aid, self-help aid, and work aid. We also reviewed how most families use a combination of these three types in order to afford college.

Next, we looked at the different financial aid programs, separating them by need-based and merit-based programs. We then looked at each program by breaking them down further into gift aid programs, self-help programs, and work aid programs. Gift aid programs covered various grants and scholarships, while self-help programs discussed the loans available to pay for college. Then, work aid programs discussed ways students can reduce college expenses by working on campus. Finally, the chapter gave a quick list of rights and responsibilities every parent and student should know when applying for financial aid.

In the next chapter, you'll learn how to navigate the financial aid process. We'll be discussing the applications, forms, and documents involved in applying for financial aid, as well as what you can expect once the paperwork is completed. But before you move on, take a look at the checklist for this chapter.

✓ CHECKLIST:

1. Have your student begin looking for merit-based financial aid opportunities.
   - Contact prospective universities to find out what they offer.
   - Ask your employer if they offer scholarships.
   - Contact local businesses and organizations.
   - Use the Internet and your student's high school for assistance.

2. Begin learning about federal financial aid opportunities you may be interested in.
   - What programs do you qualify for?
   - Are you eligible for grants as well as loans?
   - What are the advantages and disadvantages of various loans?
   - How much can you borrow?
   - What are the program's deadlines for application?

3. Contact your state's higher education agency to find out what state grants and loans are available. Request paperwork for any programs you are interested in.

4. Discuss work-study programs with your student.

5. Begin contacting lenders about various types of student loans. Be sure to compare interest rates, fees, as well as repayment terms and deferment options to find one that best suits your needs. Also, compare the differences in taking a loan out in your name versus your student's.

WEBSITES

FastWeb
www.fastweb.com

CollegeScholarships.com
www.collegescholarships.com

Scholarships.com
www.scholarships.com

Federal Financial Aid
www.studentaid.ed.gov

PELL Grants
www.pellgrantsonline.ed.gov

Perkins Loans, Federal Family Education Loan Program (FFELP),
William D. Ford Direct Loan Program
www.studentaid.ed.gov

Stafford Loans
www.ed.gov

PLUS Loans
www.ed.gov

Federal Supplemental Educational Opportunity Grant (FSEOG)
www.ed.gov

SallieMae
www.salliemae.com

NellieMae
www.nelliemae.com

## CHAPTER SEVEN

Navigate the Process

There's no doubt that applying for financial aid can be an overwhelming and confusing process. (After all, that's probably why you bought this book.) And although you may not realize it, you're much better prepared to navigate the applications and forms involved than when you first started. Now that you know how much financial aid you need and the types of programs available, applying for aid will be much easier.

The process of applying for financial aid can vary from school to school, although the same basic forms are used by almost every college and university. To start, you'll learn about the different forms, and then we'll look at each one individually.

> ## TRENT & SEPPY SAY...
>
> **Trent:**
>
> *For some people, just the thought of forms makes them nervous. Fortunately, it's not a lot of paperwork, and not all of them are going to apply to you.*
>
> **Seppy:**
>
> *Plus, the form for federal aid has gotten much easier in the last ten years. And once you get to the institutional forms for each college, they'll probably ask for the same information.*

FINANCIAL AID FORMS

There are essentially nine kinds of financial aid forms, and they fall into three categories: core forms, supplemental forms, and verification forms. Each of these categories has three forms.

Core Forms

These are the mandatory forms that you and your son or daughter will need to fill out and file before doing anything else. Because they form the core of your financial aid applications, they're the first step in the financial aid process.

FAFSA

The Free Application for Federal Student Aid (FAFSA) is the basic form required to apply for any federal financial aid. In previous chapters, you learned that the federal government uses your income tax information to determine how much aid your family qualifies for. The FAFSA form is what you'll use to provide that income tax information to the government. In turn, those numbers will be used in the government's need analysis process to decide how much your EFC will be, as well as how much aid you can receive. When filing the FAFSA, your information can be forwarded to potential colleges, which will help in their financial aid process. A new FAFSA must be completed every year, and is required by all colleges.

CSS Profile Form

The College Scholarship Service (CSS) is part of the College Board, a private educational organization best known for developing college entrance examination tests like the SAT. The Profile form is a financial aid form required by some colleges and universities. It is designed to provide more complete and accurate information than the FAFSA, and since the CSS is not part of the federal government, this form is separate from your FAFSA information. The Profile form is most often used by private colleges that have their own funds to award and need additional information in order to make their financial aid decisions.

State Grant Application

In the last chapter, you learned that some states offer grants and student loans supported by state funds. The FAFSA is used only for federal financial aid, so if you're interested in applying for any state-supported aid, you'll need to file the necessary forms to do so. Using the Regional Resources section in part two, contact your state's higher education agency for forms and deadlines.

Supplemental Forms

In addition to these essential core forms, you may also have to file some supplemental forms depending upon your financial status and your family's situation.

Institutional Aid Application

As we discussed last chapter, institutional aid is financial aid offered by the college or university itself. Although colleges use the FAFSA and Profile forms in their need analysis of your family, some schools may require you to fill out their own institutional aid form. You will need to contact each prospective college to find out if they offer an institutional aid application.

But not all will. "We don't have a separate application for institutional aid," explains Jade Kolb, manager of financial aid at New York University. "But everyone is considered for those awards."

Divorced/Separated Parents Form

This form is a supplement to the CSS Profile. If a student's parents or custodians are divorced or separated, the parent who does not have custody of the student will be required to fill out this form. The instructions for the Profile form explain the Divorced/Separated Parents form in more detail.

Business/Farm Supplemental Form

This form is also a supplement to the CSS Profile. Parents who are farmers or who own their own businesses will be required to fill out this form. The instructions for the Profile form will explain the Business/Farm supplement in more detail.

Tax Documents

Finally, you'll need to have your tax documents handy in order to fill out these forms. Financial aid forms often refer to specific line items on your income tax forms, such as your 1040, so you'll need to be able to look that information up as you complete your applications. If you have your completed tax forms handy as you fill out the FAFSA and Profile forms, you'll probably be able to simply copy numbers from one form to the other.

> ### TRENT & SEPPY SAY...
>
> **Trent:**
> *Since you'll need your income tax statements in order to file your FAFSA, you should file your income tax as soon after January 1 as possible.*
>
> **Seppy:**
> *No one likes doing their taxes, but the sooner you finish them, the better—especially if it means you're eligible for more financial aid.*

Parent's Federal Tax and W-2 Forms

Naturally, you'll need your federal tax forms for the previous year, as well as your W-2 forms provided by your employer. If you're filing the FAFSA and Profile forms in a timely manner, you'll probably have just finished filing your income tax.

Student's Federal Tax and W-2 Forms

If your son or daughter filed an income tax return for the previous year, you will need his or her income tax forms and W-2s as well. Since most families keep their income tax records together, these forms should be handy, as well.

> **Reality 101**
> "One of the best ways a student can learn how to become responsible for their own money and job is for them to do their own income tax," says parent Karon Ray. "It's a real eye-opener."

Other Forms

Depending upon your financial situation and income tax filing, you may need to refer to other tax documents for verification. For example, 1099 forms used to represent interest on savings accounts or dividends received from stocks will need to be listed on your financial aid applications. In most cases, any additional or supplemental forms you filed with your income tax will be needed as you fill out the FAFSA and Profile forms.

Just as your income tax must be filed by April 15 every year, these financial aid forms have deadlines and timetables as well. Many students and parents assume that the financial aid deadlines for these forms and colleges are the same as the deadline for applying to attend the college, but that's not the case. Financial aid applications are based on the academic calendar, which starts when college begins in either August or September and ends when college lets out for the summer in May or June, rather than a calendar year of January to December. Because of this, you'll find yourself filing for financial aid in the fall before your student starts college, or early in the year that they start college.

If you need to fill out the CSS Profile form, this should be completed first. Since your student will be applying to colleges the fall before they graduate from high school, the Profile form can be filled out and filed at the same time they are completing their college applications. Most students and parents start the Profile form after October of their student's senior year.

"We filled out the Profile first," says Joe Sanseverino, whose daughter recently applied to state and private schools that required the CSS Profile. "The Profile didn't rely solely on your tax information, so we could get it out of the way earlier. Besides, after doing that, the FAFSA was a breeze."

The FAFSA form is usually completed early the next year, ideally as soon as possible after January 1. You'll need to find out what your college's deadlines are for these forms, and attempt to finish the process as soon as possible. Although many families don't realize it, most financial aid is awarded on a first-come, first-served basis, so the sooner you and your student apply for financial aid the more financial aid he or she will be eligible for.

"Not meeting deadlines for filing is the biggest concern at most colleges," insists Jack Toney, director of financial aid at Marshall University in West Virginia. "Many families wait so long to file the FAFSA, that they don't file the school's financial aid form in time. When that happens, students lose out on aid they could have been eligible for."

THE PROCESS

Since you now understand the types of financial aid applications and how they work, it's time to look at the process itself. To make things easier, we'll go over how to apply for financial aid step-by-step in the order you should follow.

Selecting Schools for Application

The first step in applying for any financial aid is knowing which schools your son or daughter is applying to. This certainly doesn't mean that they must have selected their college, but any school that you and your student are seriously considering should receive your FAFSA results, as well as a CSS Profile form if necessary. Be sure your list of prospective colleges includes your student's safety school, as well as his or her dream school, and everything in between.

Is the CSS Profile Necessary?

You already know that the CSS Profile form should be filled out before the FAFSA form, so you'll need to find out which prospective colleges, if any, require it. The best way to do this is to contact the financial aid offices at your colleges directly and ask them. This is also a perfect time to ask about supplemental and institutional forms they may require, and request that they be mailed to you. If any of your prospective colleges require the CSS Profile form, then you'll need to read "Filling Out the CSS Profile" below. If not, skip this section.

Filling Out the CSS Profile

There are five easy steps to completing the CSS Profile form, and you'll need to do them in the following order:

Complete the Registration Worksheet

The first thing you're required to do for the Profile form is complete a worksheet. It's called the Profile Registration worksheet, and it asks for basic information about you and your student. On it, you'll also list which schools need to receive the results of your Profile. This worksheet is used to provide you with a customized Profile form and is available online at *www.collegeboard.com* or by calling (305)829-9793. A sample worksheet is shown at the end of this chapter, and you'll notice that while the worksheet is free, you can expect to pay a fee when filing the Profile form with the CSS.

> ### TRENT & SEPPY SAY...
>
> **Trent:**
>
> *Just because your student is applying to a private college, don't assume that school requires the CSS Profile. Call the financial aid office and find out for certain before you pay the fee.*
>
> **Seppy:**
>
> *Over the past few years, more and more schools are opting to use their own institutional aid forms instead of the Profile. (As a famous comedian once said, "Not that there's anything wrong with that!")*

File the Worksheet and Pay the Fee

Once you have filled out the Profile Registration Worksheet, you'll need to file it with the CSS. You can register by phone or via the Internet by calling (305)829-9793 or by logging on to *www.collegeboard.com*. When you contact the CSS to file the worksheet, you will be expected to pay a registration fee, as well as a processing fee that will be charged for each school receiving your Profile. If you file online, you will have immediate access to your Profile form. If you file by telephone, your CSS will be mailed to you.

Complete the Profile Form

Once you have the Profile form, you'll need to fill it out and return it to the CSS. Each Profile form is customized based on your financial situation and needs, with questions or information that may be specific to your prospective colleges. A sample Profile Form is shown at the end of this chapter, but yours may look different depending upon your financial situation.

Provide Additional Information If Necessary

If you are divorced or separated, or own your own business, you'll be required to fill out and file the supplemental forms we discussed earlier in this chapter. Also, some of your prospective colleges may include additional questions or sheets. These forms will need to be completed and filed with the Profile form.

File the Form and Receive Your Summary

Once the Profile form and any supplements are filed, the CSS will automatically share this information with your prospective colleges. This means that once you finish the Profile form, it's not necessary to give it to colleges yourself. Once the process is complete, you'll receive an acknowledgement or confirmation from the CSS which will summarize your information and let you know that it has been sent to your prospective schools.

Filling Out the FAFSA

Next, you'll file a FAFSA to apply for any federal aid, including things like PLUS or Stafford loans, as well as any federal grants you and your son or daughter might qualify for. There are five (or sometimes six) steps to completing the FAFSA, and you'll need to do them in the following order.

Get a Form

No matter where your son or daughter decides to go to college, you'll need to fill out a FAFSA, and thanks to the Internet, you have a few options as to how you'll do it. Most high school guidance offices offer the paper form, or you can request one by calling the Federal Student Aid Information Center at 800-4-FED-AID. But as the Internet becomes more popular, you'll find that it's easier and faster to fill out the FAFSA online at *www.fafsa.ed.gov*. A sample FAFSA can be found at the end of this chapter.

Fill Out the Form

If you request a paper FAFSA, follow the directions included to complete the form. If you're going to fill out the FAFSA online, you'll want to print out and complete the website's worksheets beforehand. This will make the online process faster and less time-consuming. Instead of sitting in front of a computer while you sort though papers hunting for a particular amount or number, a completed worksheet will allow you to type everything online in much less time. But regardless of which method you use, you'll need your tax documents to complete a FAFSA. You'll also want to indicate which prospective colleges and universities should receive this information.

Review the Form

When you finish the FAFSA, take a few minutes to double check all your information. Corrections can be made to your FAFSA later, but doing so will slow down the financial aid process and may impact how much financial aid you qualify for. "One common problem we see is when parents put the wrong information on the FAFSA form," explains Samuel Ellison, a student employment manager and financial aid adviser at Morehouse College. "If parents and students file for extensions, they may end up putting incorrect information on the FAFSA without knowing it."

Ellison also reminds students to make sure they've selected the correct school codes for prospective colleges. "Other students forget to put school codes on the form, and when that happens we never get their information. Luckily, if they forget, they can call or go online to correct that."

Submit the Form

Once you're satisfied with your information, you'll need to submit the FAFSA. If you're using a paper form, you'll need to sign it and send it in with the included postcard. This postcard will be mailed back to you to let you know that your FAFSA is being processed. If you're filing your FAFSA online, you have two options. You can either print out the FAFSA, sign it, and mail it in, or use a government-issued pin number that works much like the pin numbers for ATM cards. If you decide to use a pin number, you'll need to register for this online at *www.pin.ed.gov*. It takes a few days to process the request, so you'll have to wait for your pin before filling out the FAFSA. Still, this is faster than mailing in your signature. The earliest a FAFSA can be submitted is January 1, but the earlier the better.

"Don't wait until summer to file your FAFSA," advises Jack Toney, director of financial aid at Marshall University. "File it as soon as possible after January 1. You can always make changes to it later, but schools need your FAFSA as soon as possible if you don't want to miss the deadlines for certain aid opportunities."

"We want students to be able to make an informed decision when considering which college to attend," explains Ellen Frishberg of Johns Hopkins, "And knowing their financial aid options are part of that, we've set a school deadline of February 15 for students to file their institutional aid form and have completed their FAFSA, because we're then able to give them our package to help their decision."

"Families with unique situations should provide additional financial information to colleges as soon as possible," adds Connie Gores, who is both a vice president for enrollment at a college and a parent. "I recommend they don't wait until after they receive their aid package, but instead, send a letter to the college's financial aid office right after submitting their FAFSA. If a family has a significant event, such as a parent losing a job, caring for an additional family member, or even something like a significant one-time bonus that might increase their income more than usual, it's smart to let schools know early on."

But remember: No matter how much you've put off applying for financial aid, you should know that it's never too late to start. In fact, you and your son or daughter can file a FAFSA even after he or she has already started college. Even if you have just a few weeks until he or she'll pack up and head off for school, you still have time to start the process and get some financial aid. Granted, you'll have to work a little harder and cram some things into a short period of time, but it's worth it. So don't give up because you think you waited too long. But don't use this as an excuse to put things off. You may lose out on other significant sources of aid that may otherwise have been available to you.

Receive Your SAR

After your FAFSA is processed, you will receive a Student Aid Report (SAR) in the mail. This will tell you the results of your need analysis and let you know how much your Expected Family Contribution (EFC) is. This same information will be reported to your prospective colleges. As we discussed earlier, your EFC is not negotiable, so even if the amount is more than you can afford, there is no way to change this number (unless some of your information is incorrect, and you correct those amounts on your FAFSA).

"For me, the troubling thing about my FAFSA was that the calculations don't take your cost of living into consideration," says Joe Sanseverino. "We live on Long Island, close to New York City, and our SAR certainly didn't seem to reflect how expensive it is to live here." As anyone who's visited New York knows, a dollar isn't always worth a dollar. "It just didn't feel accurate for where we live," he admits. Ellen Frishberg of Johns Hopkins acknowledges the sentiment. "Unfortunately, the FAFSA doesn't take your cost of living into account," she says.

Verify Your Information

About 30 percent of all FAFSA applications are randomly selected for verification, and if it happens to you, don't worry. Unlike a tax audit, this doesn't mean you've made a mistake or have incorrect information. Your prospective colleges will send you a verification worksheet and ask for copies of certain documents. This may include tax returns, bank statements, statements from investment accounts, or other supplemental information. You should make every effort to provide the college with those documents and information as soon as possible. When colleges request additional information, it means that your need analysis has not been completed, and the longer the process takes, the less financial aid you may receive. And verification is usually a simple, straightforward process. "When we verify students, we'll ask for tax documents from the families," says Kolb. "If we think something like a family's amount of tax paid is wrong—for example, if someone got a refund and wrote "zero" on their form—we'll correct that for them."

"Students are normally selected for verification by the Department of Education, not by colleges," explains Karen Krause of the University of Texas at Arlington. "We verify those students, and it can be more than 30 percent of applicants." Krause also notes that while the Department of Education can flag a student for verification, colleges are able to do so as well. "We have the option to do it as well, if something doesn't seem right. It's really about quality control."

> ## TRENT & SEPPY SAY...
>
> **Trent:**
>
> *When a FAFSA application is selected for verification, colleges can't complete that student's financial aid calculations until they receive the requested documents.*
>
> **Seppy:**
>
> *So if you're one of the lucky individuals chosen for verification, don't put it off. Supplying the requested documents can be frustrating, but at least it's not a tax audit!*

Filling Out State Forms

Once you and your student have filed a FAFSA (and a CSS Profile form, if necessary), your next step should be applying for state-supported financial aid. You've learned that state-supported financial aid opportunities vary from state to state, so you'll need to research what's available in your state and what you qualify for. Some states provide grants for students attending an in-state private college, while others offer loans to supplement federal programs. Use the Regional Resources section of this book to contact your state's higher education agency and request forms.

Filing Institutional Forms

If your prospective colleges offer institutional aid, make sure you remember to fill out and file those forms as well. These may rely on your FAFSA and CSS Profile information, so once those are completed, institutional aid forms are often easier and faster to complete.

Applying for Private Aid

This includes grants and scholarships from businesses and corporations, as well as other sources beyond federal, state, and college-funded financial aid. Ideally, you and your student should be constantly seeking and applying for these types of aid throughout the whole financial aid process. But once the federal, state, and college forms are completed and filed, you'll be able to focus solely on other sources.

Start Ups

"You need to go out and beat the bushes," insists Barry Simmons, director of financial aid at Virginia Tech. "Even if you ask a local organization, and they don't have a scholarship, sometimes they'll decide it's a good idea to start one. I've seen that happen, and the student who first asked about the scholarship ended up receiving it because they got the organization started."

Your student should constantly be on the lookout for local and national scholarships that can help them afford college. Some may be as little as $100, but they may not require a lot of time and energy to apply. Local clubs, service organizations, businesses, and groups should all be contacted. For most students, a few inquiries a week can lead to a steady number of opportunities without overburdening them.

Following Up

By this point, you'll probably be sick and tired of forms, pencils, and more acronyms than a spy movie. But give yourself a pat on the back; you've gotten all the financial aid applications out of the way! We're not completely finished with the financial aid process, but you've gotten over the hardest part. Now you'll start to receive acknowledgement letters from the programs you applied to; FAFSA, CSS Profile, institutional aid, private scholarships, and any other sources. These will confirm in writing that you have applied for the programs, and may review the information you provided. As we mentioned earlier, they may also ask for additional information. If so, be sure to provide that information. Now is not the time be lazy; certainly not after you've worked so hard!

Some colleges or financial aid programs will send letters stating that they are missing information. When this happens, the college or program cannot complete your need analysis, which means you can't get any financial aid. If you receive one of these letters, address it immediately. If you're confused or have already supplied the information they are requesting, call the college or program and clarify what is needed. These kinds of letters should always be treated with a high priority.

TRENT & SEPPY SAY...

Trent:

Financial aid packages usually include not just an award letter, but instructions or paperwork you'll need to begin the process of getting that aid.

Seppy:

Everyone likes getting gifts in the mail, and that's what financial aid packages feel like when you open them. (I guess that's why they're called "award" letters.)

AWARD LETTERS

All this labor will pay off when you and your son or daughter receive your award letters. These are sent out by programs and colleges to let you know how much financial aid your student has received. They are not mailed until your student has been notified that he or she has been accepted to that college, and they'll list the financial aid awards offered to your student in detail.

The Financial Aid Package

The amount offered to students is often called a financial aid "package" because it is a combination of gift aid, self-help aid, and work aid. This package is the total amount of financial aid your student receives (unless there are grants and scholarships from outside sources, such as corporations, being paid directly to your student).

"We send out financial aid information with our acceptance letters," says Jade Kolb of NYU. "but we also refer students to our website. It's comprehensive and up-to-date, and can provide a lot more information than the packets we send out."

Ideally, your student's financial aid package will cover the complete amount of money you'll need to afford college (in other words, whatever the difference is between the cost of the college and what you can afford to pay). Unfortunately, this is seldom the case. When the combination of your student's financial aid package and the amount you can pay falls short of the cost of the college, you're faced with a few choices.

When this happens, you and your student may decide to take out loans to cover this difference; you may try to reduce the cost of the college further; or you may decide that your student shouldn't attend this particular college. But most families don't make these kind of decisions until the student has received his or her financial aid package from every college to which they have applied. Because of that, we'll look at these choices in more detail later, including how you can attempt to negotiate your financial aid package if it's less than what's offered by other colleges. For now, remember that an informed decision will be based on all your prospective colleges, not just one award letter.

Filling Out Loan Applications

Once your son or daughter has decided which college he or she will be attending, the last forms you may need to fill out are federal loan applications. If you qualify for a Stafford Loan, or Federal Direct Loan, or a Perkins Loan, you will have to fill out a supplemental loan application. In addition, students receiving a Stafford Loan are required to take an entrance interview, which explains the rights and expectations involved in the loan. Stafford loans will also require you to select a lender, so if you've done some research, you may already have a lender in mind. If not, ask the school's financial aid office for assistance.

MOVING ON

To wrap up, we began by comparing the three types of forms involved in applying for financial aid: core forms, supplemental forms, and verification documents. Within each of these categories, we looked at the various forms involved, learning the difference between the FAFSA and the CSS Profile form.* We also discussed how business owners and farmers may have to file additional forms in this process. Next, we went through the process of applying for financial aid step-by-step. We looked at why the CSS Profile form should be completed before the FAFSA, and what steps are involved in completing each. We also discussed where state, institutional, and other forms fit into this process. Finally, we reviewed the importance of providing additional information when it's requested, and what is involved in the award letters you can expect to receive. Once your student selects the college they will attend, you'll need to fill out loan applications if you qualify for federal student aid.

In the next chapter, you'll learn how the government and colleges determine the amount of financial aid you'll receive. We'll take an in-depth look at how applicants are evaluated, and you'll learn the formulas used by the federal government and colleges in this process. But before you move on, take a look at the checklist for this chapter.

CHECKLIST:

1. Determine which (if any) potential colleges need the CSS Profile form. Request institutional aid forms at this time.

2. Request the CSS Profile and FAFSA forms in paper or get them online.

3. Collect federal tax returns and W-2 forms for both you and your student.

4. Find out deadlines for filing the FAFSA and CSS Profile with your prospective schools.

5. Complete and submit the CSS Profile form (if necessary).

6. If you want to file your FAFSA online, request a pin number from *www.pin.ed.gov*

7. Complete and submit your FAFSA form.

8. Complete any state, institutional, and other financial aid forms necessary.

9. Review your acknowledgement letters from various programs and submit additional information for verification (if necessary).

10. Review your award letters.

11. Begin the student loan application process once your student has selected his or her college or university.

*The forms can be found at the end of this chapter.

WEBSITES

FAFSA
www.fafsa.ed.gov

U.S. Department of Education PIN Registration
www.pin.ed.gov

College Board
www.collegeboard.com

Internal Revenue Service
www.irs.gov

FAFSA
FREE APPLICATION FOR FEDERAL STUDENT AID
We Help Put America Through School

2003-2004 FAFSA on the Web
Pre-Application Worksheet

www.fafsa.ed.gov

Complete this worksheet only if you plan to use *FAFSA on the Web* to apply for financial aid.
Please **DO NOT** mail in this worksheet.

Instructions:

1. Use this worksheet to collect your (and your parents') information before beginning your 2003-2004 online Free Application for Federal Student Aid (FAFSA). The worksheet does not include all questions asked on the online FAFSA, just the ones that you might not know off the top of your head.
2. Questions on this worksheet are in the same order as they appear on the online FAFSA; however, because the online FAFSA allows you to skip some questions based on your answers to earlier questions, you may not have to answer all of the questions on this worksheet.
3. The numbers in parentheses to the right of each question correspond to the question numbers on the paper FAFSA.
4. In addition to completing the Pre-Application Worksheet, you might want to complete student (and parent) Worksheets A, B, and C before beginning your online FAFSA. To print Worksheets A, B, and C, go to www.fafsa.ed.gov/worksheet.htm.
5. Do not use this worksheet if you plan to fill out a paper FAFSA.

Question	Answer
The first part of the online FAFSA will ask you some basic questions about you, the student, such as your name, address, and Social Security Number (SSN).	
Student's Citizenship Status (13)	❑ U.S. Citizen ❑ Eligible Noncitizen ❑ Neither See notes on page 4
Student's Alien Registration Number (14)	A _ _ _ _ _ _ _ _ See notes on page 4
Student's Marital Status (15)	❑ Single, Divorced or Widowed ❑ Married/Remarried ❑ Separated
Student's Date of Marital Status (16)	(Month and Year; e.g., 05/1995)
Student's Enrollment Summer 2003 (17)	❑ Full time/Not sure ❑ ¾ time ❑ Half time ❑ Less than half ❑ Not attending
Student's Enrollment Fall 2003 (18)	❑ Full time/Not sure ❑ ¾ time ❑ Half time ❑ Less than half ❑ Not attending
Student's Enrollment Winter 2003-2004 (19)	❑ Full time/Not sure ❑ ¾ time ❑ Half time ❑ Less than half ❑ Not attending
Student's Enrollment Spring 2004 (20)	❑ Full time/Not sure ❑ ¾ time ❑ Half time ❑ Less than half ❑ Not attending
Student's Enrollment Summer 2004 (21)	❑ Full time/Not sure ❑ ¾ time ❑ Half time ❑ Less than half ❑ Not attending
Student's Father's Educational Level (22)	❑ Middle school/Jr. High ❑ High school ❑ College or beyond ❑ Other/unknown
Student's Mother's Educational Level (23)	❑ Middle school/Jr. High ❑ High school ❑ College or beyond ❑ Other/unknown
What is the student's state of legal residence? (24)	
Did you, the student, become a legal resident of this state before January 1, 1998? (25)	❑ Yes ❑ No
If no, what date did you become a legal resident of your state? (26)	(Month and Year; e.g., 05/1995)
If you, the student, are male, age 18-25, and not already registered with the Selective Service, if you answer "Yes" to this question on the online FAFSA, the Selective Service will register you. (28)	❑ Yes ❑ No
Student's type of degree or certificate (29)	❑ 1 (1st Bachelor's degree) ❑ 2 (2nd Bachelor's degree) ❑ 3 (Associate degree - occupational/technical program) ❑ 4 (Associate degree - general education or transfer program) ❑ 5 (Certificate or diploma for completing an occupational, technical, or educational program of less than two years) ❑ 6 (Certificate or diploma for completing an occupational, technical, or educational program of at least two years) ❑ 7 (Teaching credential program nondegree) ❑ 8 (Graduate or professional degree) ❑ 9 (Other/Undecided)

Page 1 of 4

Question	Answer	
Student's grade level in college in 2003-2004 (30)	❏ 0 (1st yr, Never Attended) ❏ 1 (1st yr, Previously Attended) ❏ 2 (2nd yr/Sophomore) ❏ 3 (3rd yr/Junior)	❏ 4 (4th yr/Senior) ❏ 5 (5th yr or More) ❏ 6 (1st Year Graduate/Professional) ❏ 7 (Continuing Graduate/Professional)
Will you, the student, have a high school diploma or GED before you enroll? (31)	❏ Yes ❏ No	
Will you, the student, have your first bachelor's degree by July 1, 2003? (32)	❏ Yes ❏ No	
Are you, the student, interested in student loans? (33)	❏ Yes ❏ No	
Are you, the student, interested in work-study? (34)	❏ Yes ❏ No	
Does the student have a drug conviction that will affect eligibility for aid? (35)	See notes on page 4	
Were you, the student, born before January 1, 1980? (52)	❏ Yes ❏ No	
In 2003-2004, will you, the student, be working on a master's or doctorate program? (53)	❏ Yes ❏ No	
As of today, are you, the student, married? (54)	❏ Yes ❏ No	
Do you, the student, have children who receive more than half of their support from you? (55)	❏ Yes ❏ No	
Do you, the student, have dependents other than your children/spouse? (56)	❏ Yes ❏ No	
Is the student an orphan, or are you or were you (until age 18) a ward/dependent of the court? (57)	❏ Yes ❏ No	
Are you, the student, a veteran of the U.S. Armed Forces? (58)	❏ Yes ❏ No See notes on page 4	
Has the student completed a 2002 IRS or other income tax return? (36)	❏ Have already completed ❏ Will file, have not yet completed ❏ Not going to file	
What income tax return did you, the student, file or will you file for 2002? (37)	❏ 1 – IRS 1040 ❏ 2 – IRS 1040A, 1040EZ, or 1040 Telefile ❏ 3 – A Foreign tax return	❏ 4 – A tax return for Puerto Rico, Guam, American Samoa, the U.S. Virgin Islands, the Marshall Islands, the Federated States of Micronesia, or Palau
If you, the student, filed a 1040, were you eligible to file a 1040A or 1040EZ? (38)	❏ Yes ❏ No See notes on page 4	
What was the student's (and spouse's) 2002 adjusted gross income from IRS form? (39) (Adjusted Gross Income is on IRS form 1040-line 35; 1040A-line 21; 1040EZ-line 4; or Telefile-line I.)	$	
What was the amount of the student's (and spouse's) income tax for 2002? (40) (Income tax amount is on IRS form 1040-line 55; 1040A-line 36; 1040EZ-line 10; or Telefile-line K(2).)	$	
Enter the student's (and spouse's) exemptions for 2002. (41) (Exemptions are on IRS form 1040-line 6d or 1040A-line 6d. For Form 1040EZ, if a person answered "Yes" on line 5, use EZ worksheet line F to determine the number of exemptions ($3,000 equals one exemption). If a person answered "No" on line 5, enter 01 if he or she is single, or 02 if he or she is married. For Form Telefile, use line J(2) to determine the number of exemptions ($3,000 equals one exemption).		
How much did you the student (and spouse) earn from working (wages, salaries, tips, etc.) in 2002? (42 and 43) (Answer these questions whether or not you, the student, filed a tax return. This information may be on your W-2 forms, or on IRS Form 1040-lines 7+12+18; 1040A-line 7; or 1040EZ-line 1. Telefilers should use their W-2 forms.)	Student (42) $ Spouse (43) $	
Student's household size (85)	See notes on page 4	
Student's number in college (86)	See notes on page 4	

Who is considered a Parent? Read the notes listed on page 4 to determine who is considered a parent for the purpose of the form. You **must** answer questions about your parent(s) if you answered "No" to all dependency questions (questions 52-58 on the paper FAFSA) listed on page 2 of this worksheet, even if you did not live with them. Please note: all questions related to your parent(s) are shaded. (Note that grandparents and legal guardians are not parents.)

Question	Answer	
What is your parents' marital status as of today? (59)	❏ Married/Remarried ❏ Single ❏ Divorced/Separated ❏ Widowed	
Month and year your parents were married, separated, divorced, or widowed (60)	(Month and Year; e.g., 05/1995)	
Have your parents completed a 2002 IRS or other income tax return? (71)	❏ Have already completed ❏ Will file, have not yet completed ❏ Not going to file	

Question	Answer	
What type of tax return did your parents file, or will they file in 2002? (72)	❏ 1 – IRS 1040 ❏ 2 – IRS 1040A, 1040EZ, or 1040 Telefile ❏ 3 – A Foreign tax return	❏ 4 – A tax return for Puerto Rico, Guam, American Samoa, the U.S. Virgin Islands, the Marshall Islands, the Federated States of Micronesia, or Palau
If your parent filed a 1040, were they eligible to file a 1040A or 1040EZ? (73)	❏ Yes ❏ No	See notes on page 4
What was your parents' adjusted gross income from IRS form? (74) (Adjusted Gross Income is on IRS form 1040-line 35; 1040A-line 21; 1040EZ-line 4; or Telefile-line I.)	$	
How much did your parents earn from working (wages, salaries, tips, etc.) in 2002? (77 and 78) (Answer these questions whether or not your parents filed a tax return. This information may be on their W-2 forms, or on IRS Form 1040-lines 7+12+18; 1040A-line 7; or 1040EZ-line 1. Telefilers should use their W-2 forms.)	Father (77) $ Mother (78) $	
Student's amount from FAFSA Worksheet A (44)	$	See notes on page 4
Student's amount from FAFSA Worksheet B (45)	$	See notes on page 4
Student's amount from FAFSA Worksheet C (46)	$	See notes on page 4
As of today, student's (and spouse's) amount for net worth of current investments, including real estate (not your home) (47)	$	Net Worth means current value minus debt
As of today, student's (and spouse's) amount for net worth of current business and/or investment farms (48)	$	Net Worth means current value minus debt
As of today, student's (and spouse's) amount of cash, savings, and checking accounts (49)	$	
Number of months student will receive veterans' education (VA) benefits (50)		Use 01 to 12
Student's monthly VA benefits amount (51)	$	
Student's father's (or stepfather's) Social Security Number (61)		
Students father's (or stepfather's) last name (62)		
Student's mother's (or stepmother's) Social Security Number (63)		
Student's mother's (or stepmother's) last name (64)		
Student's parents' household size (65)		See notes on page 4
Student's parents' number in college (66)		See notes on page 4
Student's parents' state of legal residence (67)		
Did the student's parents become legal residents of the state before January 1, 1998? (68)	❏ Yes ❏ No	
If "No," date the student's parent became a legal resident of this state (69)		(Month and Year; e.g., 05/1995)
What is the age of the student's older parent? (70)		
What was the amount the student's parents paid in income tax for 2002? (75) (Income tax amount is on IRS form 1040-line 55; 1040A-line 36; 1040EZ-line 10; or Telefile-line K(2).)	$	
Enter the student's parents' exemptions for 2002 (76) (Exemptions are on IRS form 1040-line 6d or 1040A-line 6d. For Form 1040EZ, if a person answered "Yes" on line 5, use EZ worksheet line f to determine the number of exemptions ($3,000 equals one exemption). If a person answered "No" on line 5 enter 01 if he or she is single, or 02 if he or she is married. For Form Telefile, use line J(2) to determine the number of exemptions ($3,000 equals one exemption).		
Student's parents' amount from FAFSA Worksheet A (79)	$	See notes on page 4
Student's parents' amount from FAFSA Worksheet B (80)	$	See notes on page 4
Student's parents' amount from FAFSA Worksheet C (81)	$	See notes on page 4
As of today, student's parent's amount for net worth of current investments, including real estate (not your home) (82)	$	Net Worth means current value minus debt
As of today, student's parent's amount for net worth of current business and/or investment farms (83)	$	Net Worth means current value minus debt
As of today, student's parent's amount in cash, savings, and checking accounts (84)	$	

Near the end of the application, the online FAFSA will help you to list the schools you would like to receive your FAFSA information. In addition, if someone other than you, your spouse, or your parents completed the online FAFSA for you, you will be asked to report information about that person.

Notes Section:

Notes for Student's Citizenship Status and Alien Registration Number:

Generally you are an eligible noncitizen if you are: (1) a U.S. permanent resident and you have an Alien Registration Receipt card (I-551); (2) a conditional permanent resident (I-551C); or (3) an other eligible noncitizen with an Arrival-Department Record (I-94) from the U.S. Immigration and Naturalization Service showing any of the following designations: "Refugee", "Asylum Granted", "Indefinite Parole", "Humanitarian Parole", or "Cuban-Haitian Entrant". If you're not sure how to answer, FAFSA on the Web (www.fafsa.ed.gov/help.htm) provides additional information to help you answer these questions.

If you are an eligible noncitizen, enter your eight or nine digit Alien Registration Number.

Notes for Student's Drug Conviction Affecting Eligibility:

If you have a conviction for possessing or selling illegal drugs go to FAFSA on the Web (www.fafsa.ed.gov/worksheet.htm). The worksheet will walk you through a series of questions to help you figure out if your conviction affects your eligibility.

Notes for Was Student Eligible to File a 1040A or 1040EZ:

In general, a person is eligible to file a 1040A or 1040EZ if he or she makes less than $50,000, does not itemize deductions, doesn't receive income from his or her business farm, does not receive alimony, and is not required to file Schedule D for capital gains. If you filed a 1040 only to claim Hope and Lifetime Learning credits, and you would have otherwise been eligible to file a 1040A or 1040EZ, you should answer "Yes."

Notes for Are You, the Student, a Veteran of the U.S. Armed Forces:

Answer **"No"** (you are not a veteran) if you (1) have never engaged in active duty in the U.S. Armed Forces, (2) are currently an ROTC student or cadet or midshipman at a service academy, or (3) are a National Guard or Reserves enlistee activated only for training. Also answer "No" if you are currently serving in the U.S. Armed Forces and will continue to serve through June 30, 2004.

Answer **"Yes"** (you are a veteran) if you (1) have engaged in active duty in the U.S. Armed Forces (Army, Navy, Air Force, Marines, or Coast Guard) or as a member National Guard or Reserves who was called to active duty for purposes other than training, or were a cadet or midshipman at one of the service academies, **and** (2) were released under a condition other than dishonorable. Also answer "Yes" if you are not a veteran now but will be one by June 30, 2004.

Notes for Student's Household Size:

Include in your (and your spouse's) household: (1) Yourself (and your spouse, if you have one), and (2) your children if you will provide more than half of their support from July 1, 2003 through June 30, 2004, and (3) other people if they now live with you, and you provide more than half of their support, and you will continue to provide more than half of their support from July 1, 2003 through June 30, 2004.

Notes for Student's Number in College:

Always count yourself as a college student. **Don't include your parents.** Include others only if they will attend at least half time in a 2003-2004 program that leads to a college degree or certificate.

Notes for Who is Considered a Parent:

If your parents are both living and married to each other, answer the questions about them.

If your parent is widowed or single, answer the questions about that parent. If your widowed parent is remarried as of today, answer the questions about that parent **and** the person to whom your parent is married (your stepparent).

If your parents are divorced or separated, answer the questions about the parent you lived with during the past 12 months. (If you did not live with one parent more than the other, give answers about the parent who provided more financial support during the past 12 months, or during the most recent year that you actually received support from that parent.) If this parent is remarried as of today, answer the questions on the rest of this form about that parent **and** the person to whom your parent is married (your stepparent).

Notes for Were Your Parents Eligible to File a 1040A or 1040EZ:

In general, a person is eligible to file a 1040A or 1040EZ if he or she makes less than $50,000, does not itemize deductions, doesn't receive income from his or her business farm, does not receive alimony, and is not required to file Schedule D for capital gains. If your parents filed a 1040 only to claim Hope and Lifetime Learning credits, and would have otherwise been eligible to file a 1040A or 1040EZ, they should answer "Yes" to this question.

Notes for Student's Worksheets A, B and C:

For help with answering these questions, go to www.fafsa.ed.gov/worksheet.htm. Print out copies of all Worksheets and complete them prior to filling out the online FAFSA.

Notes for Parents' Household Size:

Include in your parents' household; (1) Your parents and yourself, even if you don't live with parents, and (2) your parents' other children if (a) your parents will provide more than half of their support from July 1, 2003 through June 30, 2004, or (b) the children could answer "No" to all of the dependency questions listed on page 2 of this Worksheet (questions 52-58 on the paper FAFSA), and (3) other people if they live with your parents, and your parents provide more than half of their support, and your parents will continue to provide more than half of their support from July 1, 2003 through June 30, 2004.

Notes for Parent's Number in College:

Always count yourself as a college student. **Don't include your parents.** Include others only if they will attend at least half time in a 2003-2004 program that leads to a college degree or certificate.

Notes for Parent's Worksheets A, B and C:

For help with answering these questions, go to www.fafsa.ed.gov/worksheet.htm. Print out copies of all Worksheets and complete them prior to filling out the online FAFSA.

FAFSA
We Help Put America Through School

July 1, 2003 — June 30, 2004

FREE APPLICATION FOR FEDERAL STUDENT AID

OMB # 1845-0001

Use this free form to apply for federal and state* student grants, work-study, and loans.

Apply free over the internet at www.fafsa.ed.gov

1 If you are filing a **2002 federal income tax return,** we recommend that you complete it before filling out this form. However, you do not need to file your income tax return with the IRS before you submit this form.

If you or your family has **unusual circumstances not shown on this form** (such as loss of employment) that might affect your need for student financial aid, submit this form and then consult with the financial aid office at the college you plan to attend.

You may also use this form to apply for **aid from other sources, such as your state or college.** The deadlines for states (see table to right) or colleges may be as early as January 2003 and may differ. You may be required to complete additional forms. Check with your high school guidance counselor or a financial aid administrator at your college about state and college sources of student aid and deadlines.

2 Your answers on this form will be read electronically. Therefore:

- use black ink and fill in ovals completely:
- print clearly in CAPITAL letters and skip a box between words:
- report dollar amounts (such as $12,356.41) like this:

Correct ●   Incorrect ⊗ ⊘

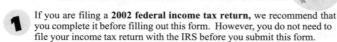

| I | 5 | | E | L | M | | S | T |

$ | | 1 | 2 | , | 3 | 5 | 6 | **no cents**

Yellow is for students and purple is for parents.

If you have questions about this application, or for more information on eligibility requirements and the U.S. Department of Education's student aid programs, look on the internet at **www.studentaid.ed.gov.** You can also call 1-800-4-FED-AID (1-800-433-3243). TTY users may call 1-800-730-8913.

3 After you complete this application, make a copy of pages 3 through 6 for your records. Then **mail the original of only pages 3 through 6** in the attached envelope or send it to: Federal Student Aid Programs, P.O. Box 7001, Mt. Vernon, IL 62864-0071. Be sure to keep the worksheets on page 8.

You should submit your application as early as possible, but no earlier than January 1, 2003. **We must receive your application no later than June 30, 2004.** Your college must have your correct, complete information by your last day of enrollment in the 2003-2004 school year.

You should hear from us within four weeks. If you do not, please check online at **www.fafsa.ed.gov** or call 1-800-433-3243. If you would like us to contact you through e-mail, please provide your e-mail address in question 99. You will then receive information about your application within a few days after we process it.

4 Now go to page 3, detach the application form, and begin filling it out. Refer to the notes as instructed.

STATE AID DEADLINES

AR	April 1, 2003 *(date received)*
AZ	June 30, 2004 *(date received)*
*^CA	For initial awards – March 3, 2003
	For additional community college awards – September 2, 2003 *(date postmarked)*
* DC	June 28, 2003 *(date received by state)*
DE	April 15, 2003 *(date received)*
FL	May 15, 2003 *(date processed)*
^ IA	July 1, 2003 *(date received)*
# IL	First-time applicants – September 30, 2003
	Continuing applicants – August 15, 2003 *(date received)*
I N	March 10, 2003 *(date received, no longer date postmarked)*
#*KS	April 1, 2003 *(date received)*
# KY	March 15, 2003 *(date received)*
#^LA	May 1, 2003
	Final deadline – July 1, 2003 *(date received)*
#^MA	May 1, 2003 *(date received)*
MD	March 1, 2003 *(date postmarked)*
ME	May 1, 2003 *(date received)*
MI	High school seniors – February 21, 2003
	College students – March 21, 2003 *(date received)*
MN	June 30, 2004 *(date received)*
MO	April 1, 2003 *(date received)*
# MT	March 1, 2003 *(date processed, no longer date postmarked)*
NC	March 15, 2003 *(date received)*
ND	April 15, 2003 *(date processed)*
NH	May 1, 2003 *(date received)*
^ NJ	June 1, 2003 if you received a Tuition Aid Grant in 2002-2003
	All other applicants – October 1, 2003, fall & spring term – March 1, 2004, spring term only *(date received)*
*^NY	May 1, 2004 *(date postmarked)*
OH	October 1, 2003 *(date received)*
# OK	April 30, 2003
	Final deadline – June 30, 2003 *(date received)*
# OR	March 1, 2003 *(date received)*
* PA	All 2002-2003 State Grant recipients & all non-2002-2003 State Grant recipients in degree programs – May 1, 2003
	All other applicants – August 1, 2003 *(date received)*
PR	May 2, 2004 *(date application signed)*
# RI	March 1, 2003 *(date received)*
SC	June 30, 2003 *(date received)*
TN	May 1, 2003 *(date processed)*
*^ WV	March 1, 2003 *(date received)*

Check with your financial aid administrator for these states: AK, AL, *AS, *CT, CO, *FM, GA, *GU, *HI, ID, *MH, *MP, MS, *NE, *NM, *NV, *PW, *SD, *TX, UT, *VA, *VI, *VT, WA, WI, and *WY.

\# For priority consideration, submit application by date specified.

^ Applicants encouraged to obtain proof of mailing.

* Additional form may be required.

STATE AID DEADLINES

Notes for questions 13–14 (page 3)

If you are an eligible noncitizen, write in your eight- or nine-digit Alien Registration Number. Generally, you are an eligible noncitizen if you are: (1) a U.S. permanent resident and you have an Alien Registration Receipt Card (I-551); (2) a conditional permanent resident (I-551C); or (3) an other eligible noncitizen with an Arrival-Departure Record (I-94) from the U.S. Immigration and Naturalization Service showing any one of the following designations: "Refugee," "Asylum Granted," "Indefinite Parole," "Humanitarian Parole," or "Cuban-Haitian Entrant." If you are in the U.S. on an F1 or F2 student visa, or a J1 or J2 exchange visitor visa, or a G series visa (pertaining to international organizations), you must fill in oval **c**. If you are neither a citizen nor an eligible noncitizen, you are not eligible for federal student aid. However, you may be eligible for state or college aid.

Notes for questions 17–21 (page 3)

For undergraduates, full time generally means taking at least 12 credit hours in a term or 24 clock hours per week. 3/4 time generally means taking at least 9 credit hours in a term or 18 clock hours per week. Half time generally means taking at least 6 credit hours in a term or 12 clock hours per week. Provide this information about the college you are most likely to attend.

Notes for question 29 (page 3) — Enter the correct number in the box in question 29.

Enter **1** for 1st bachelor's degree

Enter **2** for 2nd bachelor's degree

Enter **3** for associate degree (occupational or technical program)

Enter **4** for associate degree (general education or transfer program)

Enter **5** for certificate or diploma for completing an occupational, technical, or educational program of less than two years

Enter **6** for certificate or diploma for completing an occupational, technical, or educational program of at least two years

Enter **7** for teaching credential program (nondegree program)

Enter **8** for graduate or professional degree

Enter **9** for other/undecided

Notes for question 30 (page 3) — Enter the correct number in the box in question 30.

Enter **0** for never attended college & 1st year undergraduate

Enter **1** for attended college before & 1st year undergraduate

Enter **2** for 2nd year undergraduate/sophomore

Enter **3** for 3rd year undergraduate/junior

Enter **4** for 4th year undergraduate/senior

Enter **5** for 5th year/other undergraduate

Enter **6** for 1st year graduate/professional

Enter **7** for continuing graduate/professional or beyond

Notes for questions 37 c. and d. (page 4) and 72 c. and d. (page 5)

If you filed or will file a foreign tax return, or a tax return with Puerto Rico, Guam, American Samoa, the U.S. Virgin Islands, the Marshall Islands, the Federated States of Micronesia, or Palau, use the information from that return to fill out this form. If you filed a foreign return, convert all figures to U.S. dollars, using the exchange rate that is in effect today.

Notes for questions 38 (page 4) and 73 (page 5)

In general, a person is eligible to file a 1040A or 1040EZ if he or she makes less than $50,000, does not itemize deductions, does not receive income from his or her own business or farm, and does not receive alimony. A person is not eligible if he or she itemizes deductions, receives self-employment income or alimony, or is required to file Schedule D for capital gains. If you filed a 1040 only to claim Hope or Lifetime Learning credits, and you would have otherwise been eligible for a 1040A or 1040EZ, you should answer "Yes" to this question.

Notes for questions 41 (page 4) and 76 (page 5) — only for people who filed a 1040EZ or Telefile

On the 1040EZ, if a person answered "Yes" on line 5, use EZ worksheet line F to determine the number of exemptions ($3,000 equals one exemption). If a person answered "No" on line 5, enter 01 if he or she is single, or 02 if he or she is married.

On the Telefile, use line J(2) to determine the number of exemptions ($3,000 equals one exemption).

Notes for questions 47–48 (page 4) and 82–83 (page 5)

You may be eligible to skip some questions. Use FAFSA on the Web (www.fafsa.ed.gov) to guide you through the form, and find out. If you do not have internet access, completing questions 47-49 will not penalize you.

Net worth means current value minus debt. If net worth is one million or more, enter $999,999. If net worth is negative, enter 0.

Investments include real estate (do not include the home you live in), trust funds, money market funds, mutual funds, certificates of deposit, stocks, stock options, bonds, other securities, education IRAs, college savings plans, installment and land sale contracts (including mortgages held), commodities, etc. Investment value includes the market value of these investments as of today. Investment debt means only those debts that are related to the investments.

Investments do not include the home you live in, cash, savings, checking accounts, the value of life insurance and retirement plans (pension funds, annuities, noneducation IRAs, Keogh plans, etc.), or the value of prepaid tuition plans.

Business and/or investment farm value includes the market value of land, buildings, machinery, equipment, inventory, etc. Business and/or investment farm debt means only those debts for which the business or investment farm was used as collateral.

Notes for question 58 (page 4)

Answer **"No"** (you are not a veteran) if you (1) have never engaged in active duty in the U.S. Armed Forces, (2) are currently an ROTC student or a cadet or midshipman at a service academy, or (3) are a National Guard or Reserves enlistee activated only for training. Also answer "No" if you are currently serving in the U.S. Armed Forces and will continue to serve through June 30, 2004.

Answer **"Yes"** (you are a veteran) if you (1) have engaged in active duty in the U.S. Armed Forces (Army, Navy, Air Force, Marines, or Coast Guard) or as a member of the National Guard or Reserves who was called to active duty for purposes other than training, or were a cadet or midshipman at one of the service academies, **and** (2) were released under a condition other than dishonorable. Also answer "Yes" if you are not a veteran now but will be one by June 30, 2004. **Page 2**

FAFSA

JULY 1, 2003 — JUNE 30, 2004
FREE APPLICATION FOR FEDERAL STUDENT AID
We Help Put America Through School
OMB # 1845-0001

Step One: For questions 1-34, leave blank any questions that do not apply to you (the student).

1-3. Your full name (as it appears on your Social Security card)

1. LAST NAME	2. FIRST NAME	3. MIDDLE INITIAL
FOR INFORMATION ONLY	DO NOT SUBMIT	

4-7. Your permanent mailing address

4. NUMBER AND STREET (INCLUDE APT. NUMBER)

5. CITY (AND COUNTRY IF NOT U.S.) **6.** STATE **7.** ZIP CODE

8. Your Social Security Number
X X X – X X – X X X X

9. Your date of birth
/ / 1 9

10. Your permanent telephone number
( ) –

11-12. Your driver's license number and state (if any)

11. LICENSE NUMBER **12.** STATE

13. Are you a U.S. citizen? Pick one. **See page 2.**
a. Yes, I am a U.S. citizen. **Skip to question 15** .... ○ 1
b. No, but I am an eligible noncitizen. **Fill in question 14.** .... ○ 2
c. No, I am not a citizen or eligible noncitizen. .... ○ 3

14. ALIEN REGISTRATION NUMBER
A

15. What is your marital status as of today?
I am single, divorced, or widowed .... ○ 1
I am married/remarried .... ○ 2
I am separated .... ○ 3

16. Month and year you were married, separated, divorced, or widowed
MONTH YEAR
/

For each question (17 - 21), please mark whether you will be full time, 3/4 time, half time, less than half time, or not attending. **See page 2.**

		Full time/Not sure		3/4 time		Half time		Less than half time		Not attending	
17.	Summer 2003	Full time/Not sure	○ 1	3/4 time	○ 2	Half time	○ 3	Less than half time	○ 4	Not attending	○ 5
18.	Fall 2003	Full time/Not sure	○ 1	3/4 time	○ 2	Half time	○ 3	Less than half time	○ 4	Not attending	○ 5
19.	Winter 2003-2004	Full time/Not sure	○ 1	3/4 time	○ 2	Half time	○ 3	Less than half time	○ 4	Not attending	○ 5
20.	Spring 2004	Full time/Not sure	○ 1	3/4 time	○ 2	Half time	○ 3	Less than half time	○ 4	Not attending	○ 5
21.	Summer 2004	Full time/Not sure	○ 1	3/4 time	○ 2	Half time	○ 3	Less than half time	○ 4	Not attending	○ 5

22. Highest school your father completed Middle school/Jr. High ○ 1 High school ○ 2 College or beyond ○ 3 Other/unknown ○ 4
23. Highest school your mother completed Middle school/Jr. High ○ 1 High school ○ 2 College or beyond ○ 3 Other/unknown ○ 4

24. What is your state of legal residence?
STATE

25. Did you become a legal resident of this state before January 1, 1998?
Yes ○ 1 No ○ 2

26. If the answer to question 25 is **"No,"** give month and year you became a legal resident.
MONTH YEAR
/

27. Are you male? (Most male students must register with Selective Service to get federal aid.)
Yes ○ 1 No ○ 2
28. If you are male (age 18-25) and not registered, answer "Yes" and Selective Service will register you.
Yes ○ 1 No ○ 2

29. What degree or certificate will you be working on during 2003-2004? **See page 2** and enter the correct number in the box.

30. What will be your grade level when you begin the 2003-2004 school year? **See page 2** and enter the correct number in the box.

31. Will you have a high school diploma or GED before you begin the 2003-2004 school year? Yes ○ 1 No ○ 2
32. Will you have your first bachelor's degree before July 1, 2003? Yes ○ 1 No ○ 2
33. In addition to grants, are you interested in student loans (which you must pay back)? Yes ○ 1 No ○ 2
34. In addition to grants, are you interested in "work-study" (which you earn through work)? Yes ○ 1 No ○ 2

35. Do not leave this question blank. Have you ever been convicted of possessing or selling illegal drugs? If you have, answer "Yes," complete and submit this application, and we will send you a worksheet in the mail for you to determine if your conviction affects your eligibility for aid.
No ○ 1 Yes ○ 3
DO NOT LEAVE QUESTION 35 BLANK

Page 3 For Help — 1-800- 433-3243

Step Two: For questions 36-49, report your (the student's) income and assets. If you are married today, report your and your spouse's income and assets, even if you were not married in 2002. Ignore references to "spouse" if you are currently single, separated, divorced, or widowed.

36. For 2002, have you (the student) completed your IRS income tax return or another tax return listed in **question 37**?

   a. I have already completed my return. ○ 1   **b.** I will file, but I have not yet completed my return. ○ 2   **c.** I'm not going to file. **(Skip to question 42.)** ○ 3

37. What income tax return did you file or will you file for 2002?

   a. IRS 1040 .... ○ 1   **d.** A tax return for Puerto Rico, Guam, American Samoa, the U.S. Virgin Islands, the
   b. IRS 1040A, 1040EZ, 1040Telefile .... ○ 2   Marshall Islands, the Federated States of Micronesia, or Palau. **See page 2.** .... ○ 4
   c. A foreign tax return. **See page 2.** .... ○ 3

38. If you have filed or will file a 1040, were you eligible to file a 1040A or 1040EZ? **See page 2.**   Yes ○ 1 No ○ 2 Don't Know ○ 3

For questions 39-51, if the answer is zero or the question does not apply to you, enter 0.

39. What was your (and spouse's) adjusted gross income for 2002? Adjusted gross income is on IRS Form 1040–line 35; 1040A–line 21; 1040EZ–line 4; or Telefile–line I. $ ☐☐☐ , ☐☐☐

40. Enter the total amount of your (and spouse's) income tax for 2002. Income tax amount is on IRS Form 1040–line 55; 1040A–line 36; 1040EZ–line 10; or Telefile–line K(2). $ ☐☐☐ , ☐☐☐

41. Enter your (and spouse's) exemptions for 2002. Exemptions are on IRS Form 1040–line 6d or on Form 1040A–line 6d. For Form 1040EZ or Telefile, **see page 2.**   ☐☐

42-43. How much did you (and spouse) earn from working (wages, salaries, tips, etc.) in 2002? Answer this question whether or not you filed a tax return. This information may be on your W-2 forms, or on IRS Form 1040–lines 7 + 12 + 18; 1040A–line 7; or 1040EZ–line 1. Telefilers should use their W-2 forms.   **You (42)** $ ☐☐☐ , ☐☐☐   **Your Spouse (43)** $ ☐☐☐ , ☐☐☐

Student (and Spouse) Worksheets (44-46)

44-46. Go to page 8 and complete the columns on the left of Worksheets A, B, and C. Enter the student (and spouse) totals in questions 44, 45, and 46, respectively. Even though you may have few of the Worksheet items, check each line carefully.   **Worksheet A (44)** $ ☐☐☐ , ☐☐☐   **Worksheet B (45)** $ ☐☐☐ , ☐☐☐   **Worksheet C (46)** $ ☐☐☐ , ☐☐☐

47. As of today, what is the net worth of your (and spouse's) **investments,** including real estate (not your home)? **See page 2.** $ ☐☐☐ , ☐☐☐

48. As of today, what is the net worth of your (and spouse's) current **businesses and/or investment farms**? Do not include a farm that you live on and operate. **See page 2.** $ ☐☐☐ , ☐☐☐

49. As of today, what is your (and spouse's) total current balance of **cash, savings, and checking accounts**? Do not include student financial aid. $ ☐☐☐ , ☐☐☐

50-51. If you receive veterans' education benefits, for **how many months** from July 1, 2003 through June 30, 2004 will you receive these benefits, and **what amount** will you receive per month? Do not include your spouse's veterans education benefits.   **Months (50)** ☐☐   **Amount (51)** $ ☐ , ☐☐☐

Step Three: Answer all seven questions in this step.

52. Were you born before January 1, 1980? ....   Yes ○ 1 No ○ 2

53. During the school year 2003-2004, will you be working on a master's or doctorate program (such as an MA, MBA, MD, JD, PhD, EdD, or graduate certificate, etc.)? ....   Yes ○ 1 No ○ 2

54. As of today, are you married? (Answer "Yes" if you are separated but not divorced.) ....   Yes ○ 1 No ○ 2

55. Do you have children who receive more than half of their support from you? ....   Yes ○ 1 No ○ 2

56. Do you have dependents (other than your children or spouse) who live with you and who receive more than half of their support from you, now and through June 30, 2004? ....   Yes ○ 1 No ○ 2

57. Are you an orphan, or are you or were you (until age 18) a ward/dependent of the court? ....   Yes ○ 1 No ○ 2

58. Are you a veteran of the U.S. Armed Forces? **See page 2.** ....   Yes ○ 1 No ○ 2

If you (the student) answer "No" to every question in Step Three, go to Step Four.

If you answer "Yes" to any question in Step Three, skip Step Four and go to Step Five on page 6.

(If you are a health profession student, your school may require you to complete Step Four even if you answered "Yes" in Step Three.)

Step Four: Complete this step if you (the student) answered "No" to all questions in Step Three. Go to page 7 to determine who is a parent for this step.

59. What is your parents' marital status as of today?

Married/Remarried ○ 1   Divorced/Separated ○ 3

Single ○ 2   Widowed ○ 4

60. Month and year they were married, separated, divorced, or widowed

MONTH ☐☐ / YEAR ☐☐☐☐

61-64. What are the Social Security Numbers and last names of the parents reporting information on this form? If your parent does not have a Social Security Number, you must enter 000-00-0000

61. FATHER'S/STEPFATHER'S SOCIAL SECURITY NUMBER ☐☐☐ – ☐☐ – ☐☐☐☐

62. FATHER'S/STEPFATHER'S LAST NAME ☐☐☐☐☐☐☐☐☐☐☐☐☐☐☐

63. MOTHER'S/STEPMOTHER'S SOCIAL SECURITY NUMBER ☐☐☐ – ☐☐ – ☐☐☐☐

64. MOTHER'S/STEPMOTHER'S LAST NAME ☐☐☐☐☐☐☐☐☐☐☐☐☐☐☐

65. Go to page 7 to determine how many people are in your parents' household. ☐☐

66. Go to page 7 to determine how many in question 65 **(exclude your parents)** will be college students between July 1, 2003 and June 30, 2004. ☐

67. What is your parents' state of legal residence? STATE ☐☐

68. Did your parents become legal residents of this state before January 1, 1998?   Yes ○ 1   No ○ 2

69. If the answer to question 68 is "No," give the month and year legal residency began for the parent who has lived in the state the longest.

MONTH ☐☐ / YEAR ☐☐☐☐

70. What is the age of your older parent? ☐☐

71. For 2002, have your parents completed their IRS income tax return or another tax return listed in **question 72**?

a My parents have already completed their return. ○ 1

b My parents will file, but they have not yet completed their return. ○ 2

c. My parents are not going to file. **(Skip to question 77.)** ○ 3

72. What income tax return did your parents file or will they file for 2002?

a. IRS 1040 ...... ○ 1

b. IRS 1040A, 1040EZ, 1040Telefile ...... ○ 2

c. A foreign tax return. **See page 2.** ...... ○ 3

d. A tax return for Puerto Rico, Guam, American Samoa, the U.S. Virgin Islands, the Marshall Islands, the Federated States of Micronesia, or Palau. **See page 2.** ...... ○ 4

73. If your parents have filed or will file a 1040, were they eligible to file a 1040A or 1040EZ? **See page 2.**   Yes ○ 1   No ○ 2   Don't Know ○ 3

For questions 74 - 84, if the answer is zero or the question does not apply, enter 0.

74. What was your parents' adjusted gross income for 2002? Adjusted gross income is on IRS Form 1040–line 35; 1040A–line 21; 1040EZ–line 4; or Telefile–line I. $ ☐☐☐,☐☐☐

75. Enter the total amount of your parents' income tax for 2002. Income tax amount is on IRS Form 1040–line 55; 1040A–line 36; 1040EZ–line 10; or Telefile–line K(2). $ ☐☐☐,☐☐☐

76. Enter your parents' exemptions for 2002. Exemptions are on IRS Form 1040–line 6d or on Form 1040A–line 6d. For Form 1040EZ or Telefile, **see page 2.**   ☐☐

77-78. How much did your parents earn from working (wages, salaries, tips, etc.) in 2002? Answer this question whether or not your parents filed a tax return. This information may be on their W-2 forms, or on IRS Form 1040–lines 7 + 12 + 18; 1040A–line 7; or 1040EZ–line 1. Telefilers should use their W-2 forms.

Father/ Stepfather (77) $ ☐☐☐,☐☐☐

Mother/ Stepmother (78) $ ☐☐☐,☐☐☐

Parent Worksheets (79-81)

79-81. Go to page 8 and complete the columns on the right of Worksheets A, B, and C. Enter the parent totals in questions 79, 80, and 81, respectively. Even though your parents may have few of the worksheet items, check each line carefully.

Worksheet A (79) $ ☐☐☐,☐☐☐

Worksheet B (80) $ ☐☐☐,☐☐☐

Worksheet C (81) $ ☐☐☐,☐☐☐

82. As of today, what is the net worth of your parents' **investments,** including real estate (not their home)? **See page 2.** $ ☐☐☐,☐☐☐

83. As of today, what is the net worth of your parents' current **businesses and/or investment farms?** Do not include a farm that your parents live on and operate. **See page 2.** $ ☐☐☐,☐☐☐

84. As of today, what is your parents' total current balance of **cash, savings, and checking accounts?** $ ☐☐☐,☐☐☐

Now go to Step Six.

Step Five: Complete this step only if you (the student) answered "Yes" to any question in Step Three.

85. **Go to page 7** to determine how many people are in your (and your spouse's) household.

86. **Go to page 7** to determine how many in question 85 will be college students, attending at least half time between July 1, 2003 and June 30, 2004.

Step Six: Please tell us which schools should receive your information.

Enter the 6-digit federal school code and your housing plans. Look for the federal school codes at **www.fafsa.ed.gov**, at your college financial aid office, at your public library, or by asking your high school guidance counselor. If you cannot get the federal school code, write in the complete name, address, city, and state of the college. For state aid, you may wish to list your preferred school first.

1ST FEDERAL SCHOOL CODE
87. ☐☐☐☐☐☐ OR NAME OF COLLEGE / ADDRESS AND CITY — STATE ☐☐ HOUSING PLANS
88. on campus ○ 1 / off campus ○ 2 / with parent ○ 3

2ND FEDERAL SCHOOL CODE
89. ☐☐☐☐☐☐ OR NAME OF COLLEGE / ADDRESS AND CITY — STATE ☐☐
90. on campus ○ 1 / off campus ○ 2 / with parent ○ 3

3RD FEDERAL SCHOOL CODE
91. ☐☐☐☐☐☐ OR NAME OF COLLEGE / ADDRESS AND CITY — STATE ☐☐
92. on campus ○ 1 / off campus ○ 2 / with parent ○ 3

4TH FEDERAL SCHOOL CODE
93. ☐☐☐☐☐☐ OR NAME OF COLLEGE / ADDRESS AND CITY — STATE ☐☐
94. on campus ○ 1 / off campus ○ 2 / with parent ○ 3

5TH FEDERAL SCHOOL CODE
95. ☐☐☐☐☐☐ OR NAME OF COLLEGE / ADDRESS AND CITY — STATE ☐☐
96. on campus ○ 1 / off campus ○ 2 / with parent ○ 3

6TH FEDERAL SCHOOL CODE
97. ☐☐☐☐☐☐ OR NAME OF COLLEGE / ADDRESS AND CITY — STATE ☐☐
98. on campus ○ 1 / off campus ○ 2 / with parent ○ 3

99. For contact by internet, provide e-mail address: ☐☐☐☐☐☐☐☐☐☐☐☐☐☐☐☐☐☐ @ ☐☐☐☐☐☐☐☐☐☐☐☐☐☐☐☐☐☐☐☐

Step Seven: Please read, sign, and date.

If you are the student, by signing this application you certify that you (1) will use federal and/or state student financial aid only to pay the cost of attending an institution of higher education, (2) are not in default on a federal student loan or have made satisfactory arrangements to repay it, (3) do not owe money back on a federal student grant or have made satisfactory arrangements to repay it, and (4) will notify your school if you default on a federal student loan.

If you are the parent or the student, by signing this application you agree, if asked, to provide information that will verify the accuracy of your completed form. This information may include your U.S. or state income tax forms. Also, you certify that you understand that **the Secretary of Education has the authority to verify information reported on this application with the Internal Revenue Service and other federal agencies**. If you purposely give false or misleading information, you may be fined $20,000, sent to prison, or both.

100. Date this form was completed.

MONTH ☐☐ / DAY ☐☐ / 2003 ○ or 2004 ○

101. Student (Sign below)

1 FOR INFORMATION ONLY.

Parent (A parent from Step Four sign below)

2 DO NOT SUBMIT.

If this form was filled out by someone other than you, your spouse, or your parent(s), that person must complete this part.

Preparer's name, firm, and address

_____
_____

102. Preparer's Social Security Number (or 103)
☐☐☐ — ☐☐ — ☐☐☐☐

103. Employer ID number (or 102)
☐☐ — ☐☐☐☐☐☐☐

104. Preparer's signature and date
1

SCHOOL USE ONLY:
D/O ○ 1
FAA SIGNATURE
1

Federal School Code
☐☐☐☐☐☐

MDE USE ONLY:
○ P ○ * ○ L ○ E

Page 6

For Help — www.ed.gov/prog_info/SFA/FAFSA

 97

Worksheets
Calendar Year 2002

Do not mail these worksheets in with your application.
Keep these worksheets; your school may ask to see them.

Worksheet A

Student/Spouse — For question 44		Parent(s) — For question 79
$	Earned income credit from IRS Form 1040–line 64; 1040A–line 41; 1040EZ–line 8; or Telefile–line L.	$
$	Additional child tax credit from IRS Form 1040–line 66 or 1040A–line 42	$
$	Welfare benefits, including Temporary Assistance for Needy Families (TANF). Don't include food stamps or subsidized housing.	$
$	Social Security benefits received that were not taxed (such as SSI)	$
$ — Enter in question 44.		Enter in question 79. — $

Worksheet B

For question 45		For question 80
$	Payments to tax-deferred pension and savings plans (paid directly or withheld from earnings), including, but not limited to, amounts reported on the W-2 Form in Boxes 12a through 12d, codes D, E, F, G, H, and S	$
$	IRA deductions and payments to self-employed SEP, SIMPLE, and Keogh and other qualified plans from IRS Form 1040–total of lines 24 + 31 or 1040A–line 17	$
$	Child support **received** for all children. Don't include foster care or adoption payments.	$
$	Tax exempt interest income from IRS Form 1040–line 8b or 1040A–line 8b	$
$	Foreign income exclusion from IRS Form 2555–line 43 or 2555EZ–line 18	$
$	Untaxed portions of IRA distributions from IRS Form 1040–lines (15a minus 15b) or 1040A–lines (11a minus 11b). Exclude rollovers. If negative, enter a zero here.	$
$	Untaxed portions of pensions from IRS From 1040–lines (16a minus 16b) or 1040A–lines (12a minus 12b). Exclude rollovers. If negative, enter a zero here.	$
$	Credit for federal tax on special fuels from IRS Form 4136–line 10–nonfarmers only	$
$	Housing, food, and other living allowances paid to members of the military, clergy, and others (including cash payments and cash value of benefits)	$
$	Veterans' noneducation benefits such as Disability, Death Pension, or Dependency & Indemnity Compensation (DIC) and/or VA Educational Work-Study allowances	$
$	Any other untaxed income or benefits not reported elsewhere on Worksheets A and B, such as workers' compensation, untaxed portions of railroad retirement benefits, Black Lung Benefits, disability, etc. **Don't include** student aid, Workforce Investment Act educational benefits, or benefits from flexible spending arrangements, e.g., cafeteria plans.	$
$	Money **received**, or paid on your behalf (e.g., bills), not reported elsewhere on this form	XXXXXXXX
$ — Enter in question 45.		Enter in question 80. — $

Worksheet C

For question 46		For question 81
$	Education credits (Hope and Lifetime Learning tax credits) from IRS Form 1040-line 48 or 1040A-line 31	$
$	Child support **paid** because of divorce or separation or as a result of a legal requirement. Don't include support for children in your (or your parents') household, as reported in question 85 (or question 65 for your parents).	$
$	Taxable earnings from need-based employment programs, such as Federal Work-Study and need-based employment portions of fellowships and assistantships	$
$	Student grant and scholarship aid reported to the IRS in your (or your parents') adjusted gross income. Includes AmeriCorps benefits (awards, living allowances, and interest accrual payments), as well as grant or scholarship portions of fellowships and assistantships.	$
$ — Enter in question 46.		Enter in question 81. — $

Page 8

Registration Guide
2003–2004 School Year

Read this booklet
to find out about
the PROFILE process

Register for your
personalized PROFILE
Application via the Internet:
www.collegeboard.com

Registrations accepted
beginning September 13, 2002

Complete PROFILE Online—
the fastest and easiest way
to complete your
PROFILE Application!
•Online Instructions • Online Help
www.collegeboard.com

Pre-Application Worksheet

You can use this worksheet to help you collect your family's financial information before you begin your online PROFILE Application. You can print instructions by returning to the previous screen and clicking on "application instructions/help". As you are completing your online application, you will find more detailed online help.

The worksheet contains questions found in Sections A through P of the PROFILE Application. In general, these are standard questions that all families must complete.

• When you complete your online application, you may find additional questions in Section Q that are not found on the pre-application worksheet. These are questions required by one or more of the colleges or scholarship programs to which you are applying. If your customized application does not contain a Section Q, it means that none of the colleges and programs to which you are applying require questions beyond those collected in Sections A through P.

• Based on your dependency status, you may not be required to complete all of the questions in Sections A through O. When you complete your online PROFILE Application, these questions will not be presented to you for completion. For example, if you are a dependent student, you will not be asked to complete Questions 1 and 2, or Questions 24 and 25.

Do not mail this form to the College Board. It is a Pre-Application Worksheet and cannot be processed. Any worksheet s received for processing will be destroyed.

Pre-Application Worksheet
Section A - Student's Information
(If you are a dependent student, skip Questions 1 and 2.)

1. How many people are in the student's (and spouse's) household? <u>Always include the student (and spouse).</u> List their names and give information about them in Section M. ☐

2. Of the number in 1, how many will be college students enrolled at least half-time between July 1, 2003 and June 30, 2004? Include yourself. ☐

3. What is the student's state of legal residence? ☐☐

4 a What is the student's citizenship status?
- O U.S. citizen (Skip to question 5.)
- O Eligible non-citizen (Skip to Question 5.)
- O Neither of the above (Answer 'b' and 'c' below.)

b Country of citizenship? ☐

c Visa classification? O F1   O F2   O J   O J2   O G   O Other

Section B - Student's 2002 Income & Benefits
Questions 5-14 ask for information about the student's (and spouse's) income and benefits. If married, include spouse's information in Sections B, C, D, E and F.

5. The following 2002 U.S. Income Tax return figures are: (Fill in only one oval.)
- O estimated. Will file IRS Form 1040EZ, 1040A, or Telefile. Go to 6.
- O estimated. Will file IRS Form 1040. Go to 6.
- O from a completed IRS Form 1040EZ, 1040A, or Telefile. Go to 6.
- O from a completed IRS Form 1040. Go to 6.
- O a tax return will not be filed. Skip to 10.

6. 2002 total number of exemptions (IRS Form 1040, line 6d or 1040A, line 6d or 1040EZ or Telefile) ☐

7. 2002 Adjusted Gross Income from IRS Form 1040, line 35 or 1040A, line 21 or 1040EZ, line 4 or Telefile, line I $

8 a 2002 U.S. income tax paid (IRS Form 1040, line 55 or 1040A, line 33 or 1040EZ, line 10 or Telefile, line K) $

b 2002 Education Credits - Hope and Lifetime Learning (IRS Form 1040, line 48 or 1040a, line 31) $

9. 2002 itemized deductions (IRS Form 1040, Schedule A, line 28. Fill in "0" if deductions were not itemized.) $

10. 2002 income earned from work by student $

11. 2002 income earned from work by student's spouse $

12. 2002 dividend and interest income $

13. 2002 untaxed income and benefits (Give total amount for year.)
- a Social security benefits (untaxed portion only) $
- b Welfare benefits, including TANF $
- c Child support received for all children $
- d Earned Income Credit (IRS Form 1040, line 64 or 1040A, line 41 or 1040EZ, line 8 or Telefile, line L) $
- e Other - write total from instruction worksheet at the end of this document. $

14. 2002 earnings from Federal Work-Study or other need-based work programs plus any grant, fellowship, scholarship, and assistantship aid reported to the IRS in your adjusted gross income $

Section C - Student's Assets
Questions 15-22 ask for information about the student's (and spouse's) assets. Include trust accounts in Section D.

15. Cash, savings, and checking accounts (as of today) $

16. Total value of IRA, Keogh, 401k, 403b, etc. accounts as of December 31, 2002 $

17. Investments (Including Uniform Gifts to Minors)
What is it worth today? $
What is owed on it? $

18. Home

What is it worth today? (Renters write in "0") $ _____

What is owed on it? $ _____

19. Other real estate

What is it worth today? $ _____

What is owed on it? $ _____

20. Business and farm

What is it worth today? $ _____

What is owed on it? $ _____

21. If a farm is included in 20, is the student living on the farm?   O Yes   O No

22. If student owns home, give

a year purchased _____

b purchase price $ _____

Section D - Student's Trust Information

23.a Total value of all trust(s) $ _____

b Is any income or part of the principal currently available?   O Yes   O No

c Who established the trust(s)?   O Student's parents   O Other

Section E - Student's 2002 Expenses

(If you are a dependent student, skip Questions 24 and 25.)

24. 2002 child support paid because of divorce or separation $ _____

25. 2002 medical and dental expenses not covered by insurance $ _____

Section F - Student's Expected Summer/School-Year Resources for 2003-2004

26. Student's veterans benefits (July 1, 2003 - June 30, 2004)

Amount per month $ _____

Number of months _____

27. Student's (and spouse's) resources (Don't enter monthly amounts.)

a Student's wages, salaries, tips, etc.

Summer 2003 (3 months) $ _____

School year 2003-2004 (9 months) $ _____

b Spouse's wages, salaries, tips, etc.

Summer 2003 (3 months) $ _____

School year 2003-2004 (9 months) $ _____

c Other taxable income

Summer 2003 (3 months) $ _____

School year 2003-2004 (9 months) $ _____

d Untaxed income and benefits

Summer 2003 (3 months) $ _____

School year 2003-2004 (9 months) $ _____

e Grants, scholarships, fellowships, etc. from sources other than the colleges or universities

to which the student is applying (List sources in Section P) $ _____

f Tuition benefits from the parents' and/or the student's or spouse's employer $ _____

g Amount the student's parent(s) think they will be able to pay for 2003-2004 college expenses $ _____

h Amounts expected from prepaid tuition plan withdrawals, other relatives, spouse's parents, and all $ _____

other sources (List sources and amounts in Section P.)

Section G - Parents' Household Information

28. How many people are in your parents' household? <u>Always include the student and parents</u>. List their names and give

information about them in Section M. _____

29. Of the number in 28, how many will be college students enrolled at least half-time between July 1, 2003 and June 30, 2004?
Do not include parents. Include the student. ☐

30. How many parents will be in college at least half-time in 2003-2004? O Neither Parent O One Parent O Both Parent

31. What is the current marital status of your parents?   O Single   O Separated   O Widowed
(Fill in only one oval.)   O Married/Remarried   O Divorced

32. What is your parents' state of legal residence? ☐

Section H - Parents' Expenses

33. Child support paid because of divorce or separation
2002 $
Expected 2003 $

34. Repayment of parents' educational loans
2002 $
Expected 2003 $

35. Medical and dental expenses not covered by insurance
2002 $
Expected 2003 $

36. Total elementary, junior high school, and high school tuition paid for dependent children
a Amount paid (Don't include tuition paid for the student)
2002 $
Expected 2003 $
b For how many dependent children? (Don't include the student.)
2002   ☐
Expected 2003   ☐

Section I - Parents' Assets

If parents own all or part of a business or farm, enter its name and the percent of ownership in Section P.

37. Cash, savings, and checking accounts (as of today) ☐

38.a Total value of assets held in the names of the student's brothers
and sisters who are under age 19 and not college students $
b Total value of assets held in Section 529 prepaid tuition plans
for the student's brothers and sisters $
c Total value of assets held in Section 529 prepaid tuition plans
for the student $

39. Investments
What is it worth today? $
What is owed on it? $

40. Home
a What is it worth today? (Renters fill in "0" and skip to 40d.) $
What is owed on it? $
b Year purchased   ☐
c Purchase price $
d Monthly home mortgage or rental payment (If none, explain in Section P) $

41. Business
What is it worth today? $
What is owed on it? $

42. Farm
a What is it worth today? $
What is owed on it? $
b Does family live on the farm?   O Yes   O No

43. Other real estate

  a What is it worth today? $ _____

     What is owed on it? $ _____

  b Year purchased _____

  c Purchase price $ _____

Section J - Parents' 2001 Income & Benefits

44. 2001 Adjusted Gross Income (IRS Form 1040, line 33 or 1040A, line 19 or 1040EZ, line 4 or Telefile, line I) $ _____

45. 2001 U.S. income tax paid (IRS Form 1040, line 52 or, 1040A, line 34 or 1040EZ, line 11 or Telefile, line K) $ _____

46. 2001 itemized deductions (IRS Form 1040, Schedule A, line 28. Enter "0" if deductions were not itemized.) $ _____

47. 2001 untaxed income and benefits (Include the same types of income that are listed in 55 a-k.) $ _____

Section K - Parents' 2002 Income & Benefits

48. The following 2002 U.S. income tax return figures are (Fill in only one oval.)

    O estimated. Will file IRS Form 1040EZ, 1040A, or Telefile. Go to 49.

    O estimated. Will file IRS Form 1040. Go to 49.

    O from a completed IRS Form 1040EZ, 1040A, or Telefile. Go to 49.

    O from a completed IRS Form 1040. Go to 49.

    O a tax return will not be filed. Skip to 53.

49. 2002 total number of exemptions (IRS Form 1040, line 6d or 1040A, line 6d or 1040EZ or Telefile.)

50.a Wages, salaries, tips (IRS Form 1040, line 7 or 1040A, line 7 or 1040EZ, line 1) $ _____

  b Interest income (IRS Form 1040, line 8a or 1040A, line 8a or 1040EZ, line 2 or Telefile, line C) $ _____

  c Dividend income (IRS Form 1040, line 9 or 1040A, line 9) $ _____

  d Net income (or loss) from business, farm, rents, royalties, partnerships, estates,
trusts, etc. (IRS Form 1040, lines 12, 17, and 18) (If a loss, enter the amount in (parentheses). $ _____

  e Other taxable income such as alimony received, capital gains (or losses), pensions,
annuities, etc. (IRS Form 1040, lines 10, 11, 13, 14, 15b, 16b, 19, 20b and 21 or 1040A,
lines 10, 11b, 12b, 13, and 14b or 1040EZ, line 3 or Telefile, line D) $ _____

  f Adjustments to income (IRS Form 1040, line 34 or 1040A, line 20) $ _____

  g 2002 Adjusted Gross Income (IRS Form 1040, line 35 or 1040A, line 21 or 1040EZ, line 4 or
Telefile line I). This entry is the sum of 50a to 50e, minus 50f. $ _____

51.a 2002 U.S. income tax paid (IRS Form 1040, line 55, 1040A, line 36 or 1040EZ, line 10 or Telefile, line K) $ _____

  b 2002 Education Credits - Hope and Lifetime Learning (IRS Form 1040, line 48 or 1040A, line 31) $ _____

52. 2002 itemized deductions (IRS Form 1040, Schedule A, line 28. Fill in "0" if deductions were not itemized.) $ _____

53. 2002 income earned from work by father/stepfather $ _____

54. 2002 income earned from work by mother/stepmother $ _____

55. 2002 untaxed income and benefits (Give total amount for the year. Do not give monthly amounts.)

  a Social security benefits received (untaxed portion only) $ _____

  b Welfare benefits, including TANF $ _____

  c Child support received for all children $ _____

  d Deductible IRA and/or SEP, SIMPLE, or Keogh payments $ _____

  e Payments to tax-deferred pension and savings plans $ _____

  f Amounts withheld from wages for dependent care and medical spending accounts $ _____

  g Earned Income Credit (IRS Form 1040, line 64 or 1040A, line 41 or 1040EZ, line 8 or Telefile, line L) $ _____

  h Housing, food, and other living allowances received by military, clergy, and others $ _____

  i Tax-exempt interest income (IRS Form 1040, line 8b or 1040A, line 8b) $ _____

  j Foreign income exclusion (IRS Form 2555, line 43 or Form 2555EZ, line 18) $ _____

  k Other - write in the total from the worksheet in the instructions at the end of this document. $ _____

Section L - Parents' 2003 Expected Income & Benefits

If the expected total income and benefits will differ from the 2002 total income by $3,000 or more, explain in Section P.

56. 2003 income earned from work by father $ _____

57. 2003 income earned from work by mother $ _____

58. 2003 other taxable income $ _____

59. 2003 untaxed income and benefits (See 55a-k.) $ _____

Section M - Family Member Listing

Give information for all family members entered in question 1 or 28. Only six family members are shown here but you will be able to enter up to seven family members in addition to the student on our website. **Failure to complete all information could reduce your aid eligibility** *If there are more than seven, list first those who will be in school or college at least half-time. List the others in Section P.*

Question 60.

Student- Family Member 1

Full name of family member _____   Claimed by parents as tax exemption in 2002?   O Yes   O No

2002-2003 school year

Name of school or college _____   Year in school _____

Scholarships and grants $ _____   Parents' contribution $ _____

Family Member 2

Full name of family member _____   Claimed by parents as tax exemption in 2002?   O Yes   O No

Relationship to student: O Student's parent   O Student's stepparent   O Student's brother or sister

Age: O Student's husband or wife   O Student's son or daughter   O Student's grandparent

O Student's stepbrother/stepsister   O Other (explain in Section P)

2002-2003 school year

Name of school or college _____   Year in school _____

Scholarships and grants _____   Parents' contribution $ _____

2003-2004 school year

Attend college at least one term   O Full-time   O Half-time   O Does not apply

College or university name _____

Type: O 2-year public college   O 2-year private college   O 4-year public college/university

O 4-year private college/university   O graduate/professional school   O proprietary school

---

Family Member 3

Full name of family member _____   Claimed by parents as tax exemption in 2002?   O Yes   O No

Relationship to student: O Student's parent   O Student's stepparent   O Student's brother or sister

Age: ____   O Student's husband or wife   O Student's son or daughter   O Student's grandparent

O Student's stepbrother/stepsister   O Other (explain in Section P)

2002-2003 school year

Name of school or college _____   Year in school _____

Scholarships and grants $ _____   Parents' contribution $ _____

2003-2004 school year

Attend college at least one term   O Full-time   O Half-time   O Does not apply

College or university name _____

Type: O 2-year public college   O 2-year private college   O 4-year public college/university

O 4-year private college/university   O graduate/professional school   O proprietary school

Family Member 4

Full name of family member _____   Claimed by parents
                                                    as tax exemption in 2002?   O Yes   O No

Relationship to student: O Student's parent   O Student's stepparent   O Student's brother or sister
Age: _____   O Student's husband or wife O Student's son or daughter   O Student's grandparent
                           O Student's stepbrother/stepsister O Other (explain in Section P)

2002-2003 school year
Name of school or college _____   Year in school _____
Scholarships and grants $ _____   Parents' contribution $ _____
2003-2004 school year
Attend college at least one term   O Full-time   O Half-time   O Does not apply
College or university name _____
Type: O 2-year public college   O 2-year private college   O 4-year public college/university
         O 4-year private college/university   O graduate/professional school   O proprietary school

Family Member 5

Full name of family member _____   Claimed by parents
                                                    as tax exemption in 2002?   O Yes   O No

Relationship to student: O Student's parent   O Student's stepparent   O Student's brother or sister
Age: _____   O Student's husband or wife O Student's son or daughter   O Student's grandparent
                           O Student's stepbrother/stepsister O Other (explain in Section P)

2002-2003 school year
Name of school or college _____   Year in school _____
Scholarships and grants $ _____   Parents' contribution $ _____
2003-2004 school year
Attend college at least one term   O Full-time   O Half-time   O Does not apply
College or university name _____
Type: O 2-year public college   O 2-year private college   O 4-year public college/university
         O 4-year private college/university   O graduate/professional school   O proprietary school

Family Member 6

Full name of family member _____   Claimed by parents
                                                    as tax exemption in 2002?   O Yes   O No

Relationship to student: O Student's parent   O Student's stepparent   O Student's brother or sister
Age: _____   O Student's husband or wife O Student's son or daughter   O Student's grandparent
                           O Student's stepbrother/stepsister O Other (explain in Section P)

2002-2003 school year
Name of school or college _____   Year in school _____
Scholarships and grants $ _____   Parents' contribution $ _____
2003-2004 school year
Attend college at least one term   O Full-time   O Half-time   O Does not apply
College or university name _____
Type: O 2-year public college   O 2-year private college   O 4-year public college/university
         O 4-year private college/university   O graduate/professional school   O proprietary school

Section N - Parents' Information
(to be answeredby the parent(s)completing this form)

61.a Select one: ○ Father ○ Stepfather ○ Legal guardian ○ Other (Explain in Section P)

  b Name

  c Age

  d Select if: ○ Self-employed ○ Unemployed

  e If unemployed enter date unemployment began:

  f Occupation

  g Employer

  h Number of years employed by employer listed above

  i Work telephone

  j Retirement plans available (Check all that apply.)

    ○ Social security ○ Civil service/state ○ Military

    ○ Union/employer ○ IRA/Keogh/tax-deferred ○ Other

62.a Select one: ○ Mother ○ Stepmother ○ Legal guardian ○ Other (Explain in Section P)

  b Name

  c Age

  d Select if: ○ Self-employed ○ Unemployed

  e If unemployed enter date unemployment began:

  f Occupation

  g Employer

  h Number of years employed by employer listed above

  i Work telephone

  j Retirement plans available (Check all that apply.)

    ○ Social security ○ Civil service/state ○ Military

    ○ Union/employer ○ IRA/Keogh/tax-deferred ○ Other

Parent Loan Information

The questions that follow are intended to provide the student's family with options for financing the parents' share of the student's college costs. Many families choose to borrow through the Federal Parent Loan for Undergraduate Students (PLUS) Program to supplement the financial aid offer. This program, as well as most private loan programs, requires a check of parent credit worthiness to qualify.

Families that answer the questions on this page will:

- get information about their eligibility to borrow through the PLUS program.
- learn what their monthly payment responsibilities would be, should they decide to borrow (a valid email address is required to receive financing guidance).
- learn about loan programs sponsored by the College Board.

By answering Questions **B-G** below, you are authorizing the College Board (or its agent), to use the information you provide below and the student's name to evaluate the parents' credit record and report the results of the credit evaluation to the parent whose information is provided below. A positive credit rating will mean that the parent is pre-approved to borrow a PLUS Loan from most lenders, including the College Board's CollegeCredit PLUS Loan program, should additional financial assistance be necessary. (Most other lenders use the same criteria in approving families' applications for PLUS Loans.) The College Board will not share this information with the student, the student's colleges, or anyone else. Reporting of credit worthiness results will begin in February 2003 to ensure that your credit results remain valid when you are ready to apply for a PLUS loan. (The results are valid for only 180 days.)

You may skip the questions below if you are not interested in learning about your eligibility for the Federal PLUS program.

A. Does the parent want to be considered for an educational loan to cover college costs? ○ Yes ○ No

If you answered "Yes", complete Questions **B-G**.

B. Parent's name:

        Lastname   *Firstname*   M .I.

C. Parent's home address:

        Number, street, and apartment number

        City   *State*   *Zip code*

D. Telephone number:

        Areacode

E. Parent's social security number:

F. Parent's date of birth:

        Month   *Day*   *Year*

G. Parent's e-mail address:

Section O - Information About Noncustodial Parent

(to be answered by the parent who completes this form if the student's biological or adoptive parents are divorced, separated, or were never married to each other)

63 a Noncustodial parent's name:

    b Home address- street

    c Home address- city, state, zip

    d Occupation/Employer

    e Year of separation

    f Year of divorce

    g According to court order, when will support for the student end? (MM/YYYY)

    h Who last claimed the student as a tax exemption?

    i Year last claimed?

    j How much does the noncustodial parent plan to contribute to the student's education for the 2003-2004 school year? (Do not include this amount in 27g.)

    k Is there an agreement specifying this contribution for the student's education?   O Yes   O No

Section P - Explanations/Special Circumstances

Use this space to explain any unusual expenses such as high medical or dental expenses, educational and other debts, child care, elder care, or special circumstances. Also give information for any outside scholarships you have been awarded. If more space is needed, use sheets of paper and send them directly to your schools and programs. When online, please limit your responses to no more than 27 lines of information.

PROFILE Online 2003-2004 Worksheet

Question 13e

Complete the worksheet below and calculate the total at the end of the questions. Enter the total in question 13e. **Dont include:** *any income reported elsewhere on the PROFILE Application, money from student financial aid, foodstamps, "rollover" pensions, Workforce Investments Act educational benefits, or gifts and support, other than money received from friends or relatives.*

Deductible IRA and/or SEP, SIMPLE, or Keogh payments from IRS Form 1040, total of lines 24 and 31 or 1040A, line 17	$
Tax exempt interest income from IRS Form 1040, line 8b or 1040A, line 8b	+
Payments to tax-deferred pension and savings plans (paid directly or withheld from earnings), including but not limited to, amounts reported on the W-2 Form in Boxes 12a-12d, codes D, E, F, G, H, and S on the W-2 Form. Include untaxed payments to 401(k) and 403(b) plans.	+
Additional child tax credit from IRS Form 1040, line 66 or 1040A, line 42	+
Workers' Compensation	+
Veterans non-educational benefits such as Death Pension, Disability, etc.	+
Housing, food, and other living allowances paid to members of the military, clergy, and others (including cash payments and cash value of benefits)	+
Cash received or any money paid on the student's behalf, not reported elsewhere on this form	+
VA educational work-study allowances	+
Any other untaxed income and benefits	+
TOTAL =	$

Question 55k

Complete the worksheet below and calculate the total at the end of the questions. Enter the total in question 55k. **Dont include:** *any income reported elsewhere on the PROFILE Application, money from student financial aid, Workforce Investments Act educational benefits, or gifts and support, other than money received from friends or relatives.*

Untaxed portions of IRA distributions from IRS forms (excluding "rollovers")	$
Untaxed portions of pensions from IRS forms (excluding "rollovers")	+
Additional child tax credit from IRS Form 1040, line 66 or 1040A, line 42	+
Veterans non-educational benefits such as Disability, Death Pension, Dependency & Indemnity Compensation	+
Workers' Compensation	+
Cash received or any money paid on your behalf (Don't include child support.)	+
Black Lung Benefits, Refugee Assistance	+
Credit for federal tax on special fuels	+
Untaxed portions of Railroad Retirement benefits	+
Any other untaxed income and benefits	+
TOTAL =	$

## CHAPTER EIGHT

How You're Evaluated

Now that you've completed your applications for financial aid, you may wonder just how the federal government and colleges determine the amount of financial aid you'll receive. If so, this chapter will explain the process and take you step by step through a sample case. While this is not a mandatory part of applying for financial aid, some parents and families who want to better understand their financial aid status will find this chapter helpful. If you are starting your federal financial aid application process in fall 2004, be sure to read the section on changes in the federal need analysis methodology.

"If you're starting early, this can be helpful in understanding the process," says Barry Simmons at Virginia Tech. "Hearing about EFC and calculations may not do much good, but doing it yourself step-by-step can be beneficial."

As you've already learned, financial aid programs and offices take your information and conduct a need analysis, which is designed to determine the amount of money your son or daughter will need to afford college. Before we get into the specifics of this work, it helps to know the four basic principles on which all need analysis is based.

1. Parents are expected to shoulder as much of the financial responsibility for their student's education as they can afford.

2. Students are expected to contribute to the cost of their education.

3. Families are evaluated based upon their current financial situation—not on the future or past.

TRENT & SEPPY SAY...

Trent:

Many financial aid officers don't think it's necessary for parents to calculate their EFC, unless they want to better understand the process. So don't feel like you have to do it.

Seppy:

If you're an accountant, or just want to know what goes on "behind the scenes," you'll find this chapter interesting. But if you're happy with the results of your FAFSA and CSS Profile, a quick glance through the chapter may be enough for you.

4. Families are treated in a consistent and equal manner, while recognizing that special circumstances may exist in some situations.

THE TWO METHODOLOGIES

When it comes to calculating need analysis, there are two methods to doing so: the Federal Methodology and the Institutional Methodology.

Federal Methodology (FM) is the formula used to calculate your need analysis for the FAFSA. This method was developed by Congress to determine your eligibility for federally funded financial aid programs.

Institutional Methodology (IM) is an alternative formula for calculating need analysis and is used for the CSS Profile. IM is also used by some colleges for determining institutional aid.

You'll find that these two formulas overlap a bit, but that Federal Methodology is generally more lenient for families and students. When it comes to calculating the Institutional Methodology, there's no one way to go about it. "As many schools use the Institutional Methodology, there are different types of IM," says Ellen Frishberg of Johns Hopkins University. Regardless, she notes that practically all IM calculations use the same factors. "Five things are really key to any IM calculation," she explains. "First, who's counted in college? Some Institutional Methodology calculations may not count a sibling or parent who is a grad school student. Second, the treatment of assets is different from the FAFSA. Third, medical expenses are also treated differently. Fourth, home equity is important to an IM calculation. And fifth, Institutional Methodology has regional tables for calculations, but not every school can afford to use them."

YOUR EFC

As you've learned from previous chapters, EFC stands for Expected Family Contribution, and is the amount your family is expected to pay for your student's education. We've also discussed how this EFC is almost always quite different from how much a family can truly afford to pay out-of-pocket for college. Because of this, your "need" analysis may not accurately represent how much you and your student realistically need to afford college.

It's important to remember that financial aid programs and colleges define "need" very differently than you do. As you learned earlier, your need is determined by subtracting the amount you are expected to contribute to your student's education from the total cost of college. In other words,

Cost of Attending College (COA)
− Your Expected Family Contribution (EFC)
Your "Need" / Eligibility for Need-Based Aid

The bottom line is, you are expected to contribute at least a portion of your income to your student's education. Regardless of what your need is determined to be, you are responsible for meeting your EFC, whether you have that money or not.

HOW YOUR ASSETS AND INCOME ARE ASSESSED

In order to determine just how much your family is expected to contribute, it's necessary to assess your family's assets and income. Since it's believed that people with more assets and income can afford to pay more for their student's college education, this is essential to calculating need analysis.

To determine this, your income includes not only your salary and wages from your job, but your interest from bank accounts, dividends from stocks, profits from the sale of investments, and any other sources of income your family receives. Your assets are anything of value that you own: your home, stocks, bonds, savings accounts, CDs, and other investments that are not considered to be cash.

We'll repeat a point we made earlier here: remember that the more assets and investments your student has, the less financial aid he or she may qualify for. When schools determine a family's EFC for college, they expect 35 percent of a student's assets to be used for college, while as little as 6 percent is expected to come from the parent's assets. Because of this huge difference, it's wise to transfer assets in your son's or daughter's name to yours.

Protection Allowances

The good news is that a need analysis attempts to be fair, so a protection allowance is built into the calculations. The process takes into account that you've probably been saving for other things instead of, or in addition to, your student's education. Since people save for things like retirement, or the down payment on a house, certain allowances are allowed for such saving. This means that you're able to deduct a certain amount of your assets for these purposes, and the amount that's left after this deduction is used to determine your EFC. The chart on the next page gives the amount of allowances for the 2003–2004 school year.

EDUCATION SAVINGS AND ASSET PROTECTION ALLOWANCE (FOR FEDERAL EFC FORMULA)		
Age of older parent	Allowance if there are two parents	Allowance if there is only one parent
25 or less	0	0
26	2,300	1,100
27	4,600	2,200
28	6,900	3,300
29	9,100	4,500
30	11,400	5,600
31	13,700	6,700
32	16,000	7,800
33	18,300	8,900
34	20,600	10,000
35	22,900	11,100
36	25,200	12,200
37	27,400	13,400
38	29,700	14,500
39	32,000	15,600
40	34,300	16,700
41	35,200	17,000
42	36,100	17,400
43	36,700	17,800
44	37,700	18,200
45	38,600	18,600
46	39,600	18,900
47	40,600	19,400
48	41,900	19,900
49	42,900	20,300
50	44,000	20,800
51	45,100	21,200
52	46,500	21,700
53	47,600	22,400
54	49,100	22,900
55	50,300	23,400
56	51,800	24,000
57	53,300	24,700
58	54,900	25,300
59	56,600	26,000
60	58,300	26,600
61	60,000	27,400
62	62,000	28,100
63	63,800	28,900
64	66,000	29,700
65	68,200	30,700

Discretionary Net Worth

This term refers to the amount of your assets after subtracting your protection allowance. So, based on the chart above, if you are a single parent aged 45, and you have $57,000 in savings, and your protection allowance is $18,600, $57,000 − $18,600 = $38,400 is the amount of your discretionary net worth.

COMPARING THE FORMULAS

Since both Federal Methodology and Institutional Methodology use slightly different formulas, let's look at each individually. Afterwards, we're going to take a sample family and calculate their need using each method. If you wish to do these calculations yourself, see the Financial Aid Resources section for the forms and charts necessary to complete these calculations.

> ## TRENT & SEPPY SAY...
>
> **Trent:**
>
> *You'll notice in this chart that the older you are, the higher your subtracted protection allowance for savings will be.*
>
> **Seppy:**
>
> *This is because the older a student's parents are, the more they need to keep for retirement. (Unless your student becomes incredibly rich and takes care of you so you never have to work again.)*

In addition to the worksheets provided in this book, you can find them online at *www.finaid.org*. Also, these worksheets are not meant to be submitted to any financial aid program, but are offered solely for the benefit of parents and families who wish to calculate their EFC for their own purposes. If you prefer not to fill out worksheets, online sites such as *finaid.org* and *salliemae.com* provide calculators that allow you to create an estimate of your EFC without the detailed paperwork. Regardless of which method you choose to calculate your EFC, you'll need your tax documents and records of your assets.

"The calculators were a great help for us," says Joe Sanseverino, of Rocky Point, NY. "It's much easier than doing it by hand, and it only took minutes."

Federal Methodology

When doing a need analysis with FM, several things are taken in consideration, including:

- The parent's and student's income from the previous year
- Total income tax paid by the family
- Number of people in the family
- Number of people in the family attending college
- The family's assets (excluding equity in their house)

- The parents' ages
- The cost of living, based on the state in which the family lives

Take a look at the sample calculations for the Doe family for a step-by-step example of how FM is done. Worksheets that you can use for your own calculations are found in the Financial Aid Resources section.

Calculating the FM—A Case History

Calculating your Federal Methodology is basically a matter of determining your EFC through the same process the government uses when you file your FAFSA. To make the process easier to understand, let's go through a sample case.

Jane Doe is a high school senior who is about to start her first year of college. She is an only child and lives with her parents in New York. Jane works part time, and last year she made $4,000. She also has $300 in a savings account. Her father, who is 42 years old, earns $40,000 a year, while her mother, who is 41 years old and works part time, earns $26,136 per year. The Does have $10,000 in investments and $3,000 in savings, and Mr. Doe invests $200 each month into his 401(k).

Since the Does have already filed a FAFSA, they had a completed copy handy when determining their EFC.

THE DOES' FM: LINE BY LINE

Line 1:

The **parents' adjusted gross income** for last year was $60,290. Using his FAFSA form, Mr. Doe was able to copy this number from line 74 of the FAFSA.

Line 2a:

Mr. Doe's **income from work** was $40,000. This was copied from line 77 of the completed FAFSA.

Line 2b:

Mrs. Doe's **income from work** was $26,136. This was copied from line 78 of the completed FAFSA.

By adding these two incomes together, the **total parents' income** earned from work was $66,136.

Line 3:

As tax filers, the Does used the amount listed on line 1, making their **parents' taxable income** $60,290.

Line 4:

Using the FAFSA Worksheets A & B, the Does did not have any dollar amount from Worksheet A. But because Mr. Doe contributed $200 each month into his 401(k), the total dollar amount for Worksheet B was $4,200. This made their total **untaxed income and benefits** $2,400.

Line 5:

By adding Lines 3 and 4, the Does determined their **taxable and untaxed income**.

$60,290 (Line 3) + $2,400 (Line 4) = $62,690

Line 6:

The Does did not have any dollar amount from FAFSA Worksheet C, so this line was $0.00.

Line 7:

By subtracting Line 6 from Line 5, the Does' **total income** was $62,690.

Line 8:

The Does' 2002 income tax paid was $10,020. This amount was copied from line 75 of the completed FAFSA.

THE DOES' FM: LINE BY LINE (CONT.)

Line 9:

Looking at Table A1*, the Does' tax allowance was 10%. Since New York gives a tax allowance of 11% for anyone earning less than $15,000, and 10% for anyone earning more than $15,000, the Does qualified for the 10% allowance.

According the instructions at the bottom of the table, the Does' multiplied their total income (Line 7) by this percentage.

$62,690 × 10% = $6,269

So the Doe's **state tax allowance** is $6,269.

Line 10:

Looking at Table A2*, Mr. Doe's social security tax allowance was 7.65%, since he earns less than $84,900 per year. So multiplying this percentage by the total income, Mr. Doe's **social security tax allowance** was determined to be $3,060.

$40,000 × 7.65% = $3,060

Line 11:

Mrs. Doe's social security tax allowance was also 7.65%, since she earns less than $84,900 per year. Multiplying this percentage by her income of $26,136, her **social security tax allowance** was determined to be $1,999.

$26,136 × 7.65% = $1,999

Line 12:

Looking at Table A3*, the Does' **income protection allowance** was $16,770. This is because there is one college student in the household (Jane), and there are three adults in the household.

Line 13:

Since both parents work, the Does' employment expense allowance is either 35% of the lesser of their incomes, or $3,000, whichever is less. Mrs. Doe earns less than her husband, so her income was used.

$26,136 × 35% = $9,147

Since 35% of Mrs. Does income is well over $3,000, the Does' **employment expense allowance** was $3,000.

Line 14:

Adding Lines 8 through 13, the Does' **total allowances** were $41,118.

*See Part Two, Financial Aid Resources, section three, EFC Worksheets, for charts A1–A7.

THE DOES' FM: LINE BY LINE (CONT.)

Line 15:

To determine their **available income (AI)**, the Does subtracted Line 14 from Line 7.

$62,690 − $41,118 = $21,572

The Does' AI was $21,572.

Line 16:

Since the Does have $10,000 in **investments**, this amount was copied from line 82 of the FAFSA.

Line 19:

Since the Does have $3,000 in **savings**, this amount was copied from line 84 of the FAFSA.

Line 20:

To determine their net worth, the Does added Line 16 and 19.

$10,000 + $3,000 = $13,000

This makes their **net worth** $13,000.

Line 21:

Looking at Table A5*, the Does' used Mr. Doe's age of 42, since he is the older of the two parents. Since there are two parents and Mr. Doe is 42, their **education savings and asset protection allowance** was $39,200.

Line 22:

Subtracting Line 21 from Line 20, the Does got a negative number.

$13,000 − $39,200 = −$26,200

Line 24:

Multiplying Line 22 by .12, the Does got a negative number.

−$26,200 × .12 = −$3,144

Since the instructions indicate that if this number is negative to enter zero, the Does' **contribution from assets** is $0.00.

Line 25:

Subtracting the zero dollar amount contributed from assets from their AI on Line 15, the Does' **adjusted available income (AAI)** is the same as their AI.

$21,572 − $0.00 = $21,572

THE DOES' FM: LINE BY LINE (CONT.)

Line 26:

Using table A6*, the Does determined their contribution from AAI. Since their AAI is between $21,201 and $24,300, their contribution is $5,334, plus 40% of their income over $21,200.

By subtracting the $21,200 from their AAI of $21,572, the Does learn how much income they will have to calculate at 40%.

$21,572 – $21,200 = $372

So $372 of their AAI will be assessed at 40%.

$372 × 40% = $148

So this means that in addition to the flat $5,334, the Does need to add $148 to that amount.

$5,334 + $148 = $5,482

This makes the **total parents' contribution from AAI** $5,482.

Line 27:

The Does have **one child in college**, so this line is 1.

Line 28:

Dividing Line 26 by the 1 in Line 27, the Does' **parent contribution** is the same as their AAI, $5,482.

Next comes the income and information for Jane herself:

Line 29:

Copied from the completed FAFSA, **Jane's adjusted gross income** was $4,000.

Line 31:

As a tax filer, her **taxable income** was the same as Line 29, $4,000.

Line 32:

Since Jane did not have any additional income, she had a zero on both the FAFSA Worksheet A and B. This made her **untaxed income** $0.00, as well.

Line 33:

As the sum of Line 31 and 32, Jane's **income** remained at $4,000.

Line 34:

Jane had a zero on the FAFSA Worksheet C, so this line was $0.00 as well.

THE DOES' FM: LINE BY LINE (CONT.)

Line 35:

This makes Jane's **total income** $4,000.

Line 36:

To qualify for tax liability, a person's income must be more than $4,550. Because her income was less than this amount, Jane was **exempt from withholding**. This means her 2002 income tax paid was $0.00.

Line 37:

Using Table A7, Jane's **state tax allowance** is 7%, since she lives in New York. So multiplying this percentage by her income, Jane's state tax allowance is $280.

$4,000 × 7% = $280

Line 38:

Like her parents, Jane's social security tax allowance is 7.65%, according to Table A2. $4000 × 7.65% = $306

This makes her **social security tax allowance** $306.

Line 40:

According to the instructions, since Line 25 is a positive number, this line is zero.

Line 41:

Adding Lines 36 through 40, Jane's **total allowances** are $2,966.

Line 42:

Subtracting Line 41 from Line 35, Jane's **available income (AI)** is $1,034.

$4,000 − $2,966 = $1,034

Line 44:

By multiplying Line 42 by .50, Jane's contribution from her AI is $517.

$1,034 × 0.50 = $517

Line 47:

Since Jane has $300 in **savings**, this amount is copied from line 49 of the FAFSA.

Line 48:

Since Jane has no other **investments**, the sum of Lines 45 through 47 is $300.

THE DOES' FM: LINE BY LINE (CONT.)

Line 50:

Multiplying the $300 in Line 48 by the .35 in Line 49, Jane's **contribution from assets** is $105.

$300 × 0.35 = $105

Line 51:

To determine the **Expected Family Contribution**, the Does added Line 28 (the parents' contribution of $5,482), Line 44 (Jane's contribution from AI of $517), and Line 50 (Jane's contribution from assets of $105).

$5,482 + $517 + $105 = $6,104

This means the Does' EFC is $6,104.

TRENT & SEPPY SAY...

Trent:

Just as Institutional Methodology looks at more information than FM when calculating your EFC, it also uses more allowances.

Seppy:

And more abbreviations! CESA, ERA, IM, EFC . . . It's like listening to a baseball game!

Institutional Methodology

Just as the CSS Profile form is more detailed than the FAFSA, you can expect the information involved in calculating your EFC using IM to be more detailed than when using FM. This is true because IM is used in the CSS Profile form, as well as other types of institutional aid, where more detailed financial information about a family is desired.

For example, rather than one protection allowance, IM involves several allowances. The Emergency Reserve Allowance (ERA) is one of them. This allowance is designed to protect a family's assets for use in unexpected emergencies such as medical emergencies, unemployment, or other urgent and expensive needs a family may face.

Other kinds of allowances involved in IM include the Cumulative Education Savings Allowance (CESA), which is designed to protect a family's savings that are designated for their son or daughter's college expenses. Another allowance is the Low Income Asset Allowance, which acknowledges that low income families need additional protection because basic living expenses often take the majority of their income. Beyond these allowances, detailed information such as medical and dental expenses, elementary and secondary school tuitions, and home equity are taken into consideration.

One important factor needed for an IM calculation that's not necessary when doing an FM calculation is home equity. As you'll see, you'll need to know how much equity you have in your home. "One of the things that impacted us," admits Karon Ray, parent of three, "is that because we live in military quarters, in a house on post, our housing situation is different from most families. If we chose to buy a house off post, we'd probably qualify for financial aid because of the mortgage. But because that's not the case, the money is in financial assets instead." Medical expenses also come into play.

Also, whereas the FM calculations combined the parents and the dependent student into one worksheet, the College Board uses two different worksheets for parents and dependent students. Calculating your Institutional Methodology can be different from college to college, but in order to understand the basics, we'll use the same sample family we used for the FM calculations.

Calculating the IM—A Case History

Let's return to the Doe family and calculate their IM EFC. Once again, Jane Doe is a high school senior who is about to start her first year of college. She is an only child and lives with her parents in New York. Jane works part time, and last year she made $4,000. She also has $300 in a savings account. Her father, who is 42 years old, earns $40,000 a year, while her mother, who is 41 years old and works part time, earns $26,136 per year. The Does have $10,000 in investments and $3,000 in savings, and Mr. Doe invests $200 each month into his 401(k).

THE DOES' IM: LINE BY LINE

Let's start with the worksheet for Parents of Dependent Students.

Line 1:

The **AGI (or adjusted gross income)** for last year was $60,290. This was the same amount used on the FM calculations, and was copied from the Does' tax forms.

Line 2:

The family's **untaxed income and benefits** were $2,400. This amount reflects the $200 Mr. Doe put in his 401(k) each month.

Line 4:

By adding the above lines, their **total parents' income** was $62,690.

$60,290 (Line 1) + $2,400 (Line 2) = $62,690

Line 5:

The amount of U.S. **income tax paid** by the Does was $10,020. This was the same amount used in the FM calculations, and was copied from the Does' tax forms.

THE DOES' IM: LINE BY LINE (CONT.)

Line 6:

Looking at Table 1*, the Does' tax percentage was 12.5%, since they lived in New York and made between $60,001 and $70,000 per year. Multiplying that percentage by Line 4 gave them a **state tax allowance** of $7,836.

$62,690 (Line 4) × 12.5% = $7,836

Line 7:

Looking at Table 2*, the Does' FICA allowance was the same amount as for the FM calculation—7.65%. Multiplying this percent by Line 4 gave them a **FICA allowance** of $4,795.

$62,690 (Line 4) × 7.65% = $4,795

Line 8:

According to Table 2*, the medical and dental allowance is any unreimbursed expenses in excess of 3.5% of total income. Mr. Doe had surgery last year, and the family paid $3,000 in out of pocket expenses and bills that were not covered by his insurance. To determine this amount, they started by determining the 3.5% of their income.

$62,690 × 3.5% = $2,194

Since the $3,000 they paid was greater than 3.5% of their income, the Does could use the difference between the two.

$3,000 − $2,194 = $806.

So, the Does' **medical and dental allowance** was $806.

Line 9:

Looking at Table 2*, the **employment allowance** is 38% of the lesser earned income, with a maximum of $3,470. Mrs. Doe earns less than her husband, so her income was used.

$26,136 × 38% = $9,931

Since 38% of Mrs. Doe's income is higher than the maximum allowance of $3,470, the **maximum allowance** was used.

Line 10:

To determine the **annual savings goal** in Line a, the Does multiplied 1.52% by Line 4.

$26,136 (Line 4) × 1.52% = $952

However, since there are no other children besides Jane, and the student applicant is excluded, the amount in line b was zero. Therefore, the multiplication of $952 by 0 is 0 for Line c.

Line 11:

According to Table 3a*, the family's **income protection allowance** is $19,310, since there are three members in the family, and one person in college.

*See Part Two, section three, EFC Worksheets, for Tables 1–11.

THE DOES' IM: LINE BY LINE (CONT.)

Line 12:

By adding Lines 5 through 11, the **total allowances** were $46,237.

Line 13:

By subtracting Line 12 from Line 4, the Does' **available income** was $16,453.

$62,690 (Line 4) − $46,237 (Line 12) = $16,453

Line 14:

Using Table 5*, the Does determined their contribution from available income (AI). Since their AI (which is the amount on Line 13) is between $14,110 and $19,050, their contribution is $3,104, plus 26% of their income over $14,110.

By subtracting the $14,110 from their AI of $16,453, the Does learn how much income they will have to calculate at 26%.

$16,453 − $14,110 = $2,343

So $2,343 of their AI will be assessed at 26%.

$2,343 × 26% = $609

So this means that in addition to the flat $3,104, the Does need to add $609 to that amount.

$3,104 + $609 = $3,713

This makes the **total parents' contribution from income** $3,713.

Line 15:

The Does have $3,000 in **savings**.

Line 16:

The Does have $35,000 in **home equity**.

Line 17:

The Does have $10,000 in **investment equity**.

Line 21:

By adding Lines 15–20, the Does' **net worth** is $48,000.

Line 22a:

Using Table 8, the Does have an **emergency reserve allowance** of $17,610, since there are three people in their family.

Line 22b:

Using Table 4*, the Does calculated their **cumulative education savings allowance (CESA)**. Since their calculation came out to be less than the standard $16,540, and the table indicates that the greater amount should be used, the Does use $16,540 for this amount.

THE DOES' IM: LINE BY LINE (CONT.)
Line 22d: The sum of Lines 22a, 22b, and 22c is $34,150.
Line 23:   The Does' **discretionary net worth** was found by subtracting Line 22d from Line 21. $48,000 (Line 21) − $34,150 (Line 22d) = $13,850
Line 24:   Using Table 9, the Does' contribution from assets is 3%, since their discretionary net worth is less than $26,520. So by multiplying this percentage by Line 23, their **contribution from assets** is $415. $13,850 × 3% = $415
Line 25:   By adding Lines 14 and 24, the Does' **total parent contribution** is $4,128. $3,713 (Line 14) + $415 (Line 24) = $4,128
Line 26:   Using Table 10, the Does multiply this amount by 100%, since they have one child in college.
Line 27:   Multiplying the $4,128 in Line 25 by 100%, the Does **parent contribution** for Jane is $4,128.

Now, there's a shorter, but similar form for Jane.

JANE DOE'S IM: LINE BY LINE
Line 1:
Jane's **AGI (or adjusted gross income)** for last year was $4,000. This was the same amount used on the FM calculations, and was copied from Jane's tax forms.
Lines 2 & 3:
Jane did not have any **untaxed income or taxable student aid**.
Line 4:
By adding the above lines, Jane's **total income** was $4,000.
Line 5:
Since Jane made less than $4,550, she did not qualify for tax liability. Because her income was less than this amount, Jane was exempt from withholding. This means her 2002 **income tax paid** was $0.00.
Line 6:
Looking at Table 1, Jane's tax percentage was 12.5%, since she lived in New York and made less than $30,000. Multiplying that percentage by Line 4 gave Jane a **state tax allowance** of $500. $4,000 (Line 4) × 12.5% = $500
Line 7:
Looking at Table 2, Jane's **FICA allowance** was the same amount as for the FM calculation— 7.65%. Multiplying this percent by Line 4 gave her a FICA allowance of $306. $4,000 (Line 4) × 7.65% = $306
Line 8:
By adding Lines 5 through 7, Jane's **total allowances** were $806.
Line 9:
By subtracting Line 8 from Line 4, Jane's **available income** was $3,194. $4,000 (Line 4) − $806 (Line 8) = $3,194
Line 10:
Using Table 11, **Jane's contribution** was calculated. Multiplying Line 9 by 50%, she compared that amount to the minimum contribution in the table. $3,194 × 50% = $1,597 Since this $1,597 was greater than the minimum standard contribution for freshmen dependent students of $1,150, Jane used the higher amount of $1,597.
Line 11:
Jane has $300 in **savings**.
Line 17:
By adding Lines 11 through 16, Jane's **net worth** is $300.

JANE DOE'S IM: LINE BY LINE (CONT.)
Line 18:
By multiplying Line 17 by 0.25, Jane calculated her **contribution from assets** to be $75.
$300 × 0.25 = $75
Line 19:
Jane's **total student contribution** was found by adding Lines 10 and 18.
$1,597 (Line 10) + $75 (Line 18) = $1,672
So **Jane's expected total contribution** was $1,672.
Add It Up
You'll note that the IM worksheets don't combine the parents and student's expected contributions into one number, as the FM calculations did. If you want to find your **IM Expected Family Contribution (EFC)**, just add the total contribution on both worksheets.
When combined, the Does' EFC for the entire family was $5,800.
$4,128 (the Does' parent contribution) + $1,672 (Jane's student contribution) = $5,800 in total EFC.

CREATING NEW FORMULAS

It's interesting to note that over the past few years, the CSS Profile form and its version of Institutional Methodology may be falling out of favor with some private colleges across the country. Some who support this change have criticized the method with creating "bidding wars" over potential students, essentially overlooking the neediest families this analysis is intended to assist. Other colleges site the fees and charges involved in the CSS Profile and prefer to conduct their own need analysis.

Because of this, some private colleges no longer request the CSS Profile, but have developed their own institutional aid form that uses a variation of the Institutional Method. If your student is applying to a private college that requires its own institutional financial aid form rather than the CSS Profile, this may be the case.

"We use our own application for institutional aid, instead of the CSS Profile form, because we don't think families should pay to apply for financial aid," comments Ellen Frishberg, director of Student Financial Services at Johns Hopkins University. "The irony is that low income families need the most help with financial aid, yet they're the ones who can't afford to pay the fee."

It's uncertain if this shift will continue in the future, or what this will mean to the financial aid process. But regardless, this demonstrates that financial aid is an ever-changing process designed to accurately meet the needs of families like yours.

CHANGES IN FEDERAL NEED ANALYSIS COMING IN FALL 2004

Like the federal income tax, the federal need analysis formula allows families to deduct some of what they pay in state and local taxes. But in fall 2004, the Department of Education plans to significantly reduce that amount, in some cases cutting it in half. The controversial change means that the amount of money you're expected to pay for college will increase. If it stands, it might be to your benefit to apply for aid sooner (in 2003) than later.

HOW COLLEGES USE YOUR EFC

Naturally, calculating your EFC is one thing, but determining just how prospective colleges will use their need analysis is another. Once a college knows how much your student's need is going to be, it has to decide how it will meet that need. By deciding this, the college is creating your student's financial aid package.

A college may decide to meet your student's need by offering grants, work study opportunities, or other types of institutional aid. Colleges have different kinds and amounts of aid available, which is why your student's financial aid packages will differ from school to school.

Also, since the costs of your prospective colleges differ, those colleges are going to have calculated different amounts of need in order for your student to attend. So ideally, this would mean that the more expensive colleges and universities your student applies to would offer more financial aid. Unfortunately, this is not always true.

Most colleges insist that they follow your EFC strictly as it is provided by the FAFSA or their own calculations. Your EFC is used to determine your student's need-based aid, but financial aid administrators use their professional judgment to decide how much and what types of financial aid are offered to accepted students. More often than not, this is where a student's grades, background, achievements, and potential come in. In these situations, this may translate into offers of merit-based aid in addition to need-based aid.

And depending on the college, need-based aid is not always calculated first. "We actually consider

TRENT & SEPPY SAY...

Trent:

Even with all the calculations and methodologies, determining a student's financial aid is not a simple process.

Seppy:

Financial aid officers do more than plug a few numbers into a calculator and send out an award letter. They evaluate each student's financial situation and attempt to give them as much financial aid as possible, while still being fair. It can be a stressful job—so be nice to them!

students for merit-based aid first, before we calculate a student's need-based aid," explains Jade Kolb, manager of financial aid at New York University. "If they have a merit scholarship, the need-based aid would complement that."

You're probably well aware that the more a college wants your son or daughter to attend, the more financial aid they are willing to offer. The ultimate example of this is when a college offers to pay the complete cost of a student's education. And since private colleges often have more leeway than public schools because of increased institutional funds, this type of competition tends to be more common at these schools. But remember that while your EFC reflects the need-based aid your son or daughter is eligible for, merit based aid is another matter.

INDEPENDENT STUDENTS

In some situations, students may find themselves paying for college on their own and without any assistance from parents or family. For these independent students, most of what we've discussed throughout this book still applies. However, there are myths about the idea of independent students that must be addressed.

Some parents believe that if their student does not live at home and "becomes" independent, he or she will receive more financial aid than if they help them. These parents may encourage their student to claim that he or she is independent and therefore, not offer to help pay for college. However, this approach does not improve a student's chances of receiving financial aid, and actually reduces them.

TRENT & SEPPY SAY...

Trent:

Each year, thousands of parents try to get out of paying for college by having their student apply as an independent student. The federal government has strict guidelines for identifying independent students, and this approach doesn't work.

Seppy:

An independent student needs additional financial aid because there's no one to help them—not because they move out of their parent's house and pay their own bills.

Requirements to Be Truly Independent

The government's standards for independent students are designed to help adults who do not rely on anyone else for financial assistance. Usually, this occurs when the student is married, has children, or has no family or relatives. In order to be considered an independent student, the student must meet at least one of the following six criteria, which are asked on the FAFSA:

- Were you born before January 1, 1980?
- Will you be working on a degree beyond a bachelor's degree in the coming school year?

- As of today, are you married?
- Are you an orphan or ward of the court, or were you one until age 18?
- Are you a veteran of the U.S. Armed Forces?
- Do you have legal dependents (children who receive more than half their financial support from you); or do you have dependents (other than your children or spouse) who live with you and receive more than half their financial support from you?

If the student meets at least one of these six criteria, they will be considered an independent student. So based on these guidelines, even if your student has moved away from home, or you no longer claim the student as a dependent on your income tax, these reasons are not enough for your student to be considered independent.

Exceptions

The federal government does allow for exceptions, so if you do not meet the above criteria, but have a unique situation that should qualify you as an independent student, talk to your college's financial aid office. These types of situations are considered on a case-by-case basis, and the college's decision is final. Because of this, a student with a unique situation could be considered independent by one college, but not by another.

"We follow federal guidelines when it comes to independent students," says Ellen Frishberg of Johns Hopkins University, "unless there is an exception, or other unique circumstance. For example, one student rejected their parents' Amish background, and currently supports themselves without financial assistance. But such exceptions are rare."

Need Analysis for Independent Students

When colleges consider you to be an independent student, they will calculate your need analysis slightly differently than we originally discussed in this book. Just how a college will calculate your need analysis depends on whether or not you have dependents that rely on you financially, or if you are responsible only for yourself. Therefore, when a single mother is going back to school, the college will also consider the financial impact this has on the individual's child, while an independent student without children will have different financial needs. To better understand your differences in need analysis, contact your college for assistance.

Anything Else?

For the most part, the financial aid process of independent students does not differ that much from dependent students. Financial aid packages are created the same way, and are given the same consideration. However, the one real difference involved is that independent students usually receive more self-help aid than other students. This is because independent students have different needs than dependent students, and this extra aid is necessary to afford college. Because of this, independent students are automatically eligible for additional federal loan funds, particularly in the Stafford loan program.

As you can tell, being an independent student means more than moving away from home and filing your own taxes. But for those who are truly independent and do not have financial support from parents or a family, additional financial aid is available.

MOVING ON

To wrap up, we began by discussing the basic beliefs on which all need analysis is based. We then looked at the differences between Federal and Institutional Methodologies, briefly describing each. After recapping the definition of an EFC and how it is calculated, we then went over how your assets and income are viewed in this process. We looked at allowances and discretionary net worth before comparing FM and IM in more detail.

We demonstrated these methodologies by calculating a sample family's EFC using both methods. Afterward, we discussed how new institutional formulas are being created and how colleges use your EFC in determining financial aid. Finally, we looked at the definition of an independent student, and how the government and colleges evaluate them for aid.

In the next chapter, you'll get a better understanding of what goes into a college's financial aid offer, and learn more about the various elements involved in a financial aid package. You'll also learn how to compare and negotiate these packages. But before you move on, take a look at the checklist for this chapter.

✔ CHECKLIST:

1. Gather your family's federal tax and W-2 forms for calculating your EFC.
2. Refer to part two, section three, EFC Worksheets, for the necessary terms to complete your Federal Methodology and Institutional Methodology EFCs.
3. Complete the Federal Methodology worksheet.
4. Complete the Institutional Methodology worksheet (if applicable).
5. Save your calculations for comparison to your student's financial aid packages.

WEBSITES

Methodology Calculators:
College Board
www.collegeboard.com

FinAid
www.finaid.org

## CHAPTER NINE

Compare and Negotiate Aid Packages

As we've discussed, colleges and universities use the results of your need analysis to create a financial aid package for your student, and these packages vary from student to student, as well as from school to school. In this chapter you'll learn about the various elements of a financial aid package, as well as how you can negotiate for more financial aid.

If you used chapter eight to calculate your EFC, some of this information may be a review for you. But in order to bring others up to speed, let's backtrack for a moment and discuss these aid packages in more detail.

UNDERSTANDING A COLLEGE'S OFFER

You've already learned that a financial aid package usually contains a combination of gift aid, self-help aid, and work aid, and that this represents the total amount of financial aid your student will receive from the college. When colleges create these packages, they use your need analysis to decide how much financial aid to offer your student. Part of that process involves deciding which types of aid the college will offer to meet that need.

In addition, since your prospective colleges cost different amounts, these schools are going to have calculated different amounts of need in order for your student to attend. Because of this, you might assume that private and out-of-state colleges are

TRENT & SEPPY SAY...

Trent:

You shouldn't assume that the most expensive school is going to be the one offering your student the most financial aid.

Seppy:

Say your honor roll student is considered just another applicant to a private Ivy League school, but an up-and-coming state college really wants them to attend. Which do you think will offer more financial aid?

going to provide your student with more financial aid than a local public school. Yet you may be surprised by the award letters you receive.

While your EFC is used to determine need-based aid, financial aid administrators at colleges use their professional judgment to decide if additional aid will be offered. As you might guess, your student's academic record, as well as his or her achievements and potential will influence this. If you're fortunate, some merit-based aid will be included in your student's aid packages.

Most families understand the competitiveness involved in getting merit-based aid. The more a college wants a certain student to attend, the greater the amount of financial aid that is offered. And because private schools tend to have more institutional aid than public colleges, such competition is more common at these schools.

LOOKING AT THE GAP

The first thing you'll probably do when you receive each financial aid package is review the big picture—in other words, you'll immediately look to see if the amount of financial aid being offered is going to be enough for your and your student. If it's not, then this is what colleges call your "unmet need."

Gapping is another term for this difference, and it's the difference between your need (as calculated by the college) and the amount of financial aid they offer your student. If a college determines your need to be $8,000 a year, but your student's aid package offers $5,000 in financial aid, then your unmet need is $3,000.

> ### TRENT & SEPPY SAY...
>
> **Trent:**
>
> *Most families face some gapping in financial aid packages, but that amount can differ vastly from school to school.*
>
> **Seppy:**
>
> *And that difference could be like comparing a crack in the sidewalk to the Grand Canyon. (Now that's a gap!)*

Remember that colleges determine your "need" by subtracting your EFC from the cost of attending that college, so different amounts of unmet need are not going to necessarily reflect the dollar amount of your aid package. For example, let's say your student applies to his dream school and his safety school. His dream school may offer a $12,000 aid package, while the safety school offers a $4,000 aid package. At first, the dream school may look like the better choice. But what if that dream school is going to cost $20,000 a year, while your son could attend his safety school for only $6,000 a year? Even with this significant difference in financial aid offers, the unmet need for your student's dream school would be $8,000 a year, while the unmet need for the safety school would be only $2,000 a year.

But don't assume that all gapping is intentionally done by colleges. "For the most part, there is some unmet need with our students," admits Barry Simmons, director of financial aid at Virginia Tech, "but we don't necessarily gap. When the funds for that student run out, there's not much else we can do."

This difference alone shouldn't be the deciding factor in which college your student will attend, but it will tell you how much you'd actually pay for your student to attend various colleges. Deciding the impact of those differences will be up to you.

PACKAGE ELEMENTS

Now that you've got an overall sense of how to compare aid packages, let's look at the elements involved in them. The various parts of any financial aid package are going to break down into need-based aid, merit-based aid, and other sources of aid. You'll notice as we go through these areas that they review much of what we discussed in chapter six when we first introduced these various types of financial aid.

Need-Based Aid

As you're aware, need-based aid can either be self-help aid, work aid, or gift aid. Many colleges and universities attempt to balance out these three areas, so that no one student is unfairly overburdened with loans. Because of this, most need-based aid is spread out among students fairly equally. It's unlikely in most situations that a low income student would receive a need-based grant covering the majority of their tuition while a student with a similar economic situation would not receive any gift aid. When colleges award need-based aid, their processes are usually standardized with little room for interpretation.

However, it's important to understand that the amount of need-based aid your student receives will not necessarily be consistent throughout the time they attend college. Using aid to attract students, many colleges change the amount of aid offered to students after they attend the school for a year or two. Not surprisingly, this means incoming freshmen may receive more aid than other students. This is done because once a student begins to attend a college, that school no longer feels it has to attract the person to keep them there. The student is already attending the college and is committed to their education. Also, some schools find it unfair to burden freshmen with high loans, since some students do not complete college. As students get closer to completing their degree, they are more likely to be able to afford the burden of those higher loans.

Merit-Based Aid

This is the most flexible area of aid available to colleges, and merit-based aid is used to attract particularly gifted students. An academically gifted student may receive grants to tempt them to attend a school, just as a talented athlete may be offered a significant scholarship in hopes that they will play for the college's team. These kinds of aid can be anywhere from grants given to students with high SAT scores to a scholarship for a teenager who may be musically gifted.

"Once a student gets their aid packages, they should find out what aid is guaranteed, if it changes after freshman year, and what they need to do to keep it," says Jade Kolb, manager of financial aid at NYU. "That goes for all colleges they're looking at."

Colleges that are well known for a particular major, area of study, or athletic team can expect a significantly high number of applicants for those areas. For example, if a school has a particularly good basketball team, that school will likely get a large number of applications from high school basketball players. Because of this, some colleges are placed into a "highly competitive" category, be it for a sport or major. Merit-based aid can also be used to diversify a campus by attracting minorities or other populations.

But competition can be fierce. "I frequently have to explain to parents that no matter what a student's achievements, they're compared to the whole applicant pool for that year," explains NYU's Kolb. "A student could have a 3.5 GPA, but if our applicant pool for that year has an average of 3.7, they'll have a tough time. It can change from year to year."

> ### Multitask
>
> Even if your student has a good chance of getting an athletic scholarship, encourage them to apply for academic ones. "That's the best situation to be in," says parent Joe Sanseverino, "because coaches will set aside money for the student's scholarship, then go to the admission office and say, 'I want this person to play for us, and here's what I can give them. What can you offer to help?' If the student has good grades, they're likely to get more aid because of academics."

And even when a student receives merit-based aid, it may not be as much as you expect. "People whose children excel at sports think this will turn into lots of financial aid," explains Joe Sanseverino, whose daughter was offered a lacrosse scholarship. "Parents think there's a good chance their child will get a free ride. That may be true if your child plays football or basketball, but for other sports I don't think it's true. I've had coaches tell me that there's not enough money in lesser-known sports to do that."

Due to the flexibility involved in merit-based aid, these types of awards continue to be the most controversial type of financial aid. Some consider merit-based aid to be unfair, saying that colleges do not have enough money to offer such high awards to a handful of students. Supporters of merit-based aid insist that high achievements and accomplishments should be rewarded.

Private Scholarships

We've also briefly mentioned that your son or daughter may receive other types of aid, including scholarships or grants from corporations, local organizations, and private foundations. Because they are not offered through the college itself, they may not be included in your aid package. However, this depends on the source of the outside aid. They may choose to notify the college directly, or it may be your responsibility. Remember, looking for private scholarships should be an ongoing process. "Parents usually do scholarship searches once, and then forget it," says Virginia Tech's Simmons. "But searches should be done quarterly, because new scholarships pop up every few months."

The easiest example of this is when your student receives gift aid that can be used for any college they attend. For example, let's say your employer grants your student a set amount of money that can be used for any in-state college. In this situation, the award letter would come from the corporation itself, rather than a school. Once your son or daughter decides which in-state college he or she will attend, you'll need to notify the corporation, which then might pay the college directly. In other situations, a check may be sent to your student, and it would be his or her responsibility to pay the college.

If your son or daughter is awarded one of these scholarships or grants, you'll need to contact the financial aid office at the college your student has decided to attend and inform them of the award. In many situations, this may impact your aid package. Your student's financial aid package cannot exceed the cost of that college, so should a private scholarship cause this to happen, your other sources of aid will be reduced. Fortunately, this seldom occurs, and if it does, at least you'll be better off with a grant that doesn't have to be repaid instead of more student loans.

> ### TRENT & SEPPY SAY...
>
> **Trent:**
>
> *There's no question that private scholarships and grants are the most under-utilized financial aid out there. Thousands of private scholarships remain unawarded each year, simply because students don't apply.*
>
> **Seppy:**
>
> *These kinds of grants and scholarships are awarded for everything from archery to zoo keeping, so no matter what your student's interests or hobbies, there's something available.*

COMPARING AID PACKAGES

By now, you've probably taken a good look at your son or daughter's financial aid packages and have an understanding of what each school offers. As we've mentioned, now comes the difficult part of comparing these packages.

We've already discussed the idea of unmet need and how you should look at this difference instead of the dollar amounts offered by each package. Recognizing this gap is one aspect of comparing packages, but let's look at a few other things you and your student should consider.

Don't assume that the college offering the most gift aid has the best financial aid package. Instead, add up the self-help and work aid. It's possible that your student could attend an expensive college with less debt than if they attended a cheaper school. "For us, private colleges turned out to be cheaper in the long-term than public schools," admits Connie Gores, a parent and a financial aid manager. "My daughter was offered grants by a private school to study abroad, which significantly impacts one year of her education, while public schools didn't have such a program. Plus, the cost of public colleges is increasing faster than private schools."

When comparing your unmet need from each college, keep things in perspective. An expensive college may offer more gift aid than other schools, but if your EFC is higher, that college may be less attractive. Students who borrow heavily in order to cover a higher EFC will graduate with more debt.

"How a school meets need is also important," says Ellen Frishberg, director of Student Financial Services at Johns Hopkins University. "For example, what percent of your aid package is grants, and what percent is loans? Regardless of the dollar amount, a package that is 70 percent grants and 30 percent loans is better than a package with 30 percent grants and 70 percent loans."

Consider the budget you've created for each college (use your COA worksheets). Expenses that are not taken into consideration by the college, such as personal expenses and travel, may have a large impact on your actual needs. If these amounts are significant, will you need to borrow more? Also, can these expenses be reduced?

"Without a doubt, this [comparing packages] is the hardest part," says Joe Sanseverino. His daughter was offered a combination of financial aid awards from several schools, and his family is trying to make a decision. "She applied to both state and private schools, and we're trying to determine if the private schools are comparable in price. It's not easy."

If you receive a scholarship or grant from a private source, notify the college to determine the effect it will have on your aid package. An adjusted aid package may make a college more (or less) attractive than before.

If a financial aid package includes loans, compare the terms of different loans to determine which is best suited for you. Borrowing a smaller amount from a lender who charges more interest may cost you more in the long run than a larger amount with less interest.

Also, be careful of borrowing from several lenders, since this can end up costing more. If you're considering consolidating these loans, be sure to compare the rates and terms.

Remember that not all schools send out loan paperwork with financial aid packages. "We wait for students to accept the loans in their financial aid package," explains financial aid director Karen Krause, "then we send out the forms for them to start the loan process."

Find out if the awards your son or daughter is offered will remain consistent in future years. Although a college may offer more financial aid than your other prospective schools, that school may decrease its aid the following year—sometimes to less than what other colleges offer.

Above all, remember that there's more to picking the best school for your student than just the cost. Your student may only have to pay $1,000 a year to go to her safety school, but what if she gets accepted to an Ivy League university and had to pay a few thousand dollars more to attend? Wouldn't the long-term benefits of an Ivy League degree outweigh the short-term debt? As we've discussed, college debt is an investment in your student's future, and sometimes that investment can turn out to be a bargain.

You're probably going to find that there are advantages and disadvantages to each financial aid package you receive, and sometimes the benefits and differences between them are difficult to figure out. When this happens, you may want to make a list of the advantages and disadvantages of each. If you're having trouble, go through everything in the aid package. Jot down the consequences of each type of aid you're offered, and you'll start to realize the differences immediately.

NEGOTIATING YOUR FINANCIAL AID PACKAGE

As you and your son or daughter compare these financial aid packages, you may notice a significant difference between colleges. Let's say that one school offers your student a need-based grant for low-income families, and that this grant will pay for most of the cost of that college. But what if the college your student really wants to attend didn't offer any kind of grant at all?

Not too long ago, families were stuck with what they were offered. "Take it or leave it" pretty much summed up financial aid packages, but that's no longer true. Today, it's becoming more and more common for families to negotiate their financial aid. Many parents argue that if schools want to

> ## TRENT & SEPPY SAY...
>
> **Trent:**
>
> *Have you ever seen someone draw a line down the middle of a sheet of paper, then make a list of pros and cons when making a difficult decision? It might help compare similar aid packages.*
>
> **Seppy:**
>
> *For example, one plus might be "offers work study." But the negative to that might be, "will take away study time." (Then again, students might think the opposite.)*

compete for students, they should be willing to reconsider a financial aid package if another college has made a significantly better offer.

This attitude is slowly changing the financial aid process, and you'll find that colleges react to this differently. Some actually encourage parents to provide them with offers from competing colleges so they can attempt to improve a student's aid. Other schools refuse to reconsider their package, insisting the quality of the education and the reputation of the college makes up for the difference in financial aid. Most, however, fall somewhere in the middle and are willing to hear you out, assuming the college overlooked something or that your financial situation has changed.

Remember, however, that most schools won't admit that they negotiate. "We call it a reconsideration, rather than a negotiation," explains Ellen Frishberg. "We will take things into consideration, but we won't pay for your daughter's wedding. But we do make mistakes, and we're human."

Virginia Tech, however, is completely different. "We don't negotiate," explains Barry Simmons, director of financial aid, "and there's a couple of reasons colleges don't do it. Some think that the words *negotiate* and *need* don't belong in the same sentence. Others say financial aid should provide students the opportunity to attend a school, not a guarantee."

> ## TRENT & SEPPY SAY...
>
> ### Trent:
>
> *Some colleges are adamant in refusing to negotiate financial aid. Yet there's a difference between asking for more aid and letting the college know that they have incorrect or incomplete information.*
>
> ### Seppy:
>
> *Even schools that don't negotiate want to know if something's wrong, so no matter what a college's policy is, don't be afraid to call and ask when you think a mistake's been made.*

Simmons also cited that the practice is beginning to create financial problems for some schools. "It can be dangerous because increasing a student's aid often means discounting, and when that happens, schools have to turn around and increase the cost of tuition to cover these losses." Based on Simmon's explanation, this can create a vicious circle of discounting a student's cost, then turning right around and increasing it the following year.

Despite these opposing viewpoints, you should feel comfortable asking colleges about their policies, especially if there's significant differences between financial aid packages. While no school is going to guarantee that it will change their offer, you should take advantage of their willingness to listen to you. What have you got to lose?

HOW TO NEGOTIATE

If you decide to negotiate your financial aid package, you'll need to be prepared before contacting the school. First of all, make sure you have a legitimate reason for asking a college to reconsider its financial aid package. Also, treat the process as if you're making a request, because really, that's what you're doing. Having a negative, angry attitude and insisting that a college increase its aid will destroy any chance of success.

You may choose to call the financial aid office, or write a letter making your request. Whichever method you chose, be sure to do the following:

- Remind the school that your student is interested in attending (if not, you wouldn't be asking them to do this).
- Ask if there is a possibility you and your student can receive more help with expenses (preferably a grant).
- Give some reason for your request (maybe another college offered a low income grant, or you recently were forced to take a pay cut at your job). If you mention another school's offer, be up front and honest. Explain how your student qualified for that particular aid and ask if this college had considered your student for something similar.
- Stay calm and polite.
- Acknowledge that you appreciate the person's time and consideration, and that they are welcome to contact you if they have questions.

> ### The Flexibility Factor
>
> "One of the best things you can do is factor in how amenable a college is with regard to unique situations when you're considering schools," says financial aid officer Connie Gores. "If a college tells you they strictly go by the FAFSA and seem reluctant to consider other information, then you won't get far if you have financial troubles later.

Here's how a phone negotiation might work:

PARENT: My daughter is very interested in attending your college. In fact, it's probably her number-one choice. But I have some questions about her financial aid.

FINANCIAL AID OFFICER: What would you like to know?

PARENT: There are a couple of things, actually. First, I'm a bit concerned about the family contribution that was calculated. I don't know how I can possibly come up with that amount. As it is, our income barely meets our expenses. Is there anything you can do to lower that expected contribution?

FINANCIAL AID OFFICER: First, why don't you review the numbers you reported on your application. If there are any errors, let us know and we'll recalculate. Second, if there are any unusually high expenses that aren't reflected in these numbers—high medical bills, for example—

let us know. We may have some flexibility there. Third, as you know, you can always take out a PLUS loan to meet your family share.

PARENT: Thanks. I'll let you know. But there's something else that bothers us. As I said, your school is probably my daughter's first choice, but frankly the financial aid award isn't as attractive as some others she's received. She's going to have to borrow an awful lot to make it through. Is there any possibility of increased scholarships or grants?

FINANCIAL AID OFFICER: Well, you know, we spend a great deal of time working up packaging guidelines for students. I'll be happy to review hers to make sure we didn't make any errors. Also, if there are any special expenses that she'll have that are not usually considered in our budgets, let me know so we can consider whether the budget we used for her is appropriate.

PARENT: We don't have any unusual expenses. We're just concerned that the two other colleges that have accepted her have made significantly better offers in terms of how much she'll have to borrow or work. If it were just a few dollars difference, I wouldn't say anything. But these are pretty big differences. Big enough that we may have to recommend that she go to one of those other schools. Are you sure you can't do something?

FINANCIAL AID OFFICER: Tell you what. Why don't you send me a copy of the offer letters from those other schools. I'll look at them and see what I can do. No guarantees, you understand. But we'd very much like your daughter to come here so I promise I'll give her every possible consideration.

PARENT: Thanks. That's all I can ask.

Be sure to follow up with the college aid office.

You should know within a short period of time if your request is being considered. Colleges that want to be competitive will usually make a point of letting you know that. Likewise, schools that do not negotiate will also let you know right away. If you call the financial aid office, they'll probably tell you right then if they'll consider your request. If you write, it may take longer.

And remember to be realistic. "When it comes to negotiation, two car payments and a mortgage is not a special circumstance," notes financial aid director Karen Krause. "Neither is significant credit card debt."

"Still, it never hurts to ask."

MOVING ON

To wrap up, we began by discussing how a college creates a financial aid package, looking at the decisions financial aid administrators make. We defined "gapping" or unmet need as an important factor in comparing aid packages. We then looked at the different elements involved in a financial aid package, which reflect the different types of financial aid: gift aid (grants and scholarships), self-help aid (loans), and work aid. We also discussed private scholarships, addressing the impact they have on an aid package. Finally, we talked about negotiating packages, and how this is an ongoing change in the financial aid process. We discussed why this may be a good idea, as well as how and when families should go about doing it.

In the next chapter, we'll discuss things your family can do to meet your share of college expenses. You'll learn about various types of loans, what kinds of tax credits you can receive, and what it takes to qualify as an independent student. But before you move on, take a look at the checklist for this chapter.

✔ CHECKLIST:

1. After receiving your financial aid packages, determine your unmet need for each school.

2. If your student has received any private aid, notify your colleges and find out if it will impact their aid packages.

3. Compare your financial aid packages. Try to get a sense of the pros and cons of what each school offers.

4. If necessary, negotiate your financial aid packages.

CHAPTER TEN

Meet Your Share of Expenses

Before we go any further, give yourself a pat on the back. You're in the home stretch, and we're almost done. By now you've applied for financial aid, gotten aid packages from all your son's or daughter's prospective colleges, and compared the pros and cons of each. At this point, you should feel pretty good about the work you've done and be comfortable knowing that nothing has been left to chance.

Now comes the last step—actually paying for your share of college. In chapter five, we discussed the various incomes and investments parents can use to pay for college, but now that the process is over, it's time to start making some decisions. You and your son or daughter probably already know which school he or she is going to attend and how much financial aid he or she is going to get. And if you know your unmet need, you probably know just how much money is going to come out of your pocket.

Depending upon your situation, you may have enough money in the bank or investments to cover your share of college expenses. If so, consider yourself lucky. Other families may have enough to pay for their share of expenses, but don't want to because it would have a significant impact on their savings. For most of us, though, scraping all that money together isn't possible. When that happens, it usually means a trip to the bank for a loan.

In this chapter, we're going to discuss several topics that will help you make an informed decision about paying for your share of college. To start, let's look at just when you'll be forced to write that check.

WHEN WILL I BE EXPECTED TO PAY?

That's often the big question on parent's minds at this point. "Just exactly when am I going to have to send the school a check?" Well, ideally, most financial aid administrators and college planners recommend that you be prepared to pay half of your college costs up front. But beyond that suggestion, there are certain times throughout the school year when you'll be expected to pay.

TRENT & SEPPY SAY...

Trent:

You can expect to pay half your tuition, room, and board to the college at the beginning of each semester. But for books and supplies, as well as other expenses facing your student, you're on your own.

Seppy:

Most parents set their students up with a bank account, and then deposit the money they'll need. If your kid is good with cash, you might be able to deposit enough for the whole semester at once. Then again, if money burns a hole in his pocket, monthly transfers to his account are probably smarter.

If your student's college operates by semesters, you'll need to make a payment when the school year starts (around the beginning of September) and again when the following semester starts (usually in January). If your student's college operates by quarters, you'll be expected to make a payment when each quarter starts.

It might be helpful to separate expenses by when they'll need to be paid, so use the list below with the amounts you calculated on your COA worksheet for the college.

By Fall Registration
- One-half of the year's tuition
- One-half of the year's room and board

When Your Student Arrives for the Fall Semester
- Travel costs for getting to college
- Relocation costs for moving your student
- Personal expenses associated with relocating

When Classes Start for the Fall Semester
- One-half of the year's books and supplies

When Spring Semester Starts
- Balance of the year's tuition
- Balance of the year's room and board
- Balance of the year's books and supplies

As Necessary
- Fees for classes, labs, and other activities
- Phone and utility bills
- Clothing and laundry expenses
- Transportation costs
- Medical and dental expenses
- Personal and miscellaneous expenses

As you realized when doing your COA worksheets, these expenses really add up. Every family has a different way of handling expenses: some parents pay for things themselves, some give their students a monthly allowance to cover items, and some set aside a certain amount for each semester without budgeting. Only you'll know what method is going to work best for your son or daughter, depending on your (and his or her) spending habits.

YOU DON'T HAVE TO PAY EVERYTHING UP FRONT

Obviously, the good news about all these expenses and bills is that you won't have to pay for everything up front. You may have to stick to a budget so you won't come up short, but many parents prefer to have these expenses spread out. After all, how many people walk into a dealership and write a check for the full amount of a new car?

Tuition Payment Plans

Colleges realize that many parents want to make monthly payments for school, just as they do for a car. Because of this, many colleges offer tuition payment plans. These spread the tuition, room, and board costs out over time. Most plans start in May or June before the fall semester and run until February or March, and can include anywhere from 9 to 12 monthly payments.

You should realize that these plans are not loans, although some companies that offer tuition payment plans also offer consolidation loans, so don't get confused. Families do not pay interest on tuition payment plans, and they are not need-based. There usually are a few fees involved, so be sure you ask before signing up. Colleges that offer these plans do so themselves, or they may partner with an outside provider who administers the plan.

"I'm actually looking at these right now," says Joe Sanseverino, whose daughter starts college next fall. "I'm still undecided at this point. I think for most people, it comes down to deciding where they want financially to be when their student graduates. Is it better to have cash in the bank, but have loans over your head, or to be broke, but have paid for school?"

If you intend to budget your share of college expenses, tuition payment plans can be very

> ### TRENT & SEPPY SAY...
>
> **Trent:**
>
> *Tuition payment plans can be one of the best options available, especially if you're more comfortable making smaller payments each month instead of writing a few big checks.*
>
> **Seppy:**
>
> *But as with anything else, make sure you understand everything before your sign your John Hancock on the dotted line.*

helpful since they force you to be structured and consistent—something that can be difficult if a bill is not technically due.

HOW MUCH CAN YOU AFFORD TO PAY EACH MONTH?

When buying a car or house, many families begin by determining how much they can afford to pay each month. Doing so gives the family an idea of how expensive a purchase they can make based on what the monthly payments will be, and when you start planning monthly payments for college, you should do the same. This is especially true if you intend to take out a loan for college.

Debt-to-Income Ratio

A good way to go about this is by using the criteria lenders use when you apply for a loan, which is called a debt-to-income ratio. To do this, compare the amount you make each month to how much you pay in loan payments. Your total monthly payments for housing (in other words, your mortgage and home equity loans) should be less than 28 percent of your monthly income. Your combined monthly payments for all other loans (including education loans, credit cards, and other installment loans such as car loans) should be less than nine percent of your monthly income. So if you add all the monthly payments for these loans up, the total amount should be less than 37 percent of your monthly income. If so, the difference between that amount and 37 percent is how much you would be able to afford to pay each month for a college loan.

For example, let's say your family's income is $4,000 each month, and you pay $1,200 each month in loan payments. Start by finding out how much you can afford to make in loan payments:

$$\$4,000 \times 0.37 = \$1,480$$

(Percents are represented by two decimal places, so 37 percent = 0.37)

This means that of the $4,000 your family makes each month, up to $1,480 of that amount can be used for loans. Next, add up the loan payments you make each month. For example:

Monthly Rent	$900
Monthly Car Payment	$200
+ Monthly Payments on Credit Cards	$100
Total Monthly Payments	$1,200

So, your family would pay $1,200 each month in housing and existing loans. Finally, you'll need to subtract the difference between these two numbers:

37% of Your Monthly Income	$1,480
−Total Monthly Payments	$1,280
Amount You Can Afford to Pay	$200

In this case, your family could afford to make a $200 loan payment each month for your student's college education.

WHICH LOAN IS BEST FOR YOU?

Now that you know how much your family can afford to pay in student loans each month, let's discuss the types of loans out there and try to determine which type of loan is best suited to you.

Home Equity Loan

> **TRENT & SEPPY SAY...**
>
> **Trent:**
>
> In chapter six, we discussed the various terms associated with loans, so if you haven't had much exposure to them, you may want to review those definitions.
>
> **Seppy:**
>
> There will be a test at the end of class. Just kidding!

These loans allow you to borrow against the equity in your home, and are fixed amounts given for a defined term. This means you take the entire amount of your loan in one lump sum and then make payments for a predetermined number of months. Often, home equity loans have a lower interest rate and better terms than other loans, making it the least expensive loan available. Also, in some situations the interest from these loans can be written off for income taxes.

Borrowing against the equity in your home can be an excellent way to pay for college, but you risk losing your home if your family can't make payments. This option is best suited to the following situations:

- When your college doesn't offer a tuition payment plan
- When the monthly payments of a tuition payment would be too high
- When you need to borrow funds to meet smaller costs of your student's education, such as books and supplies, or transportation expenses
- When you need to borrow the entire amount you'll pay the college

A similar option is a home equity line of credit, which is similar to a home equity loan, except that you receive a credit card rather than the lump sum. The credit card is used as needed, up until the credit limit has been met.

Federal PLUS Loan

As you learned in chapter six, PLUS loans are non-need based loans for parents of undergraduate students. PLUS loans can be included in financial aid packages, and parents can borrow up to the total unmet need for the college. Borrowers must begin payments 60 days after receiving the funds, and repayment can take up to 10 years, depending on the amount you borrow.

Federal Perkins Loan

If your son or daughter is eligible for a Perkins loan, you'll be notified by his or her college, and they'll instruct you on the paperwork and your options. Since these loans are not available to all families, you may find the terms and rates are better suited to your needs than other loans.

Federal Stafford Loans

Most colleges participate in the Stafford loan program, so your award letters may notify you if you qualify, and for how much. Remember that even if you don't qualify for a need-based subsidized loan, you can still apply for an unsubsidized Stafford loan because it's not need-based. Both unsubsidized and subsidized Stafford Loans are offered by private lenders such as banks and credit unions, so you'll need to shop around to compare rates and interest. Although interest may be more than a PLUS loan, remember that repayment doesn't start until after your son or daughter graduates from college.

Federal Direct Student Loan

If your college does not participate in the Stafford loan program, it probably is part of this program. These loans are similar to Stafford loans, except that they are offered directly by the federal government. You'll need to ask your student's college for information if you're interested.

Many colleges are working to make the loan process easier to complete and understand. "We try to make our instructions as user-friendly as possible," says Karen Krause, director of financial aid at the University of Texas at Arlington. "And we're finding that our website is a good way to do this. It makes things easier to digest than getting pages upon pages of information with your paperwork."

Private Loans

About twenty years ago, private companies began realizing that government-funded financial aid was not keeping up with the rising cost of college. Because of this, private lenders started to offer loans for college, and today these private loans are some of the cheapest options available.

Depending upon your credit, you can borrow up to the full amount of your unmet need. And because these companies compete for business, you can expect lower fees, more time to repay the loan, and competitive interest rates. Terms for repayment and interest will vary from lender to lender, so be sure to shop around.

To determine if you qualify for a private loan, lending companies look at three things:

- Your debt-to-income ratio (which we explained earlier in this chapter)
- Your credit history
- Your income (if you're self-employed, you'll need to have been in business for at least a year)

Several factors will influence which kind of loan is best suited for you and your son or daughter. Your income, financial situation, credit history, mortgage or rent, the cost of your student's college, and how much money you need are all going to impact your choices. As we discussed about comparing financial aid packages, you may want to compare loans by looking at the pros and cons of each, paying special attention to interest and repayment terms.

TRENT & SEPPY SAY...

Trent:

Loans can be confusing, so ask for help. No matter where you go to borrow money for college, it's your right to completely understand all the details.

Seppy:

Loan officers are employed by lenders for the sole purpose of helping you understand your options and select which one is right for you, so don't be embarrassed to ask questions. And if you're unhappy with the answers, shop around. There are plenty of banks and lenders in the business of loaning money, and they all want your business!

WHAT SAVINGS SHOULD I USE?

In chapter five, we discussed various types of savings and investments you could use to help pay for college. Some are better suited to help pay for college than others.

Tax Benefits

When it comes to tax benefits, your best choices are 529 plans and education saving accounts. Both of these are tax-free and the most obvious places to get money for college, if you have them. Other types of investments will help you pay for college, but you'll have to pay taxes on the money you made from them.

Stocks and Bonds

If you don't have a 529 or education savings account, your next best bet might be to sell some stocks, mutual funds, or bonds to help pay for your student's education. Unlike 529 plans and educational savings accounts, anytime you sell these investments, you'll have to pay income tax on them. But to your advantage, you'll only need to sell as many shares as you need to cover the expense. This, combined with the ever-changing price of investments, makes them a good choice in helping to pay for college when flexibility is important.

401(k)s and IRAs

You should avoid using your retirement account to pay for college at all costs. Although many people don't realize this, you'll pay a whopping a 27 percent tax if you take money out of your 401(k) before retirement! Are you willing to throw away a quarter of the money you've saved? IRAs also have similar penalties. Since these accounts were designed to help pay for retirement, not college, you can expect to lose money if you take money out of them—so don't do it!

Some of these options may not be available to you, while others may not be appropriate to use. In fact, in some situations, it might even be a good idea to borrow money for college rather than use savings and investments. There's no easy answer, and if you have significant investments and savings, contact your financial consultant for their advice.

Transfer Assets From Student to Adult

As we discussed earlier, the more assets and investments your student has, the less financial aid they may qualify for. Remember that when schools determine a family's expected contribution (EFC) for college, they expect 35 percent of a student's assets to be used for college, while as little as six percent is expected to come from the parent's assets. Because of this huge difference, it's wise to transfer assets in your son's or daughter's name to yours.

HELP YOUR STUDENT MANAGE COLLEGE EXPENSES

Budgeting: Closing the Communication Gap

As your son or daughter actually begins to attend college, your Cost of Attending worksheet is facing a reality check. Suddenly, your student "must have" more money. And in some cases, there may be new and unforeseen expenses, essential and pressing (at least in the mind of your student).

Now's the time for a heart-to-heart with your son or daughter about a budget. Impress upon him or her that there has to be one. Whether you choose to give your student a lump sum to last a semester, or make monthly deposits into a checking account depends on the nature and habits of your son or daughter. You know them pretty well by now, so choose the best plan of action.

Money management skills aren't genetically inherited: They're learned and can always be improved. College can be an opportunity for your student to acquire financial habits, knowledge, and skills that can last a prosperous lifetime.

Work

As we've said before, studies show that students who work reasonable part-time hours may actually do better in college. And the money earned can help pay for essentials like books as well as the extras, like parking fees on campus or a weekly pizza with everything (many students might think of that as an essential). If your son or daughter is eligible for a work-study program, that's great. If not, there are usually jobs on campus and in nearby towns—catering, library reference desk work, babysitting, even paid research opportunies with professors in some cases. Ask your son or daughter to consider this option, but remember not to overdo it. Part-time work is great, but a full-time job might make grades suffer.

Credit Cards

Most of us have learned the hard way about the dangers of credit cards. Millions of Americans each year rack up debt by using these plastic cards for convenience, then realize they've spent more than they earn. Often, this means paying off debt for years to come, or worse, declaring bankruptcy.

It used to be that you had to have a job before you could qualify for a credit card. But today, teenagers with part-time jobs are offered credit cards with a limit high enough to buy a car. By the time your student starts college, they will be bombarded with credit card offers (even more so if they already have one)! If you've had problems with them, make sure your son or daughter learns from your mistakes!

> ### TRENT & SEPPY SAY...
>
> **Trent:**
>
> *Lots of companies today offer "student" credit cards. Not only is there no real advantage to them, but there are almost always hidden fees and higher rates involved.*
>
> **Seppy:**
>
> *For example, one of these cards charged a student a $5 transaction fee to take $20 out of an ATM. That's a 25% transaction fee! (Usually it's 3-5%.) Ouch!*

"We believe that a sixteen year old needs to learn about credit, so we let our children get a card with a $500 limit," says Karon Ray. "By the time they started college, they were aware of the dangers of credit cards." Karon's husband, Clark, noted that sometimes technology may actually help students be more responsible. "I'd recommend that students get a credit card where they can have their monthly statements and bills emailed to them, and have a monthly payment taken out of their checking account. I know from experience that college students can let mail and bills stack up until it's too late, but they always check their email."

Credit cards can be good to have for emergencies and limited use, but your son or daughter will have to be mature and show restraint if he or she wants to stay out of trouble. Your student needs to build a good credit history, and the best way to do that is to limit him or her to one credit card, and make sure it has a reasonable interest rate and credit limit.

When starting out, students should treat their credit cards as a type of insurance—something they'll use only in emergencies when there's not enough cash on hand and they know they'll have the money to pay for the purchase in the near future. But as with any insurance, they should only be used when completely necessary. (Actually, we'd all be a lot better off if everyone thought of credit cards in this way.)

TRENT & SEPPY SAY...

Trent:

Why do college students get so many credit card offers?

Seppy:

Because it's a safe bet that students won't read the fine print (or else their parents will bail them out).

SOLIDIFY YOUR PLAN

So you've taken a look at various ways to pay for your share of college, and it's time to put together a plan. Here's a few strategies for you to try out and compare as you make a decision:

- Pay as you go from your income and assets (savings, investments, etc).
- Borrow your share of college costs from the Federal PLUS program.
- Pay your share through a combination of the Federal PLUS program, your income and assets, and other loans.
- Borrow your share of college costs from other loan programs (Stafford loans, private loans, etc.)
- Borrow your share using a home equity loan or line of credit.

"Many people don't seem to realize that it's possible to use a combination of options when paying for college," says financial aid officer Connie Gore. "For example, I know a family that has put half of their student's college costs on loans, and are paying off the other half through tuition payment plans. This way, the monthly payments aren't too much, and the loans aren't overwhelming, either."

Depending upon your income and investments, you may already have a financial adviser. If not, you may want to consider getting one. These professionals are often known as stockbrokers, but there are individuals who assist families in everything from planning for retirement, to creating a budget, to (you guessed it)—paying for college. If you don't have a financial adviser, ask around for recommendations. Check with your lawyer, accountant, or friends.

IN A PINCH, CONSULT A FINANCIAL AID COUNSELOR

For a fee, you and your student can get help from a financial aid counselor. These individuals can be costly, and if you've understood most of this book, you probably won't need one. But if you continue to have problems along the way, or can afford to pay an expert for their advice, it may be worth the money. Odds are, however, their advice and information will be very similar to this book.

THE HOME STRETCH

Well, you made it. We're done. Hopefully, this book didn't just help you apply for financial aid, but also to understand the programs available and decide which options are best for your family. Like we mentioned in the beginning, there's no easy, one-size-fits-all answer for financial aid, but you should feel educated and well-prepared to make an informed decision for yourself.

To wrap up, we began this chapter by discussing just when you can be expected to pay for your son or daughter's college. We then looked at how tuition payment plans can keep you from having to pay everything up front, as well as how you can determine how much of a loan you can afford.

TRENT & SEPPY SAY...

Trent:

Although not required by the government, there are optional designations and titles a financial adviser can earn to indicate that they have training and experience in planning issues such as affording college.

Seppy:

For example, the Certified Financial Planner Board of Standards provides a designation for stockbrokers called the CFP, or Certified Financial Planner. These types of certifications aren't guarantees, but you'll know that the adviser understands your planning needs. You can search for a CFP through their website at www.cfp.net.

TRENT & SEPPY SAY...

Trent:

Very few financial aid officers recommend financial aid counselors to families and prospective students.

Seppy:

Some even say they've seen parents pay for a financial planner, only to have the individual file late and miss deadlines!

Next, we reviewed the various loans available to you, and mentioned why credit cards are almost always a bad idea. You learned about a few tax cuts that might help you in the future, and compared investments to see which are best suited to help pay for an education.

Remember, this book is not meant to be the final word in paying for college. Hopefully, it's provided you with a roadmap along the way, but there are plenty of other places you can learn about the things we've discussed in greater detail. Websites, college financial aid offices, government brochures and information, and even high school guidance counselors can help you learn how to best pay for college. The more places you get help, the more prepared you'll be. Good luck!

✔ CHECKLIST:

1. Contact the college your student is attending to find out key dates in the payment cycle. Work these dates into your household budget and calendar to help prepare in advance.

2. Ask your college about payment tuition plans. Request information and consider the pros and cons of such a plan.

3. If your college doesn't offer a payment plan, contact a few outside organizations to find out what private loan programs are available.

4. Calculate your debt-to-income ratio before agreeing to a plan. Learn the amount you can afford for a monthly debt payment.

5. Research various types of loans to determine which is best for you and your son or daughter.

6. Discuss the hazards and benefits of a credit card with your student.

7. Research the advantages and disadvantages of using your savings and investments to help pay for your share of college costs. If you have a financial adviser or attorney, consult them before establishing any savings or loan plan.

WEBSITES

FinAid
www.Finaid.org

Internal Revenue Service
www.irs.gov

The Motley Fool
www.motleyfool.com

Equifax
www.equifax.com

Experian
www.experian.com

Trans Union Corporation
www.transunion.com

Certified Financial Planner Board of Standards
www.cfp.net

Financial Planning Association
www.fpanet.org

Stafford Loans
www.ed.gov

PLUS Loans
www.ed.gov

Perkins Loans, Federal Family Education Loan Program (FFELP),
William D. Ford Direct Loan Program
www.studentaid.ed.gov

PART TWO

FINANCIAL AID RESOURCES

Regional Resources

State Financial Aid Agencies

Alabama

State and Federal Aid Programs
Alabama Commission on Higher Education
100 North Union Street
P.O. Box 302000
Montgomery, AL 36130-2000
(334) 242-1998
Fax: (334) 242-0268
Email: wwall@ache.state.al.us
Website: *www.ache.state.al.us*

Alaska

State Aid Programs
Alaska Commission on Postsecondary
Education
3030 Vintage Boulevard
Juneau, AK 99801-7100
(907)465-2962
800-441-2962
Fax: (907) 465-5316
Email: customer_service@acpe.state.ak.us
Website: *www.state.ak.us/acpe*

Federal Aid Programs
Sallie Mae
116600 Sallie Mae Drive
Reston, VA 20193
888-2-SALLIE
Website: *www.salliemae.com*

Arizona

State Aid Programs
Arizona Commission for Postsecondary
Education
2020 North Central Avenue, Suite 275
Phoenix, AZ 85004-4503
(602) 229-2435
Fax: (602) 229-2483
Email: dan_lee@acpe.asu.edu
Website: *www.acpe.asu.edu*

Federal Aid Programs
Sallie Mae
116600 Sallie Mae Drive
Reston, VA 20193
888-2-SALLIE
Website: *www.salliemae.com*

Arkansas

State Aid Programs
Arkansas Department of Higher Education
Financial Aid Division
114 East Capitol Avenue
Little Rock, AR 72201-3818
(501) 371-2050
Fax: (501) 371-2001
Email: finaid@adhe.arknet.edu
Website: *www.arkansashighered.com*

Federal Aid Programs
Student Loan Guarantee Foundation of Arkansas
219 South Victory Street
Little Rock, AR 72201-1884
800-622-3446
Fax: (501) 688-7675
Email: slgfa@slgfa.org
Website: *www.slgfa.org*

California

State and Federal Aid Programs
California Student Aid Commission
P.O. Box 419026 (State)
P.O. Box 419046 (Federal)
Ranch Cordova, CA 95741
888-CA-GRANT (State)
888-294-0105 (Federal)
Fax: (916)526-8002(State)
Fax: (916) 526-7937(Federal)
Website: *www.csac.ca.gov*

Colorado

State and Federal Aid Programs
Colorado Student Loan Program
999 18th Street, Suite 425
Denver, CO 80202
(303) 305-3000
Fax: (303)294-5076
Email: service@cslp.org
Website: *www.cslp.org*

Connecticut

State Aid Programs
Connecticut Department of Higher Education
Student Financial Assistance
61 Woodland Street
Hartford, CT 06105-2326
(860) 947-1800
Fax: (860) 947-1310
Email: info@ctdhe.org
Website: *www.ctdhe.org*

Federal Aid Programs
Connecticut Student Loan Foundation
525 Brook Street, P.O. Box 1009
Rocky Hill, CT 06067
(860) 257-4001
800-237-9721
Fax: (860) 563 3247
Email: CustomerSupport@mail.cslf.org
Website: *www.cslf.com*

Delaware

State and Federal Aid Programs
Delaware Higher Education Commission
Carvel State Office Building
820 North French Street
Wilmington, DE 19801
(302) 577-3240
800-292-7935
Fax: (302) 577-6765
Email: dhec@doe.K12.de.us
Website: *www.doe.state.de.us/high-ed*

District of Columbia

State Aid Programs
District of Columbia State Education Office
Financial Aid
441 4th Street NW, Suite 350
North Washington, DC 20001
(202) 727-6436
Email: seo.dc.gov
Website: *seo.dc.gov/main_shtm*

Federal Aid Programs
American Student Assistance
330 Stuart Street
Boston, MA 02116-5292
800-999-9080
Fax: (617) 728-4670
Email: info@amsa.com
Website: *www.amsa.com*

Florida

State and Federal Aid Programs
Florida Department of Education
Student Financial Assistance
1940 North Monroe Street, Suite 70
Tallahassee, FL 32303-4759
800-366-3475 (State)
888-827-2004 (Federal)
Email: osfa@fldoe.org
Website: *www.fldoe.org*

Georgia

State and Federal Aid Programs
Georgia Student Finance Commission
Scholarship and Grant Division
2082 East Exchange Place
Tucker, GA 30084-5305
(770) 724-9000
800-776-6878
Fax: (770) 724-9089
Website: *www.gsfc.org*

Hawaii

State Aid Programs
Hawaii State Postsecondary Education
Commission
Bachman Hall, Room 209
University of Hawaii
2444 Dole Street
Honolulu, HI 96822-2394
(808) 956-8213
Email: iha@hawaii.edu

Federal Aid Programs
Sallie Mae
116600 Sallie Mae Drive
Reston, VA 20193
888-2-SALLIE
Website: *www.salliemae.com*

Idaho

State Aid Programs
Idaho Board of Education
P.O. Box 83720
Boise, ID 83720-0037
(208) 334-2270
Fax: (208) 334-2632
Email: lhumphre@osbe.state.id.us
Website: *www.idahoboardofed.org/scholarships.asp*

Federal Aid Programs
Student Loan Fund of Idaho, Inc.
Processing Center
6905 Highway 95, P.O. Box #7
Fruitland, ID 83619
(208) 452-4058

Illinois

State and Federal Aid Programs
Illinois Student Assistance Commission
Scholarship and Grant Services
1755 Lake Cook Road
Deerfield, IL 60015
(847) 948-8500
800-899-ISAC
Email: cssupport@isac.org
Website: *www.isac-online.org*

Indiana

State Aid Programs
State Student Assistance Commission of Indiana
ISTA Center Building
150 West Market Street, Suite 500
Indianapolis, IN 46204-2811
(317) 232-2350
888-528-4719
Fax: (317) 232-3260
Email: grants@ssaci.state.in.us
Website: *www.in.gov/ssaci*

Federal Aid Programs
Sallie Mae
116600 Sallie Mae Drive
Reston, VA 20193
888-2-SALLIE
Website: *www.salliemae.com*

Iowa

State and Federal Aid Programs
Iowa College Student Aid Commission
200 10th Street, Fourth Floor
Des Moines, IA 50309-3609
(515) 242-3344
800-383-4222
Fax: (515) 242-3388
Email: csac@max.state.ia.us
Website: *www.iowacollegeaid.org*

Kansas

State Aid Programs
Kansas Board of Regents
Student Financial Aid
700 SW Harrison Street, Suite 520
Topeka, KS 66612-3518
(785) 296-3518
Fax: (785) 296-0983
Email: dlindeman@ksbor.org
Website: *www.kansasboardofregents.org*

Federal Aid Programs
Sallie Mae
116600 Sallie Mae Drive
Reston, VA 20193
888-2-SALLIE
Website: *www.salliemae.com*

Kentucky

State and Federal Aid Programs
Kentucky Higher Education Assistance
Student Aid Programs
P.O. Box 798
Frankfort, KY 40602-0798
(502) 696-7393
800-928-8926
Fax: (502) 696-7496
Email: inquiries@kheaa.com
Website: *www.kheaa.com*

Louisiana

State and Federal Aid Programs
Office of Student Financial Assistance
P.O. Box 91202
Baton Rouge, LA 70821-9202
(225) 922-1012
800-259-5626
Fax: (225) 922-0790
Email: custserv@osfa.state.la.us
Website: *www.osfa.state.la.us*

Maine

State and Federal Aid Programs
Finance Authority of Maine
Education Assistance Division
5 Community Drive
P.O. Box 949
Augusta, ME 04332-0949
(207) 626-3263
800-228-3734
Fax: (207) 626-0095
METYY: (207) 626-2717
Email: info@famemaine.com
Website: *www.famemaine.com*

Maryland

State Aid Programs
Maryland Higher Education Commission
Student Financial Assistance
839 Bestgate Road
Annapolis, MD 21401-3013
(410) 260-4565
800-735-2258
Fax: (410) 974-1024
Email: osfamail@mhec.state.md.us
Website: *www.mhec.state.md.us*

Federal Aid Programs
Sallie Mae
116600 Sallie Mae Drive
Reston, VA 20193
888-2-SALLIE
Website: *www.salliemae.com*

Massachusetts

State Aid Programs
Massachusetts Office of Student Financial
Assistance
454 Broadway, Suite 200
Revere, MA 02151
(617) 727-9420
Fax: (617) 727-0667
Email: osfa@ofsa.mass.edu
Website: *www.osfa.mass.edu*

Federal Aid Programs
American Student Assistance
330 Stuart Street
Boston, MA 02116-5292
800-999-9080
Fax: (617) 728-4670
Email: info@amsa.com
Website: *www.amsa.com*

Michigan

State Aid Programs
Office of Scholarships and Grants
P.O. Box 30462
Lansing, MI 48909-7962
(517) 373-3394
888-447-2687
Email: treasscholgrant@michigan.gov
Website: *www.michigan.gov/mistudentaid*

Federal Aid Programs
Michigan Guarantee Agency
P.O. Box 30047
Lansing, MI 48909
(517) 373-0760
800-642-5626
Fax: (517) 335-5984
Email: mga@michigan.gov
Website: *www.michigan.gov/mistudentaid*

Minnesota

State Aid Programs
Minnesota Higher Education Services Office
1450 Energy Park Drive, Suite 350
St. Paul, MN 55108
(651) 642-0567
800-657-3866
Email: info@heso.state.mn.us
Website: *www.mheso.state.mn.us*

Federal Aid Programs
Total Higher Education/Northstar
444 Cedar Street, Suite 500
P.O. Box 64722
St. Paul, MN 55164-0722
800-366-0604
888-843-3099
Email: service@northstar.org
Website: *www.northstar.org*

Mississippi

State Aid Programs
Mississippi Office of Financial Aid
3825 Ridgewood Road
Jackson, MI 39221-6453
(601) 432-6997; 800-327-2980
Email: sfa@ihl.state.ms.us
Website: *www.ihl.state.ms.us/financialaid/default.asp*

Federal Aid Programs
Sallie Mae
116600 Sallie Mae Drive
Reston, VA 20193
888-2-SALLIE
Website: *www.salliemae.com*

Missouri

State and Federal Aid Programs
Missouri Coordinating Board for Higher
Education
3515 Amazonas Drive
Jefferson City, MO 65109-5717
(573) 751-2361
800-473-6757
Fax: (573) 751-6635
Website: *www.mocbhe.gov*

Montana

State and Federal Aid Programs
Montana Guaranteed Student Loan Program
2500 Broadway, P.O. Box 203101
Helena, MT 59620-3101
800-537-7508
Website: *www.mgslp.state.mt.us*

Nebraska

State Aid Programs
Coordinating Commission for Postsecondary
Education
P.O. Box 95005
Lincoln, NE 68509-5005
(402) 471-2847
Fax: (402) 471-2886
Website: *www.ccpe.state.ne.us*

Federal Aid Programs
Nebraska Student Loan Program, Inc.
1300 O Street
P.O. Box 82507
Lincoln, NE 68501-2507
(402) 475-8686
800-735-8778
Fax: (402) 479-6658
Email: nslpcs@nslp.com
Website: *www.nslp.com*

Nevada

State Aid Programs
Nevada State Department of Education
700 East Fifth Street
Carson City, NV 89701
(775) 687-9200
Fax: (775) 687-9101
Website: *www.nde.state.nv.us*

Federal Aid Programs
Sallie Mae
116600 Sallie Mae Drive
Reston, VA 20193
888-2-SALLIE
Website: *www.salliemae.com*

New Hampshire

State Aid Programs
New Hampshire Postsecondary Education
Commission
3 Barrell Court Suite 300
Concord, NH 03301-8543
(603) 271-2555
Fax: (603) 271-2696
Website: *www.state.nh.us/postsecondary*

Federal Aid Programs
New Hampshire Higher Education Assistance
Foundation
4 Barrell Court
P.O. Box 877
Concord, NH 03302-0877
(603) 225-6612
800-525-2577
Email: info@gsmr.org
Website: *www.nhheaf.org*

New Jersey

State and Federal Aid Programs
New Jersey Office of Student Assistance
P.O. Box 540
Trenton, NJ 08625
800-792-8670
(609) 588-7389
Website: *www.hesaa.org*

New Mexico

State Aid Programs
New Mexico Commission on Higher Education
Financial Aid and Student Services
1068 Cerillos Road
Santa Fe, NM 87505
(505) 476-6500
Fax: (505) 476-6511
Email: highered@che.state.nm.us
Website: *www.nmche.org*

Federal Aid Programs
New Mexico Student Loan Guarantee
Corporation
3900 Osuna Road, N.E.
P.O. Box 92230
Albuquerque, NM 87199-2230
(505) 345-8821
800-279-3070
Email: guarantee@nmslgc.org
Website: *www.nmslgc.org*

New York

State and Federal Aid Programs
New York State Higher Education Services
Corporation
99 Washington Avenue
Albany, NY 12255
(518) 473-1574
888-NYS-HESC
Email: webmail@hesc.com
Website: *www.hesc.com*

North Carolina

State and Federal Aid Programs
North Carolina State Education Assistance
Authority
P.O. Box 14103
Research Triangle Park, NC 27709
(919) 549-8614
Fax: (919) 549-8481
Email: info@ncseaa.edu
Website: *www.ncseaa.edu*

North Dakota

State Aid Programs
North Dakota University System
Student Financial Assistance Program
State Capitol 10th Floor
600 East Boulevard Avenue
Dept 215
Bismark, ND 58505-0230
(701) 328-2960
Fax: (701) 328-2961
Email: ndus.office@ndus.nodak.edu
Website: *www.ndus.edu*

Federal Aid Programs
Student Loans of North Dakota
P.O. Box 5524
Bismark, 58506-5524
800-472-2166
TDD: 800-643-3916
Fax:(701) 328-5716
Email: bndsl@state.nd.us
Website: *www.mystudentloanonline.com*

Northern Marianas

State Aid Programs
Northern Marianas College
P.O. Box 501250
Saipan, North Marianas Island 96950
(670) 234-3690
Fax: (670) 234-0759
Email: webmaster@nmcnet.edu
Website: *www.nmcnet.edu*

Federal Aid Programs
Sallie Mae
116600 Sallie Mae Drive
Reston, VA 20193
888-2-SALLIE
Website: *www.salliemae.com*

Ohio

State Aid Programs
Ohio Board of Regents
State Grants and Scholarships
P.O. Box 182542
Columbus, OH 43218-2452
(614) 466-7420
888-833-1133
Fax: (614) 752-5903
Email: sminturn@regents.state.oh.us
Website: *www.regents.state.oh.us/sgs*

Federal Aid Programs
Great Lakes Higher Education
2401 International Lane
Madison, WI 53704-3192
866-464-7855
Email: marketing@mygreatlakes.com
Website: *www.glhec.org*

Oklahoma

State Aid Programs
Oklahoma State Regents for Higher Education
655 Research Parkway, Suite 200
Oklahoma City, OK 73104
(405) 524-9100
Fax: (405) 524-9230
Email: tsimonton@osrhe.edu
Website: *www.okhighered.org*

Federal Aid Programs
Oklahoma Guaranteed Student Loan Program
999 NW Grand Boulevard, Suite 300
P.O. Box 3000
Oklahoma City, OK 73101-3000
(405) 234-4300
Fax: (405) 234-4390
Email: info@ogslp.orgwwwogslp.org

Oregon

State and Federal Aid Programs
Oregon Student Assistance Commission
1500 Valley River Drive, Suite 100
Eugene, OR 97401-2130
(541) 687-7400
800-452-8807
Fax: (541) 687-7419
Email : awardinfo@mercury.osac.state.or.us
Website: *www.osac.state.or.us*

Pennsylvania

State and Federal Aid Programs
Pennsylvania Higher Education
Assistance Agency
1200 North Seventh Street
Harrisburg, PA 17102-1444
800-692-7392
Fax: (717) 720-2860 (federal)
Email: info@pheaa.org
Website: *www.pheaa.org*

Puerto Rico

State Aid Programs
State Financial Aid Programs
Council on Higher Education
Box 23305
UPR Station, Rio Piedras, Puerto Rico 00931
(809) 758-3350

Federal Aid Programs
Great Lakes Higher Education
2401 International Lane
Madison, WI 53704-3192
866-464-7855
Email: marketing@mygreatlakes.comwww.glhec.org

Rhode Island

State and Federal Aid Programs
Rhode Island Higher Education Assistance Authority
560 Jefferson Boulevard
Warwick, RI 02886
(401) 736-1100
800-922-9855
Fax: (401) 736-3541
Email: info@riheaa.org
Website: *www.riheaa.org*

South Carolina

State Aid Programs
South Carolina Commission on Higher Education
1333 Main Street, Suite 200
Columbia, SC 29201
(803) 737-2260
Fax: (803) 737-2297
Email: kwoodfau@che.sc.gov
Website: *www.che400.state.sc.us*

Federal Aid Programs
South Carolina Student Loan Corporation
Interstate Center
P.O. Box 21487
Columbia, SC 29221
(803) 798-0916
800-347-2752
Fax: (803) 772-9410
Website: *www.slc.sc.edu*

South Dakota

State Aid Programs
South Dakota Board of Regents
306 East Capitol Avenue, Suite 200
Pierre, SD 57501-2545
(605) 773-3455
Email: info@ris.sdbor.edu
Website: *www.ris.sdbor.edu*

Federal Aid Programs
South Dakota Education Assistance
Corporation
115 First Avenue SW
Aberdeen, SD 57401
800-592-1802
Email: eac@eac-easci.org
Website: *www.eac-easci.org*

Tennessee

State and Federal Aid Programs
Tennessee Student Assistance Corporation
Parkway Towers
404 James Robertson Parkway
Suite 1950
Nashville, TN 37243-0820
(615) 741-1346
800-2576526
Fax: (615) 741-6101
Website: *www.state.tn.us/tsac*

Texas

State Aid Programs
Texas Higher Education Coordinating Board
Student Services
P.O. Box 12788
Capitol Station
Austin, TX 78711
(512) 427-6340
800-242-3062
Fax: (512) 427-6127
Website: *www.thecb.state.tx.us*

Federal Aid Programs
Texas Guaranteed Student Loan Corporation
P.O. Box 201725
Austin, TX 78720-1725
(512) 219-5700
800-252-9743
Email: customer.services@tgslc.org
Website: *www.tgslc.org*

Utah

State Aid Programs
Utah System of Higher Education
3 Triad Center, Suite 550
60 South 400 West
Salt Lake City, UT 84101-1248
(801) 321-7101
Website: *www.utahsbr.edu*

Federal Aid Programs
Utah Higher Education Assistance Authority
3 Triad Center, Suite 550
60 South 400 West
Salt Lake City, UT 84101-1248
(801) 321-7200
800-418-8757
Fax: (801) 321-7299
Email: uheaa@utahsbr.edu
Website: *www.uheaa.org*

Vermont

State and Federal Aid Programs
Vermont Student Assistance Corporation
P.O. Box 2000
Champlain Mill
Winooski, VT 05404
(802) 655-9602
800-642-3177
Fax: (802) 654-3765
Email: info@vsac.org
Website: *www.vsac.org*

Virgin Islands

State Aid Programs
Virgin Islands Board of Education
No. 44-46 Kongens Gade
Charlotte Amalie
US Virgin Islands, VI 00802
(340) 774-0100
Fax: (340) 779-7153
Email: education@usvi.org

Federal Aid Programs
Great Lakes Higher Education
2401 International Lane
Madison, WI 53704-3192
866-464-7855
Email: marketing@mygreatlakes.com
Website: *www.glhec.org*

Virginia

State Aid Programs
State Council of Higher Education for Virginia
Financial Aid Office
James Monroe Building
101 North 14th Street
Richmond, VA 23219-3659
(804) 225-2600
Fax: (804) 225-2604
Email: andes@schev.edu
Website: *www.schev.edu*

Federal Aid Programs
Educational Credit Management Corporation
Boulders, Building VII
7325 Beaufont Springs Drive
Suite 200
Richmond, VA 23225
(804) 267-7100
888-775-3262
Website: *www.ecmc.org*

Washington

State Aid Programs
Washington State Higher Education
Coordinating Board
917 Lakeridge Way
P.O. Box 43430
Olympia, WA 98504-3430
(360) 753-7800
Email: info@hecb.wa.gov
Website: *www.hecb.wa.gov*

Federal Aid Programs
Northwest Education Loan Association
190 Queen Avenue North
Suite 300
Seattle, WA 98109
800-979-4441
Email: loaninfo@nela.net
Website: *www.nela.net*

West Virginia

State Aid Programs
West Virginia Higher Education Policy
Commission
1018 Kanwah Boulevard
East Suite 700
Charleston, WV 25301
(304) 558-2101
Fax: (304) 558-5719
Website: *www.hepc.wvnet.edu*

Federal Aid Programs
Pennsylvania Higher Education Assistance
Agency
1200 North Seventh Street
Harrisburg, PA 17102-1444
800-692-7392
Fax: (717) 720-2860
Website: *www.pheaa.org*

Wisconsin

State Aid Programs
Wisconsin Higher Educational Aids Board
P.O. Box 7885
Madison, WI 53707-7885
(608) 267-2206
Fax: (608) 267-2808
Email: HEABmail@heab.state.wi.usheab.state.wi.us

Federal Aid Programs
Great Lakes Higher Education
2401 International Lane
Madison, WI 53704-3192
866-464-7855
Email: marketing@mygreatlakes.com
Website: *www.glhec.org*

Wyoming

State Aid Programs
Wyoming Community College Commission
2020 Carey Avenue 8th Floor
Cheyenne, WY 82002
(307) 777-7763
Fax: (307) 777-6567
Email: diverson@commission.wcc.educommission.wcc.edu

Federal Aid Programs
Sallie Mae
116600 Sallie Mae Drive
Reston, VA 20193
888-2-SALLIE
Website: *www.salliemae.com*

Website Reference List

Accreditation

Office of Postsecondary Education
Accreditation Information
www.ed.gov/offices/OPE/accreditation

College Savings

College Savings Plan Network
www.collegesavings.org

The Motley Fool
www.fool.com

Savingforcollege.com
www.savingforcollege.com

Upromise
www.upromise.com

Community Colleges

American Association of Community Colleges
www.aacc.nche.edu

Credit Report Services

Equifax
www.equifax.com
Experian
www.experian.com
Trans Union Corporation
www.transunion.com

CSS Profile

College Board
www.collegeboard.com

EFC Methodology Calculators

College Board
www.collegeboard.com

FinAid
www.finaid.org

FAFSA

FAFSA
www.fafsa.ed.gov

U.S. Department of Education PIN
Registration
www.pin.ed.gov

Internal Revenue Service
www.irs.gov

Financial Aid (General)

EdFund
www.edfund.org

FinAid
www.finaid.org

Financial Aid/Admission Awareness Month
www.faam.org

Financial Aid (General) Cont.

U.S. Department of Education—Student Guide
to Financial Aid
www.ed.gov

National Association of Student Financial Aid
Administrators
www.nasfaa.org

National Center for Public Policy and Higher
Education
www.highereducation.org

NellieMae
www.nelliemae.com

SallieMae
www.salliemae.com

Financial Planning

Certified Financial Planner Board of Standards
www.cfp.net

Financial Planning Association
www.fpanet.org

Grants and Scholarships

CollegeScholarships.com
www.collegescholarships.com

FastWeb
www.fastweb.com

NellieMae
www.nelliemae.com

PELL Grants
www.pellgrantsonline.ed.gov

SallieMae
www.salliemae.com

Scholarships.com
www.scholarships.com

Loans

Federal Family Education Loan Program (FFELP)
www.studentaid.ed.gov

Federal Supplemental Educational
Opportunity Grant (FSEOG)
www.ed.gov

Perkins Loans
www.studentaid.ed.gov

PLUS Loans
www.ed.gov

Stafford Loans
www.ed.gov

William D. Ford Direct Loan Program
www.studentaid.ed.gov

Study Abroad

Association of Universities and Colleges of Canada
www.aucc.ca

Institute of International Education
www.IIEpassport.org

Council on International Education
www.ciee.org

Textbooks

efollett.com
www.efollett.com

VarsityBooks.com
www.varsitybooks.com

Travel

Amtrak
www.amtrak.com

Greyhound
www.greyhound.com

Travelocity.com
www.travelocity.com

EFC Worksheets

2003-2004 EFC FORMULA A : DEPENDENT STUDENT

PARENTS' INCOME IN 2002

1. Parents' Adjusted Gross Income (FAFSA/SAR #74)
(If negative, enter zero.)

2. a. Father's income earned from work
(FAFSA/SAR #77) _____

2. b. Mother's income earned from work
(FAFSA/SAR #78) + _____

Total parents' income earned from work =

3. Parents' Taxable Income
(If tax filers, enter the amount from line 1 above.
If non-tax filers, enter the amount from line 2.)*

4. Untaxed income and benefits:

• Total from FAFSA Worksheet A
(FAFSA/SAR #79) _____

• Total from FAFSA Worksheet B
(FAFSA/SAR #80) + _____

Total untaxed income and benefits =

5. Taxable and untaxed income (sum of line 3 and line 4)

6. Total from FAFSA Worksheet C (FAFSA/SAR #81) -

7. TOTAL INCOME
(line 5 minus line 6) May be a negative number. =

ALLOWANCES AGAINST PARENTS' INCOME

8. 2002 U.S. income tax paid (FAFSA/SAR #75)
(tax filers only); if negative, enter zero.

9. State and other tax allowance
(Table A1. If negative, enter zero.) +

10. Father's Social Security tax allow. (Table A2) +

11. Mother's Social Security tax allow. (Table A2) +

12. Income protection allowance (Table A3) +

13. Employment expense allowance:

• Two working parents: 35% of the lesser of the
earned incomes, or $3,000, whichever is less

• One-parent families: 35% of earned income,
or $3,000, whichever is less

• Two-parent families, one working
parent: enter zero +

14. TOTAL ALLOWANCES =

AVAILABLE INCOME

Total income (from line 7)

Total allowances (from line 14) -

15. AVAILABLE INCOME (AI)
May be a negative number. =

*STOP HERE if **both** of the following are true: line 3 is $15,000 or less,
plus the student **and** parents are eligible to file a 2002 IRS Form
1040A or 1040EZ (they are not required to file a 2002 Form 1040), or
they are not required to file any income tax return. If both circumstances are true, the Expected Family Contribution is automatically
zero.

16. Net worth of investments**
(FAFSA/SAR #82)
If negative, enter zero.

17. Net worth of business and/or investment farm
(FAFSA/SAR #83)
If negative, enter zero.

18. Adjusted net worth of business/farm
(Calculate using Table A4.) +

19. Cash, savings, & checking (FAFSA/SAR #84) +

20. Net worth (sum of lines 16, 18, and 19) =

21. Education savings and asset
protection allowance (Table A5) -

22. Discretionary net worth
(line 20 minus line 21) =

23. Asset conversion rate X .12

24. CONTRIBUTION FROM ASSETS
If negative, enter zero. =

PARENTS' CONTRIBUTION

Available Income (AI) (from line 15)

Contribution from assets (from line 24) +

25. Adjusted Available Income (AAI)
May be a negative number. =

26. Total parents' contribution from AAI
(Calculate using Table A6; if negative, enter zero.)

27. Number in college in 2003-2004
(Exclude parents) (FAFSA/SAR #66) ÷

28. PARENTS' CONTRIBUTION (standard
contribution for 9-month enrollment)***
If negative, enter zero. =

**Do not include the family's home.

***To calculate the parents' contribution for other than 9-
month enrollment, see page 11.

continued on reverse

REGULAR WORKSHEET Page 2 **A**

29. Adjusted Gross Income (FAFSA/SAR #39) (If negative, enter zero.)	
30. Income earned from work (FAFSA/SAR #42)	
31. Taxable Income (If tax filer, enter the amount from line 29. If non-tax filer, enter the amount from line 30.)	/////
32. Untaxed income and benefits: Total from FAFSA Worksheet A FAFSA/SAR #44) _____ Total from FAFSA Worksheet B (FAFSA/SAR #45) + _____ Total untaxed income and benefits =	/////
33. Taxable and untaxed income (sum of line 31 and line 32)	
34. Total from FAFSA Worksheet C (FAFSA/SAR #46) -	
35. **TOTAL INCOME** (line 33 minus line 34) May be a negative number. =	

ALLOWANCES AGAINST STUDENT INCOME		
36. 2002 U.S. income tax paid (FAFSA/SAR #40) (tax filers only); if negative, enter zero.		
37. State and other tax allowance (Table A7. If negative, enter zero.)	+	
38. Social Security tax allowance (Table A2)	+	
39. Income protection allowance	+	2,380
40. Allowance for parents' negative Adjusted Available Income (If line 25 is negative, enter line 25 as a positive number in line 40. If line 25 is zero or positive, enter zero in line 40.)	+	
41. **TOTAL ALLOWANCES**	=	

STUDENT'S CONTRIBUTION FROM INCOME		
Total income (from line 35)		
Total allowances (from line 41)	-	
42. **Available income (AI)**	=	
43. **Assessment of AI**	X	.50
44. **STUDENT'S CONTRIBUTION FROM AI** If negative, enter zero.	=	

STUDENT'S CONTRIBUTION FROM ASSETS		
45. Net worth of investments* (FAFSA/SAR #47) If negative, enter zero.		
46. Net worth of business and/or investment farm (FAFSA/SAR #48) If negative, enter zero.	+	
47. Cash, savings, & checking (FAFSA/SAR #49)	+	
48. **Net worth** (sum of lines 45 through 47)	=	
49. Assessment rate	X	.35
50. **STUDENT'S CONTRIBUTION FROM ASSETS**	=	

EXPECTED FAMILY CONTRIBUTION		
PARENTS' CONTRIBUTION (from line 28)		
STUDENT'S CONTRIBUTION FROM AI (from line 44)	+	
STUDENT'S CONTRIBUTION FROM ASSETS (from line 50)	+	
51. **EXPECTED FAMILY CONTRIBUTION** (standard contribution for 9-month enrollment)** If negative, enter zero.	=	

*Do not include the student's home.

** To calculate the EFC for other than 9-month enrollment, see the next page.

NOTE: *Use this additional page to prorate the EFC only if the student will be enrolled for other than 9 months and only to determine the student's need for campus-based aid, a subsidized Federal Stafford Loan, or a subsidized Federal Direct Stafford/Ford Loan. Do not use this page to prorate the EFC for a Federal Pell Grant. The EFC for the Federal Pell Grant Program is the 9-month EFC used in conjunction with the cost of attendance to determine a Federal Pell Grant award from the Payment or Disbursement Schedule.*

REGULAR WORKSHEET Page 3 — **A**

Calculation of Parents' Contribution for a Student Enrolled LESS Than 9 Months		
A1. Parents' contribution (standard contribution for 9-month enrollment, from line 28)		
A2. Divide by 9	÷	9
A3. Parents' contribution per month	=	
A4. Multiply by number of months of enrollment	X	
A5. Parents' contribution for LESS than 9-month enrollment	=	

Calculation of Parents' Contribution for a Student Enrolled MORE Than 9 Months		
B1. Parents' Adjusted Available Income (AAI) (from line 25—may be a negative number)		
B2. Difference between the income protection allowance for a family of four and a family of five, with one in college	+	3,730
B3. Alternate parents' AAI for more than 9-month enrollment (line B1 + line B2)	=	
B4. Total parents' contribution from alternate AAI (calculate using Table A6)		
B5. Number in college (FAFSA/SAR #66)	÷	
B6. Alternate parents' contribution for student (line B4 divided by line B5)	=	
B7. Standard parents' contribution for the student for 9-month enrollment (from line 28)	-	
B8. Difference (line B6 minus line B7)	=	
B9. Divide line B8 by 12 months	÷	12
B10. Parents' contribution per month	=	
B11. Number of months student will be enrolled that exceed 9	X	
B12. Adjustment to parents' contribution for months that exceed 9 (multiply line B10 by line B11)	=	
B13. Standard parents' contribution for 9-month enrollment (from line 28)	+	
B14. Parents' contribution for MORE than 9-month enrollment	=	

Calculation of Student's Contribution from Available Income (AI) for a Student Enrolled LESS Than 9 Months*		
C1. Student's contribution from AI (standard contribution for 9-month enrollment, from line 44)		
C2. Divide by 9	÷	9
C3. Student's contribution from AI per month	=	
C4. Multiply by number of months of enrollment	X	
C5. Student's contribution from AI for LESS than 9-month enrollment	=	

*For students enrolled more than 9 months, the standard contribution from AI is used (the amount from line 44).

REGULAR
WORKSHEET
Page 4

A

Calculation of Total Expected Family Contribution for Periods of Enrollment Other Than 9 Months

Parents' Contribution—use ONE appropriate amount from previous page: • Enter amount from line A5 for enrollment periods less than 9 months **OR** • Enter amount from line B14 for enrollment periods greater than 9 months	
Student's Contribution from Available Income—use ONE appropriate amount from previous page: • Enter amount from line C5 for enrollment periods less than 9 months **OR** + • Enter amount from line 44 for enrollment periods greater than 9 months	
Student's Contribution from Assets • Enter amount from line 50 +	
Expected Family Contribution for periods of enrollment other than 9 months =	

2003-2004 EFC FORMULA A : DEPENDENT STUDENT

SIMPLIFIED WORKSHEET Page 1 **A**

PARENTS' INCOME IN 2002

1. Parents' Adjusted Gross Income (FAFSA/SAR #74)
(If negative, enter zero.)

2. **a.** Father's income earned from work
(FAFSA/SAR #77) _____

2. **b.** Mother's income earned from work
(FAFSA/SAR #78) + _____

Total parents' income earned from work =

3. Parents' Taxable Income
(If tax filers, enter the amount from line 1 above.
If non-tax filers, enter the amount from line 2.)*

4. Untaxed income and benefits:

• Total from FAFSA Worksheet A
(FAFSA/SAR #79) _____

• Total from FAFSA Worksheet B
(FAFSA/SAR #80) + _____

Total untaxed income and benefits =

5. Taxable and untaxed income (sum of line 3 and line 4)

6. Total from FAFSA Worksheet C (FAFSA/SAR #81) –

7. **TOTAL INCOME**
(line 5 minus line 6) May be a negative number. =

ALLOWANCES AGAINST PARENTS' INCOME

8. 2002 U.S. income tax paid (FAFSA/SAR #75)
(tax filers only); if negative, enter zero.

9. State and other tax allowance
(Table A1. If negative, enter zero.) +

10. Father's Social Security tax allow. (Table A2) +

11. Mother's Social Security tax allow. (Table A2) +

12. Income protection allowance (Table A3) +

13. Employment expense allowance:

• Two working parents: 35% of the lesser of the
earned incomes, or $3,000, whichever is less

• One-parent families: 35% of earned income,
or $3,000, whichever is less

• Two-parent families, one working
parent: enter zero +

14. **TOTAL ALLOWANCES** =

AVAILABLE INCOME

Total income (from line 7)

Total allowances (from line 14) –

15. **AVAILABLE INCOME (AI)**
May be a negative number. =

*STOP HERE if **both** of the following are true: line 3 is $15,000 or less, **plus** the student **and** parents are eligible to file a 2002 IRS Form 1040A or 1040EZ (they are not required to file a 2002 Form 1040), or they are not required to file any income tax return. If both circumstances are true, the Expected Family Contribution is automatically zero.

PARENTS' CONTRIBUTION FROM ASSETS

16. Net worth of investments**
(FAFSA/SAR #82)
If negative, enter zero.

17. Net worth of business and/or investment farm
(FAFSA/SAR #83)
If negative, enter zero.

18. Adjusted net worth of business/farm
(Calculate using Table A4.) +

19. Cash, savings, & checking (FAFSA/SAR #84) +

20. **Net worth** (sum of lines 16, 18, and 19) =

21. Education savings and asset
protection allowance (Table A5) –

22. Discretionary net worth
(line 20 minus line 21) =

23. Asset conversion rate X .12

24. **CONTRIBUTION FROM ASSETS**
If negative, enter zero. =

PARENTS' CONTRIBUTION

Available Income (AI) (from line 15)

Contribution from assets (from line 24) +

25. **Adjusted Available Income (AAI)**
May be a negative number. =

26. **Total parents' contribution from AAI**
(Calculate using Table A6; if negative, enter zero.)

27. **Number in college in 2003-2004**
(Exclude parents) (FAFSA/SAR #66) ÷

28. **PARENTS' CONTRIBUTION** (standard
contribution for 9-month enrollment)***
If negative, enter zero. =

**Do not include the family's home.

***To calculate the parents' contribution for other than 9-month enrollment, see page 15.

NOTE: Do NOT complete the shaded areas; asset information is not required in the simplified formula.

continued on reverse

SIMPLIFIED WORKSHEET Page 2 **A**

29.	Adjusted Gross Income (FAFSA/SAR #39) (If negative, enter zero.)	
30.	Income earned from work (FAFSA/SAR #42)	
31.	Taxable Income (If tax filer, enter the amount from line 29. If non-tax filer, enter the amount from line 30.)	
32.	Untaxed income and benefits:	
	Total from FAFSA Worksheet A FAFSA/SAR #44) _____	
	Total from FAFSA Worksheet B (FAFSA/SAR #45) +_____	
	Total untaxed income and benefits =	
33.	Taxable and untaxed income (sum of line 31 and line 32)	
34.	Total from FAFSA Worksheet C (FAFSA/SAR #46) -	
35.	**TOTAL INCOME** (line 33 minus line 34) May be a negative number. =	

ALLOWANCES AGAINST STUDENT INCOME

36.	2002 U.S. income tax paid (FAFSA/SAR #40) (tax filers only); if negative, enter zero.	
37.	State and other tax allowance (Table A7. If negative, enter zero.) +	
38.	Social Security tax allowance (Table A2) +	
39.	Income protection allowance +	2,380
40.	Allowance for parents' negative Adjusted Available Income (If line 25 is negative, enter line 25 as a positive number in line 40. If line 25 is zero or positive, enter zero in line 40.) +	
41.	**TOTAL ALLOWANCES** =	

STUDENT'S CONTRIBUTION FROM INCOME

Total income (from line 35)		
Total allowances (from line 41)	-	
42.	**Available income (AI)** =	
43.	**Assessment of AI** X	.50
44.	**STUDENT'S CONTRIBUTION FROM AI** = If negative, enter zero.	

STUDENT'S CONTRIBUTION FROM ASSETS

45.	Net worth of investments* (FAFSA/SAR #47) If negative, enter zero.	
46.	Net worth of business and/or investment farm (FAFSA/SAR #48) If negative, enter zero. +	
47.	Cash, savings, & checking (FAFSA/SAR #49) +	
48.	**Net worth** (sum of lines 45 through 47) =	
49.	Assessment rate X	.35
50.	**STUDENT'S CONTRIBUTION FROM ASSETS =**	

EXPECTED FAMILY CONTRIBUTION

PARENTS' CONTRIBUTION (from line 28)	
STUDENT'S CONTRIBUTION FROM AI (from line 44) +	
STUDENT'S CONTRIBUTION FROM ASSETS (from line 50) +	
51. **EXPECTED FAMILY CONTRIBUTION** standard contribution for 9-month enrollment** (If negative, enter zero.) =	

*Do not include the student's home.

** To calculate the EFC for other than 9-month enrollment, see the next page.

NOTE: Do NOT complete the shaded areas; asset information is not required in the simplified formula.

Financial Aid Resources

NOTE: *Use this additional page to prorate the EFC only if the student will be enrolled for other than 9 months and only to determine the student's need for campus-based aid, a subsidized Federal Stafford Loan, or a subsidized Federal Direct Stafford/Ford Loan. Do not use this page to prorate the EFC for a Federal Pell Grant. The EFC for the Federal Pell Grant Program is the 9-month EFC used in conjunction with the cost of attendance to determine a Federal Pell Grant award from the Payment or Disbursement Schedule.*

SIMPLIFIED WORKSHEET Page 3 **A**

Calculation of Parents' Contribution for a Student Enrolled LESS Than 9 Months		
A1. Parents' contribution (standard contribution for 9-month enrollment, from line 28)		
A2. Divide by 9	÷	9
A3. Parents' contribution per month	=	
A4. Multiply by number of months of enrollment	X	
A5. Parents' contribution for LESS than 9-month enrollment	=	

Calculation of Parents' Contribution for a Student Enrolled MORE Than 9 Months		
B1. Parents' Adjusted Available Income (AAI) (from line 25—may be a negative number)		
B2. Difference between the income protection allowance for a family of four and a family of five, with one in college	+	3,730
B3. Alternate parents' AAI for more than 9-month enrollment (line B1 + line B2)	=	
B4. Total parents' contribution from alternate AAI (calculate using Table A6)		
B5. Number in college (FAFSA/SAR #66)	÷	
B6. Alternate parents' contribution for student (line B4 divided by line B5)	=	
B7. Standard parents' contribution for the student for 9-month enrollment (from line 28)	-	
B8. Difference (line B6 minus line B7)	=	
B9. Divide line B8 by 12 months	÷	12
B10. Parents' contribution per month	=	
B11. Number of months student will be enrolled that exceed 9	X	
B12. Adjustment to parents' contribution for months that exceed 9 (multiply line B10 by line B11)	=	
B13. Standard parents' contribution for 9-month enrollment (from line 28)	+	
B14. Parents' contribution for MORE than 9-month enrollment	=	

Calculation of Student's Contribution from Available Income (AI) for a Student Enrolled LESS Than 9 Months*		
C1. Student's contribution from AI (standard contribution for 9-month enrollment, from line 44)		
C2. Divide by 9	÷	9
C3. Student's contribution from AI per month	=	
C4. Multiply by number of months of enrollment	X	
C5. Student's contribution from AI for LESS than 9-month enrollment	=	

*For students enrolled more than 9 months, the standard contribution from AI is used (the amount from line 44).

Use next page to calculate total EFC for enrollment periods other than 9 months

Parents' Contribution—use ONE appropriate amount from previous page: • Enter amount from line A5 for enrollment periods less than 9 months **OR** • Enter amount from line B14 for enrollment periods greather than 9 months	
Student's Contribution from Available Income—use ONE appropriate amount from previous page: • Enter amount from line C5 for enrollment periods less than 9 months **OR** + • Enter amount from line 44 for enrollment periods greater than 9 months	
Expected Family Contribution for periods of enrollment other than 9 months =	

Table A1: State and Other Tax Allowance
for Worksheet A (parents only)

STATE	PERCENT OF TOTAL INCOME		STATE	PERCENT OF TOTAL INCOME	
	$0-14,999	$15,000 or more		$0-14,999	$15,000 or more
Alabama	5%	4%	Missouri	6%	5%
Alaska	3%	2%	Montana	8%	7%
American Samoa	4%	3%	Nebraska	8%	7%
Arizona	6%	5%	Nevada	3%	2%
Arkansas	6%	5%	New Hampshire	7%	6%
California	8%	7%	New Jersey	8%	7%
Canada	4%	3%	New Mexico	6%	5%
Colorado	7%	6%	New York	11%	10%
Connecticut	6%	5%	North Carolina	8%	7%
Delaware	8%	7%	North Dakota	6%	5%
District of Columbia	10%	9%	Northern Mariana Islands	4%	3%
Federated States of Micronesia	4%	3%	Ohio	8%	7%
Florida	4%	3%	Oklahoma	6%	5%
Georgia	7%	6%	Oregon	10%	9%
Guam	4%	3%	Palau	4%	3%
Hawaii	8%	7%	Pennsylvania	7%	6%
Idaho	7%	6%	Puerto Rico	4%	3%
Illinois	6%	5%	Rhode Island	9%	8%
Indiana	6%	5%	South Carolina	8%	7%
Iowa	8%	7%	South Dakota	4%	3%
Kansas	7%	6%	Tennessee	3%	2%
Kentucky	7%	6%	Texas	3%	2%
Louisiana	4%	3%	Utah	8%	7%
Maine	9%	8%	Vermont	8%	7%
Marshall Islands	4%	3%	Virgin Islands	4%	3%
Maryland	9%	8%	Virginia	8%	7%
Massachusetts	9%	8%	Washington	4%	3%
Mexico	4%	3%	West Virginia	6%	5%
Michigan	9%	8%	Wisconsin	10%	9%
Minnesota	9%	8%	Wyoming	3%	2%
Mississippi	5%	4%	Blank or Invalid State	4%	3%
			OTHER	4%	3%

Multiply parents' total income (EFC Worksheet A, line 7) by the appropriate rate from the table above to get the "state and other tax allowance" (Worksheet A, line 9). Use the parents' *state of legal residence* (FAFSA/SAR #67). If this item is blank or invalid, use the student's *state of legal residence* (FAFSA/SAR #24). If both items are blank or invalid, use the *state* in the student's mailing address (FAFSA/SAR #6). If all three items are blank or invalid, use the rate for a blank or invalid state above.

Table A2: Social Security Tax

Calculate separately the Social Security tax of father, mother, and student.

Income Earned from Work*	Social Security Tax
$0 - $84,900	7.65% of income
$84,901 or greater	$6,494.85 + 1.45% of amount over $84,900

*Father's 2002 income earned from work is FAFSA/SAR #77.
Mother's 2002 income earned from work is FAFSA/SAR #78.
Student's 2002 income earned from work is FAFSA/SAR #42.
Social Security tax will never be less than zero.

Table A3: Income Protection Allowance

Number in parents' household, including student (FAFSA/SAR #65)	Number of college students in household (FAFSA/SAR #66)				
	1	2	3	4	5
2	$13,470	$11,160	——	——	——
3	16,770	14,480	$12,170	——	——
4	20,710	18,410	16,120	$13,810	——
5	24,440	22,130	19,840	17,540	$15,240
6	28,580	26,280	23,990	21,680	19,390

NOTE: For each additional family member, add $3,230.
For each additional college student (except parents), subtract $2,290.

Table A4: Business/Farm Net Worth Adjustment
for EFC Formula Worksheet A (parents only)

If the net worth of a business or farm is—	Then the adjusted net worth is—
Less than $1	$0
$1 to $95,000	40% of net worth of business/farm
$95,001 to $290,000	$ 38,000 + 50% of excess over $95,000
$290,001 to $480,000	$135,500 + 60% of excess over $290,000
$480,001 or more	$249,500 + 100% of excess over $480,000

Table A5: Education Savings and Asset Protection Allowance
for EFC Formula Worksheet A (parents only)

Age of older parent*	Allowance if there are two parents	Allowance if there is only one parent	Age of older parent*	Allowance if there are two parents	Allowance if there is only one parent
25 or less..	0	0	45	42,200	20,700
26	2,500	1,200	46	43,300	21,100
27	5,000	2,500	47	44,300	21,600
28	7,500	3,700	48	45,400	22,200
29	9,900	5,000	49	46,600	22,600
30	12,400	6,200	50	47,700	23,100
31	14,900	7,400	51	49,200	23,700
32	17,400	8,700	52	50,400	24,200
33	19,900	9,900	53	51,700	24,800
34	22,400	11,200	54	53,200	25,400
35	24,900	12,400	55	54,500	26,200
36	27,400	13,600	56	56,200	26,800
37	29,800	14,900	57	57,900	27,400
38	32,300	16,100	58	59,600	28,200
39	34,800	17,400	59	61,400	28,900
40	37,300	18,600	60	63,200	29,700
41	38,200	19,000	61	65,100	30,500
42	39,200	19,400	62	67,300	31,200
43	40,200	19,800	63	69,200	32,100
44	41,200	20,300	64	71,600	33,100
			65 or more	74,000	34,100

*If age of older parent (FAFSA/SAR #70) is blank, use age 45 on the table.

Table A6: Parents' Contribution From AAI

If parents' AAI is—	The parents' contribution from AAI is—
-$3,410 or less	-$750
-$3,409 to $12,000	22% of AAI
$12,001 to $15,100	$2,640 + 25% of AAI over $12,000
$15,101 to $18,200	$3,415 + 29% of AAI over $15,100
$18,201 to $21,200	$4,314 + 34% of AAI over $18,200
$21,201 to $24,300	$5,334 + 40% of AAI over $21,200
$24,301 or more	$6,574 + 47% of AAI over $24,300

Table A7: State and Other Tax Allowance
for Worksheet A (student only)

Alabama	3%	Missouri	3%
Alaska	0%	Montana	5%
American Samoa	2%	Nebraska	4%
Arizona	3%	Nevada	0%
Arkansas	4%	New Hampshire	1%
California	5%	New Jersey	3%
Canada	2%	New Mexico	4%
Colorado	4%	New York	7%
Connecticut	2%	North Carolina	5%
Delaware	5%	North Dakota	2%
District of Columbia	7%	Northern Mariana Islands	2%
Federated States		Ohio	5%
of Micronesia	2%	Oklahoma	4%
Florida	1%	Oregon	6%
Georgia	4%	Palau	2%
Guam	2%	Pennsylvania	3%
Hawaii	6%	Puerto Rico	2%
Idaho	5%	Rhode Island	4%
Illinois	2%	South Carolina	5%
Indiana	4%	South Dakota	0%
Iowa	5%	Tennessee	0%
Kansas	4%	Texas	0%
Kentucky	5%	Utah	5%
Louisiana	2%	Vermont	4%
Maine	5%	Virgin Islands	2%
Marshall Islands	2%	Virginia	4%
Maryland	6%	Washington	0%
Massachusetts	5%	West Virginia	4%
Mexico	2%	Wisconsin	5%
Michigan	4%	Wyoming	0%
Minnesota	6%	Blank or Invalid State	2%
Mississippi	3%	OTHER	2%

Multiply the total income of student (EFC Worksheet A, line 35) by the appropriate rate from the table above to get the "state and other tax allowance" (Worksheet A, line 37). Use the student's *state of legal residence* (FAFSA/SAR #24). If this item is blank or invalid, use the *state* in the student's mailing address (FAFSA/SAR #6). If both items are blank or invalid, use the parents' *state of legal residence* (FAFSA/SAR #67). If all three items are blank or invalid, use the rate for a blank or invalid state above.

The College Board

2003-2004 Institutional Methodology (IM) Worksheet

Computational Model

Parent(s) of dependent student

Student's name:

INCOME OF PARENT(S)		
1. AGI/taxable income		$
a. Add back losses from business, farm, etc., and capital losses		+
2. Untaxed income & benefits		+
3. Child support paid		-
4. Total parents' income (sum of lines 1, 1a, 2, minus 3)		=
ALLOWANCES		
5. U.S. income tax		
6. State and other taxes (% from Table 1 X line 4)		+
7. F.I.C.A. (Table 2)		+
8. Medical/dental expense allowance (Table 2)		+
9. Employment allowance (Table 2)		+
10. Annual education savings allowance (AESA) (Table 4):		
a. Annual savings goal (1.52% X line 4, up to $1,930)	=	
b. Number of pre-college children, excluding student	=	
c. Total AESA (line 10a X 10b)		+
11. Income protection allowance (Table 3a)		+
12. Total allowances (sum of lines 5 - 11)		=
13. Available income (line 4 minus line 12)		=
14. Total PC from income (calculate using line 13 and Table 5 - may not be negative)		=
ASSETS		
15. Cash, savings, and checking accounts		
16. Home equity		+
17. Investment equity		+
18. Other real estate equity		+
19. Adjusted business/farm equity (Table 7)		+
20. Assets in siblings' names/Prepaid tuition plans:		
a. Parents' assets held in names of siblings	+	
b. Prepaid tuition plan assets for siblings	+	
c. Prepaid tuition plan assets for student	+	
d. Total assets in siblings' name/Prepaid tuition plans (sum of a + b + c)		+
21. Net worth (sum of lines 15 - 20d)		=
22. Asset protection allowances:		
a. Emergency reserve allowance (Table 8):	=	
b. Cumulative education savings allowance (CESA) (Table 4)	=	
c. Low income asset allowance (amount from line 13, if negative)	=	
d. Total asset allowances (sum of a + b + c)		-
23. Discretionary net worth (line 21 minus line 22d - may not be negative)		=
24. Total PC from assets (calculate using line 23 and Table 9)		=
CONTRIBUTION		
25. Total parent contribution (sum of line 14 and line 24)		=
26. Number in college adjustment (Table 10)	X	%
27. Parent contribution for student (line 25 X line 26)		=

2003-2004 Institutional Methodology (IM) Worksheet

Computational Model	
Dependent student	
Student's name:	
INCOME OF STUDENT	
1. AGI/taxable income	$
2. Untaxed income/benefits	+
3. Taxable student aid	-
4. Total income (sum of lines 1 and 2, minus 3)	=
ALLOWANCES	
5. U.S. income tax	
6. State and other taxes (% from Table 1 X line 1)	+
7. F.I.C.A. (Table 2)	+
8. Total allowances (sum of lines 5 - 7)	=
9. Available income (line 4 minus line 8)	=
10. SC from income (line 9 X 50%) or minimum student contribution (Table 11), whichever is greater	=
ASSETS	
11. Cash, savings, and checking accounts	
12. Home equity	+
13. Investment equity	+
14. Other real estate equity	+
15. Business/farm equity	+
16. Trust value	+
17. Net worth (sum of lines 11 - 16)	=
18. SC from assets (line 17 X .25)	=
CONTRIBUTION	
19. Total student contribution (sum of line 10 and line 18)	=

The College Board

2003-2004
Institutional Methodology (IM)
Computation Tables

TABLE 1. ALLOWANCES FOR STATE AND OTHER TAXES

State/Territory/Country Of Residence	$0- 30,000	30,001- 40,000	40,001- 50,000	50,001- 60,000	60,001- 70,000	70,001- 80,000	80,001- or more	$0- 20,000	20,001- or more
Alabama (AL)	9.0%	8.5%	8.0%	7.5%	7.0%	6.5%	6.5%	2.5%	3.0%
Alaska (AK)	4.5	4.0	3.5	3.0	2.5	2.0	2.0	0.0	0.0
American Samoa (AS)	4.5	4.0	3.5	3.0	2.5	2.0	2.0	0.0	0.0
Arizona (AZ)	8.0	7.5	7.0	7.0	7.0	6.5	6.5	0.5	1.0
Arkansas (AR)	9.0	8.5	8.0	8.0	8.0	8.0	8.0	1.5	2.0
California (CA)	8.0	8.0	7.5	7.5	8.0	8.0	8.0	0.5	1.0
Canada (CN)	4.5	4.0	3.5	3.0	2.5	2.0	2.0	4.0	5.0
Colorado (CO)	8.0	8.0	7.5	7.5	7.5	7.5	7.0	1.5	2.0
Connecticut (CT)	10.0	9.5	9.0	9.0	9.5	9.5	9.5	0.5	1.0
Delaware (DE)	6.0	6.0	6.0	6.0	6.5	7.0	7.0	2.5	3.0
District of Columbia (DC)	8.5	8.5	8.5	9.0	9.0	9.0	9.0	3.5	4.0
Federated States of Micronesia (FM)	4.5	4.0	3.5	3.0	2.5	2.0	2.0	0.0	0.0
Florida (FL)	7.5	7.0	6.5	6.0	5.5	5.0	4.5	0.0	0.0
Georgia (GA)	9.0	8.5	8.5	8.5	8.0	8.0	8.0	1.5	2.0
Guam (GU)	4.5	4.0	3.5	3.0	2.5	2.0	2.0	0.0	0.0
Hawaii (HI)	9.0	9.0	9.0	9.0	8.5	8.5	8.5	3.0	3.5
Idaho (ID)	8.5	8.5	8.5	8.5	8.5	8.5	8.5	1.0	1.5
Illinois (IL)	10.0	9.5	9.0	8.5	8.0	8.0	7.5	1.5	2.0
Indiana (IN)	9.5	9.0	8.5	8.0	7.5	7.5	7.5	2.5	3.0
Iowa (IA)	10.0	9.5	9.0	9.0	9.0	9.0	9.0	2.0	2.5
Kansas (KS)	9.0	8.5	8.5	8.5	8.5	8.0	8.0	1.5	2.0
Kentucky (KY)	9.5	9.5	9.5	9.5	9.5	9.5	9.5	3.0	3.5
Louisiana (LA)	9.0	8.5	8.0	7.5	7.0	7.0	6.5	1.0	1.5
Maine (ME)	9.0	9.0	9.0	9.5	9.5	9.5	9.5	1.0	1.5
Marshall Islands (MH)	4.5	4.0	3.5	3.0	2.5	2.0	2.0	0.0	0.0
Maryland (MD)	11.0	10.5	10.5	10.5	10.5	10.5	10.5	3.5	4.0
Massachusetts (MA)	10.5	10.0	9.5	9.5	9.5	9.5	9.5	3.0	3.5
Mexico (MX)	4.5	4.0	3.5	3.0	2.5	2.0	2.0	4.0	5.0
Michigan (MI)	11.0	10.5	10.0	9.5	9.0	9.0	8.5	2.5	3.0
Minnesota (MN)	9.0	9.0	9.0	9.0	9.0	9.0	9.0	1.5	2.0
Mississippi	8.0	8.0	8.0	8.0	8.0	7.5	7.0	0.5	1.0
Missouri (MO)	9.0	9.0	9.0	8.5	8.5	8.5	8.0	2.0	2.5
Montana (MT)	6.0	6.0	6.0	6.0	6.5	6.5	6.5	1.5	2.0
Nebraska (NE)	9.0	9.0	9.0	9.0	9.0	9.0	9.0	1.0	1.5
Nevada (NV)	6.0	5.5	5.0	4.5	4.0	3.5	3.5	0.0	0.0
New Hampshire (NH)	7.5	7.0	6.5	6.0	5.5	5.5	5.5	0.0	0.0
New Jersey (NJ)	12.0	11.5	11.0	10.5	10.0	9.5	9.0	1.0	1.5
New Mexico (NM)	9.0	9.0	8.5	8.5	8.0	8.0	8.0	0.5	1.0
New York (NY)	12.5	12.5	12.5	12.5	12.5	12.5	12.5	1.5	2.0
North Carolina (NC)	8.5	8.5	8.5	8.5	8.5	8.5	8.5	1.5	2.0
North Dakota (ND)	7.5	7.0	6.5	6.5	6.5	6.0	6.0	0.5	1.0
Northern Mariana Islands (MP)	4.5	4.0	3.5	3.0	2.5	2.0	2.0	0.0	0.0
Ohio (OH)	9.5	9.0	9.0	9.0	9.0	9.0	9.0	2.5	3.0
Oklahoma (OK)	8.5	8.5	8.5	8.5	8.0	8.0	8.0	1.0	1.5
Oregon (OR)	9.5	9.5	9.5	10.0	10.0	10.0	10.0	3.0	3.5
Palau (PW)	4.5	4.0	3.5	3.0	2.5	2.0	2.0	0.0	0.0
Pennsylvania (PA)	10.5	10.0	9.5	9.0	9.0	8.5	8.5	2.5	3.0
Puerto Rico (PR)	4.5	4.0	3.5	3.0	2.5	2.0	2.0	1.0	1.0
Rhode Island (RI)	10.5	10.0	9.5	9.5	9.5	9.5	9.5	1.0	1.5
South Carolina (SC)	6.5	6.5	7.0	7.5	7.5	7.5	7.5	0.5	1.0
South Dakota (SD)	7.5	7.0	6.5	6.0	5.5	5.0	5.0	0.0	0.0
Tennessee (TN)	7.5	7.0	6.5	6.0	5.5	5.0	4.5	0.0	0.0
Texas (TX)	7.5	7.0	6.5	6.0	5.5	5.5	5.0	0.0	0.0

TABLE 1., continued

State/Territory/Country Of Residence	$0- 30,000	30,001- 40,000	40,001- 50,000	50,001- 60,000	60,001- 70,000	70,001- 80,000	80,001- or more	$0- 20,000	20,001- or more
Utah (UT)	10.0%	10.0%	10.0%	9.5%	9.0%	9.0%	8.5%	1.5%	2.0%
Vermont (VT)	8.0	8.0	8.0	8.0	8.0	8.0	8.0	0.5	1.0
Virgin Islands (VI)	4.5	4.0	3.5	3.0	2.5	2.0	2.0	0.0	0.0
Virginia (VA)	8.0	8.0	8.0	8.0	8.0	8.0	8.0	2.0	2.5
Washington (WA)	10.0	9.5	9.0	8.5	8.0	7.5	7.0	0.0	0.0
West Virginia (WV)	8.0	7.5	7.5	7.5	7.5	7.5	7.5	2.0	2.5
Wisconsin (WI)	11.5	11.5	11.5	11.5	11.5	11.0	10.5	1.5	2.0
Wyoming (WY)	5.5	5.0	4.5	4.0	4.0	3.5	3.0	0.0	0.0
Not Reported (NR)	9.5	9.0	8.5	8.5	8.0	8.0	8.0	1.5	2.0

TABLE 2. ALLOWANCES AGAINST INCOME

FICA: Wages

$1 to $84,900 .... 7.65% of income earned by each wage earner (maximum $6,494.85 per person)

$84,901 or more ...... $6,494.85 + 1.45% of income earned above $84,900 by each wage earner

Elementary/secondary tuition allowance .... Reported tuition paid to maximum $7,340 per eligilble child

Employment allowance ..... 38% of lesser earned income to a maximum $3,470 (single parent: 38% of earned income to a maximum of $3,470)

Medical/dental expense allowance .... Unreimbursed expenses in excess of 3.5% of total income

TABLE 3a. INCOME PROTECTION ALLOWANCE (IPA)
(Parents of Dependent Students)

Family Size* (including student)	Number in College** 1	2	3	4	5
2	$ 15,900	$ 15,140			
3	19,310	18,550	$ 17,790		
4	22,720	21,960	21,200	$ 20,440	
5	26,130	25,370	24,610	23,850	$ 23,090
6	29,080	28,320	27,560	26,800	26,040

*For each additional family member, add $2,730.
**For each additional college student, subtract $760.

2003-2004
Institutional Methodology (IM)
Computation Tables

TABLE 3b. MONTHLY MAINTENANCE ALLOWANCE
(Independent Students)

Single Student .... $1,490 per month during
period of non-enrollment

Married Student .... $1,020 per month during period
of non-enrollment (calculated
for student and spouse)

Children of Independent Students .... $440 per month during period
of non-enrollment for each child

TABLE 4. EDUCATION SAVINGS ALLOWANCES

Annual Savings Goal (ASG) =
1.52% of Total Income, to a maximum of $1,930

Annual Education Savings Allowance (AESA) =
ASG x number of pre-college children, excluding the
student applicant

Cumulative Education Savings Allowance (CESA) =
[(Number of college students x ASG x 18 x .625) +
(ASG x total ages of pre-college children)]
OR
$16,540, whichever is greater*

Minimum CESA applies to parents of dependent students only

TABLE 5. CONTRIBUTION FROM AVAILABLE INCOME (AI)
(Parents of Dependent Students)

Available
Income (AI)   Total Contributions from Income

Less than $ 14,110	22% of AI	
$ 14,111 to 19,050..........	$ 3,104 +	26% of AI over $ 14,110
$ 19,051 to 23,990	$ 4,388 +	30% of AI over $ 19,050
$ 23,991 to 28,930	$ 5,870 +	34% of AI over $ 23,990
$ 28,931 to 33,860	$ 7,550 +	38% of AI over $ 28,930
$ 33,861 to 38,800..........	$ 9,423 +	42% of AI over $ 33,860
$ 38,801 or more	$11,498 +	46% of AI over $ 38,800

TABLE 6. STUDENT INCOME ASSESSMENT RATES

Dependent Students .... 50 % of Available Income (AI)
Independent Students .... 70 % of Available Income (AI)

TABLE 7. ADJUSTED NET WORTH OF A BUSINESS OR FARM

Net Worth (NW)	Adjusted Net Worth			
Less than $1	$	0		
$ 1 to 95,000	$	0 +	40% of NW	
$ 95,001 to 290,000	$	38,000 +	50% of NW over $	95,000
$ 290,001 to 480,000	$	135,500 +	60% of NW over $	290,000
$ 480,001 or more	$	249,500 +	100% of NW over $	480,000

TABLE 8. EMERGENCY RESERVE ALLOWANCE (ERA)

Parents of Dependents and Independent Students with Dependents:

Family Size	ERA
2	$14,500
3	17,610
4	20,720
5	23,830
6	26,520
Each additional family member	+ 2,690

Single Independent Students without Dependents: .... $ 1,490
Married Independent Students without Dependents: .... $ 2,040

TABLE 9. ASSET CONVERSION RATE

Parents of Dependent Students

Discretionary Net Worth	Total Contribution From Assets
Up to $ 26,520	3%
26,521 to 53,040	$ 800 + 4% of DNW over $ 26,520
53,041 or more	$ 1,860 + 5% of DNW over $ 53,040

All Students:
Asset conversion rate is 25% of discretionary net worth

TABLE 10. NUMBER IN COLLEGE ADJUSTMENT

Number of Children in College	Adjustment Rate
1	100 % of PC
2	60 %
3	45 %
4 or more	35 %

For independent students, the adjustment rate is determined
by the total number in college, including the student, spouse, and
dependent children.

TABLE 11. STUDENT MINIMUM STANDARD CONTRIBUTION

$ 1,150 .... Freshman Dependent Students
1,400 .... All Other Dependent Students
1,900 .... All Independent Students

Sample Appeal Letters

Dear Upperhill Financial Aid Office:

I am writing to explain our financial status in the hopes that you will better understand our family's approach to financial planning, both for our children's education and our retirement.

In 1993, we moved from New York to Portsmouth, RI. The main reason for the move was to capitalize on the equity we had in our home in order to create a retirement fund. We had lived in the house for 20 years and experienced a substantial gain due to its appreciation. Although selling our home was a difficult decision to make, we knew it was the only way to establish a retirement fund and some security for our future. It was also necessary to take advantage of the volatile real estate market when the opportunity was presented.

Also, my husband and I both have our own businesses, and have been self-employed throughout our professional careers. These businesses have little net worth beyond our talent and human resources. Other than standard office equipment, such as a computer, desk, fax machine, and copier, our businesses have no other capital investments. While I've been in the field of psychology for the last 17 years, my husband has tried a number of entrepreneurial pursuits. And like many entrepreneurs, we've had our ups and downs when it comes to finances. While our children were young, we were unable to put away the necessary dollars to save for retirement and the growing costs of a college education.

Please note that we have put one child through college and that another is graduating in the spring of 2004. To finance these tuitions, we have used our salaries, investments, and loans. At the moment, we still have large amounts to pay on these loans. We owe over $15,000 for our oldest son's education, and $22,000 for our daughter who graduates next year. We also owe roughly $7,000 for Joseph's prep school education. I also need to continue my own education in order to remain in practice. For the next three years, I will be enrolled in a professional training program that will cost $7,000 during 2003–2004, $7,500 during 2004–2005, and $8,000 during 2005–2006. In addition to these educational expenses, we have spent over $13,000 for our eldest son's drug treatment program at the Hope Rehabilitation Center in Florida, and we still owe $4,000 toward that bill. (Please also note that we pay our own medical and dental expenses.)

The principal we have accumulated has been through the sale of our home and monies we received from my parents' estate. The other real estate listed on our application is a warehouse in Washington, DC, which is located in one of the worst sections of the city. We have been unsuccessful in attempting to sell that property.

As you can see by our salaries and ages, we are not in a position to repay large loans. We also have plans to move again to be closer to our families, now that our children are out of the house. Because of this, it is necessary that we have access to our funds. I will have to start a new practice all over again, and my husband is contemplating retirement at 62. As you can see by our home, we are modest people who do not live beyond our means.

Our net worth is a misleading representation of our financial situation, because our only assets are our retirement funds. When we decided how to invest our resources for retirement, we did not know the consequences these actions would have on the financial aid process. Had we been advised on this, our financial picture might look dramatically different today. Please understand that we do intend to contribute toward Joseph's education, but cannot afford to deplete our assets by $120,000–$150,000 to pay for an Upperhill education.

I hope this gives you an accurate picture of what we are dealing with as our son prepares to apply as an early decision applicant to Upperhill. Joseph has a lot to offer the Upperhill community, and we would greatly appreciate your consideration of our request for assistance in the spirit of a potentially long and satisfying relationship.

Please do not hesitate to contact me if you have any questions about our application.

Sincerely,

Marya Young
Mother of Joseph Young (Joseph's social security number)

Dear Mrs. Smith:

Thank you for your April 2003 letter showing an estimated financial aid package for our son's attendance at Alwin University. We were thrilled that Rudy was admitted to Alwin, but are still very nervous about affording his education.

In hopes of helping you better understand our financial situation, I have enclosed updated information regarding our finances. Please consider this new information when putting together Rudy's finalized aid offer from Alwin.

Our actual 2003 AGI was $13,523 less than we projected and $9,785 less than our actual 2002 AGI.

We incurred substantial capital losses during 2003. Like many investors, we continued to be impacted by the poor performance of the stock market. As you know, federal tax laws allow us to claim only a $3,000 capital loss in one year. However, as our Schedule D illustrates, our actual loss was much greater than this amount.

We are still providing support to our son Mark (as noted on our tax return).

We have relocated to Ohio to be closer to family, and in order to get our house ready for the real estate market, it was necessary to make some rather costly home improvements. This move has been important to us for personal and family reasons, but it has also had professional ramifications. My husband, George, and I are starting over with our businesses. Because of this, it is uncertain how the move will impact our income this year.

I hope this has helped explain our rather unique situation, and that the information provides more insight when putting together a financial aid offer for Rudy.

Please feel free to contact me if you have questions or need additional information.

Sincerely,

Angela Andrews
Mother of Rudy Andrews (Rudy's social security number)

Enclosed:
• A copy of our CSS/Profile with updated 2003 information.
• A copy of our 2002 Federal Income Tax Return (Rudy does not file). (Our interest income grew in 2002 due to the sale of our Washington, D.C. home.)
• A copy of the FAFSA form as filed with the processor.

Glossary

Listed below is a glossary of common abbreviations. A full glossary of financial aid terms follows this section.

ACT	American College Testing Program
ADC	Aid to Dependent Children
AFDC	Aid to Families with Dependent Children
AY	Academic Year
BIA	Bureau of Indian Affairs
COA	Cost of Attendance
CPS	Central Processing System
DOE	U.S. Department of Education
ED	U.S. Department of Education
EFC	Expected Family Contribution
EFT	Electronic Funds Transfer
FAFSA	Free Application for Federal Student Aid
FAA	Financial Aid Administrator
FAO	Financial Aid Office
FAT	Financial Aid Transcript
FC	Family Contribution
FDLP	Federal Direct Loan Program
FFELP	Federal Family Education Loan Program

FM	Federal Methodology
FWS	Federal Work-Study
GPA	Grade Point Average
NMSQT	National Merit Scholarship Qualifying Test
INS	U.S. Department of Immigrants and Naturalization Services
ISIR	Institutional Student Information Report
PC	Parent Contribution
PCA	Parent Contribution from Assets
PCI	Parent Contribution from Income
PJ	Professional Judgment
PLUS	Federal Parent Loan for Undergraduate Students
PSAT	Preliminary Scholastic Assessment Test
RA	Research Assistantship
RA	Residence Assistant
ROTC	Reserve Officer Training Corps
SAP	Satisfactory Academic Progress
SAT	Scholastic Assessment Test
SC	Student Contribution
SCA	Student Contribution from Assets
SCI	Student Contribution from Income
SEOG	Federal Supplemental Educational Opportunity Grant
SFS	Student Financial Services
SSIG	State Student Incentive Grant
TA	Teaching Assistantship
USED	U.S. Department of Education
VA	Veterans Administration

529 Savings Plans: Plans for the purpose of saving for college. All fifty states offer these investment plans, and contributions to a 529 savings plan are made with after-tax dollars. Since 2002, earnings on these plans have been granted federal tax exemption when used to pay for qualified higher education expenses. When the plan makes a distribution to pay for the beneficiary's college costs, the distribution is free from federal taxes

529 Prepaid Tuition Plans: Plans that allow buyers to purchase tuition credits for colleges at current prices and use them at a later date, even if prices have gone up.

Academic Period: A measured period of enrollment (e.g., a semester, trimester, quarter, or credit hours).

Academic Year: A period of at least 30 weeks of instructional time that usually consists of semesters, quarters, or trimesters.

Accrediting Agency: An agency that sets educational standards for schools, evaluates schools, and certifies that schools have met these standards. The U.S. Department of Education publishes a list of nationally recognized accrediting agencies. These agencies may be used as reliable authorities as to the quality of education or training offered.

Accredited Institution: Any school that meets standards established by a nationally recognized accrediting agency.

Accrued Interest: Interest that accumulates on loans and must be paid at a later date.

Act, the: The Higher Education Act of 1965, as amended.

Adjusted Gross Income (AGI): The income figure taken from the federal income tax form. AGI is the total of wages, interest, and dividend income minus certain adjustments.

Aggregate Loan Limit: The borrower's maximum allowable unpaid principal amount throughout the student's academic career.

Agreement: Any written contract or letter of understanding between parties that specifies the rights and duties of each party.

Aid to Families with Dependent Children (AFDC): Also called welfare. AFDC is federal grant money administered by state departments of social services.

AmeriCorps: A national and community service program created by the National and Community Service Trust Act of 1993. For each year of full-time service in the program, participants will receive educational awards to help finance their postsecondary education or pay back their student loans.

Annual Loan Limit: The maximum federal loan amount that a guarantor may guarantee for a borrower for an academic year.

Anticipated Completion (Graduation) Date: The date on which a student is expected to complete the degree requirements of an academic program.

Asset Protection Allowance: An allowance, subtracted from a family's total assets, that is used to determine the expected family contribution. This allowance increases with age, recognizing that more assets should be available as you get closer to retirement age.

Assets: Financial holdings such as checking and savings accounts, stocks, bonds, trusts and other securities, loan receivables, home and other real estate equity, business equipment, and business inventory.

Associate's Degree: This degree is awarded upon completion of a program of study that usually includes two years of full-time study.

Award Letter: A college's notification of financial aid qualification. The award letter usually gives information about the types and amounts of aid offered, specific program information, and the conditions that govern the award.

Award Year: The period of a given calendar year and the following calendar year for which financial aid is granted.

Bachelor's Degree: This degree is awarded upon completion of a program of study that usually includes four years of full-time study.

Bankruptcy: Judicial action to stay the normal collection of debts against the petitioner and cause those debts to be satisfied at the direction of the court.

> **Chapter 7:** This is the most common form of bankruptcy, often referred to as "liquidation."

> **Chapter 11:** A bankruptcy in which the borrower's debts are reorganized.

> **Chapter 12:** Similar to chapter 13, but applies only to certain farms and family farm operations.

Chapter 13: A chapter 13 bankruptcy allows individuals with regular incomes to satisfy their debts though a court-directed payment plan.

Base Year: The 12-month period ending on December 31 preceding the award year. For example, calendar year 2001 is the base year for the 2002–03 award year.

Billing Servicer: A company that manages billing and loan collections for lenders.

Borrower: A student, parent (natural or adoptive), or legal guardian to whom a loan is made.

Business/Farm Supplement: A form required of parents and students who own a business or farm. This form may be provided by the College Scholarship Service as a supplement to the CSS Profile or may be provided directly from the school requesting it. In either case, the completed form is submitted directly to the college.

Campus-Based Programs: The three federal financial aid programs administered by the financial aid offices of eligible colleges which include the Federal Supplemental Educational Opportunity Grant (FSEOG), Federal Work-Study (FWS), and the Federal Perkins Loan. A student's financial aid package may contain aid from one or more of these programs.

Cancellation of Loan: A portion or all of some student loans can be canceled if the borrower performs service in certain geographic or academic fields. Some loans will be canceled upon the death of the borrower. Promissory notes outline the circumstances under which loans can be canceled.

Capitalization: An increase in the principal balance of a loan that occurs when a lender adds the interest accrued on the loan to the outstanding principal balance. Subsequent interest accrues on the new total principal balance, which includes any capitalized interest.

Certification: The act of attesting that something is true or meets a certain standard.

Collection Agency: An agency that specializes in collecting payment on defaulted or delinquent loans. Collection agencies usually receive a percentage of the amount they collect from borrowers whose payments are overdue.

College Board: A nonprofit membership organization of approximately 3,000 colleges, secondary schools, and educational associations. It administers the SAT, the CSS Profile, and other educational services.

College Scholarship Service (CSS): A division of the College Board that deals with disseminating financial aid information and processing applications.

Compound Interest: Interest that is computed on the sum of an original principal and any accrued interest.

Cooperative Education: A program offered by some colleges in which students alternate periods of enrollment with periods of employment, usually paid employment.

Cosigner: A signer of a promissory note who is secondarily liable for a loan obligation.

Cost of Attendance (COA): An estimate of the student's educational expenses for a period of enrollment, typically one academic year. Costs are determined by colleges themselves and usually include tuition and fees, room and board, books and supplies, transportation, and personal and miscellaneous expenses.

Cost-Less-Aid: The figure calculated by deducting all financial assistance the student has been awarded from the cost of attendance.

Credit Bureau: An agency that maintains credit histories and other financial information and reports this information to lenders.

CSS Profile: A financial aid application developed by the College Scholarship Service (CSS). Some colleges use this form along with the Institutional Methodology (IM) to award institutional funds.

Cumulative Loan Limit: See Aggregate Loan Limit.

Debt-Management Counseling: Counseling provided to a student about debt and accumulated indebtedness. Counseling is required both before the student receives the first disbursement of the student's first loan—often referred to as "entrance counseling" or an "entrance interview"—and again when the student completes or withdraws from an academic program—often referred to as "exit counseling" or an "exit interview". These sessions may be conducted in person or online.

Default: When a borrower (or endorser, cosigner, or comaker, if any) fails to make payments on a loan for a certain period or has failed to comply with other terms of a promissory note or written agreement.

Deferment: A specified period during which a borrower does not have to repay the principal of a loan. Depending on the type of loan, interest may or may not continue to accrue during a deferment period.

Dependent Student: A student who does not meet the eligibility requirements for an "Independent Student," under the Higher Education Act of 1965, as amended. Typically any undergraduate student under the age of 24 who is not a veteran of the U.S. Armed Forces, not married, not a ward of the court, and does not have legal dependents (i.e., children they support).

Delinquency: A period that begins on the day after the due date of a payment when the borrower fails to make the equivalent of one full payment.

Direct Costs: Education-related expenses that a family generally pays directly to the college (e.g., tuition, fees, etc.).

Disbursement: The transfer of aid proceeding by check or electronic funds transfer (EFT) from an aid program to a student's billing account.

Disclosure Statement: A statement from a lender to a borrower that provides the borrower with information about the terms of the loan and the consequences of defaulting on that loan.

Discretionary Income: In the Institutional Methodology (IM) of need analysis, this is the income that is available to a family after taxes, medical expenses, and various standardized allowances have been subtracted.

Disposable Income: That part of a borrower's compensation from an employer and other income from any source that remains after the deduction of any amounts required by law to be withheld, or any child support or alimony payments that are made under a court order or legally enforceable written agreement. Amounts required by law to be withheld include, but are not limited to, federal and state taxes, social security contributions, and wage garnishment payments.

Documentation: A written or printed paper, a supporting reference, or a record that can be used to furnish evidence, proof, or verification of information.

Doctorate Degree: This degree is awarded for advanced and intensive study in a particular discipline.

Due Diligence: The process that lenders use in attempt to resolve a delinquency and prevent default.

Education Savings Accounts: Savings accounts that allow contributions of up to $2,000 each year per student; withdrawals for qualified educational expenses are federal tax free.

Electronic Funds Transfer (EFT): The electronic transfer of loan proceeds from a lender to an account at a college.

Eligible Noncitizen: A student aid applicant who is not a U.S. citizen, but is eligible to receive federal financial aid because he or she is a permanent resident, noncitizen national, or a resident of the Trust territory of the Pacific Islands or Micronesia.

Endorser: A signer of a promissory note who is secondarily liable for a loan obligation (i.e., comaker, cosigner).

Enrollment Status: Either full-time or part-time, based on the number of credits or credit hours for which a student is enrolled.

Entrance Interview: See Debt Management Counseling. A required counseling session at which a college must inform student borrowers about their rights and responsibilities.

Exit Interview: See Debt Management Counseling. A required counseling session conducted when the student is leaving school. A student borrower's loan obligation and responsibilities are reviewed.

Expected Family Contribution (EFC): The figure that indicates how much of a family's financial resources should be available to help pay for educational expenses. This figure is calculated using the Federal Methodology (FM) and/or Institutional Methodology (IM) and determines eligibility for financial aid.

Federal Ford Direct Loan Program: A student loan program similar to FFELP, except that funding comes directly from the U.S. Treasury rather than from private lending institutions.

Federal Family Educational Loan Programs (FFELP): Federal Stafford (subsidized and unsubsidized), PLUS, and Consolidation Loan Programs which are funded by private lenders, guaranteed by guarantors, and reinsured by the federal government.

Federal Interest Benefits: The federal government's payment of accrued interest on subsidized Stafford loans to the lender on behalf of the borrower during in-school, grace, or deferment periods.

Federal Methodology (FM): The need-analysis formula developed by the government and used to calculate the expected family contribution and eligibility for Title IV financial aid.

Federal Pell Grant: A federal grant awarded to undergraduate students based on need.

Federal Perkins Loan: Awarded by colleges, a need-based federal loan.

Federal PLUS Loan: A federal loan program for parents of undergraduate students. It falls under either the Federal Family Education Loan Program or the William D. Ford Federal Direct Loan umbrella.

Federal Stafford Loan: A Federal Family Education Loan Program for students. The Federal Stafford Loan can either be government-subsidized, for which the government pays any interest while the borrower is attending college, or unsubsidized, for which interest accrues when the loan is made.

Federal State Student Incentive Grant: Federal funds that are pooled with state money and used for state grant programs.

Federal Supplemental Educational Opportunity: A federal grant awarded by colleges to the most needy undergraduate students as determined by the federal need-analysis formula.

Federal Work-Study: A federal need-based financial aid program through which eligible students can earn wages to help pay for college expenses. Colleges award work-study; a portion of the funds comes from the federal government and a portion from the college. Several states also have work-study programs that are similar to the federal program.

Financial Aid Award: A specific amount of financial assistance offered to a student through financial aid programs.

Financial Aid Package: The total amount of financial aid that a school awards to a student from all sources (federal, state, institutional, and private).

Financial Aid Transcript (FAT): An official record of federal financial aid that a student has received. This helps institutions review aid eligibility of applicants who have attended other schools. Schools obtain FAT data from the National Student Loan Data System.

Financial Need: The student's cost of attendance less the expected family contribution.

Fixed Interest: Rate of interest that does not change during the life of a loan.

Forbearance: When a lender allows a borrower to stop paying a loan temporarily or agrees to accept smaller payments than previously scheduled. The borrower is liable for the interest that accrues on the loan during the forbearance period. Usually, forbearance is given only when personal problems such as short-term unemployment or hospitalization prevent a borrower from making payments.

Free Application for Federal Student Aid (FAFSA): The official application used to apply and establish eligibility for federal aid.

Full-Time: A student enrolled at a college and carrying a full academic workload as determined by the school. Typically 12 or more credits per term.

Gapping: When a financial aid package does not meet an applicant's full need as per the need-analysis formula.

General Education Development Certification (GED): This certification is given to individuals without a high school diploma who have passed a series of high school equivalency tests.

Gift Aid: Grant and scholarship money that does not have to be repaid or earned by the student.

Grace Period: The period of time that begins when a student loan borrower graduates or ceases to be enrolled at least half-time and ends when repayment must begin. The grace period of the subsidized Stafford Loan is six months and that of the Perkins Loan is nine months.

Grade Level: A student's academic class level as determined by the school.

Graduated Repayment Schedule: A repayment schedule in which the amount of the borrower's installments is scheduled to change during the course of the repayment period. The Graduated Repayment Schedule cannot exceed 10 years.

Grant: Financial aid that does not need to be repaid (i.e., gift aid). Financial aid grants can take the form of tuition assistance paid directly to the college on the student's behalf or a direct disbursement of money to the student to help cover other educational or living expenses. Grants can be awarded on the basis of financial need or academic merit.

Guarantee Agency: A nonprofit state or private organization that insures lenders against losses due to a borrower's default, death, disability, or bankruptcy.

Guarantee Fee: An insurance fee that the guarantee agency charges a lender. The borrower usually pays this fee.

Half-Time Student: A student enrolled in at least half of the workload of a full-time student, as determined by the school. Typically, this is between 6 and 12 credits.

Holder: A lender or secondary market in possession of a loan.

Income-Contingent Repayment Schedule: A repayment schedule where the borrower's monthly payment amount is adjusted annually, based on the borrower's total loan amount, family size, and income.

Income-Sensitive Repayment Schedule: A repayment schedule where the borrower's monthly payment amount is adjusted annually based upon the borrower's monthly income.

Ineligible: Not meeting specific criteria.

Immigration and Naturalization Service (INS): The federal agency responsible for citizenship status and immigration.

Independent Student: Any student who meets any one of the following criteria: is at least 24 years old, is enrolled in a graduate or professional school, has legal dependents, is a ward orphan of the court, is a veteran of the U.S. Armed Forces, or is married.

Indirect Costs: All nondirect (i.e., may not be charged by the college) costs associated with attending college. May include transportation, medical and personal expenses, room and board, etc.

Institutional Methodology (IM): A method of need analysis used by some colleges to calculate a family contribution used to determine eligibility for institutional and nonfederal aid.

Insurance Fee: A fee (charged on certain loans) that is deducted from the principal and is used to cover defaults.

Interest: The charge made to a borrower for use of a lender's money.

Interest Subsidy: Interest payments made by the federal government to the lender on a Subsidized Federal Loan while the borrower is enrolled at least half-time or is in a grace period.

Internal Revenue Service (IRS): The federal agency responsible for collecting income taxes. Student aid applications are verified using IRS forms.

IRS Offset: An interception by the IRS of the income tax refund of a borrower with a defaulted FFELP loan.

Last Date of Attendance: The last day the student was physically present in class, as confirmed by the student's attendance records.

Late Charges: Charges that the lender may require the borrower to pay if the borrower fails to pay all or a portion of a required installment payment when due.

Leave of Absence: A break in enrollment, not including semester or spring breaks(s), that is requested by the student and sanctioned by the school.

Legal Guardian: An individual appointed by a court to be a guardian of a person and specifically required by the court to use his or her financial resources for the support of that person.

Lender: A bank or agency that loans money.

Loan Period: The period of enrollment for which a loan is certified.

Loan Proceeds: The amount of loan funds that have been guaranteed.

Master's Degree: An advanced degree that can be pursued after receiving a bachelor's degree.

Merit-Based Aid: Any form of financial aid awarded on the basis of personal achievement or individual characteristics and not based on demonstrated financial need.

National of the United States: A citizen of the United States or, as defined in the Immigration and Nationality Act, a noncitizen who owes permanent allegiance to the United States.

National Student Loan Data System (NSLDS): A database of information from guarantors, schools, lenders, and the Department of Education which contains information on Title IV aid received by students.

Need-Analysis Formula: A standardized assessment/formula that determines the ability of a student or student's family to contribute toward college expenses. This formula takes into account the family's financial strength and includes income and assets.

Office of Student Financial Assistance (OFSA): The Department of Education branch responsible for administering federal student financial aid programs and developing policies and procedures.

Origination Fee: A processing fee charged to a borrower by a lender to make the loan. This fee, like the guarantee or insurance fee, is usually subtracted from the amount of the loan proceeds.

Overaward: A situation that occurs when a student's family contribution plus any financial aid awarded exceeds the cost of attendance. Overawards result most often when a student's enrollment status changes or when additional resources become available to a student (such as an outside scholarship).

Package: Awards from a combination of two or more financial aid programs.

Permanent Resident of the United States: A person who meets certain requirements of the INS.

Principal: The face value of a loan or the total amount you borrow. This is the amount on which the interest is charged.

Professional Judgment: The flexibility given to a financial aid administrator to make adjustments to student eligibility for federal aid on a case-by-case basis. This may be done by adjusting the data elements used in the calculation based on additional information or circumstances that would lead to a more accurate assessment of the family's financial condition.

Promissory Note: A legally binding agreement that a borrower must sign when obtaining a loan. It lists the conditions under which the loan is made and the terms under which the borrower agrees to repay the loan.

Reauthorization: The legislative process carried out every five years reviewing the Higher Education Act. During this process Congress reviews, renews, terminates, or amends existing programs.

Repayment Period: The period during which interest accrues on the borrower's loan and principal payments are due.

Repayment Schedule: A plan that sets forth the interest rate on a loan, the frequency of payments, the principal and interest due in each installment, the number of payments required to pay back the loan in full, and the due date of each payment.

Satisfactory Academic Progress (SAP): A term defined by each college that describes a satisfactory rate of course completion as well as individual term performance. Regulations require that a student make satisfactory progress in order to receive any federal aid.

Scholarship: Gift aid based on merit and/or financial need.

Secondary Market: An entity that purchases education loans from lenders. The secondary market institution then becomes the owner or holder of the loan. The borrower will be notified of such changes and must send payments to the new loan holder.

Self-Help Aid: Funds from work and loan programs.

Self-Help Expectation: The philosophy that students have an obligation to help pay for a portion of their educational expenses. A standardized self-help expectation is frequently computed by schools. This amount may vary from school to school and often includes a student income contribution, loan amount, and work component.

Simplified Needs Test: A formula under the Federal Methodology (FM) for those families whose Adjusted Gross Income (AGI) is less than $50,000 and who file either the 1040A or 1040EZ IRS forms. When using this formula, the family's assets are not included.

Skiptracing: The attempt to find a valid address for a borrower who cannot be located. Any information from the borrower's loan application, the alumni or registrar's office, the U.S. Department of Education, or a professional skiptracing service may be used.

Statement of Educational Purpose: The borrower's signed statement that any Title IV aid received will be used only for education-related expenses at the school where the student is enrolled.

Student Aid Report (SAR): A summary of data submitted on the FAFSA and the calculated EFC based on that data. This form allows you to add schools and/or correct information.

Subsidized Loan: A loan for which the borrower is not responsible for all of the interest payments. For subsidized Federal Stafford Loans, the government pays interest to the lender on behalf of the borrower while the student is in school and during approved grace periods.

Title IV: The section of the Higher Education Act of 1965, as amended, that authorizes federal loan, work, and grant financial assistance programs for education.

Treasury Bill (T-bill): A note or bill issued by the U.S. Treasury as legal tender for all debts.

Undergraduate Student: A student enrolled at or below the baccalaureate level, designed to lead to a first degree.

Unmet Need: When a student's financial aid package (award) does not meet the calculated need (the difference between the cost of attendance and the family contribution).

Unsubsidized Loan: A non-need-based loan such as an unsubsidized Federal Stafford loan or a Federal PLUS loan. The borrower is responsible for paying the interest on an unsubsidized loan during in-school, grace, or deferment periods.

Variable Interest Rate: An interest rate that may change during the life of a loan and is generally tied to an index. Some student and parent loan programs have variable interest rates that change annually based on the one-year treasury bill rate.

Verification: The process of collecting additional documentation to substantiate data that a financial aid applicant reports on applications.

PART THREE

FINANCIAL INFORMATION FOR 328 POPULAR SCHOOLS

Financial Data
for 328 Popular Schools

In this section, you'll find financial data for schools listed in the popular *Unofficial, Unbiased Guide to the 328 Most Interesting Colleges 2004 Edition* published by Simon and Schuster. These schools include dream schools, best values, and hidden treasures, and can give you a sense of the college financial landscape out there. Here's a breakdown of the information you'll find in the following pages:*

Tuition and Fees: In most cases, we've provided tuition costs for a year of undergraduate study. Tuition figures are the most recent available at the time of data collection, with the year indicated ("est." means estimated). Public colleges and universities generally charge less for in-state students; we have listed both in-state and out-of-state tuitions, and have also indicated schools that offer a regional or "good neighbor" tuition. Private institutions usually do not differentiate between state residents and nonresidents. Required fees that all students must pay are included in the tuition figures provided. Usually they include activity, health, and registration fees, among others. Expenses like books and optional fees like parking costs are not included. Some schools may have special work-study programs, or full scholarship programs, that alleviate or eliminate the burden of paying for tuition. Other special situations may also be indicated.

Total Annual Expenses: Comprehensive fees are provided where a breakdown of tuition and fees and room and board is not available.

Room and Board: Here we provide estimated average costs for on-campus room and board for undergraduate students sharing a room with another student over a one-year period.

Tuition, Room and Board Paid by U.S. Government: This is seen with United States military schools. Usually the student pays a one-time fee, but their major expenses are paid by the government.

Payment Plan(s): Some schools have indicated if they have special payment plans: installment, deferred, and prepayment.

* Since schools vary in the way they report financial data, individual entries may not contain all the listed categories.

Institutional Aid, Need-Based: This is the total dollar amount of need-based institutional aid (and external funds awarded by the college) available (including non-need-based aid used to meet need). It does not include athletic awards and tuition waivers. These funds include endowment, alumni and other funds. These numbers are either for 2001–2 or estimated for 2002–3. Special cases may also be indicated.

Institutional Aid, Non-Need-Based: This is the total dollar amount of non-need-based institutional aid (and external funds awarded by the college) available (excluding non-need-based aid used to meet need). It does not include athletic awards and tuition waivers. These funds include endowment, alumni and other funds. These numbers are either for 2001–2 or estimated for 2002–3. Special cases may also be indicated.

Full-Time Undergrads Receiving Aid, and Average Amount per Student: This is the percent of full-time degree-seeking undergraduates who receive any financial aid, and the average financial aid package per student.

Full-Time Undergrads Receiving Non-Need-Based Gift Aid, and Average Amount per Student: This is the percent of full-time degree-seeking undergraduates who did not have financial need and who received gift aid that was non-need-based, and the average amount of such aid awarded to those students.

Receiving Need-Based Gift Aid, and Average Award: This is the percent of those students receiving any aid (see above) who received gift aid based on financial need, and the average gift award.

Receiving Need-Based Self-Help Aid (Loans and Work Aid), and Average Award: This is the percent of those students receiving any aid (see above) who received self-help aid based on financial need, and the average award. Keep in mind that self-help as colleges report it includes loans as well as work aid.

Average Loan Debt per Student: This is the average amount graduating students owe in loan debt (not including what they may owe their parents!). This number is usually for the 2002 graduating class, but in some cases may be from the class of 2001.

Financial Aid Deadline: This is the date by which you must submit your financial aid application, including priority dates for aid consideration where available. (Deadlines may vary for different programs within a school, and change from year to year. While this book provides general guidelines, and endeavors to provide the most up-to-date information, you must check with the individual school to ensure that you are applying on time.)**

**Note: Schools marked with an asterisk did not respond to our survey this year, and data listed in these entries may have changed. Please contact the school for the most recent cost and financial aid information.

Agnes Scott College

141 East College Avenue, Decatur, GA 30030-3797. **Admissions Phone:** (404) 471-6285; (800) 868-8602. **Fax:** (404) 471-6414. **Email:** admission@agnesscott.edu. **Website:** www.agnesscott.edu. **Costs (2003–04):** Tuition and Fees: $20,470. **Room & Board:** $7,760. **Payment Plan(s):** installment plan. **Institutional Aid (est. 2002–03):** Institutional Aid, Need-Based: $6,154,544. **Institutional Aid, Non-Need-Based:** $3,383,364. **FT Undergrads Receiving Aid:** 67%. **Avg. Amount per Student:** $16,520. **FT Undergrads Receiving Non-Need-Based Gift Aid:** 29%. **Avg. Amount per Student:** $12,090. **Of Those Receiving Any Aid:** Receiving Need-Based Gift Aid: 99%. **Avg. Award:** $13,966. **Receiving Need-Based Self-Help Aid:** 82%. **Avg. Award:** $4,837. **Upon Graduation, Avg. Loan Debt per Student:** $17,602. **Financial Aid Deadline:** 5/1, 2/15 (priority).

Albertson College of Idaho

2112 Cleveland Boulevard, Caldwell, ID 83605-4432. **Admissions Phone:** (208) 459-5305; (800) 224-3246. **Fax:** (208) 459-5757. **Email:** admission@albertson.edu. **Website:** www.albertson.edu. **Costs (2003–04):** Tuition and Fees: $14,500. **Room & Board:** $5,015. **Payment Plan(s):** installment plan. **Institutional Aid (est. 2002–03):** Institutional Aid, Need-Based: $1,054,079 **Institutional Aid, Non-Need-Based:** $5,327,806. **FT Undergrads Receiving Aid:** 69%. **Avg. Amount per Student:** $14,738. **FT Undergrads Receiving Non-Need-Based Gift Aid:** 21%. **Avg. Amount per Student:** $7,585. **Of Those Receiving Any Aid:** Receiving Need-Based Gift Aid: 63%. **Avg. Award:** $4,499. **Receiving Need-Based Self-Help Aid:** 75%. **Avg. Award:** $4,585. **Upon Graduation, Avg. Loan Debt per Student:** $17,181. **Financial Aid Deadline:** 2/15.

Albion College

611 East Porter Street, Albion, MI 49224. **Admissions Phone:** (517) 629-0321; (800) 858-6770. **Fax:** (517) 629-0569. **Email:** admission@albion.edu. **Website:** www.albion.edu. **Application Website:** www.albion.edu/admissions/apply. **Costs (2002–03):** Tuition and Fees: $20,458. **Room & Board:** $5,912. **Payment Plan(s):** installment plan. **Institutional Aid (est. 2002–03):** Institutional Aid, Need-Based: $10,745,279 **Institutional Aid, Non-Need-Based:** $5,069,169. **FT Undergrads Receiving Aid:** 61%. **Avg. Amount per**

Student: $17,700. **FT Undergrads Receiving Non-Need-Based Gift Aid:** 35%. **Avg. Amount per Student:** $10,003. **Of Those Receiving Any Aid:** Receiving Need-Based Gift Aid: 100%. **Avg. Award:** $14,529. **Receiving Need-Based Self-Help Aid:** 75%. **Avg. Award:** $4,219. **Upon Graduation, Avg. Loan Debt per Student:** $17,481. **Financial Aid Deadline:** 2/15.

Alfred University

One Saxon Drive, Alfred, NY 14802-1205. **Admissions Phone:** (607) 871-2115; (800) 541-9229. **Fax:** (607) 871-2198. **Email:** admwww@alfred.edu. **Website:** alfred.edu. **Application Website:** admissions/html/apply.html. **Costs (2002–03):** Tuition and Fees: $20,656. Tuition figure provided is a blended average. **Room & Board:** $8,478. **Payment Plan(s):** installment plan. **Institutional Aid (est. 2002–03):** Institutional Aid, Need-Based: $15,339,000. **Institutional Aid, Non-Need-Based:** $2,010,000. **FT Undergrads Receiving Aid:** 80%. **Avg. Amount per Student:** $18,740. **FT Undergrads Receiving Non-Need-Based Gift Aid:** 11%. **Avg. Amount per Student:** $6,322. **Of Those Receiving Any Aid:** Receiving Need-Based Gift Aid: 97%. **Avg. Award:** $13,488. **Receiving Need-Based Self-Help Aid:** 91%. **Avg. Award:** $5,638. **Upon Graduation, Avg. Loan Debt per Student:** $17,600. **Financial Aid Deadline:** rolling.

Allegheny College

520 North Main Street, Meadville, PA 16335. **Admissions Phone:** (814) 332-4351; (800) 521-5293. **Fax:** (814) 337-0431. **Email:** admiss@allegheny.edu. **Website:** www.allegheny.edu. **Application Website:** https://apply.embark.com/ugrad.Allegheny. **Costs (2002–03):** Tuition and Fees: $23,380. **Room & Board:** $5,600. **Payment Plan(s):** installment plan, pre-payment plan. **Institutional Aid (est. 2002–03):** Institutional Aid, Need-Based: $17,713,843. **Institutional Aid, Non-Need-Based:** $4,497,940. **FT Undergrads Receiving Aid:** 72%. **Avg. Amount per Student:** $19,120. **FT Undergrads Receiving Non-Need-Based Gift Aid:** 24%. **Avg. Amount per Student:** $8,532. **Of Those Receiving Any Aid:** Receiving Need-Based Gift Aid: 100%. **Avg. Award:** $13,408. **Receiving Need-Based Self-Help Aid:** 87%. **Avg. Award:** $5,659. **Upon Graduation, Avg. Loan Debt per Student:** $21,670. **Financial Aid Deadline:** rolling; 2/15 (priority).

American University

4400 Massachusetts Avenue N.W., Washington, DC 20016-8001. **Admissions Phone:** (202) 885-6000. **Fax:** (202) 885-1025. **Email:** afa@american.edu. **Website:** www.american.edu. **Application Website:** admissions.american.edu. **Costs (2002–03):** Tuition and Fees: $23,455. **Room & Board:** $9,488. **Payment Plan(s):** installment plan, pre-payment plan. **Institutional Aid (2001–02):** Institutional Aid, Need-Based: $22,953,672. **Institutional Aid, Non-Need-Based:** $11,038,796. **FT Undergrads Receiving Aid:** 44%. **Avg. Amount per Student:** $21,266. **FT Undergrads Receiving Non-Need-Based Gift Aid:** 10%. **Avg. Amount per Student:** $11,140. **Of Those Receiving Any Aid:** Receiving Need-Based Gift Aid: 84%. **Avg. Award:** $12,453. **Receiving Need-Based Self-Help Aid:** 94%. **Avg. Award:** $8,917. **Upon Graduation, Avg. Loan Debt per Student:** $19,953. **Financial Aid Deadline:** 3/1 (priority).

Amherst College

PO Box 5000, Amherst, MA 01002-5000. **Admissions Phone:** (413) 542-2328. **Fax:** (413) 542-2040. **Email:** admission@amherst.edu. **Website:** www.amherst.edu. **Application Website:** www.amherst.edu/admission/apply.html. **Costs (2002–03):** Tuition and Fees: $28,310. **Room & Board:** $7,380. **Payment Plan(s):** installment plan. **Institutional Aid (est. 2002–03):** Institutional Aid, Need-Based: $16,434,846. **FT Undergrads Receiving Aid:** 49%. **Avg. Amount per Student:** $26,080. **FT Undergrads Receiving Non-Need-Based Gift Aid:** 10%. **Avg. Amount per Student:** $5,081. **Of Those Receiving Any Aid:** Receiving Need-Based Gift Aid: 95%. **Avg. Award:** $24,039. **Receiving Need-Based Self-Help Aid:** 91%. **Avg. Award:** $3,333. **Upon Graduation, Avg. Loan Debt per Student:** $11,544. **Financial Aid Deadline:** 2/15.

Antioch College

795 Livermore Street, Yellow Springs, OH 45387. **Admissions Phone:** (937) 769-1100; (800) 543-9436. **Fax:** (937) 769-1111. **Website:** www.antioch-college.edu. **Costs (2003–04):** Tuition and Fees: $23,275. **Room & Board:** $5,994. **Payment Plan(s):** installment plan. **Institutional Aid (est. 2002–03):** Institutional Aid, Need-Based: $4,720,196. **Institutional Aid, Non-Need-Based:** $765,529. **FT Undergrads Receiving Aid:** 84%. **Avg. Amount per Student:** $16,692. **FT Undergrads Receiving Non-**

Need-Based Gift Aid: 19%. Avg. Amount per Student: $5,665. Of Those Receiving Any Aid: Receiving Need-Based Gift Aid: 100%. Avg. Award: $9,698. Receiving Need-Based Self-Help Aid: 76%. Avg. Award: $5,717. Upon Graduation, Avg. Loan Debt per Student: $18,534. Financial Aid Deadline: 3/1, 2/15 (priority).

Arizona State University

Box 870112, Tempe, AZ 85287. **Admissions Phone:** (480) 965-7788. **Fax:** (480) 965-3610. **Email:** ugradinq@asu.edu. **Website:** www.asu.edu. **Costs (2002–03):** Tuition and Fees, In-State: $2,585 Tuition and Fees, Out-of-State: $11,105. Room & Board: $5,866. **Institutional Aid (2001–02):** Institutional Aid, Need-Based: $11,309,483. Institutional Aid, Non-Need-Based: $9,011,743. FT Undergrads Receiving Aid: 37%. Avg. Amount per Student: $7,309. FT Undergrads Receiving Non-Need-Based Gift Aid: 25%. Avg. Amount per Student: $5,675. Of Those Receiving Any Aid: Receiving Need-Based Gift Aid: 79%. Avg. Award: $4,225. Receiving Need-Based Self-Help Aid: 80%. Avg. Award: $4,109. Upon Graduation, Avg. Loan Debt per Student: $17,357. Financial Aid Deadline: rolling; 3/1 (priority).

Auburn University

202 Mary Martin Hall, Auburn University, AL 36849-5145. **Admissions Phone:** (334) 844-4080; (800) AUBURN9 (in-state). **Email:** admissions@auburn.edu. **Website:** www.auburn.edu. **Application Website:** auburn.edu/student_info/student_affairs/admissio/admissform.html. **Costs (2002–03):** Tuition and Fees, In-State: $3,784. Tuition and Fees, Out-of-State: $11,084. Room: $2,216 (2001–02). **Institutional Aid (2001–02):** Institutional Aid, Need-Based: $2,796,118. Institutional Aid, Non-Need-Based: $1,159,860. FT Undergrads Receiving Aid: 31%. Avg. Amount per Student: $6,400. FT Undergrads Receiving Non-Need-Based Gift Aid: 4%. Avg. Amount per Student: $3,932. Of Those Receiving Any Aid: Receiving Need-Based Gift Aid: 46%. Avg. Award: $2,968. Receiving Need-Based Self-Help Aid: 83%. Avg. Award: $4,296. Upon Graduation, Avg. Loan Debt per Student: $18,585. Financial Aid Deadline: 3/1 (priority).

Austin College

900 North Grand Avenue, STE 6N, Sherman, TX 75090-4400. **Admissions Phone:** (800) 442-5363; (903) 813-3000. **Fax:** (903) 813-3198. **Email:** admission@austincollege.edu. **Website:** www.austincollege.edu. **Application Website:** www.austincollege.edu/admis. **Costs (2003–04):** Tuition and Fees: $17,900 Room & Board: $6,822. **Payment Plan(s):** installment plan, deferred payment plan, pre-payment plan. **Institutional Aid (est. 2002–03):** Institutional Aid, Need-Based: $5,510,465. Institutional Aid, Non-Need-Based: $3,734,353. FT Undergrads Receiving Aid: 61%. Avg. Amount per Student: $16,704. FT Undergrads Receiving Non-Need-Based Gift Aid: 33%. Avg. Amount per Student: $8,495. Of Those Receiving Any Aid: Receiving Need-Based Gift Aid: 99%. Avg. Award: $11,850. Receiving Need-Based Self-Help Aid: 73%. Avg. Award: $4,492. Upon Graduation, Avg. Loan Debt per Student: $22,462. Financial Aid Deadline: 4/1 (priority).

Babson College

Office of Undergraduate Admission, Babson Park, MA 02457. **Admissions Phone:** (781) 239-5522; (800) 488-3696. **Fax:** (781) 239-4006. **Email:** ugradadmission@babson.edu. **Website:** www.babson.edu. **Application Website:** http://www2.babson.edu/babson/babsonug p.nsf/Public/applynow. **Costs (2003–04):** Tuition and Fees: $27,248. Room & Board: $9,978 (est. 2002–03). **Institutional Aid (est. 2002–03):** Institutional Aid, Need-Based: $10,265,000. Institutional Aid, Non-Need-Based: $903,000. FT Undergrads Receiving Aid: 42%. Avg. Amount per Student: $22,004. FT Undergrads Receiving Non-Need-Based Gift Aid: 6%. Avg. Amount per Student: $8,135. Of Those Receiving Any Aid: Receiving Need-Based Gift Aid: 91%. Avg. Award: $17,127. Receiving Need-Based Self-Help Aid: 100%. Avg. Award: $5,480. Financial Aid Deadline: 2/15.

Bard College

PO Box 5000, Annandale-On-Hudson, NY 12504-5000. **Admissions Phone:** (845) 758-7472. **Fax:** (845) 758-5208. **Email:** admission@bard.edu. **Website:** www.bard.edu. **Costs (2002–03):** Tuition and Fees: $27,680. Room & Board: $8,134. **Payment Plan(s):** installment plan, pre-payment plan. **Institutional Aid (est. 2002–03):** Institutional Aid, Need-Based:

$10,894,679. Institutional Aid, Non-Need-Based: $664,808. FT Undergrads Receiving Aid: 61%. Avg. Amount per Student: $21,466. Of Those Receiving Any Aid: Receiving Need-Based Gift Aid: 94%. Avg. Award: $17,724. Receiving Need-Based Self-Help Aid: 85%. Avg. Award: $4,244. Upon Graduation, Avg. Loan Debt per Student: $15,400. Financial Aid Deadline: 2/15, 2/1 (priority).

Barnard College

3009 Broadway, New York, NY 10027. **Admissions Phone:** (212) 854-2014. **Fax:** (212) 854-6220. **Email:** admissions@barnard.edu. **Website:** barnard.edu. **Costs (2002–03):** Tuition and Fees: $25,270. Room & Board: $10,140. **Payment Plan(s):** installment plan, deferred payment plan, pre-payment plan. **Institutional Aid (est. 2002–03):** Institutional Aid, Need-Based: $14,072,929. FT Undergrads Receiving Aid: 41%. Avg. Amount per Student: $24,416. FT Undergrads Receiving Non-Need-Based Gift Aid: 5%. Avg. Amount per Student: $4,239. Of Those Receiving Any Aid: Receiving Need-Based Gift Aid: 94%. Avg. Award: $20,114. Receiving Need-Based Self-Help Aid: 100%. Avg. Award: $4,991. Upon Graduation, Avg. Loan Debt per Student: $14,030. Financial Aid Deadline: 2/1.

Bates College

2 Andrews Road, Lewiston, ME 04240. **Admissions Phone:** (207) 786-6000. **Fax:** (207) 786-6025. **Email:** admissions@bates.edu. **Website:** www.bates.edu. **Application Website:** www.commonapp.org. **Costs (2002–03):** Comprehensive Fee: $35,750. **Institutional Aid (est. 2002–03):** Institutional Aid, Need-Based: $12,576,577. FT Undergrads Receiving Aid: 39%. Avg. Amount per Student: $24,193. Of Those Receiving Any Aid: Receiving Need-Based Gift Aid: 98%. Avg. Award: $20,674. Recieving Need-Based Self-Help Aid: 94%. Avg. Award: $4,200. Upon Graduation, Avg. Loan Debt per Student: $17,045. Financial Aid Deadline: 2/1, 11/15 (priority).

Baylor University

P.O. Box 97056, Waco, TX 76798-7056. **Admissions Phone:** (254) 710-3435; 800-229-5678. **Fax:** (254) 710-3436. **Email:** Admission_Serv_Office@Baylor.edu. **Website:** www.baylor.edu. **Costs (2003–04):** Tuition and Fees: $18,430 Board is 11-meal plan. **Room & Board:** $5,434. **Payment Plan(s):** installment plan. **Institutional Aid (est. 2002–03): Institutional Aid, Need-Based:** $15,884,983. **Institutional Aid, Non-Need-Based:** $14,180,203. **FT Undergrads Receiving Aid:** 44%. **Avg. Amount per Student:** $11,518. **FT Undergrads Receiving Non-Need-Based Gift Aid:** 33%. **Avg. Amount per Student:** $7,004. **Of Those Receiving Any Aid: Receiving Need-Based Gift Aid:** 94%. **Avg. Award:** $7,055. **Receiving Need-Based Self-Help Aid:** 84%. **Avg. Award:** $5,236. **Financial Aid Deadline:** rolling; 3/1 (priority).

Belmont University

1900 Belmont Boulevard, Nashville, TN 37212-3757. **Admissions Phone:** (615) 460-6785; (800) 56-ENROLL. **Fax:** (615) 460-5434. **Email:** buadmission@belmont.edu. **Website:** belmont.edu. **Costs (2002–03): Tuition and Fees:** $14,450. **Room & Board:** $8,029. **Payment Plan(s):** deferred payment plan. **Institutional Aid (2001–02): Institutional Aid, Need-Based:** $1,774,877. **Institutional Aid, Non-Need-Based:** $3,574,944. **FT Undergrads Receiving Aid:** 44%. **Avg. Amount per Student:** $2,649. **FT Undergrads Receiving Non-Need-Based Gift Aid:** 19%. **Avg. Amount per Student:** $2,708. **Of Those Receiving Any Aid: Receiving Need-Based Gift Aid:** 68%. **Avg. Award:** $2,014. **Receiving Need-Based Self-Help Aid:** 84%. **Avg. Award:** $3,188. **Upon Graduation, Avg. Loan Debt per Student:** $15,954. **Financial Aid Deadline:** rolling; 3/1 (priority).

Beloit College

700 College Street, Beloit, WI 53511. **Admissions Phone:** (608) 363-2500; (800) 9-BELOIT. **Fax:** (608) 363-2075. **Email:** admiss@beloit.edu. **Website:** www.beloit.edu. **Application Website:** http://admiss.beloit.edu. **Costs (2003–04): Tuition and Fees:** $24,386. **Room & Board:** $5,478. **Payment Plan(s):** installment plan. **Institutional Aid (est. 2002–03): Institutional Aid, Need-Based:** $10,504,779. **Institutional Aid, Non-Need-Based:** $1,669,271. **FT Undergrads Receiving Aid:** 70%. **Avg. Amount per Student:** $17,839. **FT Undergrads Receiving Non-Need-Based Gift Aid:** 7%. **Avg. Amount per Student:** $6,574. **Of Those Receiving Any Aid: Receiving Need-Based Gift Aid:** 100%. **Avg. Award:** $12,812. **Receiving Need-Based Self-Help Aid:** 100%. **Avg. Award:** $2,920. **Upon Graduation, Avg. Loan Debt per Student:** $14,942. **Financial Aid Deadline:** 3/1, 2/1 (priority).

Bennington College

One College Drive, Bennington, VT 05201. **Admissions Phone:** (800) 833-6845; (802) 440-4312. **Fax:** (802) 440-4320. **Email:** admissions@bennington.edu. **Website:** www.bennington.edu. **Costs (2002–03): Tuition and Fees:** $26,540. **Room & Board:** $6,700. **Payment Plan(s):** installment plan. **Institutional Aid (est. 2002–03): Institutional Aid, Need-Based:** $4,418,434. **Institutional Aid, Non-Need-Based:** $1,258,172. **FT Undergrads Receiving Aid:** 54%. **Avg. Amount per Student:** $20,119. **FT Undergrads Receiving Non-Need-Based Gift Aid:** 26%. **Avg. Amount per Student:** $12,186. **Of Those Receiving Any Aid: Receiving Need-Based Gift Aid:** 99%. **Avg. Award:** $15,802. **Receiving Need-Based Self-Help Aid:** 95%. **Avg. Award:** $4,776. **Upon Graduation, Avg. Loan Debt per Student:** $17,100. **Financial Aid Deadline:** 3/1 (priority).

Berea College

CPO 2220, Berea, KY 40404. **Admissions Phone:** (859) 985-3500; (800) 326-5948. **Fax:** (859) 985-3512. **Email:** admissions@berea.edu. **Website:** www.berea.edu. **Application Website:** www.berea.edu/admissions/admit2.htm. **Costs: (est. 2002–03) Tuition:** $0; **Full-tuition scholarship for every student. Room and Board:** $4,303. **Institutional Aid (est. 2002–03): Institutional Aid, Need-Based:** $27,271,186. **FT Undergrads Receiving Aid:** 100%. **Avg. Amount per Student:** $21,438. **Of Those Receiving Any Aid: Receiving Need-Based Gift Aid:** 100%. **Avg. Award:** $21,084. **Receiving Need-Based Self-Help Aid:** 100%. **Avg. Award:** $1,697. **Upon Graduation, Avg. Loan Debt per Student:** $6,233. **Financial Aid Deadline:** 8/1, 4/15 (priority).

Berklee College of Music

1140 Boylston Street, Boston, MA 02215. **Admissions Phone:** (800) BER-KLEE. **Fax:** (617) 747-2047. **Email:** admissions@berklee.edu. **Website:** www.berklee.edu. **Costs (2003–04): Tuition and Fees:** $19,694. **Room & Board:** $10,280. **Payment Plan(s):** installment plan. **Institutional Aid: Financial Aid Deadline:** rolling, 4/22 (priority).

Berry College

2277 Martha Berry Highway, NW, Mount Berry, GA 30149-0159. **Admissions Phone:** (706) 236-2215. **Fax:** (706) 290-2178. **Email:** admissions@berry.edu. **Website:**

www.berry.edu. **Application Website:** www.berry.edu/admissions/printapp.html. **Costs (2002–03): Tuition and Fees:** $14,295. **Room & Board:** $5,624. **Payment Plan(s):** installment plan. **Institutional Aid (2001–02): Institutional Aid, Need-Based:** $4,865,843. **Institutional Aid, Non-Need-Based:** $2,803,668. **FT Undergrads Receiving Aid:** 54%. **Avg. Amount per Student:** $11,684. **FT Undergrads Receiving Non-Need-Based Gift Aid:** 46%. **Avg. Amount per Student:** $10,129. **Of Those Receiving Any Aid: Receiving Need-Based Gift Aid:** 99%. **Avg. Award:** $9,170. **Receiving Need-Based Self-Help Aid:** 76%. **Avg. Award:** $3,503. **Upon Graduation, Avg. Loan Debt per Student:** $11,506. **Financial Aid Deadline:** 5/15, 4/1 (priority).

Birmingham—Southern College

900 Arkadelphia Road, Birmingham, AL 35254. **Admissions Phone:** (205) 226-4698; (800) 523-5793. **Fax:** (205) 226-3074. **Email:** admission@bsc.edu. **Website:** www.bsc.edu. **Application Website:** www.bsc.edu/admission/online.htm. **Costs (est. 2002–03): Tuition and Fees:** $17,185. **Room & Board:** $5,980. **Institutional Aid (est. 2002–03): Institutional Aid, Need-Based:** $713,142. **Institutional Aid, Non-Need-Based:** $11,253,857. **FT Undergrads Receiving Aid:** 38%. **Avg. Amount per Student:** $15,639. **FT Undergrads Receiving Non-Need-Based Gift Aid:** 49%. **Avg. Amount per Student:** $9,285. **Of Those Receiving Any Aid: Receiving Need-Based Gift Aid:** 100%. **Avg. Award:** $11,834. **Receiving Need-Based Self-Help Aid:** 69%. **Avg. Award:** $5,544. **Upon Graduation, Avg. Loan Debt per Student:** $12,000. **Financial Aid Deadline:** 5/1, 3/1 (priority).

Boston College*

140 Commonwealth Avenue, Devlin Hall 208, Chestnut Hill, MA 02467-3809. **Admissions Phone:** (617) 552-3100. **Fax:** (617) 552-0798. **Email:** ugadmis@bc.edu. **Website:** www.bc.edu. **Costs (2002–03): Tuition and Fees:** $25,862. **Room & Board:** $8,990. **Institutional Aid: FT Undergrads Receiving Aid:** 42%. **Avg. Amount per Student:** $18,830. **FT Undergrads Receiving Non-Need-Based Gift Aid:** 4%. **Avg. Amount per Student:** $5,585. **Of Those Receiving Any Aid: Receiving Need-Based Gift Aid:** 92%. **Avg. Award:** $13,275. **Receiving Need-Based Self-Help Aid:** 100%.

Avg. Award: $5,554. Upon Graduation, Avg. Loan Debt per Student: $16,732. Financial Aid Deadline: 2/1 (priority).

Boston University

121 Bay State Road, Boston, MA 02215. Admissions Phone: (617) 353-2300. Fax: (617) 353-9695. Email: admissions@bu.edu; intadmis@bu.edu. Website: www.bu.edu. Application Website: www.bu.edu/admissions/apply/index.html. Costs (2003–04): Tuition and Fees: $28,906 (expenses vary w/type of accomodation/meal plan). Room & Board: $9,288. Payment Plan(s): installment plan, deferred payment plan. Institutional Aid (est. 2002–03): Institutional Aid, Need-Based: $106,015,903. Institutional Aid, Non-Need-Based: $18,799,310. FT Undergrads Receiving Aid: 46%. Avg. Amount per Student: $24,309. FT Undergrads Receiving Non-Need-Based Gift Aid: 14%. Avg. Amount per Student: $13,556. Of Those Receiving Any Aid: Receiving Need-Based Gift Aid: 94%. Avg. Award: $16,400. Receiving Need-Based Self-Help Aid: 92%. Avg. Award: $5,592. Upon Graduation, Avg. Loan Debt per Student: $17,941 (includes only graduating seniors who received student loans). Financial Aid Deadline: 2/15 (priority); 11/1 for early decision candidates.

Bowdoin College

5000 College Station, Brunswick, ME 04011-8441. Admissions Phone: (207) 725-3100. Fax: (207) 725-3101. Email: admissions@bowdoin.edu. Website: www.bowdoin.edu. Costs (2002–03): Tuition and Fees: $28,685. Room & Board: $7,305. Payment Plan(s): installment plan, deferred payment plan. Institutional Aid (est. 2002–03): Institutional Aid, Need-Based: $13,368,685. Institutional Aid, Non-Need-Based: $123,000. FT Undergrads Receiving Aid: 40%. Avg. Amount per Student: $24,675. FT Undergrads Receiving Non-Need-Based Gift Aid: 2%. Avg. Amount per Student: $1,000. Of Those Receiving Any Aid: Receiving Need-Based Gift Aid: 100%. Avg. Award: $20,890. Receiving Need-Based Self-Help Aid: 92%. Avg. Award: $3,785. Upon Graduation, Avg. Loan Debt per Student: $15,307. Financial Aid Deadline: 2/15.

Bradley University

1501 West Bradley Avenue, Peoria, IL 61625. Admissions Phone: (309) 677-1000; (800) 447-6460 Fax: (309) 677-2797. Email: admissions@bradley.edu. Website: www.bradley.edu. Costs (2002–03): Tuition and Fees: $16,110. Room & Board: $5,800. Payment Plan(s): installment plan, deferred payment plan. Institutional Aid (2001–02): Institutional Aid, Need-Based: $10,427,608. Institutional Aid, Non-Need-Based: $10,427,608. FT Undergrads Receiving Aid: 71%. Avg. Amount per Student: $11,997. FT Undergrads Receiving Non-Need-Based Gift Aid: 23%. Avg. Amount per Student: $7,807. Of Those Receiving Any Aid: Receiving Need-Based Gift Aid: 100%. Avg. Award: $8,155. Receiving Need-Based Self-Help Aid: 73%. Avg. Award: $5,278. Upon Graduation, Avg. Loan Debt per Student: $16,531. Financial Aid Deadline: rolling; 3/1 (priority).

Brandeis University

415 South Street, Waltham, MA 02454. Admissions Phone: (781) 736-3500; (800) 622-0622 (out-of-state). Fax: (781) 736-3536. Email: sendinfo@brandeis.edu. Website: www.brandeis.edu. Costs (2003–04): Tuition and Fees: $28,165. Room & Board: $7,849. Institutional Aid (est. 2002–03): Institutional Aid, Need-Based: $19,411,823. Institutional Aid, Non-Need-Based: $7,074,080. FT Undergrads Receiving Aid: 50%. Avg. Amount per Student: $21,053. FT Undergrads Receiving Non-Need-Based Gift Aid: 20%. Avg. Amount per Student: $14,846. Of Those Receiving Any Aid: Receiving Need-Based Gift Aid: 95%. Avg. Award: $16,844. Receiving Need-Based Self-Help Aid: 91%. Avg. Award: $5,218. Financial Aid Deadline: rolling; 1/31 (priority).

Brigham Young University

A-127 ASB, BYU, Provo, UT 84602. Admissions Phone: (801) 422-2507; (801) 422-1211. Fax: (801) 422-4264. Email: admissions@byu.edu. Website: www.byu.edu. Application Website: ar.byu.edu/admissions. Costs (est. 2003-04): Tuition and Fees: $3,150. Room & Board: $4,874. Payment Plan(s): deferred payment plan, pre-payment plan. Institutional Aid (2001–02): Institutional Aid, Need-Based: $1,770,000. Institutional Aid, Non-Need-Based: $20,774,000. FT Undergrads Receiving Aid: 31%. Avg. Amount per Student: $3,853. FT Undergrads Receiving Non-Need-Based Gift Aid: 27%. Avg. Amount per Student: $3,148. Of Those Receiving Any Aid: Receiving Need-Based Gift Aid: 59%. Avg. Award: $2,042. Receiving Need-Based Self-Help Aid: 65%. Avg. Award: $1,811. Upon

Graduation, Avg. Loan Debt per Student: $11,000. Financial Aid Deadline: rolling; 4/15 (priority).

Brown University

Box 1876, Providence, RI 02912. Admissions Phone: (401) 863-2378. Fax: (401) 863-9300. Website: www.brown.edu. Costs (2003–04): Tuition and Fees: $29,846. Room & Board: $8,096. Payments plan(s): installment plan. Institutional Aid (est. 2002–03): Institutional Aid, Need-Based: $39,854,532. FT Undergrads Receiving Aid: 44%. Avg. Amount per Student: $23,015. FT Undergrads Receiving Non-Need-Based Gift Aid: 12%. Avg. Amount per Student: $2,910. Of Those Receiving Any Aid: Receiving Need-Based Gift Aid: 98%. Avg. Award: $20,893. Receiving Need-Based Self-Help Aid: 80%. Avg. Award: $3,141. Upon Graduation, Avg. Loan Debt per Student: $21,700. Financial Aid Deadline: 2/1.

Bryn Mawr College

101 N. Merion Avenue, Bryn Mawr, PA 19010-2899. Admissions Phone: (610) 526-5152; (800) 262-1885. Fax: (610) 526-7471. Email: admissions@brynmawr.edu. Website: brynmawr.edu. Costs (2003–04): Tuition and Fees: $27,520. Room & Board: $9,370. Payment Plan(s): installment plan. Institutional Aid (est. 2002–03): Institutional Aid, Need-Based: $11,680,999. FT Undergrads Receiving Aid: 59%. Avg. Amount per Student: $22,634. FT Undergrads Receiving Non-Need-Based Gift Aid: 1%. Avg. Amount per Student: $1,730. Of Those Receiving Any Aid: Receiving Need-Based Gift Aid: 94%. Avg. Award: $19,613. Receiving Need-Based Self-Help Aid: 92%. Avg. Award: $4,186. Financial Aid Deadline: 2/7.

Bucknell University

Freas Hall, Lewisburg, PA 17837. Admissions Phone: (570) 577-1101. Fax: (570) 577-3538. Email: admissions@bucknell.edu. Website: www.bucknell.edu/. Application Website: www.applyweb.com/aw?buckn. Costs (2003–04): Tuition and Fees: $28,960. Room & Board: $6,302. Payment Plan(s): installment plan. Institutional Aid (est. 2002–03): Institutional Aid, Need-Based: $39,028,645. FT Undergrads Receiving Aid: 48%. Avg. Amount per Student: $18,072. Of Those Receiving Any Aid: Receiving Need-Based Gift Aid: 93%. Avg. Award: $17,000.

Receiving Need-Based Self-Help Aid: 100%. Avg. Award: $4,800. Upon Graduation, Avg. Loan Debt per Student: $16,000

California Institute of Technology

Mail Code: 328-87, Pasadena, CA 91125. Admissions Phone: (626) 395-6341. Fax: (626) 683-3026. Email: ugadmissions@caltech.edu. Website: www.caltech.edu. Application Website: www.admissions.caltech.edu. Costs (2003–04): Tuition and Fees: $24,117. Room & Board: $7,560. Payment Plan(s): installment plan. Institutional Aid (est. 2002–03): Institutional Aid, Need-Based: $10,844,030. Institutional Aid, Non-Need-Based: $2,550,099. FT Undergrads Receiving Aid: 57%. Avg. Amount per Student: $23,427. FT Undergrads Receiving Non-Need-Based Gift Aid: 19%. Avg. Amount per Student: $14,129. Of Those Receiving Any Aid: Receiving Need-Based Gift Aid: 100%. Avg. Award: $21,701. Receiving Need-Based Self-Help Aid: 76%. Avg. Award: $2,305. Upon Graduation, Avg. Loan Debt per Student: $10,244. Financial Aid Deadline: 3/2, 1/15 (priority).

California Polytechnic State University

1 Grand Avenue, San Luis Obispo, CA 93407. Admissions Phone: (805) 756-2311. Fax: (805) 756-5400. Website: www.calpoly.edu. Costs (2002–03): Fees: $2,877(Non-residents pay additional per-unit fee). Room & Board: $7,119. Payment Plan(s): installment plan, deferred payment plan, pre-payment plan. Institutional Aid (2001–02): Institutional Aid, Need-Based: $1,219,704. FT Undergrads Receiving Aid: 36%. Avg. Amount per Student: $6,847. Of Those Receiving Any Aid: Receiving Need-Based Gift Aid: 75%. Avg. Award: $1,352. Receiving Need-Based Self-Help Aid: 78%. Avg. Award: $3,943. Upon Graduation, Avg. Loan Debt per Student: $12,842. Financial Aid Deadline: 6/3, 3/2 (priority).

California State University—Chico

400 West First Street, Chico, CA 95929-0722. Admissions Phone: (530) 898-4428; (800) 542-4426. Fax: (530) 898-6456. Email: info@csuchico.edu. Website: www.csuchico.edu. Application Website: www.csumentor.edu. Costs (est. 2003-04): Tuition and Fees, In-State: $2,275 Tuition and Fees, Out-of-State: $10,735. Room &

Board: $7,312. Institutional Aid (2001–02): Institutional Aid, Non-Need-Based: $1,121,884. Financial Aid Deadline: rolling; 3/2 (priority).

Calvin College

3201 Burton Street S.E., Grand Rapids, MI 49546. Admissions Phone: (616) 957-6106; (800) 668-0122. Fax: (616) 957-8513. Email: admissions@calvin.edu. Website: www.calvin.edu. Application Website: www.calvin.edu/admin/admissions/. Costs (2003–04): Tuition and Fees: $16,775. Room & Board: $5,840. Payment Plan(s): installment plan, pre-payment plan. Institutional Aid (est. 2002–03): Institutional Aid, Need-Based: $13,281,900. Institutional Aid, Non-Need-Based: $3,706,000. FT Undergrads Receiving Aid: 64%. Avg. Amount per Student: $12,252. FT Undergrads Receiving Non-Need-Based Gift Aid: 26%. Avg. Amount per Student: $3,884. Of Those Receiving Any Aid: Receiving Need-Based Gift Aid: 99%. Avg. Award: $7,922. Receiving Need-Based Self-Help Aid: 72%. Avg. Award: $6,201. Upon Graduation, Avg. Loan Debt per Student: $17,000. Financial Aid Deadline: rolling; 2/15 (priority).

Carleton College

100 South College Street, Northfield, MN 55057. Admissions Phone: (507) 646-4190; (800) 995-2275. Fax: (507) 646-4526. Email: admissions@acs.carleton.edu. Website: www.carleton.edu. Application Website: www.carleton.edu/admissions/application/. Costs (2002–03): Tuition and Fees: $26,910. Room & Board: $5,535. Payment Plan(s): installment plan, pre-payment plan. Institutional Aid (2001–02): Institutional Aid, Need-Based: $13,798,407. Institutional Aid, Non-Need-Based: $345,685. FT Undergrads Receiving Aid: 54%. Avg. Amount per Student: $18,832. FT Undergrads Receiving Non-Need-Based Gift Aid: 8%. Avg. Amount per Student: $2,320. Of Those Receiving Any Aid: Receiving Need-Based Gift Aid: 98%. Avg. Award: $13,611. Receiving Need-Based Self-Help Aid: 99%. Avg. Award: $3,976. Upon Graduation, Avg. Loan Debt per Student: $14,543. Financial Aid Deadline: 2/15.

Carnegie Mellon University*

5000 Forbes Avenue, Pittsburgh, PA 15213. Admissions Phone: (412) 268-2082. Fax: (412) 268-7838. Email: undergraduate-admissions@andrew.cmu.edu. Website: www.cmu.edu. Application Website:

www.cmu.edu/enrollment/admission. Costs (2003–04): Tuition and Fees: $27,116. Room & Board: $7,534. Payment Plan(s): installment plan. Institutional Aid: FT Undergrads Receiving Aid: 48%. Avg. Amount per Student: $18,069. FT Undergrads Receiving Non-Need-Based Gift Aid: 15%. Avg. Amount per Student: $10,552. Of Those Receiving Any Aid: Receiving Need-Based Gift Aid: 94%. Avg. Award: $12,874. Receiving Need-Based Self-Help Aid: 96%. Avg. Award: $6,386. Upon Graduation, Avg. Loan Debt per Student: $18,280. Financial Aid Deadline: 5/1, 2/15 (priority).

Case Western Reserve University

103 Tomlinson Hall, 10900 Euclid Avenue, Cleveland, OH 44106. Admissions Phone: (216) 368-4450. Fax: (216) 368-5111. Email: admission@po.cwru.edu. Website: cwru.edu. Application Website: cwru.edu/ugadmis/. Costs (2003–04): Tuition and Fees: $24,342. Room & Board: $7,660. Payment Plan(s): installment plan, pre-payment plan. Institutional Aid (est. 2002–03): Institutional Aid, Need-Based: $19,813,104. Institutional Aid, Non-Need-Based: $12,708,124. FT Undergrads Receiving Aid: 54%. Avg. Amount per Student: $21,815. FT Undergrads Receiving Non-Need-Based Gift Aid: 36%. Avg. Amount per Student: $11,895. Of Those Receiving Any Aid: Receiving Need-Based Gift Aid: 100%. Avg. Award: $14,479. Receiving Need-Based Self-Help Aid: 90%. Avg. Award: $6,642. Upon Graduation, Avg. Loan Debt per Student: $21,830. Financial Aid Deadline: 4/15, 2/1 (priority).

Catholic University of America

110 McMahon Hall, Washington, DC 20064-0002. Admissions Phone: (800) 673-2772; (202) 319-5305. Fax: (202) 319-6533. Email: cua-admissions@cua.edu. Website: www.cua.edu. Application Website: http://admissions/cua.edu/application/. Costs (2003–04): Tuition and Fees: $23,250. Room & Board: $9,002. Payment Plan(s): installment plan, deferred payment plan. Institutional Aid (est. 2002–03): Institutional Aid, Need-Based: $18,199,736. Institutional Aid, Non-Need-Based: $2,399,634. FT Undergrads Receiving Aid: 78%. Avg. Amount per Student: $19,390. FT Undergrads Receiving Non-Need-Based Gift Aid: 11%. Avg. Amount per Student: $9,019. Of Those Receiving Any Aid: Receiving

KAPLAN 219

Need-Based Gift Aid: 35%. Avg. Award: $5,113. Receiving Need-Based Self-Help Aid: 56%. Avg. Award: $5,633. Financial Aid Deadline: 2/1, 1/15 (priority).

Centre College

600 West Walnut Street, Danville, KY 40422. **Admissions Phone:** (859) 238-5350; (800) 423-6236. **Fax:** (859) 238-5373. **Email:** admissions@centre.edu. **Website:** http://www.centre.edu. **Application Website:** http://www.centre.edu/admission/admission.html. **Costs (2002–03):** Tuition and Fees: $19,125. Room & Board: $6,475. **Payment Plan(s):** installment plan. **Institutional Aid (est. 2002–03):** Institutional Aid, Need-Based: $6,462,978. Institutional Aid, Non-Need-Based: $1,903,916. FT Undergrads Receiving Aid: 66%. Avg. Amount per Student: $19,585. FT Undergrads Receiving Non-Need-Based Gift Aid: 8%. Avg. Amount per Student: $9,527. Of Those Receiving Any Aid: Receiving Need-Based Gift Aid: 100%. Avg. Award: $12,687. Receiving Need-Based Self-Help Aid: 82%. Avg. Award: $4,072. Upon Graduation, Avg. Loan Debt per Student: $14,300. Financial Aid Deadline: 3/1.

Chatham College

Woodland Road, Pittsburgh, PA 15232. **Admissions Phone:** (412) 365-1290; (800) 837-1290. **Fax:** (412) 365-1609. **Email:** admissions@chatham.edu. **Website:** www.chatham.edu. **Costs (2002–03):** Tuition and Fees: $19,742. Room & Board: $6,688. **Payment Plan(s):** installment plan. **Institutional Aid (est. 2002–03):** Institutional Aid, Need-Based: $1,553,314. Institutional Aid, Non-Need-Based: $2,335,555. FT Undergrads Receiving Aid: 79%. Avg. Amount per Student: $22,535. FT Undergrads Receiving Non-Need-Based Gift Aid: 14%. Avg. Amount per Student: $5,198. Of Those Receiving Any Aid: Receiving Need-Based Gift Aid: 100%. Avg. Award: $7,443. Receiving Need-Based Self-Help Aid: 94%. Avg. Award: $5,591. Upon Graduation, Avg. Loan Debt per Student: $18,655. Financial Aid Deadline: 5\1

Citadel

171 Moultrie Street, Charleston, SC 29409-0204. **Admissions Phone:** (843) 953-5230; (800) 868-1842. **Fax:** (843) 953-7036. **Email:** admissions@citadel.edu. **Website:** citadel.edu. **Application Website:** http://www.citadel.edu/admission/cadmission/cadapplication.html. Costs

(2002–03): Tuition and Fees, In-State: $4,946. Tuition and Fees, Out-of-State: $12,417. (Freshman pay a $4,780 deposit & upperclass pay $1,520.) **Room & Board:** $4,575. **Payment Plan(s):** installment plan, pre-payment plan. **Institutional Aid (est. 2002–03):** Institutional Aid, Need-Based: $1,750,000. Institutional Aid, Non-Need-Based: $1,850,000. FT Undergrads Receiving Aid: 45%. Avg. Amount per Student: $6,048. FT Undergrads Receiving Non-Need-Based Gift Aid: 6%. Avg. Amount per Student: $13,986. Of Those Receiving Any Aid: Receiving Need-Based Gift Aid: 65%. Avg. Award: $7,010. Receiving Need-Based Self-Help Aid: 57%. Avg. Award: $3,900. Upon Graduation, Avg. Loan Debt per Student: $13,901. Financial Aid Deadline: 2/28, 3/17 (priority).

City University of New York—Baruch College

One Bernard Baruch Way, Box H-0720, New York, NY 10010-5585. **Admissions Phone:** (646) 312-1400. **Email:** admissions@baruch.cuny.edu. **Website:** www.baruch.cuny.edu. **Costs (est. 2003-04):** Tuition and Fees, In-State: $4,100. Tuition and Fees, Out-of-State: $7,700. **Payment Plan(s):** installment plan, deferred payment plan. **Institutional Aid (est. 2002–03):** Institutional Aid, Need-Based: $940,000. Institutional Aid, Non-Need-Based: $1,800,000. FT Undergrads Receiving Aid: 86%. Avg. Amount per Student: $4,705. FT Undergrads Receiving Non-Need-Based Gift Aid: 6%. Avg. Amount per Student: $1,600. Of Those Receiving Any Aid: Receiving Need-Based Gift Aid: 89%. Avg. Award: $4,150. Receiving Need-Based Self-Help Aid: 39%. Avg. Award: $3,471. Upon Graduation, Avg. Loan Debt per Student: $9,400. Financial Aid Deadline: 4/30, 3/15 (priority).

City University of New York—Brooklyn

2900 Bedford Avenue, Brooklyn, NY 11210-2889. **Admissions Phone:** (718) 951-5001. **Fax:** (718) 951-4506. **Email:** adminqry@brooklyn.cuny.edu. **Website:** www.brooklyn.cuny.edu. **Costs (est. 2002–03):** Tuition and Fees, In-State: $3,553. Tuition and Fees, Out-of-State: $7,153. **Payment Plan(s):** installment plan. **Institutional Aid (est. 2002–03):** Institutional Aid, Need-Based: $800,000. Institutional Aid, Non-Need-Based: $900,000. FT Undergrads Receiving Aid: 77%. Avg. Amount per Student: $4,700. FT

Undergrads Receiving Non-Need-Based Gift Aid: 10%. Avg. Amount per Student: $3,200. Of Those Receiving Any Aid: Receiving Need-Based Gift Aid: 90%. Avg. Award: $2,900. Receiving Need-Based Self-Help Aid: 88%. Avg. Award: $1,850. Upon Graduation, Avg. Loan Debt per Student: $13,200. Financial Aid Deadline: rolling; 4/1 (priority).

City University of New York—John Jay College of Criminal Justice

445 West 59th Street, New York, NY 10019-1128. **Admissions Phone:** (212) 237-8865. **Fax:** (212) 237-8777. **Email:** admiss@jjay.cuny.edu. **Website:** www.jjay.cuny.edu. **Costs (2002–03):** Tuition and Fees, In-State: $3,309. Tuition and Fees, Out-of-State: $6,509. **Payment Plan(s):** installment plan, deferred payment plan. **Institutional Aid (2001–02):** Institutional Aid, Non-Need-Based: $814,000. FT Undergrads Receiving Aid: 95%. Avg. Amount per Student: $5,100. FT Undergrads Receiving Non-Need-Based Gift Aid: 1%. Avg. Amount per Student: $500. Of Those Receiving Any Aid: Receiving Need-Based Gift Aid: 70%. Receiving Need-Based Self-Help Aid: 5%. Avg. Award: $2,500. Upon Graduation, Avg. Loan Debt per Student: $10,000. Financial Aid Deadline: 6/1 (priority).

Claremont McKenna College

890 Columbia Avenue, Claremont, CA 91711. **Admissions Phone:** (909) 621-8088. **Fax:** (909) 621-8516. **Email:** admissions@claremontmckenna.edu. **Website:** claremontmckenna.edu. **Costs (2002–03):** Tuition and Fees: $26,350. Room & Board: $8,740. **Payment Plan(s):** installment plan, pre-payment plan. **Institutional Aid (est. 2002–03):** Institutional Aid, Need-Based: $9,798,524. Institutional Aid, Non-Need-Based: $460,451. FT Undergrads Receiving Aid: 56%. Avg. Amount per Student: $23,059. FT Undergrads Receiving Non-Need-Based Gift Aid: 9%. Avg. Amount per Student: $6,160. Of Those Receiving Any Aid: Receiving Need-Based Gift Aid: 99%. Avg. Award: $19,742. Receiving Need-Based Self-Help Aid: 89%. Avg. Award: $3,692. Upon Graduation, Avg. Loan Debt per Student: $16,914. Financial Aid Deadline: 2/1.

Clark University

950 Main Street, Worcester, MA 01610. **Admissions Phone:** (508) 793-7431 (in-state); (800) GO-CLARK (out-of-state). **Fax:** (508) 793-8821. **Email:** admissions@clarku.edu. **Website:** www.clarku.edu. **Application Website:** www.clarku.edu/prospective/undergrads/. **Costs (2003–04): Tuition and Fees:** $26,965. Tuition discount for students from immediate vicinity. **Room & Board:** $5,150. **Payment Plan(s):** installment plan, pre-payment plan. **Institutional Aid (est. 2002–03): Institutional Aid, Need-Based:** $12,321,675. **Institutional Aid, Non-Need-Based:** $4,602,464. **FT Undergrads Receiving Aid:** 56%. **Avg. Amount per Student:** $20,515. **FT Undergrads Receiving Non-Need-Based Gift Aid:** 13%. **Avg. Amount per Student:** $11,924. Of Those Receiving Any Aid: Receiving Need-Based Gift Aid: 90%. **Avg. Award:** $10,920. Receiving Need-Based Self-Help Aid: 89%. **Avg. Award:** $5,003. Upon Graduation, **Avg. Loan Debt per Student:** $17,875. **Financial Aid Deadline:** 2/1 (priority).

Clemson University

105 Sikes Hall, Clemson, SC 29634. **Admissions Phone:** (864) 656-2287. **Fax:** (864) 656-2464. **Email:** cuadmissions@clemson.edu. **Website:** clemson.edu. **Application Website:** clemson.edu/attend/undrgrd/apps/apppage.htm. **Costs (2002–03): Tuition and Fees, In-State:** $5,834 **Tuition and Fees, Out-of-State:** $12,932. **Room & Board:** $4,454. **Payment Plan(s):** installment plan, pre-payment plan. **Institutional Aid (est. 2002–03): Institutional Aid, Need-Based:** $2,313,893. **Institutional Aid, Non-Need-Based:** $4,113,588. **FT Undergrads Receiving Aid:** 36%. **Avg. Amount per Student:** $8,518. **FT Undergrads Receiving Non-Need-Based Gift Aid:** 33%. **Avg. Amount per Student:** $5,696. Of Those Receiving Any Aid: Receiving Need-Based Gift Aid: 49%. **Avg. Award:** $3,497. Receiving Need-Based Self-Help Aid: 69%. **Avg. Award:** $4,552. **Financial Aid Deadline:** 4/1 (priority).

Colby College

4000 Mayflower Hill, Waterville, ME 04901-8840. **Admissions Phone:** (800) 723-3032. **Fax:** (207) 872-3474. **Email:** admissions@colby.edu. **Website:** www.colby.edu. **Application Website:** www.colby.edu/admissions. **Costs (2002–03): Comprehensive Fees:** $35,800.

Institutional Aid (est. 2002–03): Institutional Aid, Need-Based: $11,594,025. **FT Undergrads Receiving Aid:** 38%. **Avg. Amount per Student:** $22,055. Of Those Receiving Any Aid: Receiving Need-Based Gift Aid: 91%. **Avg. Award:** $20,531. Receiving Need-Based Self-Help Aid: 79%. **Avg. Award:** $4,279. Upon Graduation, **Avg. Loan Debt per Student:** $17,270. **Financial Aid Deadline:** 2/1.

Colgate University

13 Oak Drive, Hamilton, NY 13346. **Admissions Phone:** (315) 228-7401. **Fax:** (315) 228-7544. **Email:** admission@mail.colgate.edu. **Website:** www.colgate.edu. **Costs (2002–03): Tuition and Fees:** $28,355. **Room & Board:** $6,775. **Payment Plan(s):** installment plan, pre-payment plan. **Institutional Aid (est. 2002–03): Institutional Aid, Need-Based:** $23,646,531. **FT Undergrads Receiving Aid:** 45%. **Avg. Amount per Student:** $23,490. Of Those Receiving Any Aid: Receiving Need-Based Gift Aid: 94%. **Avg. Award:** $19,964. Receiving Need-Based Self-Help Aid: 73%. **Avg. Award:** $3,919. Upon Graduation, **Avg. Loan Debt per Student:** $12,984. **Financial Aid Deadline:** 2/1.

College of Charleston

66 George Street, Charleston, SC 29424. **Admissions Phone:** (843) 953-5670. **Fax:** (843) 953-6322. **Email:** admissions@cofc.edu. **Website:** www.cofc.edu. **Costs (2002–03): Tuition and Fees, In-State:** $4,858 **Tuition and Fees, Out-of-State:** $10,974. **Room & Board:** $7,717. **Institutional Aid (2001–02): Institutional Aid, Need-Based:** $736,918. **Institutional Aid, Non-Need-Based:** $2,927,892. **FT Undergrads Receiving Aid:** 34%. **Avg. Amount per Student:** $7,508. **FT Undergrads Receiving Non-Need-Based Gift Aid:** 20%. **Avg. Amount per Student:** $5,511. Of Those Receiving Any Aid: Receiving Need-Based Gift Aid: 62%. **Avg. Award:** $2,138. Receiving Need-Based Self-Help Aid: 86%. **Avg. Award:** $3,203. Upon Graduation, **Avg. Loan Debt per Student:** $15,167. **Financial Aid Deadline:** rolling; 3/15 (priority).

College of New Jersey

P.O. Box 7718, Ewing, NJ 08628-0718. **Admissions Phone:** (609) 771-2131; (800) 624-0967. **Fax:** (609) 637-5174. **Email:** admiss@vm.tcnj.edu. **Website:** tcnj.edu. **Costs (2003–04): Tuition and Fees, In-State:** $7,516 **Tuition and Fees, Out-of-**

State: $11,713. **Room & Board:** $7,416. **Payment Plan(s):** installment plan. **Institutional Aid (est. 2002–03): Institutional Aid, Need-Based:** $9,027,108. **Institutional Aid, Non-Need-Based:** $6,584,581. **FT Undergrads Receiving Aid:** 41%. **Avg. Amount per Student:** $2,449. **FT Undergrads Receiving Non-Need-Based Gift Aid:** 14%. **Avg. Amount per Student:** $2,241. Of Those Receiving Any Aid: Receiving Need-Based Gift Aid: 69%. **Avg. Award:** $2,271. Receiving Need-Based Self-Help Aid: 78%. **Avg. Award:** $2,760. Upon Graduation, **Avg. Loan Debt per Student:** $5,490. **Financial Aid Deadline:** 3/3 (priority).

College of the Atlantic

105 Eden Street, Bar Harbor, ME 04609. **Admissions Phone:** (207) 288-5015; (800) 528-0025. **Fax:** (207) 288-4126. **Email:** inquiry@ecology.coa.edu. **Website:** coa.edu. **Costs (2002–03): Tuition and Fees:** $22,536. **Room & Board:** $6,087. **Payment Plan(s):** installment plan, pre-payment plan. **Institutional Aid (est. 2002–03): Institutional Aid, Need-Based:** $1,578,651. **Institutional Aid, Non-Need-Based:** $16,000. **FT Undergrads Receiving Aid:** 80%. **Avg. Amount per Student:** $19,800. **FT Undergrads Receiving Non-Need-Based Gift Aid:** 2%. **Avg. Amount per Student:** $2,900. Of Those Receiving Any Aid: Receiving Need-Based Gift Aid: 96%. **Avg. Award:** $15,700. Receiving Need-Based Self-Help Aid: 79%. **Avg. Award:** $5,422. Upon Graduation, **Avg. Loan Debt per Student:** $12,992. **Financial Aid Deadline:** 2/15, 2/1 (priority).

College of the Holy Cross

1 College Street, Worcester, MA 01610-2395. **Admissions Phone:** (508) 793-2443; (800) 442-2421. **Fax:** (508) 793-3888. **Email:** admissions@holycross.edu. **Website:** holycross.edu. **Costs (2003–04): Tuition and Fees:** $28,011. **Room & Board:** $8,440. **Payment Plan(s):** installment plan, pre-payment plan. **Institutional Aid (2001–02): Institutional Aid, Need-Based:** $12,424,503. **Institutional Aid, Non-Need-Based:** $1,616,230. **FT Undergrads Receiving Aid:** 50%. **Avg. Amount per Student:** $18,427. **FT Undergrads Receiving Non-Need-Based Gift Aid:** 7%. **Avg. Amount per Student:** $8,470. Of Those Receiving Any Aid: Receiving Need-Based Gift Aid: 83%. **Avg. Award:** $13,005. Receiving Need-Based Self-Help Aid: 71%.

Avg. Award: $6,812. Upon Graduation, Avg. Loan Debt per Student: $16,063. Financial Aid Deadline: 2/1.

College of the Ozarks

P.O. Box 17, Point Lookout, MO 65616. Admissions Phone: (417) 334-6411; (800) 222-0525. Fax: (417) 335-2616. Email: admiss4@cofo.edu. Website: www.cofo.edu. Costs (2002–03): Fees: $200. Room & Board: $2,900. Institutional Aid (est. 2002–03): Institutional Aid, Need-Based: $10,188,809. Institutional Aid, Non-Need-Based: $145,402. FT Undergrads Receiving Aid: 19%. Avg. Amount per Student: $12,467. FT Undergrads Receiving Non-Need-Based Gift Aid: 2%. Avg. Amount per Student: $12,467. Of Those Receiving Any Aid: Receiving Need-Based Gift Aid: 91%. Avg. Award: $7,716. Receiving Need-Based Self-Help Aid: 91%. Avg. Award: $2,884. Upon Graduation, Avg. Loan Debt per Student: $6,000. Financial Aid Deadline: 3/15 (priority).

College of William and Mary

P.O. Box 8795, Williamsburg, VA 23187-8795. Admissions Phone: (757) 221-4223. Fax: (757) 221-1242. Email: admiss@wm.edu. Website: www.wm.edu. Application Website: wm.edu/admission/new/index.html. Costs (2002–03): Tuition and Fees, In-State: $5,488 Tuition and Fees, Out-of-State: $19,656. Room & Board: $5,534. Payment Plan(s): pre-payment plan. Institutional Aid (2001–02): Institutional Aid, Need-Based: $3,582,800. Institutional Aid, Non-Need-Based: $852,110. FT Undergrads Receiving Aid: 26%. Avg. Amount per Student: $8,154. FT Undergrads Receiving Non-Need-Based Gift Aid: 19%. Avg. Amount per Student: $6,284. Of Those Receiving Any Aid: Receiving Need-Based Gift Aid: 91%. Avg. Award: $6,356. Receiving Need-Based Self-Help Aid: 77%. Avg. Award: $3,115. Upon Graduation, Avg. Loan Debt per Student: $19,762. Financial Aid Deadline: 3/15, 2/15 (priority).

College of Wooster, The

1189 Beall Avenue, Wooster, OH 44691. Admissions Phone: (330) 263-2322; (800) 877-9905. Fax: (330) 263-2621. Email: admissions@wooster.edu. Website: www.wooster.edu. Costs (2003–04): Tuition and Fees: $25,040. Room & Board: $6,260. Payment Plan(s): installment plan, deferred payment plan. Institutional Aid

(est. 2002–03): Institutional Aid, Need-Based: $15,277,493. Institutional Aid, Non-Need-Based: $6,912,838. FT Undergrads Receiving Aid: 63%. Avg. Amount per Student: $20,629. FT Undergrads Receiving Non-Need-Based Gift Aid: 38%. Avg. Amount per Student: $9,955. Of Those Receiving Any Aid: Receiving Need-Based Gift Aid: 100%. Avg. Award: $15,640. Receiving Need-Based Self-Help Aid: 84%. Avg. Award: $4,660. Upon Graduation, Avg. Loan Debt per Student: $17,545. Financial Aid Deadline: rolling; 2/15 (priority).

Colorado College

14 East Cache La Poudre, Colorado Springs, CO 80903. Admissions Phone: (719) 389-6344; (800) 542-7214. Fax: (719) 389-6816. Email: admissions @coloradocollege.edu. Website: www.coloradocollege.edu. Costs (est. 2003-04): Tuition and Fees: $27,635. Room & Board: $6,840. Payment Plan(s): installment plan. Institutional Aid (est. 2002–03): Institutional Aid, Need-Based: $12,446,922. Institutional Aid, Non-Need-Based: $1,972,475. FT Undergrads Receiving Aid: 43%. Avg. Amount per Student: $21,385. FT Undergrads Receiving Non-Need-Based Gift Aid: 13%. Avg. Amount per Student: $15,630. Of Those Receiving Any Aid: Receiving Need-Based Gift Aid: 94%. Avg. Award: $18,759. Receiving Need-Based Self-Help Aid: 91%. Avg. Award: $4,543. Upon Graduation, Avg. Loan Debt per Student: $13,500. Financial Aid Deadline: 2/15.

Columbia University— Columbia College

212 Hamilton Hall, Mail Code 2807, 1130 Amsterdam Avenue, New York, NY 10027. Fax: (212) 854-1209. Website: www.columbia.edu. Application Website: www.studentaffairs.columbia.edu/admissions/. Costs (2002–03): Tuition and Fees: $28,206. Room & Board: $8,546. Payment Plan(s): installment plan, pre-payment plan. Institutional Aid (est. 2002–03): Institutional Aid, Need-Based: $28,086. FT Undergrads Receiving Aid: 41%. Avg. Amount per Student: $25,327. Of Those Receiving Any Aid: Receiving Need-Based Gift Aid: 96%. Avg. Award: $21,715. Receiving Need-Based Self-Help Aid: 92%. Avg. Award: $6,187. Upon Graduation, Avg. Loan Debt per Student: $15,331. Financial Aid Deadline: 2/10.

Connecticut College

270 Mohegan Avenue, New London, CT 06320. Admissions Phone: (860) 439-2200. Fax: (860) 439-4301. Website: www.connecticutcollege.edu. Costs (2002–03): Comprehensive Fees: $35, 625. Payment Plan(s): installment plan. Institutional Aid (est. 2002–03): Institutional Aid, Need-Based: $13,507,312. FT Undergrads Receiving Aid: 44%. Avg. Amount per Student: $23,586. Of Those Receiving Any Aid: Receiving Need-Based Gift Aid: 93%. Avg. Award: $20,237. Receiving Need-Based Self-Help Aid: 88%. Avg. Award: $5,265. Upon Graduation, Avg. Loan Debt per Student: $17,250. Financial Aid Deadline: 1/15.

Cooper Union for the Advancement of Science and Art*

30 Cooper Square, New York, NY 10003. Admissions Phone: (212) 353-4120. Fax: (212) 353-4342. Website: cooper.edu. Costs (2002–03): Tuition and Fees: $25,600 Every student receives a full tuition scholarship. Room & Board: $10,000.

Cornell College

600 First Street West, Mount Vernon, IA 52314-1098. Admissions Phone: (319) 895-4477; (800) 747-1112. Fax: (319) 895-4451. Email: admissions@cornellcollege.edu. Website: www.cornellcollege.edu. Costs (2003–04): Tuition and Fees: $21,790. Room & Board: $6,035. Payment Plan(s): installment plan. Institutional Aid (est. 2002–03): Institutional Aid, Need-Based: $9,780,769. Institutional Aid, Non-Need-Based: $2,222,783. FT Undergrads Receiving Aid: 80%. Avg. Amount per Student: $18,795. FT Undergrads Receiving Non-Need-Based Gift Aid: 20%. Avg. Amount per Student: $11,115. Of Those Receiving Any Aid: Receiving Need-Based Gift Aid: 100%. Avg. Award: $15,380. Receiving Need-Based Self-Help Aid: 77%. Avg. Award: $4,945. Upon Graduation, Avg. Loan Debt per Student: $17,650. Financial Aid Deadline: 3/1 (priority).

Cornell University

410 Thurston Avenue, Ithaca, NY 14850. Admissions Phone: (607) 255-5241. Fax: (607) 255-0659. Email: admissions@cornell.edu. Website: http://admissions.cornell.edu. Costs (2002–03): Tuition and Fees: $27,394. Room & Board: $8,980. Institutional Aid

(est. 2002–03): Institutional Aid, Need-Based: $71,862,000. FT Undergrads Receiving Aid: 47%. Avg. Amount per Student: $23,017. Of Those Receiving Any Aid: Receiving Need-Based Gift Aid: 93%. Avg. Award: $15,852. Receiving Need-Based Self-Help Aid: 96%. Avg. Award: $8,601. Upon Graduation, Avg. Loan Debt per Student: $15,587. Financial Aid Deadline: 12/1.

Creighton University

2500 California Plaza, Omaha, NE 68178. Admissions Phone: (402) 280-2703; (800) 282-5835. Fax: (402) 280-2685. Email: admissions@creighton.edu. Website: www.creighton.edu. Application Website: www.applyweb.com/apply/creighton/menu.html. Costs (2002–03): Tuition and Fees: $18,882. Room & Board: $6,438. Institutional Aid (est. 2002–03): Institutional Aid, Need-Based: $11,101,676. Institutional Aid, Non-Need-Based: $7,033,760. FT Undergrads Receiving Aid: 49%. Avg. Amount per Student: $17,972. FT Undergrads Receiving Non-Need-Based Gift Aid: 30%. Avg. Amount per Student: $10,242. Of Those Receiving Any Aid: Receiving Need-Based Gift Aid: 100%. Avg. Award: $13,052. Receiving Need-Based Self-Help Aid: 85%. Avg. Award: $6,531. Upon Graduation, Avg. Loan Debt per Student: $21,494. Financial Aid Deadline: rolling; 4/1 (priority).

Culinary Institute of America

1946 Campus Drive, Hyde Park, NY 12538. Admissions Phone: (800) 285-4627; (845) 452-9430. Fax: (845) 451-1068. Email: admissions@culinary.edu. Website: www.ciachef.edu. Application Website: https://www.applyweb.com/aw?ciachef. Costs (2003–04): Tuition and Fees: $18,295. Room & Board: $6,220. Payment Plan(s): installment plan. Institutional Aid (2001–02): Institutional Aid, Need-Based: $6,000,000. Institutional Aid, Non-Need-Based: $100,000. FT Undergrads Receiving Aid: 91%. Avg. Amount per Student: $8,500. FT Undergrads Receiving Non-Need-Based Gift Aid: 5%. Avg. Amount per Student: $2,000. Of Those Receiving Any Aid: Receiving Need-Based Gift Aid: 100%. Avg. Award: $2,000. Receiving Need-Based Self-Help Aid: 100%. Avg. Award: $5,715. Upon Graduation, Avg. Loan Debt per Student: $18,768. Financial Aid Deadline: 2/15 (priority).

Dartmouth College

Dartmouth, Hanover, NH 03755. Admissions Phone: (603) 646-2875. Fax: (603) 646-1216. Email: admissions.office@dartmouth.edu. Website: www.dartmouth.edu. Costs (2002–03): Tuition and Fees: $27,771. Room & Board: $8,217. Payment Plan(s): installment plan, pre-payment plan. Institutional Aid (2001–02): Institutional Aid, Need-Based: $28,637,644. Institutional Aid, Non-Need-Based: $19,140. FT Undergrads Receiving Aid: 47%. Avg. Amount per Student: $25,549. FT Undergrads Receiving Non-Need-Based Gift Aid: 8%. Avg. Amount per Student: $2,416. Of Those Receiving Any Aid: Receiving Need-Based Gift Aid: 87%. Avg. Award: $19,352. Receiving Need-Based Self-Help Aid: 95%. Avg. Award: $6,197. Upon Graduation, Avg. Loan Debt per Student: $15,543. Financial Aid Deadline: 2/1.

Davidson College

P.O. Box 7156, Davidson, NC 28035-7156. Admissions Phone: (800) 768-0380; (704) 894-2230. Fax: (704) 894-2016. Email: admission@davidson.edu. Website: www.davidson.edu. Costs (2002–03): Tuition and Fees: $24,930. Room & Board: $7,094. Institutional Aid (2001–02): Institutional Aid, Need-Based: $7,317,184. Institutional Aid, Non-Need-Based: $2,112,419. FT Undergrads Receiving Aid: 33%. Avg. Amount per Student: $16,108. FT Undergrads Receiving Non-Need-Based Gift Aid: 23%. Avg. Amount per Student: $6,076. Of Those Receiving Any Aid: Receiving Need-Based Gift Aid: 95%. Avg. Award: $13,251. Receiving Need-Based Self-Help Aid: 80%. Avg. Award: $4,351. Upon Graduation, Avg. Loan Debt per Student: $13,697. Financial Aid Deadline: 2/15 (priority).

Denison University

100 South Ridge Road, Granville, OH 43023. Admissions Phone: (800) 336-4766; (740) 587-6276. Fax: (740) 587-6306. Email: admissions@denison.edu. Website: www.denison.edu. Costs (2002–03): Tuition and Fees: $24,240. Room & Board: $6,880. Payment Plan(s): installment plan, pre-payment plan. Institutional Aid (est. 2002–03): Institutional Aid, Need-Based: $13,752,433. Institutional Aid, Non-Need-Based: $11,558,638. FT Undergrads Receiving Aid: 48%. Avg. Amount per Student: $21,560. FT Undergrads Receiving Non-Need-Based Gift Aid: 52%.

Avg. Amount per Student: $9,759. Of Those Receiving Any Aid: Receiving Need-Based Gift Aid: 99%. Avg. Award: $16,051. Receiving Need-Based Self-Help Aid: 74%. Avg. Award: $4,956. Upon Graduation, Avg. Loan Debt per Student: $14,077. Financial Aid Deadline: rolling; 2/15 (priority).

DePaul University

1 East Jackson, Suite 9100, Chicago, IL 60604-4100. Admissions Phone: (312) 362-8300. Fax: (312) 362-5749. Email: admitdpu@depaul.edu. Website: www.depaul.edu. Costs (2002–03): Tuition and Fees: $17,850. Room & Board: $8,750. Institutional Aid (est. 2002–03): FT Undergrads Receiving Aid: 64%. Avg. Amount per Student: $14,106. FT Undergrads Receiving Non-Need-Based Gift Aid: 2%. Avg. Amount per Student: $6,482. Of Those Receiving Any Aid: Receiving Need-Based Gift Aid: 84%. Avg. Award: $9,161. Receiving Need-Based Self-Help Aid: 93%. Avg. Award: $5,754. Financial Aid Deadline: 5/1

DePauw University

101 East Seminary St., Greencastle, IN 46135. Admissions Phone: (765) 658-4006; (800) 447-2495. Fax: (765) 658-4007. Email: admission@depauw.edu. Website: www.depauw.edu. Application Website: www.depauw.edu/admission/applyonline/. Costs (2002–03): Tuition and Fees: $22,840. Room & Board: $6,800. Payment Plan(s): installment plan, deferred payment plan. Institutional Aid (est. 2002–03): Institutional Aid, Need-Based: $19,359,177. Institutional Aid, Non-Need-Based: $8,815,346. FT Undergrads Receiving Aid: 51%. Avg. Amount per Student: $20,233. FT Undergrads Receiving Non-Need-Based Gift Aid: 42%. Avg. Amount per Student: $10,337. Of Those Receiving Any Aid: Receiving Need-Based Gift Aid: 86%. Avg. Award: $16,619. Receiving Need-Based Self-Help Aid: 85%. Avg. Award: $4,046. Upon Graduation, Avg. Loan Debt per Student: $15,048. Financial Aid Deadline: 2/15.

Dickinson College

P.O. Box 1773, Carlisle, PA 17013-2896. Admissions Phone: (717) 245-1231; (800) 644-1773. Fax: (717) 245-1442. Email: admit@dickinson.edu. Website: dickinson.edu. Application Website: http://app.commonapp.org/action/apply.nsf. Costs (2003–04): Tuition and

Fees: $28,615. Room & Board: $7,210. Payment Plan(s): installment plan. Institutional Aid (est. 2002–03): Institutional Aid, Need-Based: $17,760,411. Institutional Aid, Non-Need-Based: $3,968,372. FT Undergrads Receiving Aid: 57%. Avg. Amount per Student: $22,147. FT Undergrads Receiving Non-Need-Based Gift Aid: 14%. Avg. Amount per Student: $12,085. Of Those Receiving Any Aid: Receiving Need-Based Gift Aid: 97%. Avg. Award: $16,847. Receiving Need-Based Self-Help Aid: 82%. Avg. Award: $5,835. Upon Graduation, Avg. Loan Debt per Student: $17,586. Financial Aid Deadline: 2/1.

Drew University

36 Madison Ave., Madison, NJ 07940. Admissions Phone: (973) 408-DREW. Fax: (973) 408-3068. Email: cadm@drew.edu. Website: www.drew.edu. Costs (2002–03): Tuition and Fees: $26,346. Room & Board: $7,288. Institutional Aid (2001–02): Institutional Aid, Need-Based: $7,395,083. Institutional Aid, Non-Need-Based: $4,582,710. FT Undergrads Receiving Aid: 48%. Avg. Amount per Student: $19,403. FT Undergrads Receiving Non-Need-Based Gift Aid: 27%. Avg. Amount per Student: $11,109. Of Those Receiving Any Aid: Receiving Need-Based Gift Aid: 99%. Avg. Award: $14,485. Receiving Need-Based Self-Help Aid: 82%. Avg. Award: $5,196. Upon Graduation, Avg. Loan Debt per Student: $16,120. Financial Aid Deadline: 2/15.

Drexel University

3141 Chestnut Street, Philadelphia, PA 19104-2875. Admissions Phone: (215) 895-2400; (800) 237-3935. Fax: (215) 895-5939. Email: enroll@drexel.edu. Website: www.drexel.edu. Application Website: www.applyweb.com/apply/drexel/menu.html. Costs (2002–03): Tuition and Fees: $17,624. Room & Board: $8,695. Payment Plan(s): installment plan. Institutional Aid (est. 2002–03): Institutional Aid, Need-Based: $1,817,432. Institutional Aid, Non-Need-Based: $47,295,759. FT Undergrads Receiving Aid: 69%. Avg. Amount per Student: $9,515. FT Undergrads Receiving Non-Need-Based Gift Aid: 18%. Avg. Amount per Student: $5,920. Of Those Receiving Any Aid: Receiving Need-Based Gift Aid: 57%. Avg. Award: $4,024. Receiving Need-Based Self-Help Aid: 97%. Avg. Award: $6,337. Upon Graduation, Avg. Loan Debt per Student: $21,443. Financial Aid Deadline: 2/15.

Duke University

2138 Campus Drive, Durham, NC 27708. Admissions Phone: (919) 684-3214. Fax: (919) 684-8128. Email: askduke@admiss.duke.edu. Website: www.duke.edu. Costs (2002–03): Tuition and Fees: $27,844. Room & Board: $7,921. Payment Plan(s): installment plan, deferred payment plan, pre-payment plan. Institutional Aid (2001–02): FT Undergrads Receiving Aid: 36%. Avg. Amount per Student: $22,687. FT Undergrads Receiving Non-Need-Based Gift Aid: 2%. Avg. Amount per Student: $30,166. Of Those Receiving Any Aid: Receiving Need-Based Gift Aid: 94%. Avg. Award: $18,318. Receiving Need-Based Self-Help Aid: 87%. Avg. Award: $5,851. Upon Graduation, Avg. Loan Debt per Student: $16,502. Financial Aid Deadline: 2/1.

Duquesne University*

600 Forbes Avenue, Pittsburgh, PA 15282-0201. Admissions Phone: (412) 396-5000. Fax: (412) 396-5644. Email: admissions@duq.edu. Website: www.duq.edu. Application Website: www.duq.edu/index.html. Costs (2002–03): Tuition and Fees: $18,527. Room & Board: $7,170. Payment Plan(s): installment plan, deferred payment plan. Institutional Aid: FT Undergrads Receiving Aid: 62%. Avg. Amount per Student: $13,444. FT Undergrads Receiving Non-Need-Based Gift Aid: 22%. Avg. Amount per Student: $7,866. Of Those Receiving Any Aid: Receiving Need-Based Gift Aid: 95%. Avg. Award: $8,351. Receiving Need-Based Self-Help Aid: 95%. Avg. Award: $5,182. Upon Graduation, Avg. Loan Debt per Student: $16,461. Financial Aid Deadline: 5/1.

Earlham College

801 National Rd. W., Richmond, IN 47374. Admissions Phone: (765) 983-1600; (800) 327-5426. Fax: (765) 983-1560. Email: admission@earlham.edu. Website: www.earlham.edu. Application Website: http://www.earlham.edu/~adm/apps.html. Costs (2002–03): Tuition and Fees: $24,560. Room & Board: $5,416. Payment Plan(s): installment plan, deferred payment plan, pre-payment plan. Institutional Aid (est. 2002–03): Institutional Aid, Need-Based: $8,051,873. Institutional Aid, Non-Need-Based: $1,821,373. FT Undergrads Receiving Aid: 65%. Avg. Amount per Student: $20,439. FT Undergrads Receiving Non-Need-Based Gift Aid: 14%. Avg.

Amount per Student: $5,701. Of Those Receiving Any Aid: Receiving Need-Based Gift Aid: 96%. Avg. Award: $12,796. Receiving Need-Based Self-Help Aid: 84%. Avg. Award: $5,206. Upon Graduation, Avg. Loan Debt per Student: $15,444. Financial Aid Deadline: 3/1 (priority).

Eckerd College

4200 54th Avenue South, St. Petersburg, FL 33711. Admissions Phone: (727) 864-8331; (800) 456-9009. Fax: (727) 866-2304. Email: admissions@eckerd.edu. Website: www.eckerd.edu. Costs (2002–03): Tuition and Fees: $21,488. Room & Board: $5,688. Institutional Aid (est. 2002–03): Institutional Aid, Need-Based: $6,684,000. Institutional Aid, Non-Need-Based: $4,456,000. FT Undergrads Receiving Aid: 57%. Avg. Amount per Student: $17,500. Of Those Receiving Any Aid: Receiving Need-Based Gift Aid: 100%. Receiving Need-Based Self-Help Aid: 83%. Upon Graduation, Avg. Loan Debt per Student: $17,500. Financial Aid Deadline: 4/1 (priority).

Elon University

2700 Campus Box, Elon, NC 27244-2010. Admissions Phone: (336) 278-3566; (800) 334-8448 (out-of-state). Fax: (336) 278-7699. Email: admissions@elon.edu. Website: www.elon.edu. Application Website: www.elon.edu/admissions/apply.asp. Costs (2002–03): Tuition and Fees: $15,505. Room & Board: $5,090. Payment Plan(s): installment plan. Institutional Aid (est. 2002–03): Institutional Aid, Need-Based: $3,979,756. Institutional Aid, Non-Need-Based: $2,337,317. FT Undergrads Receiving Aid: 36%. Avg. Amount per Student: $10,694. FT Undergrads Receiving Non-Need-Based Gift Aid: 30%. Avg. Amount per Student: $4,664. Of Those Receiving Any Aid: Receiving Need-Based Gift Aid: 86%. Avg. Award: $6,025. Receiving Need-Based Self-Help Aid: 84%. Avg. Award: $4,669. Upon Graduation, Avg. Loan Debt per Student: $26,663. Financial Aid Deadline: 2/15 (priority).

Embry-Riddle Aeronautical University–Florida

600 South Clyde Morris Boulevard, Daytona Beach, FL 32114-3900. Admissions Phone: (386) 226-6100; (800) 862-2416. Fax: (386) 226-7070. Email: dbadmit@erau.edu. Website: embryriddle.edu. Costs (2003–04): Tuition and Fees: $19,960. Room & Board: $6,370.

Payment Plan(s): installment plan, deferred payment plan. **Institutional Aid (2001–02): Institutional Aid, Need-Based: $6,889,924. FT Undergrads Receiving Aid: 55%. Avg. Amount per Student: $11,350. Of Those Receiving Any Aid: Receiving Need-Based Gift Aid: 80%. Avg. Award: $7,116. Receiving Need-Based Self-Help Aid: 88%. Avg. Award: $6,021. Upon Graduation, Avg. Loan Debt per Student: $34,546. Financial Aid Deadline: 6/30, 4/15 (priority).**

Emerson College

120 Boylston Street, Boston, MA 02116-4624. **Admissions Phone:** (617) 824-8600. **Fax:** (617) 824-8609. **Email:** admission@emerson.edu. **Website:** www.emerson.edu. **Costs (2002–03): Tuition and Fees: $21,624. Room & Board: $9,542. Payment Plan(s):** installment plan. **Institutional Aid (2001–02): Institutional Aid, Need-Based: $9,250,234. Institutional Aid, Non-Need-Based: $903,680. FT Undergrads Receiving Aid: 61%. Avg. Amount per Student: $12,543. FT Undergrads Receiving Non-Need-Based Gift Aid: 5%. Avg. Amount per Student: $8,624. Of Those Receiving Any Aid: Receiving Need-Based Gift Aid: 72%. Avg. Award: $9,655. Receiving Need-Based Self-Help Aid: 100%. Avg. Award: $4,929. Upon Graduation, Avg. Loan Debt per Student: $10,550. Financial Aid Deadline: 3/1 (priority).**

Emory University

200 B. Jones Center, Atlanta, GA 30322. **Admissions Phone:** (404) 727-6036; (800) 727-6036. **Fax:** (404) 727-4303. **Email:** admiss@emory.edu. **Website:** www.emory.edu. **Application Website:** www.emory.edu/ADMISSIONS. **Costs (2002–03): Tuition and Fees: $26,932. Room & Board: $9,198. Payment Plan(s):** installment plan. **Institutional Aid (est. 2002–03): Institutional Aid, Need-Based: $30,684,281. Institutional Aid, Non-Need-Based: $7,100,605. FT Undergrads Receiving Aid: 37%. Avg. Amount per Student: $24,084. FT Undergrads Receiving Non-Need-Based Gift Aid: 17%. Avg. Amount per Student: $13,657. Of Those Receiving Any Aid: Receiving Need-Based Gift Aid: 91%. Avg. Award: $17,615. Receiving Need-Based Self-Help Aid: 89%. Avg. Award: $6,228. Upon Graduation, Avg. Loan Debt per Student: $17,675. Financial Aid Deadline: 4/1, 2/15 (priority).**

Eugene Lang College, New School University

65 West 11th Street, New York, NY 10011-8963. **Admissions Phone:** (212) 229-5665; (877) 528-3321. **Fax:** (212) 229-5166. **Email:** Lang@newschool.edu. **Website:** www.lang.edu. **Costs (2003–04): Tuition and Fees: $22,990. Room & Board: $9,896. Institutional Aid (est. 2002–03): Institutional Aid, Need-Based: $4,583,013. Institutional Aid, Non-Need-Based: $103,569. FT Undergrads Receiving Aid: 64%. Avg. Amount per Student: $17,088. FT Undergrads Receiving Non-Need-Based Gift Aid: 1%. Avg. Amount per Student: $7,930. Of Those Receiving Any Aid: Receiving Need-Based Gift Aid: 89%. Avg. Award: $13,617. Receiving Need-Based Self-Help Aid: 2%. Avg. Award: $4,520. Upon Graduation, Avg. Loan Debt per Student: $20,963. Financial Aid Deadline: rolling; 3/1 (priority).**

Evergreen State College

2700 Evergreen Parkway NW, Olympia, WA 98505. **Admissions Phone:** (360) 867-6170. **Fax:** (360) 867-6576. **Email:** admissions@evergreen.edu. **Website:** evergreen.edu. **Application Website:** www.evergreen.edu/admissions/apply.htm. **Costs (2002–03): Tuition and Fees, In-State: $3,591 Tuition and Fees, Out-of-State: $12,414. Room & Board: $5,610. Institutional Aid (2001–02): Institutional Aid, Need-Based: $598,524. Institutional Aid, Non-Need-Based: $133,254. FT Undergrads Receiving Aid: 52%. Avg. Amount per Student: $9,175. FT Undergrads Receiving Non-Need-Based Gift Aid: 1%. Avg. Amount per Student: $2,641. Of Those Receiving Any Aid: Receiving Need-Based Gift Aid: 79%. Avg. Award: $4,989. Receiving Need-Based Self-Help Aid: 82%. Avg. Award: $4,040. Upon Graduation, Avg. Loan Debt per Student: $13,000. Financial Aid Deadline: 3/15, 2/15 (priority).**

Fairfield University

1073 North Benson Road, Fairfield, CT 06824-5195. **Admissions Phone:** (203) 254-4100. **Fax:** (203) 254-4199. **Email:** admis@mail.fairfield.edu. **Website:** www.fairfield.edu. **Costs (2002–03): Tuition and Fees: $24,555. Room & Board: $8,560. Payment Plan(s):** installment plan. **Institutional Aid (est. 2002–03): FT Undergrads Receiving Aid: 53%. Avg. Amount per Student: $17, 013. FT Undergrads Receiving Non-Need-Based**

Gift Aid: 8%. **Avg. Amount per Student: $9,270. Of Those Receiving Any Aid: Receiving Need-Based Gift Aid: 98%. Avg. Award: $9,207. Receiving Need-Based Self-Help Aid: 84%. Avg. Award: $4,660. Upon Graduation, Avg. Loan Debt per Student: $17,446. Financial Aid Deadline: 2/15 (priority).**

Fashion Institute of Technology

Seventh Avenue @ 27th Street, New York, NY 10001-5992. **Admissions Phone:** (212) 217-7675. **Email:** fitinfo@fitsuny.edu. **Website:** www.fitnyc.edu. **Costs (2002–03): Tuition and Fees, In-State: $3,020. Tuition and Fees, Out-of-State: $7,520** (Tuition differs for AAS degree Bach. degree students). **Room & Board: $6,258. Institutional Aid (2001–02): Institutional Aid, Need-Based: $1,832,614. Institutional Aid, Non-Need-Based: $57,250. FT Undergrads Receiving Aid: 43%. Avg. Amount per Student: $6,118. FT Undergrads Receiving Non-Need-Based Gift Aid: 3%. Avg. Amount per Student: $2,660. Of Those Receiving Any Aid: Receiving Need-Based Gift Aid: 91%. Avg. Award: $3,578. Receiving Need-Based Self-Help Aid: 63%. Avg. Award: $3,338. Upon Graduation, Avg. Loan Debt per Student: $9,395**

Fisk University

1000 17th Ave North, Nashville, TN 37208-3051. **Admissions Phone:** (800) 443-3475. **Fax:** (615) 329-8774. **Email:** admissions@dubois.fisk.edu. **Website:** fisk.edu. **Costs (2002–03): Tuition and Fees: $10,400. Room & Board: $5,340. Payment Plan(s):** installment plan, pre-payment plan. **Institutional Aid (est. 2002–03): Institutional Aid, Non-Need-Based: $1,954,302. FT Undergrads Receiving Aid: 92%. Avg. Amount per Student: $13,000. FT Undergrads Receiving Non-Need-Based Gift Aid: 2%. Avg. Amount per Student: $6,000. Of Those Receiving Any Aid: Receiving Need-Based Gift Aid: 60%. Avg. Award: $3,600. Receiving Need-Based Self-Help Aid: 97%. Avg. Award: $3,400. Upon Graduation, Avg. Loan Debt per Student: $20,000. Financial Aid Deadline: 7/1, 3/1 (priority).**

Flagler College

P.O. Box 1027, St. Augustine, FL 32085-1027. **Admissions Phone:** (904) 819-6220; (800) 304-4208. **Fax:** (904) 829-6838. **Email:** admiss@flagler.edu. **Website:**

www.flagler.edu. Costs (2003–04): Tuition and Fees: $7,410. Room & Board: $4,450. Payment Plan(s): pre-payment plan. Institutional Aid (2001–02): Institutional Aid, Need-Based: $152,003. Institutional Aid, Non-Need-Based: $263,511. FT Undergrads Receiving Aid: 37%. Avg. Amount per Student: $6,930. FT Undergrads Receiving Non-Need-Based Gift Aid: 39%. Avg. Amount per Student: $4,086. Of Those Receiving Any Aid: Receiving Need-Based Gift Aid: 56%. Avg. Award: $2,920. Receiving Need-Based Self-Help Aid: 85%. Avg. Award: $3,275. Upon Graduation, Avg. Loan Debt per Student: $14,496. Financial Aid Deadline: rolling; 5/1 (priority).

Florida State University

Florida State University, Tallahassee, FL 32306-2400. Admissions Phone: (850) 644-6200. Fax: (850) 644-0197. Email: admissions@admin.fsu.edu. Website: www.fsu.edu. Application Website: admissions.fsu.edu/. Costs (2002–03): Tuition and Fees, In-State: $2,684. Tuition and Fees, Out-of-State: $12,228. Room & Board: $5,740. Payment Plan(s): installment plan, deferred payment plan, pre-payment plan. Institutional Aid (est. 2002–03): Institutional Aid, Need-Based: $7,193,004. Institutional Aid, Non-Need-Based: $6,785,150. FT Undergrads Receiving Aid: 42%. Avg. Amount per Student: $6,529. FT Undergrads Receiving Non-Need-Based Gift Aid: 39%. Avg. Amount per Student: $1,785. Of Those Receiving Any Aid: Receiving Need-Based Gift Aid: 63%. Avg. Award: $3,959. Receiving Need-Based Self-Help Aid: 59%. Avg. Award: $3,677. Upon Graduation, Avg. Loan Debt per Student: $16,372. Financial Aid Deadline: 2/15 (priority).

Fordham University

441 East Fordham Rd., Thebaud Hall, New York, NY 10458-9993. Admissions Phone: (718) 817-1000; (800) FORDHAM. Fax: (718) 367-9404. Email: enroll@fordham.edu. Website: fordham.edu. Costs (2002–03): Tuition and Fees: $23,540. Room & Board: $9,460. Payment Plan(s): installment plan, pre-payment plan. Institutional Aid (est. 2002–03): Financial Aid Deadline: 2/1.

Franklin and Marshall College

P.O. Box 3003, Lancaster, PA 17604-3003. Admissions Phone: (717) 291-3953. Fax: (717) 291-4389. Email: admission@FandM.edu. Website: www.FandM.edu. Costs (2002–03): Tuition and Fees: $27,280. Room & Board: $6,580. Payment Plan(s): installment plan. Institutional Aid (est. 2002–03): Institutional Aid, Need-Based: $9,969,942. Institutional Aid, Non-Need-Based: $2,595,357. FT Undergrads Receiving Aid: 45%. Avg. Amount per Student: $19,479. FT Undergrads Receiving Non-Need-Based Gift Aid: 19%. Avg. Amount per Student: $11,829. Of Those Receiving Any Aid: Receiving Need-Based Gift Aid: 91%. Avg. Award: $15,655. Receiving Need-Based Self-Help Aid: 92%. Avg. Award: $5,716. Upon Graduation, Avg. Loan Debt per Student: $19,656. Financial Aid Deadline: 2/1.

Furman University

3300 Poinsett Highway, Greenville, SC 29613. Admissions Phone: (864) 294-2034. Fax: (864) 294-3127. Email: admissions@furman.edu. Website: www.furman.edu. Application Website: www.engagefurman.com/apply. Costs (2002–03): Tuition and Fees: $21,264. Room & Board: $5,664. Payment Plan(s): installment plan. Institutional Aid (est. 2002–03): Institutional Aid, Need-Based: $8,665,920. Institutional Aid, Non-Need-Based: $7,890,888. FT Undergrads Receiving Aid: 42%. Avg. Amount per Student: $18,349. FT Undergrads Receiving Non-Need-Based Gift Aid: 34%. Avg. Amount per Student: $9,200. Of Those Receiving Any Aid: Receiving Need-Based Gift Aid: 98%. Avg. Award: $13,134. Receiving Need-Based Self-Help Aid: 77%. Avg. Award: $5,511. Upon Graduation, Avg. Loan Debt per Student: $17,741. Financial Aid Deadline: 1/15.

Gallaudet University

800 Florida Avenue NE, Washington, DC 20002. Admissions Phone: (202) 651-5750; (800) 995-0550. Fax: (202) 651-5744. Email: admissions@gallaudet.edu. Website: www.gallaudet.edu. Application Website: www.gallaudet.edu/applicationforms.htm. Costs (est. 2003-04): Tuition and Fees: $9,330. Room & Board: $8,030. Payment Plan(s): installment plan. Institutional Aid (est. 2002–03): Institutional Aid, Need-Based: $1,885,363. Institutional Aid, Non-Need-Based: $329,048. FT Undergrads

Receiving Aid: 69%. Avg. Amount per Student: $12,626. FT Undergrads Receiving Non-Need-Based Gift Aid: 4%. Avg. Amount per Student: $11,553. Of Those Receiving Any Aid: Receiving Need-Based Gift Aid: 96%. Avg. Award: $11,597. Receiving Need-Based Self-Help Aid: 45%. Avg. Award: $3,235. Upon Graduation, Avg. Loan Debt per Student: $9,333. Financial Aid Deadline: rolling; 6/15 (priority).

George Mason University*

4400 University Drive, MSN 3A4, Fairfax, VA 22030-4444. Admissions Phone: (703) 993-2400. Email: admissions@gmu.edu. Website: www.gmu.edu. Application Website: admissions@gmu.edu/onapps.html. Costs (2002–03): Tuition and Fees, In-State: $5,112. Tuition and Fees, Out-of-State: $14,952. Room & Board: varies. Payment Plan(s): installment plan. Institutional Aid: FT Undergrads Receiving Aid: 40%. Avg. Amount per Student: $6,344. FT Undergrads Receiving Non-Need-Based Gift Aid: 15%. Avg. Amount per Student: $5,755. Of Those Receiving Any Aid: Receiving Need-Based Gift Aid: 71%. Avg. Award: $3,976. Receiving Need-Based Self-Help Aid: 80%. Avg. Award: $2,358. Upon Graduation, Avg. Loan Debt per Student: $14,110. Financial Aid Deadline: 3/1 (priority).

George Washington University

2121 I Street, NW, Suite 201, Washington, DC 20052. Admissions Phone: (202) 994-6040; (800) 447-3765. Fax: (202) 994-0325. Email: gwadm@gwu.edu. Website: www.gwu.edu. Application Website: http://gwired.gwu.edu/adm/apply/index.html. Costs (2003–04): Tuition and Fees: $29,350. Room & Board: $10,040. Institutional Aid (2001–02): Institutional Aid, Need-Based: $42,451,206. Institutional Aid, Non-Need-Based: $22,553,322. FT Undergrads Receiving Aid: 37%. Avg. Amount per Student: $25,695. FT Undergrads Receiving Non-Need-Based Gift Aid: 21%. Avg. Amount per Student: $10,324. Of Those Receiving Any Aid: Receiving Need-Based Gift Aid: 97%. Avg. Award: $14,374. Receiving Need-Based Self-Help Aid: 90%. Avg. Award: $5,524. Upon Graduation, Avg. Loan Debt per Student: $22,854. Financial Aid Deadline: 1/31 (priority).

Georgetown University

37th and O Streets, NW, Washington, DC 20057. **Admissions Phone:** (202) 687-3600. **Fax:** (202) 687-5084. **Website:** georgetown.edu/. **Application Website:** georgetown.edu/undergrad/admissions. **Costs (2002–03): Tuition and Fees:** $26,853. **Room & Board:** $9,692. **Payment Plan(s):** installment plan, deferred payment plan. **Institutional Aid (est. 2002–03): Institutional Aid, Need-Based:** $29,500,000. **Institutional Aid, Non-Need-Based:** $170,000. **FT Undergrads Receiving Aid:** 41%. **Avg. Amount per Student:** $21,650. **FT Undergrads Receiving Non-Need-Based Gift Aid:** 4%. **Avg. Amount per Student:** $6,350. **Of Those Receiving Any Aid: Receiving Need-Based Gift Aid:** 86%. **Avg. Award:** $14,800. **Receiving Need-Based Self-Help Aid:** 89%. **Avg. Award:** $6,090. **Upon Graduation, Avg. Loan Debt per Student:** $20,000. **Financial Aid Deadline:** 2/1 (priority).

Georgia Institute of Technology

225 North Avenue, Atlanta, GA 30332-0320. **Admissions Phone:** (404) 894-4154. **Fax:** (404) 894-9511. **Email:** admissions@gatech.edu. **Website:** www.gatech.edu. **Application Website:** apply.gatech.edu. **Costs (2002–03): Tuition and Fees, In-State:** $3,616. **Tuition and Fees, Out-of-State:** $13,986. **Room & Board:** $5,922. **Institutional Aid (2001–02): Institutional Aid, Need-Based:** $4,456,958. **Institutional Aid, Non-Need-Based:** $1,364,213. **FT Undergrads Receiving Aid:** 30%. **Avg. Amount per Student:** $7,141. **FT Undergrads Receiving Non-Need-Based Gift Aid:** 31%. **Avg. Amount per Student:** $4,439. **Of Those Receiving Any Aid: Receiving Need-Based Gift Aid:** 76%. **Avg. Award:** $5,318. **Receiving Need-Based Self-Help Aid:** 76%. **Avg. Award:** $3,955. **Upon Graduation, Avg. Loan Debt per Student:** $17,221. **Financial Aid Deadline:** 3/1.

Gettysburg College

300 North Washington Street, Gettysburg, PA 17325. **Admissions Phone:** (800) 431-0803; (717) 337-6100. **Fax:** (717) 337-6145. **Email:** admiss@gettysburg.edu. **Website:** www.gettysburg.edu. **Costs (2002–03): Tuition and Fees:** $25,748. **Room & Board:** $6,322. **Institutional Aid (est. 2002–03): Institutional Aid, Need-Based:** $22,611,450. **Institutional Aid, Non-Need-Based:** $1,205,000. **FT Undergrads Receiving Aid:** 56%. **Avg. Amount per Student:** $22,415. **FT Undergrads Receiving Non-Need-Based**

Gift Aid: 5%. **Avg. Amount per Student:** $9,565. **Of Those Receiving Any Aid: Receiving Need-Based Gift Aid:** 99%. **Avg. Award:** $17,465. **Receiving Need-Based Self-Help Aid:** 79%. **Avg. Award:** $4,950. **Upon Graduation, Avg. Loan Debt per Student:** $15,500. **Financial Aid Deadline:** 3/15, 2/15 (priority).

Gonzaga University

502 East Boone Avenue, Spokane, WA 99258. **Admissions Phone:** (509) 323-6572; (800) 322-2584. **Fax:** (509) 324-5780. **Email:** ballinger@gu.gonzaga.edu. **Website:** www.gonzaga.edu. **Costs (2003–04): Tuition and Fees:** $20,685. **Room & Board:** $5,960. **Payment Plan(s):** installment plan, deferred payment plan. **Institutional Aid (est. 2002–03): Institutional Aid, Need-Based:** $13,303,598. **Institutional Aid, Non-Need-Based:** $6,019,818. **FT Undergrads Receiving Aid:** 63%. **Avg. Amount per Student:** $12,525. **FT Undergrads Receiving Non-Need-Based Gift Aid:** 26%. **Avg. Amount per Student:** $4,894. **Of Those Receiving Any Aid: Receiving Need-Based Gift Aid:** 84%. **Avg. Award:** $10,411. **Receiving Need-Based Self-Help Aid:** 79%. **Avg. Award:** $6,252

Goshen College

1700 S. Main St., Goshen, IN 46526-4794. **Admissions Phone:** (574) 535-7535; (800) 348-7422. **Fax:** (574) 535-7609. **Email:** admissions@goshen.edu. **Website:** www.goshen.edu. **Costs (2003–04): Tuition and Fees:** $16,650. **Room & Board:** $5,800. **Payment Plan(s):** installment plan, deferred payment plan, pre-payment plan. **Institutional Aid (est. 2002–03): Institutional Aid, Need-Based:** $2,830,384. **Institutional Aid, Non-Need-Based:** $864,064. **FT Undergrads Receiving Aid:** 63%. **Avg. Amount per Student:** $13,629. **FT Undergrads Receiving Non-Need-Based Gift Aid:** 14%. **Avg. Amount per Student:** $9,107. **Of Those Receiving Any Aid: Receiving Need-Based Gift Aid:** 98%. **Avg. Award:** $8,593. **Receiving Need-Based Self-Help Aid:** 81%. **Avg. Award:** $5,179. **Upon Graduation, Avg. Loan Debt per Student:** $15,689. **Financial Aid Deadline:** 2/15.

Goucher College

1021 Dulaney Valley Road, Baltimore, MD 21204-2794. **Admissions Phone:** (410) 337-6100; (800) 468-2437. **Fax:** (410) 337-6354. **Email:** admissions@goucher.edu. **Website:** goucher.edu. **Costs (2002–03): Tuition and Fees:** $23,250. **Room & Board:** $8,050. **Institutional Aid (2001–02): Institutional**

Aid, Need-Based: $10,517,367. **Institutional Aid, Non-Need-Based:** $1,300,164. **FT Undergrads Receiving Aid:** 57%. **Avg. Amount per Student:** $18,166. **FT Undergrads Receiving Non-Need-Based Gift Aid:** 17%. **Avg. Amount per Student:** $8,934. **Of Those Receiving Any Aid: Receiving Need-Based Gift Aid:** 100%. **Avg. Award:** $11,295. **Receiving Need-Based Self-Help Aid:** 89%. **Avg. Award:** $2,432. **Upon Graduation, Avg. Loan Debt per Student:** $15,376. **Financial Aid Deadline:** 2/15.

Grinnell College

1103 Park Street, Grinnell, IA 50112-1690. **Admissions Phone:** (641) 269-3600; (800) 247-0113. **Fax:** (641) 269-4800. **Email:** askgrin@grinnell.edu. **Website:** www.grinnell.edu. **Application Website:** www.grinnell.edu/admission/apply/. **Costs (2002–03): Tuition and Fees:** $23,530. **Room & Board:** $6,330. **Payment Plan(s):** installment plan, pre-payment plan. **Institutional Aid (est. 2002–03): Institutional Aid, Need-Based:** $10,745,908. **Institutional Aid, Non-Need-Based:** $3,482,079. **FT Undergrads Receiving Aid:** 58%. **Avg. Amount per Student:** $19,611. **FT Undergrads Receiving Non-Need-Based Gift Aid:** 30%. **Avg. Amount per Student:** $8,148. **Of Those Receiving Any Aid: Receiving Need-Based Gift Aid:** 100%. **Avg. Award:** $14,875. **Receiving Need-Based Self-Help Aid:** 88%. **Avg. Award:** $5,389. **Upon Graduation, Avg. Loan Debt per Student:** $13,854. **Financial Aid Deadline:** 2/1.

Guilford College

5800 West Friendly Avenue, Greensboro, NC 27410. **Admissions Phone:** (336) 316-2100; (800) 992-7759. **Fax:** (336) 316-2954. **Email:** admission@guilford.edu. **Website:** www.guilford.edu. **Costs (2003–04): Tuition and Fees:** $19,165. **Room & Board:** $5,940. **Payment Plan(s):** installment plan, pre-payment plan. **Institutional Aid (est. 2002–03): Institutional Aid, Need-Based:** $4,906,306. **Institutional Aid, Non-Need-Based:** $2,691,765. **FT Undergrads Receiving Aid:** 39%. **Avg. Amount per Student:** $15,200. **FT Undergrads Receiving Non-Need-Based Gift Aid:** 28%. **Avg. Amount per Student:** $7,585. **Of Those Receiving Any Aid: Receiving Need-Based Gift Aid:** 100%. **Avg. Award:** $11,900. **Receiving Need-Based Self-Help Aid:** 89%. **Avg. Award:** $5,000. **Upon Graduation, Avg. Loan Debt per Student:** $17,380. **Financial Aid Deadline:** rolling; 3/1 (priority).

Gustavus Adolphus College

800 West College Avenue, St. Peter, MN 56082. **Admissions Phone:** (507) 933-7676; (800) 487-8288. **Fax:** (507) 933-7474. **Email:** admission@gustavus.edu. **Website:** www.gustavus.edu. **Application Website:** https://www.applyweb.com/apply/gustavus/menu.html. **Costs** (2002–03): **Tuition and Fees:** $20,450. **Room & Board:** $5,170. **Payment Plan(s):** installment plan, pre-payment plan. **Institutional Aid** (2001–02): **Institutional Aid, Need-Based:** $11,328,567. **Institutional Aid, Non-Need-Based:** $4,365,306. **FT Undergrads Receiving Aid:** 65%. **Avg. Amount per Student:** $14,501. **FT Undergrads Receiving Non-Need-Based Gift Aid:** 28%. **Avg. Amount per Student:** $5,843. **Of Those Receiving Any Aid:** **Receiving Need-Based Gift Aid:** 100%. **Avg. Award:** $10,211. **Receiving Need-Based Self-Help Aid:** 84%. **Avg. Award:** $4,964. **Upon Graduation, Avg. Loan Debt per Student:** $17,400. **Financial Aid Deadline:** 6/15, 4/15 (priority).

Hamilton College

198 College Hill Road, Clinton, NY 13323. **Admissions Phone:** (315) 859-4421; (800) 843-2655. **Fax:** (315) 859-4457. **Email:** admission@hamilton.edu. **Website:** www.hamilton.edu. **Application Website:** www.hamilton.edu/admission/apply/default.html. **Costs** (2002–03): **Tuition and Fees:** $28,760. **Room & Board:** $7,040. **Payment Plan(s):** installment plan. **Institutional Aid** (est. 2002–03): **Institutional Aid, Need-Based:** $15,492,893. **Institutional Aid, Non-Need-Based:** $608,905. **FT Undergrads Receiving Aid:** 54%. **Avg. Amount per Student:** $22,460. **FT Undergrads Receiving Non-Need-Based Gift Aid:** 4%. **Avg. Amount per Student:** $8,825. **Of Those Receiving Any Aid: Receiving Need-Based Gift Aid:** 95%. **Avg. Award:** $18,989. **Receiving Need-Based Self-Help Aid:** 77%. **Avg. Award:** $4,870. **Upon Graduation, Avg. Loan Debt per Student:** $16,856. **Financial Aid Deadline:** 2/1 (priority).

Hampden–Sydney College

P.O. Box 667, Hampden-Sydney, VA 23943-0667. **Admissions Phone:** (434) 223-6120; (800) 755-0733. **Email:** hsapp@hsc.edu. **Website:** www.hsc.edu. **Costs** (2002–03): **Tuition and Fees:** $18,485. **Room & Board:** $6,386. **Payment Plan(s):** installment plan. **Institutional Aid** (2001–02): **FT Undergrads Receiving Aid:** 46%. **Avg.**

Amount per Student: $14,518. **FT Undergrads Receiving Non-Need-Based Gift Aid:** 42%. **Avg. Amount per Student:** $13,044. **Of Those Receiving Any Aid:** **Receiving Need-Based Gift Aid:** 100%. **Avg. Award:** $11,248. **Receiving Need-Based Self-Help Aid:** 74%. **Avg. Award:** $4,444. **Upon Graduation, Avg. Loan Debt per Student:** $7,071. **Financial Aid Deadline:** 5/1, 11/15 (priority).

Hampshire College

893 West Street, Amherst, MA 01002. **Admissions Phone:** (413) 559-5471; (877) 937-4267. **Fax:** (413) 559-5631. **Email:** admissions@hampshire.edu. **Website:** www.hampshire.edu. **Costs** (2002–03): **Tuition and Fees:** $27,870. **Room & Board:** $7,294. **Institutional Aid** (est. 2002–03): **Institutional Aid, Need-Based:** $9,813,800. **Institutional Aid, Non-Need-Based:** $158,000. **FT Undergrads Receiving Aid:** 52%. **Avg. Amount per Student:** $21,340. **FT Undergrads Receiving Non-Need-Based Gift Aid:** 3%. **Avg. Amount per Student:** $4,700. **Of Those Receiving Any Aid:** **Receiving Need-Based Gift Aid:** 97%. **Avg. Award:** $16,615. **Receiving Need-Based Self-Help Aid:** 96%. **Avg. Award:** $4,725. **Upon Graduation, Avg. Loan Debt per Student:** $16,200. **Financial Aid Deadline:** 2/1 (priority).

Hampton University

Hampton University, Hampton, VA 23668. **Admissions Phone:** (757) 727-5328; (800) 624-3328. **Fax:** (757) 727-5095. **Email:** admit@hamptonu.edu. **Website:** hamptonu.edu. **Costs** (2002–03): **Tuition and Fees:** $12,252. (Army ROTC pays room for select students.) **Room & Board:** $5,828. **Payment Plan(s):** deferred payment plan. **Institutional Aid** (2001–02): **Institutional Aid, Non-Need-Based:** $9,839,372. **FT Undergrads Receiving Aid:** 60%. **Avg. Amount per Student:** $8,539. **FT Undergrads Receiving Non-Need-Based Gift Aid:** 23%. **Avg. Amount per Student:** $9,515. **Of Those Receiving Any Aid:** **Receiving Need-Based Gift Aid:** 66%. **Avg. Award:** $4,297. **Receiving Need-Based Self-Help Aid:** 84%. **Avg. Award:** $3,722. **Upon Graduation, Avg. Loan Debt per Student:** $23,000. **Financial Aid Deadline:** rolling; 3/1 (priority).

Hanover College

P.O. Box 108, Hanover, IN 47243. **Admissions Phone:** (812) 866-7021; (800) 213-2178. **Fax:** (812) 866-7098. **Email:**

info@hanover.edu. **Website:** www.hanover.edu. **Costs** (2003–04): **Tuition and Fees:** $14,700. **Room & Board:** $5,900. **Institutional Aid** (est. 2002–03): **Institutional Aid, Need-Based:** $2,882,671. **Institutional Aid, Non-Need-Based:** $1,755,795. **FT Undergrads Receiving Aid:** 58%. **Avg. Amount per Student:** $12,050. **FT Undergrads Receiving Non-Need-Based Gift Aid:** 33%. **Avg. Amount per Student:** $10,657. **Of Those Receiving Any Aid:** **Receiving Need-Based Gift Aid:** 97%. **Avg. Award:** $9,445. **Receiving Need-Based Self-Help Aid:** 82%. **Avg. Award:** $3,595. **Upon Graduation, Avg. Loan Debt per Student:** $11,583. **Financial Aid Deadline:** 3/10 (priority).

Harvard University

Byerly Hall, 8 Garden Street, Cambridge, MA 02138. **Admissions Phone:** (617) 495-1551. **Fax:** (617) 495-8821. **Email:** college@fas.harvard.edu. **Website:** college.harvard.edu. **Application Website:** http://adm-is.fas.harvard.edu. **Costs** (2002–03): **Tuition and Fees:** $27,448. **Room & Board:** $8,502. **Institutional Aid** (est. 2002–03): **Institutional Aid, Need-Based:** $58,489,637. **FT Undergrads Receiving Aid:** 48%. **Avg. Amount per Student:** $23,739. **FT Undergrads Receiving Non-Need-Based Gift Aid:** 18%. **Avg. Amount per Student:** $5,630. **Of Those Receiving Any Aid: Receiving Need-Based Gift Aid:** 100%. **Avg. Award:** $21,375. **Receiving Need-Based Self-Help Aid:** 99%. **Avg. Award:** $3,113. **Upon Graduation, Avg. Loan Debt per Student:** $10,465. **Financial Aid Deadline:** 2/1 (priority).

Harvey Mudd College

301 East 12th Street, Claremont, CA 91711-5990. **Admissions Phone:** (909) 621-8011. **Fax:** (909) 607-7046. **Email:** admission@hmc.edu. **Website:** www.hmc.edu. **Costs** (2002–03): **Tuition and Fees:** $27,037. **Room & Board:** $8,971. **Payment Plan(s):** installment plan. **Institutional Aid** (est. 2002–03): **Institutional Aid, Need-Based:** $4,981,802. **Institutional Aid, Non-Need-Based:** $639,306. **FT Undergrads Receiving Aid:** 57%. **Avg. Amount per Student:** $21,358. **FT Undergrads Receiving Non-Need-Based Gift Aid:** 24%. **Avg. Amount per Student:** $5,990. **Of Those Receiving Any Aid:** **Receiving Need-Based Gift Aid:** 96%. **Avg. Award:** $16,839. **Receiving Need-Based Self-Help Aid:** 86%. **Avg. Award:** $5,771. **Upon Graduation, Avg. Loan Debt per Student:** $20,219. **Financial Aid Deadline:** 2/1.

Hastings College

800 Turner Ave., Hastings, NE 68901-7696. **Admissions Phone:** (402) 461-7403; (800) 532-7642. **Fax:** (402) 461-7490. **Email:** admissions@hastings.edu. **Website:** hastings.edu. **Application Website:** hastings.edu/html/admiss/admissions5.stm. **Costs (2002–03): Tuition and Fees:** $14,554. **Room & Board:** $4,398. **Payment Plan(s):** installment plan, pre-payment plan. **Institutional Aid (est. 2002–03): Institutional Aid, Need-Based:** $2,816,953. **Institutional Aid, Non-Need-Based:** $1,374,632. **FT Undergrads Receiving Aid:** 71%. **Avg. Amount per Student:** $11,597. **FT Undergrads Receiving Non-Need-Based Gift Aid:** 28%. **Avg. Amount per Student:** $6,624. **Of Those Receiving Any Aid: Receiving Need-Based Gift Aid:** 99%. **Avg. Award:** $8,050. **Receiving Need-Based Self-Help Aid:** 83%. **Avg. Award:** $4,331. **Upon Graduation, Avg. Loan Debt per Student:** $16,869. **Financial Aid Deadline:** 9/1, 5/1 (priority).

Haverford College

370 W. Lancaster Avenue, Haverford, PA 19041-1392. **Admissions Phone:** (610) 896-1350. **Fax:** (610) 896-1338. **Email:** admitme@haverford.edu. **Website:** www.haverford.edu. **Costs (2002–03): Tuition and Fees:** $27,260. **Room & Board:** $8,590. **Payment Plan(s):** installment plan, deferred payment plan. **Institutional Aid (est. 2002–03): Institutional Aid, Need-Based:** $8,377,748. **FT Undergrads Receiving Aid:** 44%. **Avg. Amount per Student:** $23,550. **Of Those Receiving Any Aid: Receiving Need-Based Gift Aid:** 93%. **Avg. Award:** $21,102. **Receiving Need-Based Self-Help Aid:** 87%. **Avg. Award:** $4,305. **Upon Graduation, Avg. Loan Debt per Student:** $15,253. **Financial Aid Deadline:** 1//31.

Hendrix College

1600 Washington Avenue, Conway, AR 72032. **Admissions Phone:** (501) 450-1362; (800) 277-9017. **Fax:** (501) 450-3843. **Email:** adm@hendrix.edu. **Website:** www.hendrix.edu. **Costs (2002–03): Tuition and Fees:** $15,630. **Room & Board:** $5,090. **Payment Plan(s):** installment plan. **Institutional Aid (est. 2002–03): Institutional Aid, Need-Based:** $3,449,571. **Institutional Aid, Non-Need-Based:** $2,983,974. **FT Undergrads Receiving Aid:** 52%. **Avg. Amount per Student:** $14,482. **FT Undergrads Receiving Non-Need-Based Gift Aid:** 44%. **Avg. Amount per Student:**

$12,623. **Of Those Receiving Any Aid: Receiving Need-Based Gift Aid:** 100%. **Avg. Award:** $10,945. **Receiving Need-Based Self-Help Aid:** 78%. **Avg. Award:** $4,532. **Upon Graduation, Avg. Loan Debt per Student:** $14,290. **Financial Aid Deadline:** 2/15 (priority).

Hiram College

P.O. Box 96, Hiram, OH 44234. **Admissions Phone:** (800) 362-5280; (330) 569-5169. **Fax:** (330) 569-5944. **Email:** admission@hiram.edu. **Website:** www.hiram.edu. **Costs (2003–04): Tuition and Fees:** $20,344. **Room & Board:** $7,100. **Payment Plan(s):** installment plan, pre-payment plan. **Institutional Aid (est. 2002–03): Institutional Aid, Need-Based:** $2,776,310. **Institutional Aid, Non-Need-Based:** $4,240,500. **FT Undergrads Receiving Aid:** 83%. **Avg. Amount per Student:** $17,492. **FT Undergrads Receiving Non-Need-Based Gift Aid:** 13%. **Avg. Amount per Student:** $7,799. **Of Those Receiving Any Aid: Receiving Need-Based Gift Aid:** 78%. **Avg. Award:** $7,908. **Receiving Need-Based Self-Help Aid:** 94%. **Avg. Award:** $5,170. **Upon Graduation, Avg. Loan Debt per Student:** $17,125. **Financial Aid Deadline:** rolling.

Hobart and William Smith Colleges

629 South Main Street, Geneva, NY 14456. **Admissions Phone:** (800) 852-2256; (800) 245-0100. **Fax:** (315) 781-3471. **Email:** admissions@hws.edu. **Website:** www.hws.edu. **Application Website:** www.hws.edu/admissions/adm_apply.asp. **Costs (2002–03): Tuition and Fees:** $27,348. **Room & Board:** $7,230. **Payment Plan(s):** installment plan, pre-payment plan. **Institutional Aid (est. 2002–03): Institutional Aid, Need-Based:** $17,446,767. **Institutional Aid, Non-Need-Based:** $2,091,522. **FT Undergrads Receiving Aid:** 64%. **Avg. Amount per Student:** $21,561. **FT Undergrads Receiving Non-Need-Based Gift Aid:** 12%. **Avg. Amount per Student:** $8,955. **Of Those Receiving Any Aid: Receiving Need-Based Gift Aid:** 99%. **Avg. Award:** $17,595. **Receiving Need-Based Self-Help Aid:** 88%. **Avg. Award:** $4,679. **Upon Graduation, Avg. Loan Debt per Student:** $18,642. **Financial Aid Deadline:** 2/1.

Hofstra University

100 Hofstra University, Hempstead, NY 11549-1000. **Admissions Phone:** (516) 463-6700; (800) HOFSTRA. **Fax:** (516) 463-5100. **Email:** admitme@hofstra.edu. **Website:** www.hofstra.edu. **Application Website:** www.hofstra.edu/application. **Costs (2002–03): Tuition and Fees:** $16,542. **Room & Board:** $8,450. **Payment Plan(s):** installment plan, deferred payment plan. **Institutional Aid (est. 2002–03): Institutional Aid, Need-Based:** $9,200,000. **Institutional Aid, Non-Need-Based:** $8,500,000. **FT Undergrads Receiving Aid:** 58%. **Avg. Amount per Student:** $11,197. **FT Undergrads Receiving Non-Need-Based Gift Aid:** 10%. **Avg. Amount per Student:** $4,115. **Of Those Receiving Any Aid: Receiving Need-Based Gift Aid:** 72%. **Avg. Award:** $4,380. **Receiving Need-Based Self-Help Aid:** 86%. **Avg. Award:** $5,072. **Upon Graduation, Avg. Loan Debt per Student:** $15,455. **Financial Aid Deadline:** 2/15 (priority).

Hollins University

P.O. Box 9707, Roanoke, VA 24020. **Admissions Phone:** (800) 456-9595; (540) 362-6401. **Fax:** (540) 362-6218. **Email:** huadm@hollins.edu. **Website:** www.hollins.edu. **Costs (2002–03): Tuition and Fees:** $18,450. **Room & Board:** $6,875. **Payment Plan(s):** installment plan. **Institutional Aid (est. 2002–03): Institutional Aid, Need-Based:** $4,057,467. **Institutional Aid, Non-Need-Based:** $1,932,704. **FT Undergrads Receiving Aid:** 59%. **Avg. Amount per Student:** $15,737. **FT Undergrads Receiving Non-Need-Based Gift Aid:** 34%. **Avg. Amount per Student:** $8,715. **Of Those Receiving Any Aid: Receiving Need-Based Gift Aid:** 100%. **Avg. Award:** $11,333. **Receiving Need-Based Self-Help Aid:** 79%. **Avg. Award:** $5,460. **Upon Graduation, Avg. Loan Debt per Student:** $13,477. **Financial Aid Deadline:** 3/1, 2/15 (priority).

Howard University*

2400 6th Street NW, Washington, DC 20059. **Admissions Phone:** (202) 806-2763. **Email:** admission@howard.edu. **Website:** howard.edu. **Costs (2002–03): Tuition and Fees:** $10,320. **Room & Board:** $5,166. **Payment Plan(s):** installment plan. **Institutional Aid: Financial Aid Deadline:** 4/1.

Illinois Institute of Technology

Room 101, Perlstein Hall, 10 W. 33rd St., Chicago, IL 60616-3793. **Admissions Phone:** (312) 567-3025; (800) 448-2329. **Fax:** (312) 567-6939. **Email:** admission@iit.edu. **Website:** www.iit.edu. **Application Website:** www.iit.edu/admission/undergrad/apply.html. **Costs (2003–04):** Tuition and Fees: $20,331. Room & Board: $6,282. **Payment Plan(s):** installment plan, prepayment plan. **Institutional Aid (2001–02):** Institutional Aid, Need-Based: $6,692,173. Institutional Aid, Non-Need-Based: $6,446,973. FT Undergrads Receiving Aid: 54%. Avg. Amount per Student: $18,232. FT Undergrads Receiving Non-Need-Based Gift Aid: 6%. Avg. Amount per Student: $11,197. Of Those Receiving Any Aid: Receiving Need-Based Gift Aid: 59%. Avg. Award: $9,828. Receiving Need-Based Self-Help Aid: 74%. Avg. Award: $5,624. Upon Graduation, Avg. Loan Debt per Student: $15,402. **Financial Aid Deadline:** rolling; 4/15 (priority).

Illinois Wesleyan University

1312 N. Park Street, Bloomington, IL 61702-2900. **Admissions Phone:** (309) 556-3031 (in-state); (800) 332-2498. **Fax:** (309) 556-3411. **Email:** iwuadmit@titan.iwu.edu. **Website:** www.iwu.edu. **Application Website:** www.iwu.edu/admissions/appinst.html. **Costs (2003–04):** Tuition and Fees: $24,540. Room & Board: $5,840. **Payment Plan(s):** installment plan. **Institutional Aid (est. 2002–03):** Institutional Aid, Need-Based: $10,144,755. Institutional Aid, Non-Need-Based: $5,295,883. FT Undergrads Receiving Aid: 52%. Avg. Amount per Student: $16,671. FT Undergrads Receiving Non-Need-Based Gift Aid: 35%. Avg. Amount per Student: $7,685. Of Those Receiving Any Aid: Receiving Need-Based Gift Aid: 100%. Avg. Award: $11,922. Receiving Need-Based Self-Help Aid: 96%. Avg. Award: $5,543. Upon Graduation, Avg. Loan Debt per Student: $17,722. **Financial Aid Deadline:** rolling; 3/1 (priority).

Indiana University of Pennsylvania

1011 South Drive, Sutton Hall Room 117, Indiana, PA 15705. **Admissions Phone:** (724) 357-2230; (800) 442-6830. **Email:** admissions-inquiry@iup.edu. **Website:** www.iup.edu. **Application Website:** www.iup.edu/admissions. **Costs (2002–03):** Tuition and Fees, In-State: $5,541. Tuition and Fees, Out-of-State: $12,109. Room & Board: $4,524. **Payment Plan(s):** installment plan. **Institutional Aid (2001–02):** Institutional Aid, Need-Based: $20,000. Institutional Aid, Non-Need-Based: $2,037,034. FT Undergrads Receiving Aid: 63%. Avg. Amount per Student: $6,669. FT Undergrads Receiving Non-Need-Based Gift Aid: 6%. Avg. Amount per Student: $2,763. Of Those Receiving Any Aid: Receiving Need-Based Gift Aid: 84%. Avg. Award: $3,256. Receiving Need-Based Self-Help Aid: 94%. Avg. Award: $3,678. Upon Graduation, Avg. Loan Debt per Student: $16,319. **Financial Aid Deadline:** 4/15.

Indiana University— Bloomington

300 N. Jordan Avenue, Bloomington, IN 47405-1106. **Admissions Phone:** (812) 855-0661. **Fax:** (812) 855-5102. **Email:** iuadmit@indiana.edu. **Website:** www.indiana.edu. **Costs (2002–03):** Tuition and Fees, In-State: $5,315. Tuition and Fees, Out-of-State: $15,926. Room & Board: $5,676. **Institutional Aid (est. 2002–03):** Institutional Aid, Need-Based: $4,369,617. Institutional Aid, Non-Need-Based: $21,597,821. FT Undergrads Receiving Aid: 37%. Avg. Amount per Student: $7,080. FT Undergrads Receiving Non-Need-Based Gift Aid: 18%. Avg. Amount per Student: $3,092. Of Those Receiving Any Aid: Receiving Need-Based Gift Aid: 58%. Avg. Award: $4,425. Receiving Need-Based Self-Help Aid: 89%. Avg. Award: $3,950. Upon Graduation, Avg. Loan Debt per Student: $16,930. **Financial Aid Deadline:** rolling; 3/1 (priority).

Ithaca College

100 Job Hall, Ithaca, NY 14850-7020. **Admissions Phone:** (607) 274-3124; (800) 429-4274. **Fax:** (607) 274-1900. **Email:** admission@ithaca.edu. **Website:** www.ithaca.edu. **Costs (2002–03):** Tuition and Fees: $21,102. Room & Board: $8,960. **Institutional Aid (est. 2002–03):** Institutional Aid, Need-Based: $40,351,867. Institutional Aid, Non-Need-Based: $6,500,646. FT Undergrads Receiving Aid: 68%. Avg. Amount per Student: $19,830. FT Undergrads Receiving Non-Need-Based Gift Aid: 3%. Avg. Amount per Student: $5,789. Of Those Receiving Any Aid: Receiving Need-

Based Gift Aid: 96%. Avg. Award: $12,692. Receiving Need-Based Self-Help Aid: 94%. Avg. Award: $6,533. **Financial Aid Deadline:** 2/1 (priority).

James Madison University

Sonner Hall MSC 0101, Harrisonburg, VA 22807. **Admissions Phone:** (540) 568-5681. **Fax:** (540) 568-3332. **Email:** gotojmu@jmu.edu. **Website:** www.jmu.edu. **Application Website:** www.jmu.edu/admissions/. **Costs (2002–03):** Tuition and Fees, In-State: $4,458 Tuition and Fees, Out-of-State: $11,642. Room & Board: $5,794. **Payment Plan(s):** installment plan. **Institutional Aid (est. 2002–03):** Institutional Aid, Need-Based: $146,180. Institutional Aid, Non-Need-Based: $1,622,728. FT Undergrads Receiving Aid: 28%. Avg. Amount per Student: $5,754. FT Undergrads Receiving Non-Need-Based Gift Aid: 4%. Avg. Amount per Student: $1,575. Of Those Receiving Any Aid: Receiving Need-Based Gift Aid: 45%. Avg. Award: $3,825. Receiving Need-Based Self-Help Aid: 78%. Avg. Award: $3,553. Upon Graduation, Avg. Loan Debt per Student: $11,786. **Financial Aid Deadline:** 3/1 (priority).

Johns Hopkins University*

3400 North Charles Street, Baltimore, MD 21218. **Admissions Phone:** (410) 516-8171. **Fax:** (410) 516-6025. **Email:** gotojhu@jhu.edu. **Website:** www.jhu.edu. **Application Website:** http://apply.jhu.edu/apply/application.html. **Costs (2002–03):** Tuition and Fees: $27,390. Room & Board: $8,830 (est. 2002–03). **Institutional Aid:** FT Undergrads Receiving Aid: 39%. Avg. Amount per Student: $24,285. FT Undergrads Receiving Non-Need-Based Gift Aid: 6%. Avg. Amount per Student: $13,968. Of Those Receiving Any Aid: Receiving Need-Based Gift Aid: 96%. Avg. Award: $18,894. Receiving Need-Based Self-Help Aid: 100%. Avg. Award: $5,366. Upon Graduation, Avg. Loan Debt per Student: $16,300. **Financial Aid Deadline:** 2/15, 2/1 (priority).

Juilliard School

60 Lincoln Center Plaza, New York, NY 10023-6588. **Admissions Phone:** (212) 799-5000. **Fax:** (212) 769-6420. **Email:** admissions@juilliard.edu. **Website:** www.juilliard.edu. **Costs (est. 2003-04):** Tuition and Fees: $20,300. Room & Board: $7,850. **Institutional Aid (est. 2002–03):** Institutional Aid, Need-Based: $4,765,746.

Institutional Aid, Non-Need-Based: $245,100. FT Undergrads Receiving Aid: 75%. Avg. Amount per Student: $20,791. FT Undergrads Receiving Non-Need-Based Gift Aid: 13%. Avg. Amount per Student: $4,980. Of Those Receiving Any Aid: Receiving Need-Based Gift Aid: 99%. Avg. Award: $15,191. Receiving Need-Based Self-Help Aid: 99%. Avg. Award: $5,910. Upon Graduation, Avg. Loan Debt per Student: $22,868. Financial Aid Deadline: 3/1.

Juniata College

1700 Moore Street, Huntingdon, PA 16652. Admissions Phone: (814) 641-3420; (877) JUNIATA. Fax: (814) 641-3100. Email: info@juniata.edu. Website: juniata.edu. Costs (2003–04): Tuition and Fees: $22,760. Room & Board: $6,290. Payment Plan(s): installment plan. Institutional Aid (est. 2002–03): Institutional Aid, Need-Based: $9,828,811. Institutional Aid, Non-Need-Based: $3,075,431. FT Undergrads Receiving Aid: 77%. Avg. Amount per Student: $17,938. FT Undergrads Receiving Non-Need-Based Gift Aid: 9%. Avg. Amount per Student: $8,805. Of Those Receiving Any Aid: Receiving Need-Based Gift Aid: 100%. Avg. Award: $12,797. Receiving Need-Based Self-Help Aid: 83%. Avg. Award: $4,802. Upon Graduation, Avg. Loan Debt per Student: $16,553. Financial Aid Deadline: 3/1 (priority).

Kalamazoo College

1200 Academy Street, Kalamazoo, MI 49006-3295. Admissions Phone: (269) 337-7166; (800) 253-3602. Fax: (269) 337-7390. Email: admission@kzoo.edu. Website: www.kzoo.edu. Costs (2002–03): Tuition and Fees: $21,603. Room & Board: $6,354. Payment Plan(s): installment plan. Institutional Aid (est. 2002–03): Institutional Aid, Need-Based: $5,830,890. Institutional Aid, Non-Need-Based: $4,393,375. FT Undergrads Receiving Aid: 50%. Avg. Amount per Student: $19,000. FT Undergrads Receiving Non-Need-Based Gift Aid: 49%. Avg. Amount per Student: $9,450. Of Those Receiving Any Aid: Receiving Need-Based Gift Aid: 96%. Avg. Award: $12,790. Receiving Need-Based Self-Help Aid: 91%. Avg. Award: $5,795. Upon Graduation, Avg. Loan Debt per Student: $20,000. Financial Aid Deadline: 2/15.

Kansas State University

119 Anderson Hall, Manhattan, KS 66506. Admissions Phone: (785) 532-6250; (800) 432-8270 (in-state). Fax: (785) 532-6393.

Email: kstate@ksu.edu. Website: www.ksu.edu. Application Website: www.ksu.edu/admit. Costs (2002–03): Tuition and Fees, In-State: $3,444. Tuition and Fees, Out-of-State: $10,704. Room & Board: $4,500. Payment Plan(s): installment plan, deferred payment plan. Institutional Aid (2001–02): Institutional Aid, Need-Based: $4,971,897. Institutional Aid, Non-Need-Based: $1,686,439. FT Undergrads Receiving Aid: 56%. Avg. Amount per Student: $4,882. FT Undergrads Receiving Non-Need-Based Gift Aid: 6%. Avg. Amount per Student: $1,834. Of Those Receiving Any Aid: Receiving Need-Based Gift Aid: 48%. Avg. Award: $2,522. Receiving Need-Based Self-Help Aid: 74%. Avg. Award: $3,557. Upon Graduation, Avg. Loan Debt per Student: $17,000. Financial Aid Deadline: 3/1 (priority).

Kenyon College

Ransom Hall, Gambier, OH 43022-9623. Admissions Phone: (740) 427-5776; (800) 848-2468. Fax: (740) 427-5770. Email: admissions@kenyon.edu. Website: www.kenyon.edu. Application Website: www.kenyon.edu/admissions/apply/. Costs (2003–04): Tuition and Fees: $30,330. Room & Board: $5,040. Payment Plan(s): installment plan. Institutional Aid (est. 2002–03): Institutional Aid, Need-Based: $11,003,788. FT Undergrads Receiving Aid: 43%. Avg. Amount per Student: $21,499. FT Undergrads Receiving Non-Need-Based Gift Aid: 21%. Avg. Amount per Student: $11,096. Of Those Receiving Any Aid: Receiving Need-Based Gift Aid: 97%. Avg. Award: $18,368. Receiving Need-Based Self-Help Aid: 91%. Avg. Award: $4,023. Upon Graduation, Avg. Loan Debt per Student: $20,850. Financial Aid Deadline: 2/15.

Kettering University

1700 West Third Avenue, Flint, MI 48504. Admissions Phone: (810) 762-7865; (800) 955-4464. Fax: (810) 762-9837. Email: admissions@kettering.edu. Website: www.kettering.edu. Costs (est. 2003-04): Tuition and Fees: $21,549. Room & Board: $4,752. Payment Plan(s): installment plan. Institutional Aid (2001–02): Institutional Aid, Need-Based: $5,489,087. Institutional Aid, Non-Need-Based: $1,549,481. FT Undergrads Receiving Aid: 69%. Avg. Amount per Student: $8,661. FT Undergrads Receiving Non-Need-Based Gift Aid: 14%. Avg. Amount per Student: $5,453. Of Those Receiving Any Aid: Receiving Need-Based Gift Aid: 91%. Avg.

Award: $6,811. Receiving Need-Based Self-Help Aid: 81%. Avg. Award: $10,177. Upon Graduation, Avg. Loan Debt per Student: $29,281. Financial Aid Deadline: rolling.

Knox College

Campus Box 148, Galesburg, IL 61401. Admissions Phone: (309) 341-7100; (800) 678-5669. Fax: (309) 341-7070. Email: admission@knox.edu. Website: www.knox.edu. Costs (2003–04): Tuition and Fees: $24,369. Room & Board: $5,925. Payment Plan(s): installment plan, pre-payment plan. Institutional Aid (est. 2002–03): Institutional Aid, Need-Based: $9,978,022. Institutional Aid, Non-Need-Based: $1,937,444. FT Undergrads Receiving Aid: 75%. Avg. Amount per Student: $20,356. FT Undergrads Receiving Non-Need-Based Gift Aid: 19%. Avg. Amount per Student: $9,689. Of Those Receiving Any Aid: Receiving Need-Based Gift Aid: 100%. Avg. Award: $15,400. Receiving Need-Based Self-Help Aid: 91%. Avg. Award: $5,471. Upon Graduation, Avg. Loan Debt per Student: $16,920. Financial Aid Deadline: rolling; 3/1 (priority).

Lafayette College

Lafayette College, Easton, PA 18042. Admissions Phone: (610) 330-5100. Fax: (610) 330-5355. Email: admissions@lafayette.edu. Website: lafayette.edu. Costs (2002–03): Tuition and Fees: $27,328. Room & Board: $8,418. Payment Plan(s): installment plan, deferred payment plan. Institutional Aid (2001–02): Institutional Aid, Need-Based: $20,824,263. Institutional Aid, Non-Need-Based: $2,324,824. FT Undergrads Receiving Aid: 54%. Avg. Amount per Student: $20,609. FT Undergrads Receiving Non-Need-Based Gift Aid: 8%. Avg. Amount per Student: $10,663. Of Those Receiving Any Aid: Receiving Need-Based Gift Aid: 94%. Avg. Award: $20,566. Receiving Need-Based Self-Help Aid: 72%. Avg. Award: $4,027. Upon Graduation, Avg. Loan Debt per Student: $17,380. Financial Aid Deadline: 2/1, 1/1 (priority).

Lake Forest College

555 North Sheridan Road, Lake Forest, IL 60045. Admissions Phone: (847) 735-5000. Fax: (847) 735-6271. Email: admissions@lakeforest.edu. Website: lakeforest.edu. Application Website: lakeforest.edu/admissions/applying/application.php3. Costs (2003–04): Tuition and Fees: $24,406. Room & Board: $5,764.

Payment Plan(s): installment plan. Institutional Aid (est. 2002–03): Institutional Aid, Need-Based: $11,466,218. Institutional Aid, Non-Need-Based: $2,629,471. FT Undergrads Receiving Aid: 70%. Avg. Amount per Student: $20,020. FT Undergrads Receiving Non-Need-Based Gift Aid: 20%. Avg. Amount per Student: $10,485. Of Those Receiving Any Aid: Receiving Need-Based Gift Aid: 100%. Avg. Award: $16,380. Receiving Need-Based Self-Help Aid: 82%. Avg. Award: $5,509. Upon Graduation, Avg. Loan Debt per Student: $15,486. Financial Aid Deadline: 3/1 (priority).

Lawrence University

P.O. Box 599, Appleton, WI 54912. Admissions Phone: (920) 832-6500; (800) 227-0982. Fax: (920) 832-6782. Email: excel@lawrence.edu. Website: www.lawrence.edu. Costs (2003–04): Tuition and Fees: $23,667. Room & Board: $5,457. Payment Plan(s): installment plan, pre-payment plan. Institutional Aid (est. 2002–03): Institutional Aid, Need-Based: $10,069,417. Institutional Aid, Non-Need-Based: $3,671,960. FT Undergrads Receiving Aid: 62%. Avg. Amount per Student: $20,421. FT Undergrads Receiving Non-Need-Based Gift Aid: 29%. Avg. Amount per Student: $10,317. Of Those Receiving Any Aid: Receiving Need-Based Gift Aid: 100%. Avg. Award: $14,705. Receiving Need-Based Self-Help Aid: 87%. Avg. Award: $6,140. Upon Graduation, Avg. Loan Debt per Student: $16,927. Financial Aid Deadline: 3/15 (priority).

Lehigh University

27 Memorial Drive West, Bethlehem, PA 18015. Admissions Phone: (610) 758-3100. Fax: (610) 758-4361. Email: admissions@lehigh.edu. Website: www.lehigh.edu. Application Website: http://www3.lehigh.edu/admissions/uadap pl.asp. Costs (2003–04): Tuition and Fees: $27,430. Room & Board: $7,880. Institutional Aid (est. 2002–03): Institutional Aid, Need-Based: $28,891,680. Institutional Aid, Non-Need-Based: $4,291,875. FT Undergrads Receiving Aid: 46%. Avg. Amount per Student: $22,072. FT Undergrads Receiving Non-Need-Based Gift Aid: 8%. Avg. Amount per Student: $12,439. Of Those Receiving Any Aid: Receiving Need-Based Gift Aid: 95%. Avg. Award: $16,547. Receiving Need-Based Self-Help Aid: 93%. Avg. Award: $5,684. Upon Graduation, Avg. Loan Debt per Student: $16,972

Lewis and Clark College

0615 SW Palatine Hill Road, Portland, OR 97219-7899. Admissions Phone: (503) 768-7040; (800) 444-4111. Fax: (503) 768-7055. Email: admissions@lclark.edu. Website: www.lclark.edu. Costs (2002–03): Tuition and Fees: $23,730. Room & Board: $6,630. Institutional Aid (est. 2002–03): Institutional Aid, Need-Based: $12,203,132. Institutional Aid, Non-Need-Based: $2,349,118. FT Undergrads Receiving Aid: 55%. Avg. Amount per Student: $19,545. FT Undergrads Receiving Non-Need-Based Gift Aid: 16%. Avg. Amount per Student: $8,282. Of Those Receiving Any Aid: Receiving Need-Based Gift Aid: 98%. Avg. Award: $14,909. Receiving Need-Based Self-Help Aid: 86%. Avg. Award: $5,658. Upon Graduation, Avg. Loan Debt per Student: $16,412. Financial Aid Deadline: 3/1 (priority).

Louisiana State University

110 Thomas Boyd Hall, Baton Rouge, LA 70803. Admissions Phone: (225) 578-1175. Fax: (225) 578-4433. Email: admissions@lsu.edu. Website: www.lsu.edu. Application Website: http://appl003.lsu.edu/slas/ugadmissions.nsf/index. Costs (2002–03): Tuition and Fees, In-State: $3,536 Tuition and Fees, Out-of-State: $8,836. Room & Board: $4,968 (2001–02). Institutional Aid (2001–02): Institutional Aid, Need-Based: $2,690,612. Institutional Aid, Non-Need-Based: $6,690,171. FT Undergrads Receiving Aid: 43%. Avg. Amount per Student: $6,354. FT Undergrads Receiving Non-Need-Based Gift Aid: 36%. Avg. Amount per Student: $3,579. Of Those Receiving Any Aid: Receiving Need-Based Gift Aid: 45%. Avg. Award: $2,720. Receiving Need-Based Self-Help Aid: 56%. Avg. Award: $3,716. Upon Graduation, Avg. Loan Debt per Student: $17,569. Financial Aid Deadline: rolling

Loyola College in Maryland

4501 North Charles Street, Baltimore, MD 21210. Admissions Phone: (410) 617-5012; (800) 221-9107. Fax: (410) 617-2176. Website: www.loyola.edu. Costs (2003–04): Tuition and Fees: $25,743. Room & Board: $8,630. Institutional Aid (est. 2002–03): Institutional Aid, Need-Based: $13,122,530. Institutional Aid, Non-Need-Based: $4,530,420. FT Undergrads Receiving Aid: 42%. Avg. Amount per Student: $16,950. FT Undergrads Receiving Non-Need-Based Gift Aid: 18%.

Avg. Amount per Student: $8,650. Of Those Receiving Any Aid: Receiving Need-Based Gift Aid: 72%. Avg. Award: $9,645. Receiving Need-Based Self-Help Aid: 88%. Avg. Award: $7,305. Upon Graduation, Avg. Loan Debt per Student: $15,835. Financial Aid Deadline: 2/10.

Loyola Marymount University

One LMU Drive, Los Angeles, CA 90045. Admissions Phone: (310) 338-2750; (800) 568-4636. Fax: (310) 338-2797. Email: admissions@lmu.edu. Website: www.lmu.edu. Costs (2002–03): Tuition and Fees: $22,016. Room & Board: $6,930. Payment Plan(s): installment plan, deferred payment plan. Institutional Aid (2001–02): FT Undergrads Receiving Aid: 57%. Avg. Amount per Student: $19,970. FT Undergrads Receiving Non-Need-Based Gift Aid: 3%. Avg. Amount per Student: $7,515. Of Those Receiving Any Aid: Receiving Need-Based Gift Aid: 99%. Avg. Award: $11,328. Receiving Need-Based Self-Help Aid: 85%. Avg. Award: $4,000. Upon Graduation, Avg. Loan Debt per Student: $19,970. Financial Aid Deadline: 2/15 (priority).

Loyola University New Orleans

6363 St. Charles Avenue, Campus Box 18, New Orleans, LA 70118-6195. Admissions Phone: (504) 865-3240; (800) 4-LOYOLA. Fax: (504) 865-3383. Email: admit@loyno.edu. Website: loyno.edu. Costs (2003–04): Tuition and Fees: $20,106. Room & Board: $7,660. Institutional Aid (est. 2002–03): Institutional Aid, Need-Based: $14,545,527. Institutional Aid, Non-Need-Based: $9,527,476. FT Undergrads Receiving Aid: 54%. Avg. Amount per Student: $15,288. FT Undergrads Receiving Non-Need-Based Gift Aid: 33%. Avg. Amount per Student: $8,953. Of Those Receiving Any Aid: Receiving Need-Based Gift Aid: 98%. Avg. Award: $11,920. Receiving Need-Based Self-Help Aid: 68%. Avg. Award: $5,091. Upon Graduation, Avg. Loan Debt per Student: $16,591. Financial Aid Deadline: rolling; 2/15 (priority).

Loyola University of Chicago*

820 North Michigan Avenue, Chicago, IL 60611. **Admissions Phone:** (312) 915-6500; (800) 262-2373. **Email:** admission@luc.edu. **Website:** www.luc.edu. **Costs (est. 2003-04):** Tuition and Fees: $21,054. **Room & Board:** $7,900. **Payment Plan(s):** installment plan. **Institutional Aid:** FT Undergrads Receiving Aid: 69%. **Avg. Amount per Student:** $17,836. FT Undergrads Receiving Non-Need-Based Gift Aid: 5%. **Avg. Amount per Student:** $7,978. Of Those Receiving Any Aid: Receiving Need-Based Gift Aid: 95%. **Avg. Award:** $12,292. Receiving Need-Based Self-Help Aid: 85%. **Avg. Award:** $6,545. **Upon Graduation, Avg. Loan Debt per Student:** $18,750. **Financial Aid Deadline:** 3/1 (priority).

Macalester College

1600 Grand Avenue, St. Paul, MN 55105. **Admissions Phone:** (651) 696-6357; (800) 231-7974. **Fax:** (651) 696-6724. **Email:** admissions@macalester.edu. **Website:** macalester.edu. **Costs (2003–04):** Tuition and Fees: $25,070. **Room & Board:** $6,874. **Institutional Aid (est. 2002–03):** Institutional Aid, Need-Based: $17,989,439. **Institutional Aid, Non-Need-Based:** $492,351. **FT Undergrads Receiving Aid:** 69%. **Avg. Amount per Student:** $20,539. **FT Undergrads Receiving Non-Need-Based Gift Aid:** 8%. **Avg. Amount per Student:** $5,428. **Of Those Receiving Any Aid:** Receiving Need-Based Gift Aid: 100%. **Avg. Award:** $16,453. **Receiving Need-Based Self-Help Aid:** 97%. **Avg. Award:** $4,275. **Upon Graduation, Avg. Loan Debt per Student:** $15,000. **Financial Aid Deadline:** 2/7.

Manhattanville College

2900 Purchase Street, Purchase, NY 10577. **Admissions Phone:** (914) 323-5464; (800) 328-4553. **Fax:** (914) 694-1732. **Email:** admissions@mville.edu. **Website:** www.mville.edu. **Application Website:** https://www.mville.edu/admissions/undergrad_app.asp. **Costs (2003–04):** Tuition and Fees: $23,040. **Room & Board:** $9,380. **Payment Plan(s):** installment plan, deferred payment plan. **Institutional Aid (2001–02):** Institutional Aid, Need-Based: $4,058,431. **Institutional Aid, Non-Need-Based:** $8,980,957. **FT Undergrads Receiving Aid:** 65%. **Avg. Amount per Student:** $17,432. **FT Undergrads Receiving Non-Need-Based Gift Aid:** 92%. **Avg. Amount per Student:** $8,334. Of

Those Receiving Any Aid: Receiving Need-Based Gift Aid: 91%. **Avg. Award:** $10,052. Receiving Need-Based Self-Help Aid: 97%. **Avg. Award:** $5,160. **Financial Aid Deadline:** rolling; 4/15 (priority).

Marlboro College*

P.O. Box A, Marlboro, VT 05344-0300. **Admissions Phone:** (802) 257-4333; (800) 343-0049. **Fax:** (802) 451-7555. **Email:** admissions@marlboro.edu. **Website:** www.marlboro.edu. **Costs (2002–03):** Tuition and Fees: $19,660. **Room & Board:** $6,750. **Payment Plan(s):** installment plan. **Institutional Aid:** FT Undergrads Receiving Aid: 71%. **Avg. Amount per Student:** $15,091. **FT Undergrads Receiving Non-Need-Based Gift Aid:** 1%. **Avg. Amount per Student:** $1,416. Of Those Receiving Any Aid: Receiving Need-Based Gift Aid: 100%. **Avg. Award:** $9,346. Receiving Need-Based Self-Help Aid: 92%. **Avg. Award:** $4,582. **Upon Graduation, Avg. Loan Debt per Student:** $18,212. **Financial Aid Deadline:** 3/1.

Marquette University

P.O. Box 1881, Milwaukee, WI 53201-1881. **Admissions Phone:** (414) 288-7302; (800) 222-6544. **Website:** www.marquette.edu. **Application Website:** www.marquette.edu/admissions. **Costs (2003–04):** Tuition and Fees: $20,724. **Room & Board:** $7,036. **Payment Plan(s):** installment plan, pre-payment plan(est. 2002–03)**Institutional Aid (est. 2002–03):** Institutional Aid, Need-Based: $25,225,394. **Institutional Aid, Non-Need-Based:** $19,191,023. **FT Undergrads Receiving Aid:** 60%. **Avg. Amount per Student:** $16,400. **FT Undergrads Receiving Non-Need-Based Gift Aid:** 22%. **Avg. Amount per Student:** $7,673. Of Those Receiving Any Aid: Receiving Need-Based Gift Aid: 89%. **Avg. Award:** $8,929. Receiving Need-Based Self-Help Aid: 85%. **Avg. Award:** $6,410. **Upon Graduation, Avg. Loan Debt per Student:** $21,258. **Financial Aid Deadline:** 3/1 (priority).

Mary Washington College

1301 College Avenue, Fredericksburg, VA 22401-5398. **Admissions Phone:** (540) 654-2000; (800) 468-5614. **Fax:** (540) 654-1857. **Email:** admit@mwc.edu. **Website:** www.mwc.edu. **Application Website:** www.mwc.edu/admissions. **Costs (2002–03):** Tuition and Fees, In-State: $3,706 Tuition and Fees, Out-of-State: $10,894. **Room & Board:** $5,318. **Payment Plan(s):** installment plan(2001–02).

Institutional Aid (2001–02): Institutional Aid, Need-Based: $395,050. Institutional Aid, Non-Need-Based: $436,250. FT Undergrads Receiving Aid: 39%. **Avg. Amount per Student:** $5,326. FT Undergrads Receiving Non-Need-Based Gift Aid: 12%. **Avg. Amount per Student:** $1,180. Of Those Receiving Any Aid: Receiving Need-Based Gift Aid: 89%. **Avg. Award:** $3,254. Receiving Need-Based Self-Help Aid: 93%. **Avg. Award:** $4,141. **Upon Graduation, Avg. Loan Debt per Student:** $13,100. **Financial Aid Deadline:** 3/1.

Massachusetts Institute of Technology

77 Massachusetts Avenue, 3-108, Cambridge, MA 02139-4307. **Admissions Phone:** (617) 253-4791. **Fax:** (617) 258-8304. **Website:** http://web.mit.edu. **Application Website:** web.mit.edu/admissions/www/applications/. **Costs (2002–03):** Tuition and Fees: $29,130. **Room & Board:** $7,830. **Payment Plan(s):** installment plan. **Institutional Aid (2001–02):** Institutional Aid, Need-Based: $38,876,858. FT Undergrads Receiving Aid: 57%. **Avg. Amount per Student:** $22,983. FT Undergrads Receiving Non-Need-Based Gift Aid: 16%. **Avg. Amount per Student:** $8,876. Of Those Receiving Any Aid: Receiving Need-Based Gift Aid: 89%. **Avg. Award:** $19,604. Receiving Need-Based Self-Help Aid: 85%. **Avg. Award:** $5,112. **Upon Graduation, Avg. Loan Debt per Student:** $22,855. **Financial Aid Deadline:** 2/1.

Miami University

301 S. Campus Ave., Oxford, OH 45056. **Admissions Phone:** (513) 529-2531. **Fax:** (513) 529-1550. **Email:** admission@muohio.edu. **Website:** www.muohio.edu. **Application Website:** www.muohio.edu/apply. **Costs (2002–03):** Tuition and Fees, In-State: $7,600. Tuition and Fees, Out-of-State: $16,324. (Regional or 'good neighbor' tuition available.) **Room & Board:** $6,240. **Payment Plan(s):** installment plan, deferred payment plan. **Institutional Aid (est. 2002–03):** Institutional Aid, Need-Based: $1,335,915. **Institutional Aid, Non-Need-Based:** $14,001,929. FT Undergrads Receiving Aid: 31%. **Avg. Amount per Student:** $6,997. FT Undergrads Receiving Non-Need-Based Gift Aid: 15%. **Avg. Amount per Student:** $4,301. Of Those Receiving Any Aid: Receiving Need-Based Gift Aid: 41%. **Avg. Award:** $3,366. Receiving Need-Based Self-

Help Aid: 82%. **Avg. Award:** $3,847. **Upon Graduation, Avg. Loan Debt per Student:** $17,579. **Financial Aid Deadline:** rolling; 2/15 (priority).

Michigan State University

250 Administration Building, East Lansing, MI 48824-1046. **Admissions Phone:** (517) 355-8332. **Fax:** (517) 353-1647. **Email:** admis@msu.edu. **Website:** www.msu.edu. **Application Website:** admis.msu.edu/Apply.asp. **Costs (2002–03):** **Tuition and Fees, In-State:** $6,101. **Tuition and Fees, Out-of-State:** $15,168. **Room & Board:** $4,932. **Payment Plan(s):** deferred payment plan. **Institutional Aid (est. 2002–03):** **Institutional Aid, Need-Based:** $23,103,239. **FT Undergrads Receiving Aid:** 40%. **Avg. Amount per Student:** $9,355. **FT Undergrads Receiving Non-Need-Based Gift Aid:** 23%. **Avg. Amount per Student:** $4,474. **Of Those Receiving Any Aid:** **Receiving Need-Based Gift Aid:** 65%. **Avg. Award:** $4,073. **Receiving Need-Based Self-Help Aid:** 96%. **Avg. Award:** $5,035. **Upon Graduation, Avg. Loan Debt per Student:** $18,663. **Financial Aid Deadline:** 6/30, 2/21 (priority).

Michigan Technological University

1400 Townsend Drive, Houghton, MI 49931. **Admissions Phone:** (906) 487-2335; (888) MTU-1885. **Fax:** (906) 487-2125. **Email:** mtu4u@mtu.edu. **Website:** www.mtu.edu. **Application Website:** www.mtu.edu/apply. **Costs (2002–03):** **Tuition and Fees, In-State:** $6,455. **Tuition and Fees, Out-of-State:** $14,825 (tuition figures are for lower division). **Room & Board:** $5,465. **Payment Plan(s):** installment plan. **Institutional Aid (est. 2002–03):** **Institutional Aid, Need-Based:** $5,438,758. **Institutional Aid, Non-Need-Based:** $4,010,628. **FT Undergrads Receiving Aid:** 42%. **Avg. Amount per Student:** $7,855. **FT Undergrads Receiving Non-Need-Based Gift Aid:** 26%. **Avg. Amount per Student:** $3,438. **Of Those Receiving Any Aid:** **Receiving Need-Based Gift Aid:** 90%. **Avg. Award:** $4,796. **Receiving Need-Based Self-Help Aid:** 88%. **Avg. Award:** $3,937. **Upon Graduation, Avg. Loan Debt per Student:** $15,711. **Financial Aid Deadline:** rolling; 2/21 (priority).

Middlebury College

The Emma Willard House, Middlebury, VT 05753-6002. **Admissions Phone:** (802) 443-3000. **Fax:** (802) 443-2056. **Email:** admissions@middlebury.edu. **Website:** middlebury.edu/. **Application Website:** middlebury.edu/%7Eadmit/apply-online.html. **Costs (2002–03):** **Comprehensive Fees:** $35,900. **Payment Plan(s):** installment plan, pre-payment plan. **Institutional Aid (est. 2002–03):** **Institutional Aid, Need-Based:** $16,155,998. **FT Undergrads Receiving Aid:** 36%. **Avg. Amount per Student:** $26,979. **Of Those Receiving Any Aid:** **Receiving Need-Based Gift Aid:** 100%. **Avg. Award:** $21,244. **Receiving Need-Based Self-Help Aid:** 100%. **Avg. Award:** $5,250. **Upon Graduation, Avg. Loan Debt per Student:** $21,751. **Financial Aid Deadline:** 12/31, 11/15 (priority).

Mills College*

5000 MacArthur Boulevard, Oakland, CA 94613-1301. **Admissions Phone:** (800) 87-MILLS. **Fax:** (510) 430-3314. **Email:** admission@mills.edu. **Website:** mills.edu. **Costs (2002–03):** **Tuition and Fees:** $22,280. **Room & Board:** $8,500. **Payment Plan(s):** installment plan. **Institutional Aid:** **Financial Aid Deadline:** 2/15.

Millsaps College

1701 North State Street, Jackson, MS 39210. **Admissions Phone:** (601) 974-1050; (800) 352-1050. **Fax:** (601) 974-1059. **Email:** admissions@millsaps.edu. **Website:** www.millsaps.edu. **Costs (2003–04):** **Tuition and Fees:** $18,414. **Room & Board:** $6,768. **Payment Plan(s):** installment plan, deferred payment plan. **Institutional Aid (est. 2002–03):** **Institutional Aid, Need-Based:** $5,860,109. **Institutional Aid, Non-Need-Based:** $4,369,591. **FT Undergrads Receiving Aid:** 55%. **Avg. Amount per Student:** $16,072. **FT Undergrads Receiving Non-Need-Based Gift Aid:** 41%. **Avg. Amount per Student:** $11,567. **Of Those Receiving Any Aid:** **Receiving Need-Based Gift Aid:** 100%. **Avg. Award:** $12,523. **Receiving Need-Based Self-Help Aid:** 77%. **Avg. Award:** $4,608. **Upon Graduation, Avg. Loan Debt per Student:** $11,582. **Financial Aid Deadline:** rolling; 3/1 (priority).

Morehouse College

830 Westview Drive S.W., Atlanta, GA 30314. **Admissions Phone:** (404) 681-2800; (800) 851-1254. **Fax:** (404) 524-5635.

Email: admissions@morehouse.edu. **Website:** www.morehouse.edu. **Costs (2002–03):** **Tuition and Fees:** $14,060. **Room & Board:** $8,172. **Payment Plan(s):** installment plan, deferred payment plan, pre-payment plan. **Institutional Aid (est. 2002–03):** **Institutional Aid, Need-Based:** $3,310,257. **Institutional Aid, Non-Need-Based:** $8,404,810. **FT Undergrads Receiving Aid:** 95%. **Avg. Amount per Student:** $6,416. **FT Undergrads Receiving Non-Need-Based Gift Aid:** 64%. **Avg. Amount per Student:** $4,482. **Of Those Receiving Any Aid:** **Receiving Need-Based Gift Aid:** 48%. **Avg. Award:** $2,830. **Receiving Need-Based Self-Help Aid:** 100%. **Avg. Award:** $3,193. **Financial Aid Deadline:** 2/15, 11/1 (priority).

Mount Holyoke College

50 College Street, South Hadley, MA 01075-1488. **Admissions Phone:** (413) 538-2023. **Fax:** (413) 538-2409. **Email:** admission@mtholyoke.edu. **Website:** www.mtholyoke.edu. **Application Website:** http://www.mtholyoke.edu/adm/center/applications.shtml. **Costs (2002–03):** **Tuition and Fees:** $27,708. **Room & Board:** $8,100. **Payment Plan(s):** installment plan, pre-payment plan. **Institutional Aid (est. 2002–03):** **Institutional Aid, Need-Based:** $25,350,333. **Institutional Aid, Non-Need-Based:** $680,000. **FT Undergrads Receiving Aid:** 67%. **Avg. Amount per Student:** $25,500. **FT Undergrads Receiving Non-Need-Based Gift Aid:** 3%. **Avg. Amount per Student:** $10,300. **Of Those Receiving Any Aid:** **Receiving Need-Based Gift Aid:** 95%. **Avg. Award:** $19,400. **Receiving Need-Based Self-Help Aid:** 97%. **Avg. Award:** $5,875. **Upon Graduation, Avg. Loan Debt per Student:** $14,200. **Financial Aid Deadline:** 2/1 (priority).

Muhlenberg College

2400 Chew Street, Allentown, PA 18104-5586. **Admissions Phone:** (484) 664-3200. **Fax:** (484) 664-3234. **Email:** admissions@muhlenberg.edu. **Website:** muhlenberg.edu. **Costs (est. 2003-04):** **Tuition and Fees:** $24,945. **Room & Board:** $6,540. **Payment Plan(s):** installment plan. **Institutional Aid (est. 2002–03):** **Institutional Aid, Need-Based:** $10,888,398. **Institutional Aid, Non-Need-Based:** $3,861,457. **FT Undergrads Receiving Aid:** 44%. **Avg. Amount per Student:** $16,023. **FT Undergrads Receiving Non-Need-Based Gift Aid:** 25%. **Avg. Amount per Student:** $10,136. **Of Those Receiving Any Aid: Receiving Need-**

Based Gift Aid: 97%. **Avg. Award:** $12,945. Receiving Need-Based Self-Help Aid: 72%. **Avg. Award:** $4,870. Upon Graduation, **Avg. Loan Debt per Student:** $16,848. **Financial Aid Deadline:** 2/15.

New College of Florida

5700 North Tamiami Trail, Sarasota, FL 34243-2197. **Admissions Phone:** (941) 359-4269. **Fax:** (941) 359-4435. **Email:** admissions@ncf.edu. **Website:** www.ncf.edu. **Application Website:** www.ncf.edu/admissions. **Costs (2002–03):** Tuition and Fees, In-State: $3,020 Tuition and Fees, Out-of-State: $13,810. **Room & Board:** $5,394. **Institutional Aid (2001–02):** Institutional Aid, Need-Based: $101,121. Institutional Aid, Non-Need-Based: $1,367,550. FT Undergrads Receiving Aid: 42%. **Avg. Amount per Student:** $7,669. FT Undergrads Receiving Non-Need-Based Gift Aid: 48%. **Avg. Amount per Student:** $4,992. Of Those Receiving Any Aid: Receiving Need-Based Gift Aid: 95%. **Avg. Award:** $5,334. Receiving Need-Based Self-Help Aid: 67%. **Avg. Award:** $3,373. **Financial Aid Deadline:** 3/1 (priority).

New York University

22 Washington Square North, New York, NY 10011-9108. **Admissions Phone:** (212) 998-4500. **Fax:** (212) 995-4902. **Website:** www.nyu.edu. **Application Website:** nyu.edu/ugadmissions/uga/apply/applynow.html. **Costs (2002–03):** Tuition and Fees: $26,646. **Room & Board:** $10,430. **Payment Plan(s):** installment plan, deferred payment plan, pre-payment plan. **Institutional Aid (est. 2002–03):** Institutional Aid, Need-Based: $71,367,287. Institutional Aid, Non-Need-Based: $13,500,087. FT Undergrads Receiving Aid: 55%. **Avg. Amount per Student:** $17,715. FT Undergrads Receiving Non-Need-Based Gift Aid: 15%. **Avg. Amount per Student:** $6,750. Of Those Receiving Any Aid: Receiving Need-Based Gift Aid: 92%. **Avg. Award:** $11,823. Receiving Need-Based Self-Help Aid: 93%. **Avg. Award:** $7,600. Upon Graduation, **Avg. Loan Debt per Student:** $21,495. **Financial Aid Deadline:** 2/15.

North Carolina School of the Arts

1533 South Main Street, Winston-Salem, NC 27127. **Admissions Phone:** (336) 770-3290; (336) 770-3291. **Fax:** (336) 770-3370. **Email:** admissions@ncarts.edu. **Website:** www.ncarts.edu. **Costs (2002–03):** Tuition

and Fees, In-State: $3,450. Tuition and Fees, Out-of-State: $14,050. **Room & Board:** $5,115. **Institutional Aid (2001–02):** Institutional Aid, Need-Based: $734,177. Institutional Aid, Non-Need-Based: $217,592. FT Undergrads Receiving Aid: 47%. **Avg. Amount per Student:** $8,499. FT Undergrads Receiving Non-Need-Based Gift Aid: 18%. **Avg. Amount per Student:** $2,216. Of Those Receiving Any Aid: Receiving Need-Based Gift Aid: 93%. **Avg. Award:** $4,723. Receiving Need-Based Self-Help Aid: 91%. **Avg. Award:** $2,236. Upon Graduation, **Avg. Loan Debt per Student:** $15,566. **Financial Aid Deadline:** 3/1 (priority).

North Carolina State University

Box 7103, Raleigh, NC 27695. **Admissions Phone:** (919) 515-2434. **Fax:** (919) 515-5039. **Email:** undergrad_admissions@ncsu.edu. **Website:** ncsu.edu. **Application Website:** ncsu.edu/admissions.html. **Costs (est. 2003-04):** Tuition and Fees, In-State: $3,829. Tuition and Fees, Out-of-State: $15,113. **Room & Board:** $5,917. **Payment Plan(s):** installment plan. **Institutional Aid (est. 2002–03):** Institutional Aid, Need-Based: $17,272,495. Institutional Aid, Non-Need-Based: $9,530,019. FT Undergrads Receiving Aid: 37%. **Avg. Amount per Student:** $7,321. FT Undergrads Receiving Non-Need-Based Gift Aid: 11%. **Avg. Amount per Student:** $4,867. Of Those Receiving Any Aid: Receiving Need-Based Gift Aid: 96%. **Avg. Award:** $5,180. Receiving Need-Based Self-Help Aid: 80%. **Avg. Award:** $2,877. Upon Graduation, **Avg. Loan Debt per Student:** $15,476. **Financial Aid Deadline:** rolling; 3/1 (priority).

Northeastern University

360 Huntington Avenue, 150 Richards Hall, Boston, MA 02115. **Admissions Phone:** (617) 373-2200. **Fax:** (617) 373-8780. **Email:** admissions@neu.edu. **Website:** www.neu.edu/admissions. **Costs (2002–03):** Tuition and Fees: $24,467. **Room & Board:** $9,660. **Payment Plan(s):** installment plan. **Institutional Aid (est. 2002–03):** Institutional Aid, Need-Based: $66,512,680. Institutional Aid, Non-Need-Based: $8,867,556. FT Undergrads Receiving Aid: 63%. **Avg. Amount per Student:** $14,925. FT Undergrads Receiving Non-Need-Based Gift Aid: 10%. Of Those Receiving Any Aid: Receiving Need-Based Gift Aid: 91%. **Avg. Award:**

$10,126. Receiving Need-Based Self-Help Aid: 93%. **Avg. Award:** $5,017. **Financial Aid Deadline:** rolling; 2/15 (priority).

Northern Arizona University

P.O. Box 4084, Flagstaff, AZ 86011. **Admissions Phone:** (928) 523-5511; (888) 667-3628. **Fax:** (928) 523-0226. **Email:** undergraduate.admissions@nau.edu. **Website:** www.nau.edu. **Application Website:** www4.nau.edu.uadmissions. **Costs (2002–03):** Tuition and Fees, In-State: $2,585 Tuition and Fees, Out-of-State: $11,105. **Room & Board:** $5,156. **Institutional Aid (est. 2002–03):** Institutional Aid, Need-Based: $5,607,194. Institutional Aid, Non-Need-Based: $1,770,693. FT Undergrads Receiving Aid: 49%. **Avg. Amount per Student:** $8,004. FT Undergrads Receiving Non-Need-Based Gift Aid: 15%. **Avg. Amount per Student:** $2,131. Of Those Receiving Any Aid: Receiving Need-Based Gift Aid: 87%. **Avg. Award:** $4,617. Receiving Need-Based Self-Help Aid: 78%. **Avg. Award:** $5,584. Upon Graduation, **Avg. Loan Debt per Student:** $15,795. **Financial Aid Deadline:** rolling.

Northwestern University

P.O. Box 3060, Evanston, IL 60204-3060. **Admissions Phone:** (847) 491-7271. **Email:** ug-admission@northwestern.edu. **Website:** www.northwestern.edu. **Application Website:** www.ugadm.northwestern.edu. **Costs (2002–03):** Tuition and Fees: $27,228. **Room & Board:** $8,446. **Payment Plan(s):** installment plan. **Institutional Aid (est. 2002–03):** Institutional Aid, Need-Based: $49,115,392. FT Undergrads Receiving Aid: 44%. **Avg. Amount per Student:** $23,382. FT Undergrads Receiving Non-Need-Based Gift Aid: 6%. **Avg. Amount per Student:** $2,279. Of Those Receiving Any Aid: Receiving Need-Based Gift Aid: 93%. **Avg. Award:** $18,441. Receiving Need-Based Self-Help Aid: 95%. **Avg. Award:** $5,814. Upon Graduation, **Avg. Loan Debt per Student:** $14,551. **Financial Aid Deadline:** 2/1.

Oberlin College

101 N. Professor Street, Oberlin, OH 44074. **Admissions Phone:** (440) 775-8411; (800) 622-6243. **Fax:** (440) 775-6905. **Email:** college.admissions@oberlin.edu. **Website:** www.oberlin.edu. **Application Website:** www.oberlin.edu/coladm/onlineapplication. **Costs (2002–03):** Tuition and Fees: $28,050. **Room & Board:** $6,830. **Payment Plan(s):** installment plan.

Institutional Aid (est. 2002–03): Institutional Aid, Need-Based: $27,490,175. Institutional Aid, Non-Need-Based: $3,295,849. FT Undergrads Receiving Aid: 56%. Avg. Amount per Student: $23,099. FT Undergrads Receiving Non-Need-Based Gift Aid: 12%. Avg. Amount per Student: $11,005. Of Those Receiving Any Aid: Receiving Need-Based Gift Aid: 100%. Avg. Award: $16,607. Receiving Need-Based Self-Help Aid: 87%. Avg. Award: $4,371. Upon Graduation, Avg. Loan Debt per Student: $13,034. Financial Aid Deadline: 2/15, 2/1 (priority).

Occidental College

1600 Campus Road, Los Angeles, CA 90041-3314. Admissions Phone: (323) 259-2700; (800) 825-5262. Fax: (323) 341-4875. Email: admission@oxy.edu. Website: www.oxy.edu. Application Website: http://departments.oxy.edu/admission. Costs (2003–04): Tuition and Fees: $27,734. Room & Board: $7,823. Payment Plan(s): installment plan, deferred payment plan, pre-payment plan. Institutional Aid (est. 2002–03): Institutional Aid, Need-Based: $14,909,808. Institutional Aid, Non-Need-Based: $2,880,391. FT Undergrads Receiving Aid: 56%. Avg. Amount per Student: $25,144. FT Undergrads Receiving Non-Need-Based Gift Aid: 15%. Avg. Amount per Student: $12,978. Of Those Receiving Any Aid: Receiving Need-Based Gift Aid: 99%. Avg. Award: $20,058. Receiving Need-Based Self-Help Aid: 92%. Avg. Award: $5,852. Upon Graduation, Avg. Loan Debt per Student: $15,066. Financial Aid Deadline: 2/1.

Ohio State University, The

Third Floor Lincoln Tower, 1800 Cannon Drive, Columbus, OH 43210. Admissions Phone: (614) 292-3980. Fax: (614) 292-4818. Email: askabuckeye@osu.edu. Website: www.osu.edu. Application Website: www.applyweb.com/aw?osu. Costs (2002–03): Tuition and Fees, In-State: $5,664. Tuition and Fees, Out-of-State: $15,087. Room & Board: $6,291. Institutional Aid (est. 2002–03): Institutional Aid, Need-Based: $8,130,499. Institutional Aid, Non-Need-Based: $37,447,487. FT Undergrads Receiving Aid: 48%. Avg. Amount per Student: $8,211. FT Undergrads Receiving Non-Need-Based Gift Aid: 7%. Avg. Amount per Student: $3,500. Of Those Receiving Any Aid: Receiving Need-Based Gift Aid: 54%. Avg. Award: $3,962. Receiving Need-Based Self-Help Aid: 87%. Avg. Award: $4,737. Upon

Graduation, Avg. Loan Debt per Student: $15,011. Financial Aid Deadline: 2/15 (priority).

Ohio University

120 Chubb Hall, Athens, OH 45701-2979. Admissions Phone: (740) 593-4100. Fax: (740) 593-0560. Email: admissions. freshmen@ohiou.edu. Website: www.ohiou.edu. Application Website: https://applyweb.com/aw?ohiou. Costs (2002–03): Tuition and Fees, In-State: $6,336. Tuition and Fees, Out-of-State: $13,818. Room & Board: $6,777. Payment Plan(s): installment plan. Institutional Aid (est. 2002–03): Institutional Aid, Need-Based: $478,350. Institutional Aid, Non-Need-Based: $9,428,020. FT Undergrads Receiving Aid: 46%. Avg. Amount per Student: $6,581. FT Undergrads Receiving Non-Need-Based Gift Aid: 8%. Avg. Amount per Student: $3,430. Of Those Receiving Any Aid: Receiving Need-Based Gift Aid: 42%. Avg. Award: $3,412. Receiving Need-Based Self-Help Aid: 86%. Avg. Award: $3,840. Upon Graduation, Avg. Loan Debt per Student: $15,285. Financial Aid Deadline: 3/15 (priority).

Oklahoma State University

324 Student Union, Stillwater, OK 74078. Admissions Phone: (405) 744-6858; (800) 233-5019 (in-state). Fax: (405) 744-5285. Email: admit@okstate.edu. Website: www.okstate.edu. Costs (est. 2003-04): Tuition and Fees, In-State: $3,025. Tuition and Fees, Out-of-State: $8,079. Room & Board: $5,150. Payment Plan(s): installment plan. Institutional Aid (2001–02): Institutional Aid, Need-Based: $1,971,989. Institutional Aid, Non-Need-Based: $2,718,442. FT Undergrads Receiving Aid: 45%. Avg. Amount per Student: $7,550. FT Undergrads Receiving Non-Need-Based Gift Aid: 14%. Avg. Amount per Student: $2,664. Of Those Receiving Any Aid: Receiving Need-Based Gift Aid: 71%. Avg. Award: $3,199. Receiving Need-Based Self-Help Aid: 75%. Avg. Award: $3,747. Upon Graduation, Avg. Loan Debt per Student: $15,580. Financial Aid Deadline: rolling

Oregon State University

104 Kerr Administration Building, Corvallis, OR 97331-2106. Admissions Phone: (541) 737-4411; (800) 291-4192. Fax: (541) 737-2482. Email: osuadmit@orst.edu. Website: http://oregonstate.edu. Application Website:

http://oregonstate.edu/admissions/. Costs (2002–03): Tuition and Fees, In-State: $4,014. Tuition and Fees, Out-of-State: $14,898. Room & Board: $5,976. Institutional Aid (est. 2002–03): Financial Aid Deadline: 5/1, 2/1 (priority).

Pacific Lutheran University

Pacific Lutheran University, Tacoma, WA 98447. Admissions Phone: (253) 535-7151; (800) 274-6758. Fax: (253) 536-5136. Email: admissions@plu.edu. Website: www.plu.edu. Costs (2003–04): Tuition and Fees: $19,610. Room & Board: $6,105. Payment Plan(s): installment plan. Institutional Aid (est. 2002–03): Institutional Aid, Need-Based: $12,700,615. Institutional Aid, Non-Need-Based: $6,208,513. FT Undergrads Receiving Aid: 70%. Avg. Amount per Student: $16,411. FT Undergrads Receiving Non-Need-Based Gift Aid: 17%. Avg. Amount per Student: $5,858. Of Those Receiving Any Aid: Receiving Need-Based Gift Aid: 92%. Avg. Award: $7,151. Receiving Need-Based Self-Help Aid: 92%. Avg. Award: $7,868. Upon Graduation, Avg. Loan Debt per Student: $20,585. Financial Aid Deadline: rolling; 1/31 (priority).

Parsons School of Design

66 Fifth Avenue, New York, NY 10011. Admissions Phone: (877) 528-3321. Fax: (212) 229-5166. Email: customer@ newschool.edu. Website: www.parsons.edu. Costs (2003–04): Tuition and Fees: $24,475. Room & Board: $9,896. Payment Plan(s): installment plan. Institutional Aid (est. 2002–03): Institutional Aid, Need-Based: $10,577,837. Institutional Aid, Non-Need-Based: $502,000. FT Undergrads Receiving Aid: 61%. Avg. Amount per Student: $13,156. FT Undergrads Receiving Non-Need-Based Gift Aid: 4%. Avg. Amount per Student: $3,223. Of Those Receiving Any Aid: Receiving Need-Based Gift Aid: 99%. Avg. Award: $10,165. Receiving Need-Based Self-Help Aid: 68%. Avg. Award: $4,905. Upon Graduation, Avg. Loan Debt per Student: $23,919. Financial Aid Deadline: rolling; 3/1 (priority).

Pennsylvania State University—University Park

201 Shields Building, Box 3000, University Park, PA 16804-3000. Admissions Phone: (814) 865-5471. Fax: (814) 863-7590. Email: admissions@psu.edu. Website: www.psu.edu. Application Website:

www.psu.edu/dept/admissions/apply. Costs (2002–03): Tuition and Fees, In-State: $8,382. Tuition and Fees, Out-of-State: $17,610. Room & Board: $5,660. Payment Plan(s): deferred payment plan. Institutional Aid (2001–02): Institutional Aid, Need-Based: $7,350,083. Institutional Aid, Non-Need-Based: $12,391,172. FT Undergrads Receiving Aid: 47%. Avg. Amount per Student: $10,954. FT Undergrads Receiving Non-Need-Based Gift Aid: 21%. Avg. Amount per Student: $5,492. Of Those Receiving Any Aid: Receiving Need-Based Gift Aid: 70%. Avg. Award: $4,145. Receiving Need-Based Self-Help Aid: 84%. Avg. Award: $4,220. Upon Graduation, Avg. Loan Debt per Student: $17,900. Financial Aid Deadline: rolling; 2/15 (priority).

Pepperdine University

Seaver College, 24255 Pacific Coast Highway, Malibu, CA 90263-4392. Admissions Phone: (310) 506-4392. Fax: (310) 506-4861. Website: pepperdine.edu. Application Website: pepperdine.edu/seaver/admission/App.htm. Costs (2002–03): Tuition and Fees: $26,370. Room & Board: $7,930. Payment Plan(s): installment plan. Institutional Aid (2001–02): Institutional Aid, Need-Based: $15,881,573. Institutional Aid, Non-Need-Based: $5,720,923. FT Undergrads Receiving Aid: 53%. Avg. Amount per Student: $22,611. FT Undergrads Receiving Non-Need-Based Gift Aid: 9%. Avg. Amount per Student: $14,042. Of Those Receiving Any Aid: Receiving Need-Based Gift Aid: 96%. Avg. Award: $16,191. Receiving Need-Based Self-Help Aid: 82%. Avg. Award: $5,902. Upon Graduation, Avg. Loan Debt per Student: $31,179. Financial Aid Deadline: 4/1, 2/15 (priority).

Pitzer College

1050 North Mills Avenue, Claremont, CA 91711. Admissions Phone: (909) 621-8129; (800) PITZER1. Fax: (909) 621-8770. Email: admission@pitzer.edu. Website: www.pitzer.edu. Application Website: www.pitzer.edu/admission/applic.asp. Costs (2002–03): Tuition and Fees: $28,256. Room & Board: $7,370. Payment Plan(s): installment plan. Institutional Aid (est. 2002–03): Institutional Aid, Need-Based: $6,138,193. Institutional Aid, Non-Need-Based: $280,000. FT Undergrads Receiving Aid: 45%. Avg. Amount per Student: $25,947. FT Undergrads Receiving Non-Need-Based Gift Aid: 3%. Avg. Amount per Student: $10,000. Of

Those Receiving Any Aid: Receiving Need-Based Gift Aid: 98%. Avg. Award: $20,308. Receiving Need-Based Self-Help Aid: 92%. Avg. Award: $7,326. Upon Graduation, Avg. Loan Debt per Student: $20,900. Financial Aid Deadline: 2/1.

Pomona College

333 N. College Way, Claremont, CA 91711. Admissions Phone: (909) 621-8134. Fax: (909) 621-8952. Email: admissions@pomona.edu. Website: www.pomona.edu. Application Website: www.pomona.edu/admissions/. Costs (2003–04): Tuition and Fees: $27,150. Room & Board: $9,980. Payment Plan(s): installment plan. Institutional Aid (2001–02): Institutional Aid, Need-Based: $12,891,274. FT Undergrads Receiving Aid: 52%. Avg. Amount per Student: $24,210. FT Undergrads Receiving Non-Need-Based Gift Aid: 4%. Avg. Amount per Student: $2,457. Of Those Receiving Any Aid: Receiving Need-Based Gift Aid: 100%. Avg. Award: $19,560. Receiving Need-Based Self-Help Aid: 97%. Avg. Award: $4,650. Upon Graduation, Avg. Loan Debt per Student: $15,800. Financial Aid Deadline: 2/1.

Princeton University

P.O.Box 430, Princeton, NJ 08544-0403. Admissions Phone: (609) 258-3060. Fax: (609) 258-6743. Website: www.princeton.edu. Application Website: www.princeton.edu/pr/admissions/u/appl. Costs (2003–04): Tuition and Fees: $28,540. Room & Board: $8,109. Payment Plan(s): installment plan, deferred payment plan. Institutional Aid (2001–02): Institutional Aid, Need-Based: $38,386,000. FT Undergrads Receiving Aid: 43%. Avg. Amount per Student: $23,053. Of Those Receiving Any Aid: Receiving Need-Based Gift Aid: 100%. Avg. Award: $22,309. Receiving Need-Based Self-Help Aid: 100%. Avg. Award: $1,160. Financial Aid Deadline: 2/1.

Providence College

River Avenue and Eaton Street, Providence, RI 02918-0001. Admissions Phone: (401) 865-2535; (800) 721-6444. Fax: (401) 865-2826. Email: pcadmiss@providence.edu. Website: www.providence.edu. Costs (2002–03): Tuition and Fees: $20,860. Room & Board: $8,120. Payment Plan(s): installment plan. Institutional Aid (est. 2002–03): Institutional Aid, Need-Based: $17,051,977. Institutional Aid, Non-Need-Based: $4,256,600. FT Undergrads

Receiving Aid: 52%. Avg. Amount per Student: $14,582. FT Undergrads Receiving Non-Need-Based Gift Aid: 12%. Avg. Amount per Student: $9,800. Of Those Receiving Any Aid: Receiving Need-Based Gift Aid: 98%. Avg. Award: $8,900. Receiving Need-Based Self-Help Aid: 96%. Avg. Award: $5,329. Upon Graduation, Avg. Loan Debt per Student: $19,850. Financial Aid Deadline: 2/1.

Purdue University—West Lafayette

1080 Schleman Hall, West Lafayette, IN 47907-1080. Admissions Phone: (765) 494-1776. Fax: (765) 494-0544. Email: admissions@adms.purdue.edu. Website: www.purdue.edu. Application Website: adpc.purdue.edu/Admissions. Costs (2002–03): Tuition and Fees, In-State: $5,580 Tuition and Fees, Out-of-State: $16,260 (Regional or 'good neighbor' tuition available.) Room & Board: $6,340. Payment Plan(s): installment plan, deferred payment plan, pre-payment plan. Institutional Aid (est. 2002–03): Institutional Aid, Need-Based: $14,022,778. FT Undergrads Receiving Aid: 37%. Avg. Amount per Student: $7,387. FT Undergrads Receiving Non-Need-Based Gift Aid: 13%. Avg. Amount per Student: $9,198. Of Those Receiving Any Aid: Receiving Need-Based Gift Aid: 59%. Avg. Award: $5,968. Receiving Need-Based Self-Help Aid: 90%. Avg. Award: $4,013. Upon Graduation, Avg. Loan Debt per Student: $15,677. Financial Aid Deadline: 3/2 (priority).

Randolph-Macon Woman's College

2500 Rivermont Avenue, Lynchburg, VA 24503-1526. Admissions Phone: (434) 947-8100; (800) 745-7692. Fax: (434) 947-8996. Email: admissions@rmwc.edu. Website: rmwc.edu. Costs (2002–03): Tuition and Fees: $19,280. Room & Board: $7,560. Payment Plan(s): installment plan. Institutional Aid (est. 2002–03): Institutional Aid, Need-Based: $4,581,603. Institutional Aid, Non-Need-Based: $3,422,299. FT Undergrads Receiving Aid: 62%. Avg. Amount per Student: $18,381. FT Undergrads Receiving Non-Need-Based Gift Aid: 37%. Avg. Amount per Student: $12,560. Of Those Receiving Any Aid: Receiving Need-Based Gift Aid: 100%. Avg. Award: $14,100. Receiving Need-Based Self-Help Aid: 99%. Avg. Award: $5,373.

Upon Graduation, Avg. Loan Debt per Student: $20,385. Financial Aid Deadline: rolling; 3/1 (priority).

Reed College

3203 Southeast Woodstock Boulevard, Portland, OR 97202-8199. Admissions Phone: (800) 547-4750; (503) 777-7511. Fax: (503) 777-7553. Email: admission@reed.edu. Website: www.reed.edu. Costs (2002–03): Tuition and Fees: $27,560. Room & Board: $7,380. Payment Plan(s): installment plan. Institutional Aid (est. 2002–03): Institutional Aid, Need-Based: $11,858,300. FT Undergrads Receiving Aid: 55%. Avg. Amount per Student: $21,254. Of Those Receiving Any Aid: Receiving Need-Based Gift Aid: 92%. Avg. Award: $19,096. Receiving Need-Based Self-Help Aid: 87%. Avg. Award: $4,268. Upon Graduation, Avg. Loan Debt per Student: $16,758. Financial Aid Deadline: 2/1, 1/15 (priority).

Rensselaer Polytechnic Institute

110 8th Street, Troy, NY 12180-3590. Admissions Phone: (518) 276-6216. Fax: (518) 276-4072. Email: admissions@rpi.edu. Website: www.rpi.edu. Application Website: http://admissions.rpi.edu. Costs (2002–03): Tuition and Fees: $27,170. Room & Board: $8,902. Payment Plan(s): installment plan. Institutional Aid (est. 2002–03): Institutional Aid, Need-Based: $41,304,000. Institutional Aid, Non-Need-Based: $10,326,000. FT Undergrads Receiving Aid: 71%. Avg. Amount per Student: $22,791. FT Undergrads Receiving Non-Need-Based Gift Aid: 15%. Avg. Amount per Student: $10,789. Of Those Receiving Any Aid: Receiving Need-Based Gift Aid: 100%. Avg. Award: $16,840. Receiving Need-Based Self-Help Aid: 100%. Avg. Award: $7,790. Upon Graduation, Avg. Loan Debt per Student: $24,590. Financial Aid Deadline: 2/15 (priority).

Rhode Island School of Design

2 College Street, Providence, RI 02903. Admissions Phone: (401) 454-6300. Fax: (401) 454-6309. Website: www.risd.edu. Costs (2003–04): Tuition and Fees: $24,765. Room & Board: $7,038. Payment Plan(s): deferred payment plan. Institutional Aid (est. 2002–03): Institutional Aid, Need-Based: $7,500,000.

Institutional Aid, Non-Need-Based: $50,000. FT Undergrads Receiving Aid: 48%. Avg. Amount per Student: $15,100. FT Undergrads Receiving Non-Need-Based Gift Aid: 2%. Avg. Amount per Student: $1,250. Of Those Receiving Any Aid: Receiving Need-Based Gift Aid: 84%. Avg. Award: $8,025. Receiving Need-Based Self-Help Aid: 98%. Avg. Award: $6,900. Upon Graduation, Avg. Loan Debt per Student: $21,125. Financial Aid Deadline: 2/15.

Rhodes College

2000 North Parkway, Memphis, TN 38112. Admissions Phone: (901) 843-3700; (800) 844-5969. Fax: (901) 843-3631. Email: adminfo@rhodes.edu. Website: www.rhodes.edu. Costs (2003–04): Tuition and Fees: $22,938. Room & Board: $6,382. Institutional Aid (est. 2002–03): Institutional Aid, Need-Based: $6,171,813. Institutional Aid, Non-Need-Based: $4,416,086. FT Undergrads Receiving Aid: 37%. Avg. Amount per Student: $16,054. FT Undergrads Receiving Non-Need-Based Gift Aid: 32%. Avg. Amount per Student: $8,784. Of Those Receiving Any Aid: Receiving Need-Based Gift Aid: 98%. Avg. Award: $11,181. Receiving Need-Based Self-Help Aid: 86%. Avg. Award: $4,849. Upon Graduation, Avg. Loan Debt per Student: $15,100. Financial Aid Deadline: 3/1 (priority).

Rice University

Post Office Box 1892, Houston, TX 77251-1892. Admissions Phone: (713) 348-7423; (800) 527-6957. Fax: (713) 348-5952. Email: admission@rice.edu. Website: www.rice.edu. Costs (est. 2003-04): Tuition and Fees: $19,661. Room & Board: $7,880. Payment Plan(s): installment plan. Institutional Aid (est. 2002–03): Institutional Aid, Need-Based: $8,521,008. Institutional Aid, Non-Need-Based: $3,442,271. FT Undergrads Receiving Aid: 30%. Avg. Amount per Student: $15,498. FT Undergrads Receiving Non-Need-Based Gift Aid: 25%. Avg. Amount per Student: $5,932. Of Those Receiving Any Aid: Receiving Need-Based Gift Aid: 100%. Avg. Award: $13,571. Receiving Need-Based Self-Help Aid: 86%. Avg. Award: $3,651. Upon Graduation, Avg. Loan Debt per Student: $12,705. Financial Aid Deadline: 3/1.

Ripon College

300 Seward Street, PO Box 248, Ripon, WI 54971. Admissions Phone: (920) 748-8337; (800) 947-4766. Fax: (920) 748-8335. Email:

adminfo@ripon.edu. Website: www.ripon.edu. Costs (2003–04): Tuition and Fees: $19,940. Room & Board: $5,055. Payment Plan(s): installment plan. Institutional Aid (est. 2002–03): Institutional Aid, Need-Based: $8,364,805. Institutional Aid, Non-Need-Based: $1,753,605. FT Undergrads Receiving Aid: 76%. Avg. Amount per Student: $18,573. FT Undergrads Receiving Non-Need-Based Gift Aid: 20%. Avg. Amount per Student: $10,265. Of Those Receiving Any Aid: Receiving Need-Based Gift Aid: 99%. Avg. Award: $14,844. Receiving Need-Based Self-Help Aid: 93%. Avg. Award: $4,161. Upon Graduation, Avg. Loan Debt per Student: $15,565. Financial Aid Deadline: rolling

Rochester Institute of Technology

60 Lomb Memorial Drive, Rochester, NY 14623-5604. Admissions Phone: (585) 475-6631. Fax: (585) 475-7424. Email: admissions@rit.edu. Website: www.rit.edu. Application Website: www.rit.edu/admissions. Costs (2002–03): Tuition and Fees: $19,980. Room & Board: $7,527. Payment Plan(s): installment plan, deferred payment plan, pre-payment plan. Institutional Aid (2001–02): Institutional Aid, Need-Based: $41,800,400. Institutional Aid, Non-Need-Based: $4,488,700. FT Undergrads Receiving Aid: 67%. Avg. Amount per Student: $15,250. FT Undergrads Receiving Non-Need-Based Gift Aid: 10%. Avg. Amount per Student: $5,200. Of Those Receiving Any Aid: Receiving Need-Based Gift Aid: 95%. Avg. Award: $9,400. Receiving Need-Based Self-Help Aid: 89%. Avg. Award: $5,300. Financial Aid Deadline: 3/1 (priority).

Rollins College

1000 Holt Avenue, Winter Park, FL 32789-4499. Admissions Phone: (407) 646-2161. Fax: (407) 646-1502. Email: admission@rollins.edu. Website: www.rollins.edu. Application Website: www.rollins.edu/admission/application.shtml. Costs (2002–03): Tuition and Fees: $24,958. Room & Board: $7,652. Payment Plan(s): installment plan. Institutional Aid (est. 2002–03): Institutional Aid, Need-Based: $9,683,165. Institutional Aid, Non-Need-Based: $1,897,461. FT Undergrads Receiving Aid: 42%. Avg. Amount per Student: $26,716. FT Undergrads Receiving Non-Need-Based Gift Aid: 17%. Avg. Amount per Student: $8,223. Of Those Receiving Any Aid: Receiving Need-

Based Gift Aid: 95%. Avg. Award: $19,831. Receiving Need-Based Self-Help Aid: 85%. Avg. Award: $5,642. Upon Graduation, Avg. Loan Debt per Student: $14,719. Financial Aid Deadline: 3/1, 2/15 (priority).

Rose-Hulman Institute of Technology

5500 Wabash Avenue, Terre Haute, IN 47803-3999. **Admissions Phone:** (800) 552-0725 (in-state); (800) 248-7448 (out-of-state). **Fax:** (812) 877-8941. **Email:** admis.ofc@rose-hulman.edu. **Website:** www.rose-hulman.edu. **Application Website:** www.rose-hulman.edu/admissions. **Costs (2002–03): Tuition and Fees:** $22,997. **Room & Board:** $6,348. **Payment Plan(s):** installment plan, pre-payment plan. **Institutional Aid (2001–02): Institutional Aid, Need-Based:** $5,482,983. **Institutional Aid, Non-Need-Based:** $819,296. **FT Undergrads Receiving Aid:** 73%. **Avg. Amount per Student:** $14,471. **FT Undergrads Receiving Non-Need-Based Gift Aid:** 22%. **Avg. Amount per Student:** $3,905. **Of Those Receiving Any Aid: Receiving Need-Based Gift Aid:** 83%. **Avg. Award:** $3,948. **Receiving Need-Based Self-Help Aid:** 83%. **Avg. Award:** $6,048. **Upon Graduation, Avg. Loan Debt per Student:** $27,000. **Financial Aid Deadline:** rolling; 3/1 (priority).

Rutgers, The State University of New Jersey

65 Davidson Road, Room 202, Piscataway, NJ 08854-8097. **Admissions Phone:** (732) 932-4636. **Fax:** (732) 445-0237. **Website:** http://www.rutgers.edu. **Application Website:** admissions.rutgers.edu. **Costs (2002–03): Tuition and Fees, In-State:** $7,308 **Tuition and Fees, Out-of-State:** $13,284. **Room & Board:** $6,970. **Institutional Aid (est. 2002–03): Institutional Aid, Need-Based:** $5,864,689. **Institutional Aid, Non-Need-Based:** $12,619,275. **FT Undergrads Receiving Aid:** 47%. **Avg. Amount per Student:** $9,985. **FT Undergrads Receiving Non-Need-Based Gift Aid:** 11%. **Avg. Amount per Student:** $4,671. **Of Those Receiving Any Aid: Receiving Need-Based Gift Aid:** 68%. **Avg. Award:** $6,475. **Receiving Need-Based Self-Help Aid:** 85%. **Avg. Award:** $4,504. **Upon Graduation, Avg. Loan Debt per Student:** $15,270. **Financial Aid Deadline:** rolling; 3/15 (priority).

Saint Anselm College

100 Saint Anselm Drive, Manchester, NH 03102-1310. **Admissions Phone:** (603) 641-7500; (888) 4ANSELM. **Fax:** (603) 641-7550. **Email:** admissions@anselm.edu. **Website:** http://www.anselm.edu. **Application Website:** www.anselm.edu/admissions/application/application03.pdf. **Costs (2003–04): Tuition and Fees:** $22,160. **Room & Board:** $8,090. **Payment Plan(s):** installment plan. **Institutional Aid (est. 2002–03): Institutional Aid, Need-Based:** $11,657,109. **Institutional Aid, Non-Need-Based:** $3,561,436. **FT Undergrads Receiving Aid:** 82%. **Avg. Amount per Student:** $21,933. **FT Undergrads Receiving Non-Need-Based Gift Aid:** 21%. **Avg. Amount per Student:** $5,751. **Of Those Receiving Any Aid: Receiving Need-Based Gift Aid:** 89%. **Avg. Award:** $8,178. **Receiving Need-Based Self-Help Aid:** 64%. **Avg. Award:** $8,543. **Upon Graduation, Avg. Loan Debt per Student:** $19,139. **Financial Aid Deadline:** 3/1 (priority).

Saint John's College

P.O. Box 2800, Annapolis, MD 21404. **Admissions Phone:** (800) 727-9238; (410) 626-2522. **Fax:** (410) 269-7916. **Email:** admissions@sjca.edu. **Website:** www.sjca.edu. **Costs (2002–03): Tuition and Fees:** $27,410. **Room & Board:** $6,970. **Payment Plan(s):** installment plan, pre-payment plan. **Institutional Aid (est. 2002–03): Institutional Aid, Need-Based:** $3,934,138. **FT Undergrads Receiving Aid:** 55%. **Avg. Amount per Student:** $25,854. **Of Those Receiving Any Aid: Receiving Need-Based Gift Aid:** 96%. **Avg. Award:** $17,754. **Receiving Need-Based Self-Help Aid:** 96%. **Avg. Award:** $8,100. **Upon Graduation, Avg. Loan Debt per Student:** $18,125. **Financial Aid Deadline:** rolling; 3/15 (priority).

Saint John's College

1160 Camino Cruz Blanca, Santa Fe, NM 87505-4599. **Admissions Phone:** (800) 331-5232; (505) 984-6060. **Fax:** (505) 984-6162. **Email:** admissions@mail.sjcsf.edu. **Website:** www.sjcsf.edu. **Costs (2002–03): Tuition and Fees:** $27,410. **Room & Board:** $6,970. **Payment Plan(s):** installment plan. **Institutional Aid (est. 2002–03): Institutional Aid, Need-Based:** $4,103,760. **FT Undergrads Receiving Aid:** 71%. **Avg. Amount per Student:** $20,424. **FT Undergrads Receiving Non-Need-Based Gift Aid:** 1%. **Avg. Amount per Student:** $2,150. **Of Those Receiving Any Aid:**

Receiving Need-Based Gift Aid: 96%. Avg. Award: $14,695. Receiving Need-Based Self-Help Aid: 100%. Avg. Award: $5,424. Upon Graduation, Avg. Loan Debt per Student: $20,753

Saint Lawrence University

Payson Hall, Canton, NY 13617. **Admissions Phone:** (315) 229-5261; (800) 285-1856. **Fax:** (315) 229-5818. **Email:** admissions@stlawu.edu. **Website:** www.stlawu.edu. **Application Website:** web.stlawu.edu/admis/online_app.html. **Costs (2003–04): Tuition and Fees:** $28,180. **Room & Board:** $7,775. **Payment Plan(s):** installment plan. **Institutional Aid (est. 2002–03): Institutional Aid, Need-Based:** $22,914,140. **Institutional Aid, Non-Need-Based:** $2,628,568. **FT Undergrads Receiving Aid:** 69%. **Avg. Amount per Student:** $25,373. **FT Undergrads Receiving Non-Need-Based Gift Aid:** 9%. **Avg. Amount per Student:** $9,168. **Of Those Receiving Any Aid: Receiving Need-Based Gift Aid:** 99%. **Avg. Award:** $18,076. **Receiving Need-Based Self-Help Aid:** 88%. **Avg. Award:** $6,640. **Upon Graduation, Avg. Loan Debt per Student:** $22,132. **Financial Aid Deadline:** 2/15.

Saint Louis University

221 N. Grand Boulevard, St. Louis, MO 63103. **Admissions Phone:** (314) 977-2500; (800) 758-3678. **Fax:** (314) 977-7136. **Email:** admitme@slu.edu. **Website:** www.slu.edu. **Application Website:** imagine.slu.edu. **Costs (est. 2003-04): Tuition and Fees:** $21,008. **Room & Board:** $7,310. **Payment Plan(s):** installment plan, deferred payment plan. **Institutional Aid (est. 2002–03): Institutional Aid, Need-Based:** $39,155,191. **Institutional Aid, Non-Need-Based:** $6,477,375. **FT Undergrads Receiving Aid:** 67%. **Avg. Amount per Student:** $20,707. **FT Undergrads Receiving Non-Need-Based Gift Aid:** 15%. **Avg. Amount per Student:** $8,269. **Of Those Receiving Any Aid: Receiving Need-Based Gift Aid:** 96%. **Avg. Award:** $13,081. **Receiving Need-Based Self-Help Aid:** 45%. **Avg. Award:** $5,853. **Upon Graduation, Avg. Loan Debt per Student:** $14,989. **Financial Aid Deadline:** 5/1, 4/1 (priority).

Saint Mary's College of California

P.O. Box 4800, Moraga, CA 94575-4800. **Admissions Phone:** (925) 631-4224; (800) 800-4762. **Fax:** (925) 376-7193. **Email:** smcadmit@stmarys-ca.edu. **Website:**

www.stmarys-ca.edu. **Costs (2003–04):** Tuition and Fees: $23,775. Room & Board: $9,075. **Payment Plan(s):** installment plan. **Institutional Aid (est. 2002–03):** Institutional Aid, Need-Based: $11,754,181. Institutional Aid, Non-Need-Based: $806,000. FT Undergrads Receiving Aid: 60%. Avg. Amount per Student: $20,096. FT Undergrads Receiving Non-Need-Based Gift Aid: 4%. Avg. Amount per Student: $5,763. Of Those Receiving Any Aid: Receiving Need-Based Gift Aid: 85%. Avg. Award: $15,009. Receiving Need-Based Self-Help Aid: 93%. Avg. Award: $5,038. Upon Graduation, Avg. Loan Debt per Student: $19,334. **Financial Aid Deadline:** 3/2.

Saint Mary's College of Maryland

18952 East Fisher Road, St. Mary's City, MD 20686-3001. **Admissions Phone:** (800) 492-7181; (240) 895-5000. **Fax:** (240) 895-5001. **Email:** admissions@smcm.edu. **Website:** www.smcm.edu. **Application Website:** www.smcm.edu/admissions/application/. **Costs (2003–04):** Tuition and Fees, In-State: $8,740 Tuition and Fees, Out-of-State: $15,060. Room & Board: $7,105. **Payment Plan(s):** installment plan. **Institutional Aid (est. 2002–03):** Institutional Aid, Need-Based: $774,867. Institutional Aid, Non-Need-Based: $2,114,850. FT Undergrads Receiving Aid: 45%. Avg. Amount per Student: $6,695. FT Undergrads Receiving Non-Need-Based Gift Aid: 28%. Avg. Amount per Student: $4,500. Of Those Receiving Any Aid: Receiving Need-Based Gift Aid: 58%. Avg. Award: $4,000. Receiving Need-Based Self-Help Aid: 58%. Avg. Award: $5,500. Upon Graduation, Avg. Loan Debt per Student: $17,125. **Financial Aid Deadline:** 3/1.

Saint Olaf College

1520 St. Olaf Avenue, Northfield, MN 55057-1098. **Admissions Phone:** (507) 646-3025; (800) 800-3025. **Fax:** (507) 646-3832. **Email:** admissions@stolaf.edu. **Website:** www.stolaf.edu. **Application Website:** www.stolaf.edu/admissions/onlineappl. **Costs (2003–04):** Tuition and Fees: $23,650. Room & Board: $4,850. **Payment Plan(s):** pre-payment plan. **Institutional Aid (est. 2002–03):** Institutional Aid, Need-Based: $16,451,679. Institutional Aid, Non-Need-Based: $3,563,158. FT Undergrads Receiving Aid: 58%. Avg. Amount per Student: $16,873. FT Undergrads Receiving Non-Need-Based Gift Aid: 21%.

Avg. Amount per Student: $4,625. Of Those Receiving Any Aid: Receiving Need-Based Gift Aid: 100%. Avg. Award: $4,432. Receiving Need-Based Self-Help Aid: 52%. Avg. Award: $4,478. Upon Graduation, Avg. Loan Debt per Student: $18,806. **Financial Aid Deadline:** rolling; 2/15 (priority).

Salisbury University

1101 Camden Avenue, Salisbury, MD 21801-6862. **Admissions Phone:** (410) 543-6161; (888) 543-0148. **Fax:** (410) 546-6016. **Email:** admissions@salisbury.edu. **Website:** salisbury.edu. **Application Website:** salisbury.edu/Admissions/Onlineapp.html. **Costs (2002–03):** Tuition and Fees, In-State: $6,234 Tuition and Fees, Out-of-State: $11,998. Room & Board: $6,530. **Payment Plan(s):** installment plan. **Institutional Aid (2001–02):** Institutional Aid, Need-Based: $265,906. Institutional Aid, Non-Need-Based: $867,987. FT Undergrads Receiving Aid: 40%. Avg. Amount per Student: $5,654. FT Undergrads Receiving Non-Need-Based Gift Aid: 7%. Avg. Amount per Student: $3,224. Of Those Receiving Any Aid: Receiving Need-Based Gift Aid: 53%. Avg. Award: $3,389. Receiving Need-Based Self-Help Aid: 76%. Avg. Award: $3,533. Upon Graduation, Avg. Loan Debt per Student: $14,773. **Financial Aid Deadline:** 2/1 (priority).

Santa Clara University

500 El Camino Real, Santa Clara, CA 95053-0925. **Admissions Phone:** (408) 554-4700; (408) 554-4000. **Fax:** (408) 554-5255. **Website:** www.scu.edu. **Application Website:** www.scu.edu/apply. **Costs (2002–03):** Tuition and Fees: $23,925. Room & Board: $8,904. **Payment Plan(s):** installment plan, deferred payment plan, pre-payment plan. **Institutional Aid (est. 2002–03):** Institutional Aid, Need-Based: $19,339,611. Institutional Aid, Non-Need-Based: $4,236,741. FT Undergrads Receiving Aid: 53%. Avg. Amount per Student: $14,718. FT Undergrads Receiving Non-Need-Based Gift Aid: 10%. Avg. Amount per Student: $4,146. Of Those Receiving Any Aid: Receiving Need-Based Gift Aid: 61%. Avg. Award: $12,745. Receiving Need-Based Self-Help Aid: 62%. Avg. Award: $4,694. Upon Graduation, Avg. Loan Debt per Student: $22,869. **Financial Aid Deadline:** rolling; 2/1 (priority).

Sarah Lawrence College

One Mead Way, Bronxville, NY 10708-5999. **Admissions Phone:** (914) 395-2510; (800) 888-2858. **Fax:** (914) 395-2515. **Email:** slcadmit@slc.edu. **Website:** www.sarahlawrence.edu. **Costs (2002–03):** Tuition and Fees: $29,360. Room & Board: $10,494. **Payment Plan(s):** installment plan. **Institutional Aid (est. 2002–03):** Institutional Aid, Need-Based: $9,430,232. FT Undergrads Receiving Aid: 51%. Avg. Amount per Student: $26,289. Of Those Receiving Any Aid: Receiving Need-Based Gift Aid: 97%. Avg. Award: $19,274. Receiving Need-Based Self-Help Aid: 95%. Avg. Award: $4,942. Upon Graduation, Avg. Loan Debt per Student: $13,042. **Financial Aid Deadline:** 2/1.

Scripps College

1030 Columbia Avenue, Claremont, CA 91711. **Admissions Phone:** (909) 621-8149; (800) 770-1333. **Fax:** (909) 607-7508. **Email:** admission@scrippscollege.edu. **Website:** scrippscollege.edu. **Costs (2002–03):** Tuition and Fees: $25,700. Room & Board: $8,300. **Payment Plan(s):** installment plan. **Institutional Aid (est. 2002–03):** Institutional Aid, Need-Based: $5,499,299. Institutional Aid, Non-Need-Based: $743,864. FT Undergrads Receiving Aid: 46%. Avg. Amount per Student: $23,802. FT Undergrads Receiving Non-Need-Based Gift Aid: 7%. Avg. Amount per Student: $15,145. Of Those Receiving Any Aid: Receiving Need-Based Gift Aid: 99%. Avg. Award: $18,516. Receiving Need-Based Self-Help Aid: 89%. Avg. Award: $5,286. Upon Graduation, Avg. Loan Debt per Student: $12,941. **Financial Aid Deadline:** rolling; 2/1 (priority).

Simmons College

300 The Fenway, Boston, MA 02115. **Admissions Phone:** (617) 521-2051; (800) 345-8468. **Fax:** (617) 521-3190. **Email:** ugadm@simmons.edu. **Website:** www.simmons.edu. **Costs (2003–04):** Tuition and Fees: $23,550. Room & Board: $9,450. **Payment Plan(s):** deferred-payment plan. **Institutional Aid (2001–02):** Institutional Aid, Need-Based: $7,852,200. Institutional Aid, Non-Need-Based: $441,625. FT Undergrads Receiving Aid: 66%. Avg. Amount per Student: $16,119. FT Undergrads Receiving Non-Need-Based Gift Aid: 3%. Avg. Amount per Student: $10,216. Of Those Receiving Any Aid: Receiving Need-Based Gift Aid: 95%.

Avg. Award: $12,136. Receiving Need-Based Self-Help Aid: 89%. Avg. Award: $1,735. Financial Aid Deadline: 3/1.

Skidmore College

815 North Broadway, Saratoga Springs, NY 12866. **Admissions Phone:** (800) 867-6007; (518) 580-5570. **Fax:** (518) 580-5584. **Email:** admissions@skidmore.edu. **Website:** www.skidmore.edu. **Costs (2002–03):** Tuition and Fees: $27,980. Room & Board: $7,835. Payment Plan(s): installment plan, pre-payment plan. Institutional Aid (est. 2002–03): Institutional Aid, Need-Based: $14,291,042. Institutional Aid, Non-Need-Based: $281,925. FT Undergrads Receiving Aid: 42%. Avg. Amount per Student: $23,148. FT Undergrads Receiving Non-Need-Based Gift Aid: 1%. Avg. Amount per Student: $9,400. Of Those Receiving Any Aid: Receiving Need-Based Gift Aid: 100%. Avg. Award: $17,815. Receiving Need-Based Self-Help Aid: 100%. Avg. Award: $5,333. Upon Graduation, Avg. Loan Debt per Student: $15,560. Financial Aid Deadline: 1/15.

Smith College

7 College Lane, Northampton, MA 01063. **Admissions Phone:** (413) 585-2500; (800) 383-3232. **Fax:** (413) 585-2527. **Email:** admission@smith.edu. **Website:** www.smith.edu. **Application Website:** http://www.smith.edu/admission. Costs (2002–03): Tuition and Fees: $25,986. Room & Board: $8,950. Payment Plan(s): installment plan, pre-payment plan. Institutional Aid (est. 2002–03): Institutional Aid, Need-Based: $30,485,493. Institutional Aid, Non-Need-Based: $872,530. FT Undergrads Receiving Aid: 64%. Avg. Amount per Student: $25,647. FT Undergrads Receiving Non-Need-Based Gift Aid: 4%. Avg. Amount per Student: $9,631. Of Those Receiving Any Aid: Receiving Need-Based Gift Aid: 100%. Avg. Award: $19,471. Receiving Need-Based Self-Help Aid: 100%. Avg. Award: $6,176. Upon Graduation, Avg. Loan Debt per Student: $19,911. Financial Aid Deadline: 2/1.

Southern Methodist University

P.O. Box 750221, Dallas, TX 75275-0221. **Admissions Phone:** (214) 768-2058; (800) 323-0672. **Fax:** (214) 768-0202. **Email:** enrol_serv@mail.smu.edu. **Website:** www.smu.edu. **Application Website:** smu.edu/apply. Costs (2002–03): Tuition

and Fees: $21,942. Room & Board: $7,954. Institutional Aid (est. 2002–03): Institutional Aid, Need-Based: $23,587,977. Institutional Aid, Non-Need-Based: $9,927,252. FT Undergrads Receiving Aid: 37%. Avg. Amount per Student: $20,885. FT Undergrads Receiving Non-Need-Based Gift Aid: 33%. Avg. Amount per Student: $5,033. Of Those Receiving Any Aid: Receiving Need-Based Gift Aid: 86%. Avg. Award: $13,014. Receiving Need-Based Self-Help Aid: 82%. Avg. Award: $5,201. Upon Graduation, Avg. Loan Debt per Student: $18,693. Financial Aid Deadline: rolling; 2/1 (priority).

Southwestern University

1001 East University Avenue, Georgetown, TX 78626. **Admissions Phone:** (512) 863-1200; (800) 252-3166. **Fax:** (512) 863-9601. **Email:** admission@southwestern.edu. **Website:** www.southwestern.edu. **Application Website:** www.southwestern.edu/admission-finaid/adm-apply.html. Costs (2003–04): Tuition and Fees: $18,870. Room & Board: $6,887. Payment Plan(s): installment plan, deferred payment plan, pre-payment plan. Institutional Aid (est. 2002–03): Institutional Aid, Need-Based: $4,546,151. Institutional Aid, Non-Need-Based: $2,232,496. FT Undergrads Receiving Aid: 51%. Avg. Amount per Student: $13,000. FT Undergrads Receiving Non-Need-Based Gift Aid: 25%. Avg. Amount per Student: $6,591. Of Those Receiving Any Aid: Receiving Need-Based Gift Aid: 100%. Avg. Award: $10,534. Receiving Need-Based Self-Help Aid: 83%. Avg. Award: $5,000. Upon Graduation, Avg. Loan Debt per Student: $17,505. Financial Aid Deadline: 3/1.

Spelman College*

350 Spelman Lane SW, Atlanta, GA 30314. **Admissions Phone:** (800) 982-2411; (404) 681-3643. **Email:** admiss@spelman.edu. **Website:** www.spelman.edu. **Application Website:** princess.spelman.edu/admissionsapp.nsf/introduction. Costs (2002–03): Tuition and Fees: $12,675. Room & Board: $7,300. Payment Plan(s): deferred payment plan. Institutional Aid (est. 2002–03): FT Undergrads Receiving Aid: 78%. Avg. Amount per Student: $4,500. FT Undergrads Receiving Non-Need-Based Gift Aid: 16%. Avg. Amount per Student: $2,000. Of Those Receiving Any Aid: Receiving Need-Based Gift Aid: 79%. Avg. Award: $1,500. Receiving Need-Based Self-Help Aid: 13%. Avg. Award:

$3,000. Upon Graduation, Avg. Loan Debt per Student: $16,400. Financial Aid Deadline: rolling; 2/15 (priority).

Stanford University

Old Student Union, Stanford, CA 94305-3005. **Admissions Phone:** (650) 723-2091. **Fax:** (650) 723-6050. **Email:** undergrad.admissions@forsythe.stanford.edu. **Website:** www.stanford.edu. Costs (2003–04): Tuition and Fees: $28,564. Room & Board: $9,049. Institutional Aid (2001–02): Institutional Aid, Need-Based: $47,140,338. Institutional Aid, Non-Need-Based: $2,706,159. FT Undergrads Receiving Aid: 44%. Avg. Amount per Student: $24,648. FT Undergrads Receiving Non-Need-Based Gift Aid: 19%. Avg. Amount per Student: $5,166. Of Those Receiving Any Aid: Receiving Need-Based Gift Aid: 97%. Avg. Award: $21,129. Receiving Need-Based Self-Help Aid: 69%. Avg. Award: $3,394. Upon Graduation, Avg. Loan Debt per Student: $15,782. Financial Aid Deadline: 2/1 (priority).

State University of New York—Albany

1400 Washington Avenue, Albany, NY 12222. **Admissions Phone:** (518) 442-5435; (800) 293-7869. **Fax:** (518) 442-5383. **Email:** ugadmissions@albany.edu. **Website:** www.albany.edu. **Application Website:** www.albany.edu/admissions/undergraduate/applying/. Costs (est. 2002–03): Tuition and Fees, In-State: $4,820. Tuition and Fees, Out-of-State: $9,720. Room & Board: $7,052. Payment Plan(s): installment plan. Institutional Aid (est. 2002–03): Institutional Aid, Need-Based: $386,303. Institutional Aid, Non-Need-Based: $4,859,727. FT Undergrads Receiving Aid: 53%. Avg. Amount per Student: $7,739. FT Undergrads Receiving Non-Need-Based Gift Aid: 5%. Avg. Amount per Student: $3,202. Of Those Receiving Any Aid: Receiving Need-Based Gift Aid: 90%. Avg. Award: $3,975. Receiving Need-Based Self-Help Aid: 84%. Avg. Award: $4,479. Upon Graduation, Avg. Loan Debt per Student: $15,108. Financial Aid Deadline: 3/15 (priority).

State University of New York—Binghamton University

P.O. Box 6000, Binghamton, NY 13902-6000. **Admissions Phone:** (607) 777-2171. **Fax:** (607) 777-4445. **Email:**

admit@binghamton.edu. **Website:** www.binghamton.edu. **Costs (2002–03): Tuition and Fees, In-State:** $4,717. **Tuition and Fees, Out-of-State:** $9,617. **Room & Board:** $6,412. **Payment Plan(s):** installment plan, deferred payment plan. **Institutional Aid (est. 2002–03): Institutional Aid, Need-Based:** $375,795. **Institutional Aid, Non-Need-Based:** $2,092,054. **FT Undergrads Receiving Aid:** 49%. **Avg. Amount per Student:** $9,136. **FT Undergrads Receiving Non-Need-Based Gift Aid:** 8%. **Avg. Amount per Student:** $1,995. **Of Those Receiving Any Aid: Receiving Need-Based Gift Aid:** 92%. **Avg. Award:** $4,373. **Receiving Need-Based Self-Help Aid:** 93%. **Avg. Award:** $4,671. **Upon Graduation, Avg. Loan Debt per Student:** $13,915. **Financial Aid Deadline:** 3/1 (priority).

State University of New York—College at Geneseo

1 College Circle, Geneseo, NY 14454. **Admissions Phone:** (585) 245-5571; (866) 245-5211. **Fax:** (585) 245-5550. **Email:** admissions@geneseo.edu. **Website:** www.geneseo.edu. **Costs (est. 2003-04): Tuition and Fees, In-State:** $4,310. **Tuition and Fees, Out-of-State:** $9,210. **Room & Board:** $5,660. **Payment Plan(s):** installment plan, pre-payment plan. **Institutional Aid (est. 2002–03): Institutional Aid, Non-Need-Based:** $565,745. **FT Undergrads Receiving Aid:** 47%. **Avg. Amount per Student:** $7,873. **FT Undergrads Receiving Non-Need-Based Gift Aid:** 22%. **Avg. Amount per Student:** $960. **Of Those Receiving Any Aid: Receiving Need-Based Gift Aid:** 100%. **Avg. Award:** $2,000. **Receiving Need-Based Self-Help Aid:** 93%. **Avg. Award:** $3,945. **Upon Graduation, Avg. Loan Debt per Student:** $15,000. **Financial Aid Deadline:** 2/15 (priority).

State University of New York—Purchase College

735 Anderson Hill Road, Purchase, NY 10577. **Admissions Phone:** (914) 251-6300. **Fax:** (914) 251-6314. **Email:** admissn@purchase.edu. **Website:** www.purchase.edu. **Application Website:** www.purchase.edu/admissions/adm_applyonline.asp. **Costs (2003–04): Tuition and Fees, In-State:** $4,397. **Tuition and Fees, Out-of-State:** $9,297. **Room & Board:** $6,860 (est. 2002–03). **Institutional Aid (est. 2002–03): Institutional Aid, Need-Based:** $42,780. **Institutional Aid, Non-Need-Based:** $734,820. **FT Undergrads Receiving Aid:** 48%. **Avg. Amount per Student:** $7,235. **FT Undergrads Receiving Non-Need-Based**

Gift Aid: 14%. **Avg. Amount per Student:** $11,242. **Of Those Receiving Any Aid: Receiving Need-Based Gift Aid:** 87%. **Avg. Award:** $3,975. **Receiving Need-Based Self-Help Aid:** 96%. **Avg. Award:** $3,919. **Upon Graduation, Avg. Loan Debt per Student:** $13,873. **Financial Aid Deadline:** 3/15 (priority).

State University of New York—Stony Brook

SUNY Stony Brook, Stony Brook, NY 11794. **Admissions Phone:** (631) 632-6868; (800) 872-7869. **Fax:** (631) 632-9898. **Email:** ugadmissions@notes.cc.sunysb.edu. **Website:** www.stonybrook.edu. **Costs (est. 2003-04): Tuition and Fees, In-State:** $4,358 **Tuition and Fees, Out-of-State:** $9,258. **Room & Board:** $6,974. **Payment Plan(s):** installment plan. **Institutional Aid (2001–02): Institutional Aid, Non-Need-Based:** $1,531,773. **FT Undergrads Receiving Aid:** 60%. **Avg. Amount per Student:** $7,579. **FT Undergrads Receiving Non-Need-Based Gift Aid:** 2%. **Avg. Amount per Student:** $1,842. **Of Those Receiving Any Aid: Receiving Need-Based Gift Aid:** 98%. **Avg. Award:** $3,941. **Receiving Need-Based Self-Help Aid:** 78%. **Avg. Award:** $3,687. **Upon Graduation, Avg. Loan Debt per Student:** $15,747. **Financial Aid Deadline:** rolling; 3/1 (priority).

State University of New York—University at Buffalo

17 Capen Hall, Box 601660, Buffalo, NY 14260-1660. **Admissions Phone:** (888) UBADMIT. **Email:** ubadmissions@admissions.buffalo.edu. **Website:** www.buffalo.edu. **Costs (2002–03): Tuition and Fees, In-State:** $4,850. **Tuition and Fees, Out-of-State:** $9,750. **Room & Board:** $6,512. **Payment Plan(s):** installment plan. **Institutional Aid (est. 2002–03): Institutional Aid, Need-Based:** $2,105,885. **Institutional Aid, Non-Need-Based:** $1,043,712. **FT Undergrads Receiving Aid:** 52%. **Avg. Amount per Student:** $7,525. **FT Undergrads Receiving Non-Need-Based Gift Aid:** 4%. **Avg. Amount per Student:** $2,912. **Of Those Receiving Any Aid: Receiving Need-Based Gift Aid:** 67%. **Avg. Award:** $3,466. **Receiving Need-Based Self-Help Aid:** 95%. **Avg. Award:** $4,510. **Upon Graduation, Avg. Loan Debt per Student:** $16,255. **Financial Aid Deadline:** rolling; 3/1 (priority).

Stetson University

421 N. Woodland Blvd, Unit 8378, DeLand, FL 32723. **Admissions Phone:** (386) 822-7100; (800) 688-0101. **Fax:** (386) 822-7112. **Email:** admissions@stetson.edu. **Website:** www.stetson.edu. **Application Website:** www.stetson.edu/admissions/apply/onlineapp.html. **Costs (est. 2003-04): Tuition and Fees:** $21,505. **Room & Board:** $6,855. **Payment Plan(s):** installment plan. **Institutional Aid (est. 2002–03): Institutional Aid, Need-Based:** $8,496,658. **Institutional Aid, Non-Need-Based:** $5,497,890. **FT Undergrads Receiving Aid:** 57%. **Avg. Amount per Student:** $18,791. **FT Undergrads Receiving Non-Need-Based Gift Aid:** 32%. **Avg. Amount per Student:** $10,848. **Of Those Receiving Any Aid: Receiving Need-Based Gift Aid:** 99%. **Avg. Award:** $13,548. **Receiving Need-Based Self-Help Aid:** 89%. **Avg. Award:** $6,131. **Financial Aid Deadline:** rolling; 3/15 (priority).

Stonehill College

320 Washington Street, Easton, MA 02357-5610. **Admissions Phone:** (508) 565-1373. **Fax:** (508) 565-1545. **Email:** admissions@stonehill.edu. **Website:** www.stonehill.edu. **Costs (2002–03): Tuition and Fees:** $19,908. **Room & Board:** $9,172. **Payment Plan(s):** installment plan, pre-payment plan. **Institutional Aid (est. 2002–03): Institutional Aid, Need-Based:** $13,455,260. **Institutional Aid, Non-Need-Based:** $2,801,115. **FT Undergrads Receiving Aid:** 66%. **Avg. Amount per Student:** $13,923. **FT Undergrads Receiving Non-Need-Based Gift Aid:** 23%. **Avg. Amount per Student:** $8,680. **Of Those Receiving Any Aid: Receiving Need-Based Gift Aid:** 95%. **Avg. Award:** $10,080. **Receiving Need-Based Self-Help Aid:** 87%. **Avg. Award:** $4,951. **Upon Graduation, Avg. Loan Debt per Student:** $16,504. **Financial Aid Deadline:** 2/1.

Susquehanna University

514 University Avenue, Selinsgrove, PA 17870-1040. **Admissions Phone:** (570) 372-4260; (800) 326-9672. **Fax:** (570) 372-2722. **Email:** suadmiss@susqu.edu. **Website:** susqu.edu. **Application Website:** susqu.edu/admissions/how_apply.htm. **Costs (2002–03): Tuition and Fees:** $23,480. **Room & Board:** $6,510. **Institutional Aid (est. 2002–03): Institutional Aid, Need-Based:** $11,208,915. **Institutional Aid, Non-Need-Based:** $4,684,931. **FT Undergrads**

Receiving Aid: 62%. Avg. Amount per Student: $16,624. FT Undergrads Receiving Non-Need-Based Gift Aid: 24%. Avg. Amount per Student: $8,143. Of Those Receiving Any Aid: Receiving Need-Based Gift Aid: 99%. Avg. Award: $12,878. Receiving Need-Based Self-Help Aid: 83%. Avg. Award: $4,709. Upon Graduation, Avg. Loan Debt per Student: $18,852. Financial Aid Deadline: 5/1, 3/1 (proirity).

Swarthmore College

500 College Avenue, Swarthmore, PA 19081. Admissions Phone: (610) 328-8300; (800) 667-3110. Fax: (610) 328-8580. Email: admissions@swarthmore.edu. Website: www.swarthmore.edu. Application Website: www.commonapp.org. Costs (2002–03): Tuition and Fees: $27,562. Room & Board: $8,530. Payment Plan(s): installment plan. Institutional Aid (est. 2002–03): Institutional Aid, Need-Based: $13,787,580. Institutional Aid, Non-Need-Based: $313,628. FT Undergrads Receiving Aid: 49%. Avg. Amount per Student: $25,032. FT Undergrads Receiving Non-Need-Based Gift Aid: 1%. Avg. Amount per Student: $27,272. Of Those Receiving Any Aid: Receiving Need-Based Gift Aid: 100%. Avg. Award: $21,290. Receiving Need-Based Self-Help Aid: 94%. Avg. Award: $3,964. Upon Graduation, Avg. Loan Debt per Student: $12,759. Financial Aid Deadline: mid-February.

Sweet Briar College

Sweet Briar College, Sweet Briar, VA 24595. Admissions Phone: (434) 381-6142; (800) 381-6142. Fax: (434) 381-6152. Email: admissions@sbc.edu. Website: www.sbc.edu. Application Website: www.admissions.sbc.edu/apply/. Costs (2003–04): Tuition and Fees: $19,900. Regional or 'good neighbor' tuition available.Room & Board: $8,040 (est. 2002–03). Financial Aid Deadline: 3/1 (priority).

Syracuse University

201 Tolley Administration Building, Syracuse, NY 13244. Admissions Phone: (315) 443-3611. Email: orange@syr.edu. Website: www.syracuse.edu. Application Website: http://admissions.syr.edu/adminfinaid/downloadapplication.html. Costs (2002–03): Tuition and Fees: $23,424. Room & Board: $9,510. Payment Plan(s): installment plan. Institutional Aid (est. 2002–03): Institutional Aid, Need-

Based: $64,807,128. Institutional Aid, Non-Need-Based: $13,802,645. FT Undergrads Receiving Aid: 56%. Avg. Amount per Student: $18,000. FT Undergrads Receiving Non-Need-Based Gift Aid: 18%. Avg. Amount per Student: $6,720. Of Those Receiving Any Aid: Receiving Need-Based Gift Aid: 89%. Avg. Award: $12,000. Receiving Need-Based Self-Help Aid: 94%. Avg. Award: $6,800. Upon Graduation, Avg. Loan Debt per Student: $18,925. Financial Aid Deadline: 2/1, varies for early decision.

Temple University

1801 N. Broad Street, Philadelphia, PA 19122-6096. Admissions Phone: (215) 204-7200; (888) 340-2222. Fax: (215) 204-5694. Email: TUADM@temple.edu. Website: www.temple.edu. Application Website: www.temple.edu/UGAPP. Costs (2002–03): Tuition and Fees, In-State: $8,062 Tuition and Fees, Out-of-State: $14,316. Room & Board: $7,112. Payment Plan(s): installment plan, deferred payment plan, pre-payment plan. Institutional Aid (2001–02): Institutional Aid, Need-Based: $12,038,978. Institutional Aid, Non-Need-Based: $3,880,028. FT Undergrads Receiving Aid: 67%. Avg. Amount per Student: $10,715. FT Undergrads Receiving Non-Need-Based Gift Aid: 20%. Avg. Amount per Student: $2,828. Of Those Receiving Any Aid: Receiving Need-Based Gift Aid: 100%. Avg. Award: $4,054. Receiving Need-Based Self-Help Aid: 85%. Avg. Award: $3,299. Upon Graduation, Avg. Loan Debt per Student: $20,807. Financial Aid Deadline: rolling; 3/1 (priority).

Texas A&M University

1266 TAMU, College Station, TX 77843-1266. Admissions Phone: (979) 845-3741. Fax: (979) 847-8737. Email: admissions@tamu.edu. Website: http://www.tamu.edu. Application Website: http://www.tamu.edu/admissions. Costs (2002–03): Tuition and Fees, In-State: $4,748. Tuition and Fees, Out-of-State: $11,288. Room & Board: $6,030. Payment Plan(s): installment plan. Institutional Aid (2001–02): Institutional Aid, Need-Based: $2,450,988. Institutional Aid, Non-Need-Based: $5,416,911. FT Undergrads Receiving Aid: 27%. Avg. Amount per Student: $8,415. FT Undergrads Receiving Non-Need-Based Gift Aid: 14%. Avg. Amount per Student: $6,569. Of Those Receiving Any Aid: Receiving Need-Based Gift Aid: 84%. Avg. Award: $5,506.

Receiving Need-Based Self-Help Aid: 71%. Avg. Award: $3,084. Upon Graduation, Avg. Loan Debt per Student: $14,418.

Texas Christian University

2800 S. University Drive, Fort Worth, TX 76129. Admissions Phone: (817) 257-7490; (800) 828-3764. Fax: (817) 257-7268. Email: frogmail@tcu.edu. Website: www.tcu.edu. Costs (2002–03): Tuition and Fees: $16,340. Room & Board: $5,300. Payment Plan(s): installment plan, pre-payment plan. Institutional Aid (est. 2002–03): Institutional Aid, Need-Based: $9,199,374. Institutional Aid, Non-Need-Based: $9,685,254. FT Undergrads Receiving Aid: 40%. Avg. Amount per Student: $12,268. FT Undergrads Receiving Non-Need-Based Gift Aid: 20%. Avg. Amount per Student: $6,865. Of Those Receiving Any Aid: Receiving Need-Based Gift Aid: 90%. Avg. Award: $8,348. Receiving Need-Based Self-Help Aid: 79%. Avg. Award: $6,001. Financial Aid Deadline: 5/1

Texas Tech University

Box 45005, Lubbock, TX 79409-5005. Admissions Phone: (806) 742-1480. Fax: (806) 742-0980. Email: nsr@ttu.edu. Website: www.ttu.edu. Costs (2002–03): Tuition and Fees, In-State: $3,867. Tuition and Fees, Out-of-State: $10,407. Room & Board: $5,497. Payment Plan(s): installment plan. Institutional Aid (2001–02): Institutional Aid, Need-Based: $7,046,643. Institutional Aid, Non-Need-Based: $4,339,115. FT Undergrads Receiving Aid: 37%. Avg. Amount per Student: $5,710. FT Undergrads Receiving Non-Need-Based Gift Aid: 9%. Avg. Amount per Student: $2,307. Of Those Receiving Any Aid: Receiving Need-Based Gift Aid: 75%. Avg. Award: $3,090. Receiving Need-Based Self-Help Aid: 75%. Avg. Award: $3,497. Financial Aid Deadline: 3/3.

Trinity College

300 Summit Street, Hartford, CT 06106. Admissions Phone: (860) 297-2180. Fax: (860) 297-2287. Email: admissions.office@trincoll.edu. Website: www.trincoll.edu. Costs (2002–03): Tuition and Fees: $28,602. Room & Board: $7,380. Payment Plan(s): installment plan, pre-payment plan. Institutional Aid (est. 2002–03): Institutional Aid, Need-Based: $16,072,456. Institutional Aid, Non-Need-Based: $155,692. FT Undergrads Receiving

Aid: 47%. **Avg. Amount per Student:** $24,367. **FT Undergrads Receiving Non-Need-Based Gift Aid:** 1%. **Avg. Amount per Student:** $7,699. **Of Those Receiving Any Aid: Receiving Need-Based Gift Aid:** 95%. **Avg. Award:** $21,137. **Receiving Need-Based Self-Help Aid:** 81%. **Avg. Award:** $5,137. **Upon Graduation, Avg. Loan Debt per Student:** $15,402. **Financial Aid Deadline:** 2/1.

Trinity University

715 Stadium Drive, San Antonio, TX 78212-7200. **Admissions Phone:** (210) 999-7207; (800) TRINITY. **Fax:** (210) 999-8164. **Email:** admissions@trinity.edu. **Website:** www.trinity.edu. **Application Website:** www.trinity.edu/departments/admissions/apply3.htm. **Costs (2003–04):** Tuition and Fees: $17,854. **Room & Board:** $7,040. **Institutional Aid (est. 2002–03):** Institutional Aid, Need-Based: $6,566,318. **Institutional Aid, Non-Need-Based:** $4,625,541. **FT Undergrads Receiving Aid:** 41%. **Avg. Amount per Student:** $14,518. **FT Undergrads Receiving Non-Need-Based Gift Aid:** 33%. **Avg. Amount per Student:** $5,893. **Of Those Receiving Any Aid: Receiving Need-Based Gift Aid:** 97%. **Avg. Award:** $10,380. **Receiving Need-Based Self-Help Aid:** 85%. **Avg. Award:** $4,460. **Financial Aid Deadline:** 4/1, 2/1 (priority).

Truman State University

McClain Hall 205, 100 East Normal, Kirksville, MO 63501. **Admissions Phone:** (660) 785-4114; (800) 892-7792 (in-state). **Fax:** (660) 785-7456. **Email:** admissions@truman.edu. **Website:** http://www.truman.edu. **Application Website:** http://admissions.truman.edu/Applying_to_Truman/application.stm. **Costs (2003–04):** Tuition and Fees, In-State: $4,656. **Tuition and Fees, Out-of-State:** $8,456. **Room & Board:** $5,072. **Payment Plan(s):** installment plan. **Institutional Aid (2001–02):** Institutional Aid, Need-Based: $183,817. **FT Undergrads Receiving Aid:** 36%. **Avg. Amount per Student:** $5,263. **FT Undergrads Receiving Non-Need-Based Gift Aid:** 43%. **Avg. Amount per Student:** $4,021. **Of Those Receiving Any Aid: Receiving Need-Based Gift Aid:** 43%. **Avg. Award:** $3,005. **Receiving Need-Based Self-Help Aid:** 75%. **Avg. Award:** $3,666. **Upon Graduation, Avg. Loan Debt per Student:** $14,382. **Financial Aid Deadline:** rolling; 4/1 (priority).

Tufts University

Bendetson Hall, Medford, MA 02155. **Admissions Phone:** (617) 627-3170. **Fax:** (617) 627-3860. **Email:** admissions.inquiry@ase.tufts.edu. **Website:** www.tufts.edu. **Costs (2002–03):** Tuition and Fees: $28,155. **Room & Board:** $8,310. **Payment Plan(s):** installment plan. **Institutional Aid (est. 2002–03):** Institutional Aid, Need-Based: $29,845,324. **Institutional Aid, Non-Need-Based:** $41,000. **FT Undergrads Receiving Aid:** 41%. **Avg. Amount per Student:** $22,334. **FT Undergrads Receiving Non-Need-Based Gift Aid:** 2%. **Avg. Amount per Student:** $1,696. **Of Those Receiving Any Aid: Receiving Need-Based Gift Aid:** 92%. **Avg. Award:** $19,058. **Receiving Need-Based Self-Help Aid:** 92%. **Avg. Award:** $5,262. **Upon Graduation, Avg. Loan Debt per Student:** $15,499. **Financial Aid Deadline:** 2/15.

Tulane University

210 Gibson Hall, New Orleans, LA 70118. **Admissions Phone:** (504) 865-5731(in-state); (800) 873-9283. **Fax:** (504) 862-8715. **Email:** undergrad.admission@tulane.edu. **Website:** www2.tulane.edu. **Application Website:** www.tulane.edu/~admiss. **Costs (2002–03):** Tuition and Fees: $26,100. **Room & Board:** $7,392. **Payment Plan(s):** installment plan, pre-payment plan. **Institutional Aid (2001–02):** Institutional Aid, Need-Based: $31,607,459. **Institutional Aid, Non-Need-Based:** $20,381,251. **FT Undergrads Receiving Aid:** 40%. **Avg. Amount per Student:** $23,918. **FT Undergrads Receiving Non-Need-Based Gift Aid:** 27%. **Avg. Amount per Student:** $13,765. **Of Those Receiving Any Aid: Receiving Need-Based Gift Aid:** 97%. **Avg. Award:** $16,720. **Receiving Need-Based Self-Help Aid:** 70%. **Avg. Award:** $6,141. **Upon Graduation, Avg. Loan Debt per Student:** $20,685. **Financial Aid Deadline:** 2/1.

Tuskegee University

102 Old Administration Building, Tuskegee, AL 36088-1920. **Admissions Phone:** (334) 727-8500; (800) 622-6531. **Fax:** (334) 724-4402. **Email:** adm@acd.tusk.edu. **Website:** www.tusk.edu. **Application Website:** www.abwwed.tusk. **Costs (2002–03):** Tuition and Fees: $11,310. **Room & Board:** $5,940. **Payment Plan(s):** installment plan. **Institutional Aid (est. 2002–03):** Institutional Aid, Need-Based: $1,309,702.

Institutional Aid, Non-Need-Based: $50,695. **FT Undergrads Receiving Aid:** 77%. **Avg. Amount per Student:** $13,666. **FT Undergrads Receiving Non-Need-Based Gift Aid:** 30%. **Avg. Amount per Student:** $6,000. **Of Those Receiving Any Aid: Receiving Need-Based Gift Aid:** 85%. **Avg. Award:** $8,000. **Receiving Need-Based Self-Help Aid:** 64%. **Avg. Award:** $5,666. **Upon Graduation, Avg. Loan Debt per Student:** $30,000. **Financial Aid Deadline:** 4/1, 3/31 (priority).

Union College

807 Union Street, Schenectady, NY 12308-2311. **Admissions Phone:** (518) 388-6112; (888) 843-6688. **Fax:** (518) 388-6986. **Email:** admissions@union.edu. **Website:** www.union.edu. **Application Website:** www.embark.com, or www.app.commonapp.org. **Costs (2003–04):** Tuition and Fees: $28,928. **Room & Board:** $7,077. **Payment Plan(s):** installment plan. **Institutional Aid (2001–02):** Institutional Aid, Need-Based: $15,732,988. **Institutional Aid, Non-Need-Based:** $140,000. **FT Undergrads Receiving Aid:** 51%. **Avg. Amount per Student:** $22,750. **FT Undergrads Receiving Non-Need-Based Gift Aid:** <1%. **Avg. Amount per Student:** $20,000. **Of Those Receiving Any Aid: Receiving Need-Based Gift Aid:** 100%. **Avg. Award:** $18,024. **Receiving Need-Based Self-Help Aid:** 93%. **Avg. Award:** $4,847. **Upon Graduation, Avg. Loan Debt per Student:** $15,725. **Financial Aid Deadline:** 2/1.

United States Air Force Academy

2304 Cadet Drive, Suite 200, USAF Academy, CO 80840-5025. **Admissions Phone:** (800) 443-9266; (719) 333-2520. **Fax:** (719) 333-3012. **Website:** www.usafa.edu. **Costs (2003–04):** $2,500 fee for uniforms and computer.

United States Coast Guard Academy

31 Mohegan Avenue, New London, CT 06320. **Admissions Phone:** (860) 444-8501; (800) 883-8724. **Fax:** (860) 701-6700. **Email:** admissions@cga.uscg.mil. **Website:** www.cga.edu. **Costs :** Tuition, room and board paid by U.S. government.

United States Merchant Marine Academy

300 Steamboat Road, Kings Point, NY 11024-1699. **Admissions Phone:** (516) 773-5391; (866) 546-4778. **Fax:** (516) 773-5390. **Email:** admissions@usmma.edu. **Website:** www.usmma.edu. **Costs (2002–03):** Tuition, room and board paid by U.S. government.

United States Military Academy—West Point*

606 Building, West Point, NY 10996. **Admissions Phone:** (845) 938-4041. **Email:** admissions@usma.edu. **Website:** www.usma.edu. **Costs :** Tuition, room and board paid by U.S. government.

United States Naval Academy

117 Decatur Road, Annapolis, MD 21402-5017. **Admissions Phone:** (410) 293-4361. **Fax:** (410) 293-4348. **Email:** webmail@gwmail.usna.edu. **Website:** www.usna.edu. **Costs (2003–04):** Tuition, room and board paid by U.S. government. $2,200 required fees.

University of Alabama

Box 870132, Tuscaloosa, AL 35487-0132. **Admissions Phone:** (205) 348-5666; (800) 933-BAMA. **Fax:** (205) 348-9046. **Email:** admissions@.ua.edu. **Website:** www.ua.edu. **Application Website:** http://www.ssc.ua.edu/application/. **Costs (2002–03):** Tuition and Fees, In-State: $3,556. Tuition and Fees, Out-of-State: $9,624. **Room & Board:** $4,232. **Payment Plan(s):** pre-payment plan. **Institutional Aid (est. 2002–03):** Institutional Aid, Need-Based: $130,656. Institutional Aid, Non-Need-Based: $8,816,615. FT Undergrads Receiving Aid: 46%. Avg. Amount per Student: $7,622. FT Undergrads Receiving Non-Need-Based Gift Aid: 26%. Avg. Amount per Student: $3,702. Of Those Receiving Any Aid: Receiving Need-Based Gift Aid: 51%. Avg. Award: $3,061. Receiving Need-Based Self-Help Aid: 86%. Avg. Award: $4,825. Upon Graduation, Avg. Loan Debt per Student: $18,978. Financial Aid Deadline: rolling; 3/1 (priority).

University of Arizona

P.O. Box 210011, Tucson, AZ 85721. **Admissions Phone:** (520) 621-2211. **Website:** www.arizona.edu. **Costs**

(2002–03): Tuition and Fees, In-State: $2,593. Tuition and Fees, Out-of-State: $11,113. **Room & Board:** $6,568. **Institutional Aid (2001–02):** Institutional Aid, Need-Based: $4,475,835. Institutional Aid, Non-Need-Based: $3,175,164. FT Undergrads Receiving Aid: 47%. Avg. Amount per Student: $9,502. Upon Graduation, Avg. Loan Debt per Student: $17,340. Financial Aid Deadline: 3/1 (priority).

University of Arkansas

200 Silas Hunt Hall, Fayetteville, AR 72701. **Admissions Phone:** (479) 575-5346; (800) 377-8632. **Email:** uafa@uark.edu. **Website:** www.uark.edu. **Costs (2002–03):** Tuition and Fees, In-State: $4,456. Tuition and Fees, Out-of-State: $10,828. Regional or 'good neighbor' tuition available. **Room & Board:** $4,810. **Payment Plan(s):** installment plan. **Institutional Aid (2001–02):** Institutional Aid, Non-Need-Based: $14,739,283. FT Undergrads Receiving Aid: 44%. Avg. Amount per Student: $8,028. FT Undergrads Receiving Non-Need-Based Gift Aid: 25%. Avg. Amount per Student: $5,734. Of Those Receiving Any Aid: Receiving Need-Based Gift Aid: 66%. Avg. Award: $3,377. Receiving Need-Based Self-Help Aid: 67%. Avg. Award: $4,298. Upon Graduation, Avg. Loan Debt per Student: $17,597. Financial Aid Deadline: rolling; 3/15 (priority).

University of California—Berkeley*

Berkeley, CA 94720. **Admissions Phone:** (510) 642-3175 (out-of-state); (510) 642-3246 (int'l). **Fax:** (510) 642-7333. **Email:** ouars@uclink.berkeley.edu. **Website:** www.berkeley.edu. **Application Website:** www.ucop.edu/pathways/. **Costs (2002–03):** Tuition and Fees, In-State: $4,200. Tuition and Fees, Out-of-State: $15,702. **Room & Board:** $10,047. **Payment Plan(s):** installment plan, deferred payment plan. **Institutional Aid (2001–02):** Institutional Aid, Need-Based: $32,821,448. Institutional Aid, Non-Need-Based: $2,481,060. FT Undergrads Receiving Aid: 45%. Avg. Amount per Student: $11,441. FT Undergrads Receiving Non-Need-Based Gift Aid: 11%. Avg. Amount per Student: $2,390. Of Those Receiving Any Aid: Receiving Need-Based Gift Aid: 93%. Avg. Award: $7,991. Receiving Need-Based Self-Help Aid: 78%. Avg. Award: $5,101. Upon

Graduation, Avg. Loan Debt per Student: $14,648. Financial Aid Deadline: rolling; 3/2 (priority).

University of California—Davis*

175 Mrak Hall, One Shields Avenue, Davis, CA 95616. **Admissions Phone:** (530) 752-2971. **Fax:** (530) 752-1280. **Email:** thinkucd@ucdavis.edu. **Website:** www.ucdavis.edu. **Application Website:** ucop.edu/pathways. **Costs (2002–03):** Tuition and Fees, In-State: $4,630. Tuition and Fees, Out-of-State: $16,974. Room and Board: $8,764. **Institutional Aid:** Financial Aid Deadline: 3/1.

University of California—Irvine

204 Administration Building, Irvine, CA 92697-1075. **Admissions Phone:** (949) 824-6703. **Fax:** (949) 824-2711. **Website:** http://www.uci.edu. **Application Website:** http://www.ucop.edu/pathways/. **Costs (2002–03):** Tuition and Fees, In-State: $4,556 Tuition and Fees, Out-of-State: $19,815. **Room & Board:** $7,098. **Institutional Aid (2001–02):** Institutional Aid, Need-Based: $15,801,100. Institutional Aid, Non-Need-Based: $1,805,002. FT Undergrads Receiving Aid: 48%. Avg. Amount per Student: $9,739. FT Undergrads Receiving Non-Need-Based Gift Aid: 4%. Avg. Amount per Student: $3,195. Of Those Receiving Any Aid: Receiving Need-Based Gift Aid: 87%. Avg. Award: $6,926. Receiving Need-Based Self-Help Aid: 78%. Avg. Award: $4,696. Financial Aid Deadline: 5/1, 3/2 (priority).

University of California—Los Angeles

1147 Murphy Hall, Los Angeles, CA 90095. **Admissions Phone:** (310) 825-3101. **Fax:** (310) 206-1206. **Email:** ugadm@saonet.ucla.edu. **Website:** www.ucla.edu. **Costs (2002–03):** Tuition and Fees, In-State: $4,378. Tuition and Fees, Out-of-State: $16,757. **Room & Board:** $9,480. **Institutional Aid (2001–02):** Institutional Aid, Need-Based: $33,903,967. Institutional Aid, Non-Need-Based: $1,903,859. FT Undergrads Receiving Aid: 50%. Avg. Amount per Student: $10,905. FT Undergrads Receiving Non-Need-Based Gift Aid: 7%. Avg. Amount per Student: $2,357. Of Those Receiving Any Aid: Receiving Need-Based Gift Aid: 90%. Avg. Award: $8,024.

Receiving Need-Based Self-Help Aid: 79%. Avg. Award: $4,642. Upon Graduation, Avg. Loan Debt per Student: $12,886. Financial Aid Deadline: rolling; 3/2 (priority).

University of California— San Diego

9500 Gilman Drive, 0021, La Jolla, CA 92093-0021. **Admissions Phone:** (858) 534-4831. **Fax:** (858) 534-5629. **Email:** admissionsinfo@ucsd.edu. **Website:** ucsd.edu. **Application Website:** admissions.ucsd.edu. **Costs (2002–03):** Tuition and Fees, In-State: $3,950. Tuition and Fees, Out-of-State: $16,430. **Room & Board:** $8,066. **Payment Plan(s):** installment plan, deferred payment plan. **Institutional Aid (est. 2002–03):** Institutional Aid, Need-Based: $16,275,051. Institutional Aid, Non-Need-Based: $979,150. FT Undergrads Receiving Aid: 40%. Avg. Amount per Student: $10,407. FT Undergrads Receiving Non-Need-Based Gift Aid: 7%. Avg. Amount per Student: $2,769. Of Those Receiving Any Aid: Receiving Need-Based Gift Aid: 91%. Avg. Award: $6,957. Receiving Need-Based Self-Help Aid: 86%. Avg. Award: $4,664. Upon Graduation, Avg. Loan Debt per Student: $13,275. **Financial Aid Deadline:** 6/1, 3/2 (priority).

University of California— Santa Barbara*

University of California, Santa Barbara, CA 93106. **Admissions Phone:** (805) 893-2881. **Fax:** (805) 893-2676. **Email:** appinfo@sa.ucsb.edu. **Website:** ucsb.edu. **Costs (2002–03):** Tuition and Fees, In-State: $4,363 Tuition and Fees, Out-of-State: $16,742. **Room & Board:** $8,834. **Institutional Aid:** FT Undergrads Receiving Aid: 43%. Avg. Amount per Student: $8,851. FT Undergrads Receiving Non-Need-Based Gift Aid: 10%. Avg. Amount per Student: $4,236. Of Those Receiving Any Aid: Receiving Need-Based Gift Aid: 78%. Avg. Award: $5,923. Receiving Need-Based Self-Help Aid: 87%. Avg. Award: $3,935. **Financial Aid Deadline:** 3/2 (priority).

University of California— Santa Cruz

1156 High Street, Santa Cruz, CA 95064. **Admissions Phone:** (831) 459-4008. **Fax:** (831) 459-4452. **Email:** admissions@ucsc.edu. **Website:**

www.ucsc.edu. **Application Website:** myapplication.ucsc.edu. **Costs (2003–04):** Tuition and Fees, In-State: $5,607. Tuition and Fees, Out-of-State: $18,587. **Room & Board:** $10,389. **Payment Plan(s):** deferred payment plan. **Institutional Aid (est. 2001–02):** Institutional Aid, Need-Based: $14,977,742. Institutional Aid, Non-Need-Based: $1,205,288. FT Undergrads Receiving Aid: 47%. Avg. Amount per Student: $11,334. FT Undergrads Receiving Non-Need-Based Gift Aid: 5%. Avg. Amount per Student: $3,679. Of Those Receiving Any Aid: Receiving Need-Based Gift Aid: 78%. Avg. Award: $7,589. Receiving Need-Based Self-Help Aid: 84%. Avg. Award: $4,977. Upon Graduation, Avg. Loan Debt per Student: $13,282. **Financial Aid Deadline:** rolling; 3/2 (priority).

University of Chicago

1116 East 59th Street, Chicago, IL 60637. **Admissions Phone:** (773) 702-8650. **Fax:** (773) 702-4199. **Website:** www.uchicago.edu. **Application Website:** uncommonapplication.uchicago.edu. **Costs (2002–03):** Tuition and Fees: $28,395. **Room & Board:** $8,728. **Payment Plan(s):** installment plan.

University of Cincinnati

P.O. Box 210091, Cincinnati, OH 45221-0091. **Admissions Phone:** (513) 556-1100; (800) 827-8728. **Fax:** (513) 556-1105. **Email:** admissions@uc.edu. **Website:** www.uc.edu. **Costs (2002–03):** Tuition and Fees, In-State: $6,936. Tuition and Fees, Out-of-State: $17,310. **Room & Board:** $6,774. **Institutional Aid (est. 2002–03):** Institutional Aid, Need-Based: $15,173,209. Institutional Aid, Non-Need-Based: $2,145,832. FT Undergrads Receiving Aid: 52%. Avg. Amount per Student: $7,125. FT Undergrads Receiving Non-Need-Based Gift Aid: 5%. Avg. Amount per Student: $4,084. Of Those Receiving Any Aid: Receiving Need-Based Gift Aid: 69%. Avg. Award: $3,665. Receiving Need-Based Self-Help Aid: 97%. Avg. Award: $2,831. **Financial Aid Deadline:** rolling.

University of Colorado— Boulder

552 UCB, Boulder, CO 80309-0552. **Admissions Phone:** (303) 492-6301. **Fax:** (303) 492-7115. **Email:** apply@colorado.edu. **Website:** www.colorado.edu. **Application Website:**

colorado.edu/admissions/apply.html. **Costs (2002–03):** Tuition and Fees, In-State: $3,575. Tuition and Fees, Out-of-State: $18,919. **Room & Board:** $6,272. **Payment Plan(s):** deferred payment plan. **Institutional Aid (2001–02):** Institutional Aid, Need-Based: $3,803,184. Institutional Aid, Non-Need-Based: $2,941,052. FT Undergrads Receiving Aid: 25%. Avg. Amount per Student: $9,434. FT Undergrads Receiving Non-Need-Based Gift Aid: 19%. Avg. Amount per Student: $4,547. Of Those Receiving Any Aid: Receiving Need-Based Gift Aid: 70%. Avg. Award: $4,060. Receiving Need-Based Self-Help Aid: 90%. Avg. Award: $4,387. Upon Graduation, Avg. Loan Debt per Student: $16,737. **Financial Aid Deadline:** rolling; 4/1 (priority).

University of Connecticut

2131 Hillside Road, Unit 3088, Storrs, CT 06269-3088. **Admissions Phone:** (860) 486-3137. **Email:** beahusky@uconn.edu. **Website:** www.uconn.edu. **Costs (2003–04):** Tuition and Fees, In-State: $6,800. Tuition and Fees, Out-of-State: $17,584. Regional or 'good neighbor' tuition available. **Room & Board:** $6,888. **Payment Plan(s):** installment plan. **Institutional Aid (est. 2002–03):** Institutional Aid, Need-Based: $12,661,413. Institutional Aid, Non-Need-Based: $5,064,083. FT Undergrads Receiving Aid: 47%. Avg. Amount per Student: $8,313. FT Undergrads Receiving Non-Need-Based Gift Aid: 12%. Avg. Amount per Student: $4,571. Of Those Receiving Any Aid: Receiving Need-Based Gift Aid: 70%. Avg. Award: $5,212. Receiving Need-Based Self-Help Aid: 85%. Avg. Award: $4,337. Upon Graduation, Avg. Loan Debt per Student: $16,093. **Financial Aid Deadline:** rolling; 3/1 (priority).

University of Dallas

1845 East Northgate Drive, Irving, TX 75062-4799. **Admissions Phone:** (972) 721-5266; (800) 628-6999. **Fax:** (972) 721-5017. **Email:** ugadmis@acad.udallas.edu. **Website:** www.udallas.edu. **Costs (2003–04):** Tuition and Fees: $18,062. **Room & Board:** $6,494. **Payment Plan(s):** installment plan. **Institutional Aid (est. 2002–03):** Institutional Aid, Need-Based: $3,902,715. Institutional Aid, Non-Need-Based: $4,068,524. FT Undergrads Receiving Aid: 61%. Avg. Amount per Student: $14,409. FT Undergrads Receiving Non-Need-Based Gift Aid: 32%. Avg. Amount per Student: $8,635. Of Those Receiving Any Aid:

Receiving Need-Based Gift Aid: 70%. Avg. Award: $10,393. Receiving Need-Based Self-Help Aid: 78%. Avg. Award: $5,718. Financial Aid Deadline: 3/1.

University of Dayton

300 College Park, Dayton, OH 45469-1300. **Admissions Phone:** (937) 229-4411; (800) 837-7433. **Fax:** (937) 229-4729. **Email:** admission@udayton.edu. **Website:** www.udayton.edu. **Application Website:** http://admission.udayton.edu. **Costs (2003–04): Tuition and Fees:** $20,360 (fees incl. student activities & purchase of notebook computer). **Room & Board:** $6,270. **Payment Plan(s):** deferred payment plan, pre-payment plan. **Institutional Aid (2001–02): Institutional Aid, Need-Based:** $21,332,462. **Institutional Aid, Non-Need-Based:** $9,409,562. **FT Undergrads Receiving Aid:** 56%. **Avg. Amount per Student:** $9,410. **FT Undergrads Receiving Non-Need-Based Gift Aid:** 39%. **Avg. Amount per Student:** $4,846. **Of Those Receiving Any Aid: Receiving Need-Based Gift Aid:** 99%. **Avg. Award:** $8,229. **Receiving Need-Based Self-Help Aid:** 95%. **Avg. Award:** $4,512. **Upon Graduation, Avg. Loan Debt per Student:** $18,897. **Financial Aid Deadline:** 3/31 (priority).

University of Delaware

116 Hullihen Hall, Newark, DE 19716-6210. **Admissions Phone:** (302) 831-8123. **Fax:** (302) 831-6905. **Email:** admissions@udel.edu. **Website:** www.udel.edu. **Application Website:** www.udel.edu/apply. **Costs (2002–03): Tuition and Fees, In-State:** $5,760. **Tuition and Fees, Out-of-State:** $15,290. **Room & Board:** $5,822. **Payment Plan(s):** installment plan. **Institutional Aid (est. 2002–03): Institutional Aid, Need-Based:** $8,085,000. **Institutional Aid, Non-Need-Based:** $8,510,000. **FT Undergrads Receiving Aid:** 37%. **Avg. Amount per Student:** $9,750. **FT Undergrads Receiving Non-Need-Based Gift Aid:** 21%. **Avg. Amount per Student:** $3,900. **Of Those Receiving Any Aid: Receiving Need-Based Gift Aid:** 78%. **Avg. Award:** $5,750. **Receiving Need-Based Self-Help Aid:** 72%. **Avg. Award:** $4,900. **Upon Graduation, Avg. Loan Debt per Student:** $13,610. **Financial Aid Deadline:** 3/15, 2/1 (priority).

University of Denver

2199 South University Boulevard, Denver, CO 80208. **Admissions Phone:** (303) 871-2036; (800) 525-9495. **Fax:** (303) 871-3301. **Email:** admission@du.edu. **Website:** www.du.edu. **Costs (2002–03): Tuition and Fees:** $23,259. **Room & Board:** $6,987. **Institutional Aid (2001–02): Institutional Aid, Need-Based:** $13,753,248. **Institutional Aid, Non-Need-Based:** $6,562,480. **FT Undergrads Receiving Aid:** 40%. **Avg. Amount per Student:** $19,074. **FT Undergrads Receiving Non-Need-Based Gift Aid:** 20%. **Avg. Amount per Student:** $6,385. **Of Those Receiving Any Aid: Receiving Need-Based Gift Aid:** 72%. **Avg. Award:** $7,370. **Receiving Need-Based Self-Help Aid:** 75%. **Avg. Award:** $5,659. **Upon Graduation, Avg. Loan Debt per Student:** $19,656. **Financial Aid Deadline:** 2/15 (priority).

University of Florida

201 Criser Hall, Box 114000, Gainesville, FL 32611-4000. **Admissions Phone:** (352) 392-1365. **Fax:** (352) 392-3987. **Website:** www.ufl.edu. **Application Website:** www.reg.ufl.edu/apppath.html. **Costs (2002–03): Tuition and Fees, In-State:** $2,581. **Tuition and Fees, Out-of-State:** $12,046. **Room & Board:** $5,640. **Institutional Aid (2001–02): Institutional Aid, Need-Based:** $9,911,612. **Institutional Aid, Non-Need-Based:** $11,669,313. **Financial Aid Deadline:** 3/15 (priority).

University of Georgia

212 Terrell Hall, Athens, GA 30602-1633. **Admissions Phone:** (706) 542-2112. **Fax:** (706) 542-1466. **Email:** undergrad@admissions.uga.edu. **Website:** www.uga.edu. **Application Website:** admissons.uga.edu/app_info/. **Costs (2002–03): Tuition and Fees, In-State:** $3,616. **Tuition and Fees, Out-of-State:** $12,986. **Room & Board:** $5,950. **Institutional Aid (est. 2002–03): Institutional Aid, Need-Based:** $410,227. **Institutional Aid, Non-Need-Based:** $2,329,464. **FT Undergrads Receiving Aid:** 26%. **Avg. Amount per Student:** $6,874. **FT Undergrads Receiving Non-Need-Based Gift Aid:** 50%. **Avg. Amount per Student:** $4,255. **Of Those Receiving Any Aid: Receiving Need-Based Gift Aid:** 85%. **Avg. Award:** $5,289. **Receiving Need-Based Self-Help Aid:** 63%. **Avg. Award:** $3,766. **Upon Graduation, Avg. Loan Debt per Student:** $13,550. **Financial Aid Deadline:** 8/1, 3/3 (priority).

University of Hawaii at Manoa

2600 Campus Road, Rm. 001, Honolulu, HI 96822. **Admissions Phone:** (808) 956-8975; (800) 823-9771. **Fax:** (808) 956-4148. **Email:** ar-info@hawaii.edu. **Website:** www.uhm.hawaii.edu. **Application Website:** www.hawaii.edu/admissions/. **Costs (est. 2003–04): Tuition and Fees, In-State:** $3,470. **Tuition and Fees, Out-of-State:** $9,950. **Room & Board:** $5,359. (Tuition is 03-4, fees are est. 03-4, room & board figure is for 02-3.) **Institutional Aid (est. 2002–03): Institutional Aid, Need-Based:** $277,581. **Institutional Aid, Non-Need-Based:** $751,864. **FT Undergrads Receiving Aid:** 30%. **Avg. Amount per Student:** $5,947. **FT Undergrads Receiving Non-Need-Based Gift Aid:** 8%. **Avg. Amount per Student:** $5,176. **Of Those Receiving Any Aid: Receiving Need-Based Gift Aid:** 84%. **Avg. Award:** $3,247. **Receiving Need-Based Self-Help Aid:** 67%. **Avg. Award:** $3,676. **Upon Graduation, Avg. Loan Debt per Student:** $13,629. **Financial Aid Deadline:** rolling; 3/15 (priority).

University of Houston

122 East Cullen Building, Houston, TX 77204-2023. **Admissions Phone:** (713) 743-1010. **Fax:** (713) 743-9633. **Email:** admissions@uh.edu. **Website:** www.uh.edu. **Application Website:** www.uh.edu/enroll/admis. **Costs (2002–03): Tuition and Fees, In-State:** $3,348. **Tuition and Fees, Out-of-State:** $9,888. **Room & Board:** $5,694. **Payment Plan(s):** installment plan, deferred payment plan. **Institutional Aid (est. 2002–03): Institutional Aid, Need-Based:** $7,500,000. **Institutional Aid, Non-Need-Based:** $35,000. **FT Undergrads Receiving Aid:** 56%. **Avg. Amount per Student:** $11,340. **FT Undergrads Receiving Non-Need-Based Gift Aid:** 17%. **Avg. Amount per Student:** $2,730. **Of Those Receiving Any Aid: Receiving Need-Based Gift Aid:** 81%. **Avg. Award:** $6,200. **Receiving Need-Based Self-Help Aid:** 73%. **Avg. Award:** $6,820. **Upon Graduation, Avg. Loan Debt per Student:** $12,988. **Financial Aid Deadline:** rolling; 4/1 (priority).

University of Illinois— Urbana-Champaign

901 West Illinois St., Urbana, IL 61801-3028. **Admissions Phone:** (217) 333-0302. **Fax:** (217) 244-0903. **Email:**

admissions@oar.uiuc.edu. **Website:** www.uiuc.edu. **Costs (2002–03):** Tuition and Fees, In-State: $5,748. Tuition and Fees, Out-of-State: $15,798. Room & Board: $6,360. **Payment Plan(s):** installment plan. **Institutional Aid (est. 2002–03):** Institutional Aid, Need-Based: $15,646,576. Institutional Aid, Non-Need-Based: $3,815,895. FT Undergrads Receiving Aid: 39%. Avg. Amount per Student: $10,044. FT Undergrads Receiving Non-Need-Based Gift Aid: 12%. Avg. Amount per Student: $4,293. Of Those Receiving Any Aid: Receiving Need-Based Gift Aid: 75%. Avg. Award: $6,365. Receiving Need-Based Self-Help Aid: 91%. Avg. Award: $4,952. Upon Graduation, Avg. Loan Debt per Student: $14,791. **Financial Aid Deadline:** rolling; 3/15 (priority).

University of Iowa

107 Calvin Hall, Iowa City, IA 52242-1396. **Admissions Phone:** (319) 335-3847; (800) 553-4692. **Fax:** (319) 335-1535. **Email:** admissions@uiowa.edu. **Website:** uiowa.edu. **Application Website:** uiowa.edu/admissions. **Costs (2003–04):** Tuition and Fees, In-State: $4,993. Tuition and Fees, Out-of-State: $15,285. Room & Board: $5,930. **Payment Plan(s):** installment plan. **Institutional Aid (est. 2002–03):** Institutional Aid, Need-Based: $8,182,126. Institutional Aid, Non-Need-Based: $7,134,380. FT Undergrads Receiving Aid: 41%. Avg. Amount per Student: $6,806. FT Undergrads Receiving Non-Need-Based Gift Aid: 21%. Avg. Amount per Student: $2,945. Of Those Receiving Any Aid: Receiving Need-Based Gift Aid: 61%. Avg. Award: $2,303. Receiving Need-Based Self-Help Aid: 84%. Avg. Award: $3,001. Upon Graduation, Avg. Loan Debt per Student: $15,335. **Financial Aid Deadline:** rolling; 1/3 (priority).

University of Kansas

KU Visitor Center, 1502 Iowa Street, Lawrence, KS 66045-7576. **Admissions Phone:** (785) 864-3911. **Fax:** (785) 864-5006. **Email:** adm@ku.edu. **Website:** www.ku.edu. **Application Website:** www.admissions.ku.edu. **Costs (2002–03):** Tuition and Fees, In-State: $3,484. Tuition and Fees, Out-of-State: $10,687. Room & Board: $4,642. **Institutional Aid (2001–02):** Institutional Aid, Need-Based: $5,929,775. Institutional Aid, Non-Need-Based: $6,381,930. FT Undergrads Receiving Aid: 34%. Avg. Amount per Student: $6,173. FT

Undergrads Receiving Non-Need-Based Gift Aid: 15%. Avg. Amount per Student: $3,166. Of Those Receiving Any Aid: Receiving Need-Based Gift Aid: 67%. Avg. Award: $3,407. Receiving Need-Based Self-Help Aid: 83%. Avg. Award: $3,760. Upon Graduation, Avg. Loan Debt per Student: $17,347. **Financial Aid Deadline:** rolling; 3/1 (priority).

University of Kentucky

100 W.D. Funkhouser Building, Lexington, KY 40506. **Admissions Phone:** (859) 257-2000; (800) 432-0967 (in-state). **Fax:** (859) 257-3823. **Email:** admissio@pop.uky.edu. **Website:** www.uky.edu. **Application Website:** www.uky.edu/UGAdmission/applicants/application.html. **Costs (2003–04):** Tuition and Fees, In-State: $4,547. Tuition and Fees, Out-of-State: $11,227. Room & Board: $4,285. **Payment Plan(s):** installment plan. **Institutional Aid (est. 2002–03):** Institutional Aid, Need-Based: $8,109,716. FT Undergrads Receiving Aid: 37%. Avg. Amount per Student: $8,538. FT Undergrads Receiving Non-Need-Based Gift Aid: 41%. Avg. Amount per Student: $2,561. Of Those Receiving Any Aid: Receiving Need-Based Gift Aid: 53%. Avg. Award: $3,838. Receiving Need-Based Self-Help Aid: 74%. Avg. Award: $3,624. **Financial Aid Deadline:** rolling; 2/15 (priority).

University of Maine

5713 Chadbourne Hall, Orono, ME 04469-5713. **Admissions Phone:** (207) 581-1561; (877) 486-2364. **Fax:** (207) 581-1213. **Email:** um-admit@maine.edu. **Website:** www.umaine.edu. **Application Website:** http://apply.maine.edu. **Costs (2002–03):** Tuition and Fees, In-State: $5,550. Tuition and Fees, Out-of-State: $13,620. Regional or 'good neighbor' tuition available. Room & Board: $5,922. **Payment Plan(s):** installment plan. **Institutional Aid (est. 2002–03):** Institutional Aid, Need-Based: $5,372,829. Institutional Aid, Non-Need-Based: $1,005,313. FT Undergrads Receiving Aid: 56%. Avg. Amount per Student: $7,829. FT Undergrads Receiving Non-Need-Based Gift Aid: 12%. Avg. Amount per Student: $4,535. Of Those Receiving Any Aid: Receiving Need-Based Gift Aid: 66%. Avg. Award: $4,618. Receiving Need-Based Self-Help Aid: 86%. Avg. Award: $4,365. Upon Graduation, Avg. Loan Debt per Student: $17,917. **Financial Aid Deadline:** 3/1 (priority).

University of Maryland— Baltimore County

1000 Hilltop Circle, Baltimore, MD 21250. **Admissions Phone:** (410) 455-2291; (800) UMBC-4U2. **Fax:** (410) 455-1094. **Email:** admissions@umbc.edu. **Website:** www.umbc.edu. **Application Website:** www.umbc.edu/Admissions/undergrad.html. **Costs (2002–03):** Tuition and Fees, In-State: $6,362. Tuition and Fees, Out-of-State: $12,546. Room & Board: $6,780. **Payment Plan(s):** installment plan. **Institutional Aid (2001–02):** Institutional Aid, Need-Based: $792,391. Institutional Aid, Non-Need-Based: $9,800,124. FT Undergrads Receiving Aid: 54%. Avg. Amount per Student: $6,212. FT Undergrads Receiving Non-Need-Based Gift Aid: 23%. Avg. Amount per Student: $6,021. Of Those Receiving Any Aid: Receiving Need-Based Gift Aid: 55%. Avg. Award: $3,570. Receiving Need-Based Self-Help Aid: 87%. Avg. Award: $4,809. Upon Graduation, Avg. Loan Debt per Student: $14,500. **Financial Aid Deadline:** 3/1 (priority).

University of Maryland— College Park

Mitchell Building, College Park, MD 20742-5235. **Admissions Phone:** (301) 314-8385; (800) 422-5867. **Fax:** (301) 314-9693. **Email:** um-admit@uga.umd.edu. **Website:** www.maryland.edu. **Application Website:** www.uga.umd.edu. **Costs (2002–03):** Tuition and Fees, In-State: $5,670. Tuition and Fees, Out-of-State: $14,434. Room & Board: $7,241. **Payment Plan(s):** installment plan. **Institutional Aid (2001–02):** Institutional Aid, Need-Based: $5,440,152. Institutional Aid, Non-Need-Based: $14,579,154. FT Undergrads Receiving Aid: 39%. Avg. Amount per Student: $8,051. FT Undergrads Receiving Non-Need-Based Gift Aid: 16%. Avg. Amount per Student: $5,267. Of Those Receiving Any Aid: Receiving Need-Based Gift Aid: 67%. Avg. Award: $4,081. Receiving Need-Based Self-Help Aid: 79%. Avg. Award: $3,713. Upon Graduation, Avg. Loan Debt per Student: $15,566. **Financial Aid Deadline:** 6/30, 2/15 (priority).

University of Massachusetts—Amherst

37 Mather Drive, Amherst, MA 01003-9291. **Admissions Phone:** (413) 545-0222. **Fax:** (413) 545-4312. **Website:** www.umass.edu. **Application Website:** umass.edu/home/

admissions. **Costs (2002–03): Tuition and Fees, In-State:** $6,660. **Tuition and Fees, Out-of-State:** $15,513. Regional or 'good neighbor' tuition available. **Room & Board:** $5,473. **Payment Plan(s):** installment plan, pre-payment plan. **Institutional Aid (2001–02): Institutional Aid, Need-Based:** $11,666,808. **Institutional Aid, Non-Need-Based:** $3,205,637. **FT Undergrads Receiving Aid:** 44%. **Avg. Amount per Student:** $8,439. **FT Undergrads Receiving Non-Need-Based Gift Aid:** 7%. **Avg. Amount per Student:** $3,476. **Of Those Receiving Any Aid: Receiving Need-Based Gift Aid:** 97%. **Avg. Award:** $4,766. **Receiving Need-Based Self-Help Aid:** 90%. **Avg. Award:** $4,043. **Upon Graduation, Avg. Loan Debt per Student:** $15,321. **Financial Aid Deadline:** 3/1 (priority).

University of Miami

Office of Admission, Coral Gables, FL 33124. **Admissions Phone:** (305) 284-4323. **Fax:** (305) 284-2507. **Email:** admission@miami.edu. **Website:** www.miami.edu. **Application Website:** miami.edu/apply. **Costs (2002–03): Tuition and Fees:** $24,810. **Room & Board:** $8,062. **Payment Plan(s):** installment plan, pre-payment plan. **Institutional Aid (est. 2002–03): Institutional Aid, Need-Based:** $48,331,753. **Institutional Aid, Non-Need-Based:** $23,270,721. **FT Undergrads Receiving Aid:** 54%. **Avg. Amount per Student:** $22,399. **FT Undergrads Receiving Non-Need-Based Gift Aid:** 27%. **Avg. Amount per Student:** $14,858. **Of Those Receiving Any Aid: Receiving Need-Based Gift Aid:** 99%. **Avg. Award:** $16,124. **Receiving Need-Based Self-Help Aid:** 83%. **Avg. Award:** $6,632. **Upon Graduation, Avg. Loan Debt per Student:** $25,093. **Financial Aid Deadline:** 2/15 (priority).

University of Michigan— Ann Arbor

Undergraduate Admissions, Ann Arbor, MI 48109. **Admissions Phone:** (734) 764-7433. **Fax:** (734) 936-0740. **Email:** ugadmiss@umich.edu. **Website:** www.umich.edu. **Application Website:** www.admissions.umich.edu. **Costs (2002–03): Tuition and Fees, In-State:** $7,959. **Tuition and Fees, Out-of-State:** $24,185. **Room & Board:** $6,366. **Payment Plan(s):** installment plan. **Institutional Aid (2001–02): Institutional Aid, Need-Based:** $33,379,481. **Institutional Aid, Non-Need-Based:** $19,544,007. **FT Undergrads Receiving Aid:** 38%. **Avg. Amount per Student:** $10,022. **FT Undergrads**

Receiving Non-Need-Based Gift Aid: 22%. **Avg. Amount per Student:** $4,300. **Of Those Receiving Any Aid: Receiving Need-Based Gift Aid:** 63%. **Avg. Award:** $8,010. **Receiving Need-Based Self-Help Aid:** 100%. **Avg. Award:** $6,294. **Upon Graduation, Avg. Loan Debt per Student:** $16,825. **Financial Aid Deadline:** 9/30, 2/15 (priority).

University of Minnesota— Twin Cities

240 Williamson Hall, 231 Pillsbury Drive SE, Minneapolis, MN 55455-0015. **Admissions Phone:** (612) 625-2008; (800) 752-1000. **Fax:** (612) 626-1693. **Email:** admissions@tc.umn.edu. **Website:** www.umn.edu/tc/. **Application Website:** www1.umn.edu/twincities/admissions.html. **Costs (2002–03): Tuition and Fees, In-State:** $6,280. **Tuition and Fees, Out-of-State:** $16,854. Regional or 'good neighbor' tuition available. **Room & Board:** $5,696. **Institutional Aid (est. 2002–03): Institutional Aid, Need-Based:** $15,941,773. **Institutional Aid, Non-Need-Based:** $8,505,349. **FT Undergrads Receiving Aid:** 46%. **Avg. Amount per Student:** $8,496. **FT Undergrads Receiving Non-Need-Based Gift Aid:** 11%. **Avg. Amount per Student:** $4,089. **Of Those Receiving Any Aid: Receiving Need-Based Gift Aid:** 74%. **Avg. Award:** $6,008. **Receiving Need-Based Self-Help Aid:** 87%. **Avg. Award:** $5,691. **Financial Aid Deadline:** rolling; 1/15 (priority).

University of Missouri— Columbia

230 Jesse Hall, Columbia, MO 65211. **Admissions Phone:** (573) 882-7786; (800) 225-6075 (in-state). **Fax:** (573) 882-7887. **Email:** MU4U@missouri.edu. **Website:** missouri.edu. **Application Website:** missouri.edu/~reqwww. **Costs (2002–03): Tuition and Fees, In-State:** $5,552 **Tuition and Fees, Out-of-State:** $14,705 Regional or 'good neighbor' tuition available.**Room & Board:** $5,374 (est. 2002–03). **Institutional Aid (est. 2002–03): Institutional Aid, Need-Based:** $10,505,226. **Institutional Aid, Non-Need-Based:** $10,339,859. **FT Undergrads Receiving Aid:** 41%. **Avg. Amount per Student:** $7,544. **FT Undergrads Receiving Non-Need-Based Gift Aid:** 25%. **Avg. Amount per Student:** $4,204. **Of Those Receiving Any Aid: Receiving Need-Based Gift Aid:** 84%. **Avg. Award:** $5,070. **Receiving Need-Based Self-Help Aid:** 78%. **Avg. Award:** $3,791. **Upon Graduation,**

Avg. Loan Debt per Student: $17,137. **Financial Aid Deadline:** rolling; 3/1 (priority).

University of Missouri— Rolla

106 Parker Hall, 1870 Miner Circle, Rolla, MO 65409-1060. **Admissions Phone:** (573) 341-4164; (800) 522-0938. **Fax:** (573) 341-4082. **Email:** admissions@umr.edu. **Website:** www.umr.edu. **Application Website:** www.umr.edu/admissions. **Costs (2002–03): Tuition and Fees, In-State:** $5,650. **Tuition and Fees, Out-of-State:** $14,695. (Midwest Student Exchange Program). **Room & Board:** $5,230. **Payment Plan(s):** installment plan. **Institutional Aid (est. 2002–03): FT Undergrads Receiving Aid:** 50%. **Avg. Amount per Student:** $8,330. **FT Undergrads Receiving Non-Need-Based Gift Aid:** 33%. **Avg. Amount per Student:** $5,220. **Of Those Receiving Any Aid: Receiving Need-Based Gift Aid:** 85%. **Avg. Award:** $4,922. **Receiving Need-Based Self-Help Aid:** 75%. **Avg. Award:** $4,590. **Upon Graduation, Avg. Loan Debt per Student:** $16,850. **Financial Aid Deadline:** rolling; 3/1 (priority).

University of Nebraska— Lincoln

1410 Q Street, Lincoln, NE 68588-0417. **Admissions Phone:** (402) 472-2023; (800) 742-8800. **Fax:** (402) 472-0670. **Email:** nuhusker@unl.edu. **Website:** www.unl.edu. **Costs (2002–03): Tuition and Fees, In-State:** $4,125. **Tuition and Fees, Out-of-State:** $10,718. Regional or 'good neighbor' tuition available. **Room & Board:** $4,875. **Payment Plan(s):** installment plan. **Institutional Aid (2001–02): Institutional Aid, Need-Based:** $6,446,807. **Institutional Aid, Non-Need-Based:** $8,599,483. **FT Undergrads Receiving Aid:** 40%. **Avg. Amount per Student:** $6,234. **FT Undergrads Receiving Non-Need-Based Gift Aid:** 6%. **Avg. Amount per Student:** $2,701. **Of Those Receiving Any Aid: Receiving Need-Based Gift Aid:** 71%. **Avg. Award:** $3,410. **Receiving Need-Based Self-Help Aid:** 84%. **Avg. Award:** $3,668. **Upon Graduation, Avg. Loan Debt per Student:** $15,682. **Financial Aid Deadline:** rolling.

University of Nevada—Las Vegas

4505 Maryland Parkway, Box 451021, Las Vegas, NV 89154. Admissions Phone: (702) 895-2030. Fax: (702) 895-1200. Email: Undergraduate.Recruitment@ccmail.nevada.edu. Website: www.unlv.edu. Costs (2003–04): Tuition and Fees, In-State: $2,736. Tuition and Fees, Out-of-State: $11,223. Regional or 'good neighbor' tuition available. Room & Board: $6,140. Institutional Aid (est. 2002–03): Institutional Aid, Need-Based: $225,000. Institutional Aid, Non-Need-Based: $10,000. FT Undergrads Receiving Aid: 42%. Avg. Amount per Student: $6,889. FT Undergrads Receiving Non-Need-Based Gift Aid: 28%. Avg. Amount per Student: $1,820. Of Those Receiving Any Aid: Receiving Need-Based Gift Aid: 59%. Avg. Award: $2,990. Receiving Need-Based Self-Help Aid: 62%. Avg. Award: $5,110. Upon Graduation, Avg. Loan Debt per Student: $12,900. Financial Aid Deadline: rolling; 2/1 (priority).

University of Nevada—Reno

Mail Stop 120, Reno, NV 89557. Admissions Phone: (775) 784-4700. Fax: (775) 784-4283. Email: asknevada@unr.edu. Website: www.unr.edu. Application Website: www.ss.unr.edu/admission. Costs (est. 2003-04): Tuition and Fees, In-State: $2,802. Tuition and Fees, Out-of-State: $11,289. Institutional Aid (2001–02): Institutional Aid, Need-Based: $427,718. Institutional Aid, Non-Need-Based: $888,703. FT Undergrads Receiving Aid: 31%. Avg. Amount per Student: $6,288. FT Undergrads Receiving Non-Need-Based Gift Aid: 33%. Avg. Amount per Student: $2,752. Of Those Receiving Any Aid: Receiving Need-Based Gift Aid: 57%. Avg. Award: $3,208. Receiving Need-Based Self-Help Aid: 65%. Avg. Award: $3,897. Upon Graduation, Avg. Loan Debt per Student: $15,788. Financial Aid Deadline: rolling; 2/1 (priority).

University of New Hampshire

4 Garrison Avenue, Durham, NH 03824-3510. Admissions Phone: (603) 862-1360. Fax: (603) 862-0077. Website: www.unh.edu. Application Website: www.unh.edu/admissions/apply.html. Costs : (2002–03): Tuition and Fees, In-State: $8,130. Tuition and Fees, Out-of-State: $17,830. Room & Board: $5,882. Regional or 'good neighbor' tuition available. Payment Plan(s): installment plan. Institutional Aid (est. 2002–03): Institutional Aid, Need-Based: $9,488,601. Institutional Aid, Non-Need-Based: $12,252,949. FT Undergrads Receiving Aid: 53%. Avg. Amount per Student: $13,429. FT Undergrads Receiving Non-Need-Based Gift Aid: 19%. Avg. Amount per Student: $5,315. Of Those Receiving Any Aid: Receiving Need-Based Gift Aid: 58%. Avg. Award: $2,086. Receiving Need-Based Self-Help Aid: 93%. Avg. Award: $2,993. Upon Graduation, Avg. Loan Debt per Student: $20,701. Financial Aid Deadline: 3/1 (priority).

University of New Mexico

Student Services Center 140, Albuquerque, NM 87131-2046. Admissions Phone: (505) 277-2446; (800) CALL-UNM. Fax: (505) 277-6686. Email: apply@unm.edu. Website: www.unm.edu. Application Website: www.unm.edu/preview/na_admis.htm. Costs (2002–03): Tuition and Fees, In-State: $3,169. Tuition and Fees, Out-of-State: $11,436. Room & Board: $5,300. Payment Plan(s): installment plan, deferred payment plan. Financial Aid Deadline: 3/1 (priority).

University of North Carolina—Chapel Hill

Campus Box 2200, Jackson Hall, Chapel Hill, NC 27599. Admissions Phone: (919) 966-3621. Fax: (919) 962-3045. Email: uadm@email.unc.edu. Website: unc.edu. Application Website: www.admissions.unc.edu. Costs (2002–03): Tuition and Fees, In-State: $3,856. Tuition and Fees, Out-of-State: $15,140. Room & Board: $5,805. Payment Plan(s): installment plan, deferred payment plan. Institutional Aid (2001–02): Institutional Aid, Need-Based: $12,159,952. Institutional Aid, Non-Need-Based: $3,095,460. FT Undergrads Receiving Aid: 29%. Avg. Amount per Student: $7,824. FT Undergrads Receiving Non-Need-Based Gift Aid: 14%. Avg. Amount per Student: $5,305. Of Those Receiving Any Aid: Receiving Need-Based Gift Aid: 95%. Avg. Award: $4,617. Receiving Need-Based Self-Help Aid: 61%. Avg. Award: $3,152. Upon Graduation, Avg. Loan Debt per Student: $11,156. Financial Aid Deadline: 3/1 (priority).

University of Notre Dame

220 Main Building, Notre Dame, IN 46556. Admissions Phone: (574) 631-7505. Fax: (574) 631-8865. Email: admissio.1@nd.edu. Website: www.nd.edu. Application Website: http://admissions.nd.edu. Costs (2002–03): Tuition and Fees: $25,852. Room & Board: $6,510. Payment Plan(s): installment plan. Institutional Aid (est. 2002–03): Institutional Aid, Need-Based: $46,233,684. Institutional Aid, Non-Need-Based: $2,523,012. FT Undergrads Receiving Aid: 40%. Avg. Amount per Student: $23,432. FT Undergrads Receiving Non-Need-Based Gift Aid: 11%. Avg. Amount per Student: $9,088. Of Those Receiving Any Aid: Receiving Need-Based Gift Aid: 95%. Avg. Award: $17,381. Receiving Need-Based Self-Help Aid: 87%. Avg. Award: $5,846. Upon Graduation, Avg. Loan Debt per Student: $25,595. Financial Aid Deadline: 2/15.

University of Oklahoma

1000 Asp Avenue, Norman, OK 73019-4076. Admissions Phone: (800) 234-6868; (405) 325-2252. Fax: (405) 325-7124. Email: admrec@ou.edu. Website: www.ou.edu. Application Website: www.ou.edu/admrec/admissions.htm. Costs (2002–03): Tuition and Fees, In-State: $2,929. Tuition and Fees, Out-of-State: $8,077. Room & Board: $5,030. Payment Plan(s): installment plan. Institutional Aid (2001–02): Institutional Aid, Need-Based: $1,918,091. Institutional Aid, Non-Need-Based: $1,700,748. FT Undergrads Receiving Aid: 48%. Avg. Amount per Student: $7,635. FT Undergrads Receiving Non-Need-Based Gift Aid: 14%. Avg. Amount per Student: $3,718. Of Those Receiving Any Aid: Receiving Need-Based Gift Aid: 42%. Avg. Award: $3,521. Receiving Need-Based Self-Help Aid: 68%. Avg. Award: $4,233. Upon Graduation, Avg. Loan Debt per Student: $16,886. Financial Aid Deadline: rolling; 3/1 (priority).

University of Oregon

240 Oregon Hall, Eugene, OR 97403. Admissions Phone: (541) 346-3201; (800) BE A-DUCK (out-of-state). Fax: (541) 346-5815. Email: uoadmit@oregon.uoregon.edu. Website: www.uoregon.edu. Costs (2002–03): Tuition and Fees, In-State: $4,230 Tuition and Fees, Out-of-State: $15,219. Room & Board: $6,252. Payment Plan(s): installment plan. Institutional Aid (est. 2002–03): Institutional Aid, Need-

Based: $1,387,473. Institutional Aid, Non-Need-Based: $9,563,600. FT Undergrads Receiving Aid: 46%. Avg. Amount per Student: $7,825. FT Undergrads Receiving Non-Need-Based Gift Aid: 12%. Avg. Amount per Student: $2,291. Of Those Receiving Any Aid: Receiving Need-Based Gift Aid: 60%. Avg. Award: $3,822. Receiving Need-Based Self-Help Aid: 86%. Avg. Award: $4,032. Upon Graduation, Avg. Loan Debt per Student: $22,783. Financial Aid Deadline: 3/1.

University of Pennsylvania

1 College Hall, Philadelphia, PA 19104-6376. Admissions Phone: (215) 898-7507. Fax: (215) 898-9670. Email: info@admissions.ugao.upenn.edu. Website: www.upenn.edu. Application Website: www.upenn.edu/admissions. Costs (2002–03): Tuition and Fees: $27,988. Room & Board: $8,224. Payment Plan(s): installment plan, pre-payment plan. Institutional Aid (est. 2001–02): FT Undergrads Receiving Aid: 43%. Avg. Amount per Student: $23,875. Of Those Receiving Any Aid: Receiving Need-Based Gift Aid: 90%. Avg. Award: $18,444. Receiving Need-Based Self-Help Aid: 100%. Avg. Award: $6,900. Upon Graduation, Avg. Loan Debt per Student: $20,247. Financial Aid Deadline: 1/1, 2/15 (priority).

University of Pittsburgh

Alumni Hall, 4227 Fifth Ave., Pittsburgh, PA 15260. Admissions Phone: (412) 624-7488. Fax: (412) 648-8815. Email: oafa@pitt.edu. Website: www.pitt.edu. Application Website: www.admissions.pitt.edu/freshapp/freshman.asp. Costs (2002–03): Tuition and Fees, In-State: $8,528. Tuition and Fees, Out-of-State: $17,336. Room & Board: $6,470. Payment Plan(s): installment plan, deferred payment plan. Institutional Aid (est. 2002–03): Institutional Aid, Need-Based: $2,754,283. Institutional Aid, Non-Need-Based: $15,205,198. FT Undergrads Receiving Aid: 55%. Avg. Amount per Student: $10,798. FT Undergrads Receiving Non-Need-Based Gift Aid: 11%. Avg. Amount per Student: $6,377. Of Those Receiving Any Aid: Receiving Need-Based Gift Aid: 71%. Avg. Award: $4,302. Receiving Need-Based Self-Help Aid: 86%. Avg. Award: $5,216. Upon Graduation, Avg. Loan Debt per Student: $20,154. Financial Aid Deadline: rolling; 3/1 (priority).

University of Puget Sound

1500 North Warner, Tacoma, WA 98416-1062. Admissions Phone: (253) 879-3211; (800) 396-7191. Fax: (253) 879-3993. Email: admission@ups.edu. Website: http://www.ups.edu. Costs (2002–03): Tuition and Fees: $23,945. Room & Board: $6,140. Payment Plan(s): deferred payment plan. Institutional Aid (est. 2002–03): Institutional Aid, Need-Based: $14,577,662. Institutional Aid, Non-Need-Based: $4,457,042. FT Undergrads Receiving Aid: 57%. Avg. Amount per Student: $18,963. FT Undergrads Receiving Non-Need-Based Gift Aid: 26%. Avg. Amount per Student: $6,619. Of Those Receiving Any Aid: Receiving Need-Based Gift Aid: 95%. Avg. Award: $10,571. Receiving Need-Based Self-Help Aid: 83%. Avg. Award: $7,513. Upon Graduation, Avg. Loan Debt per Student: $24,272. Financial Aid Deadline: 2/1, 1/31 (priority).

University of Redlands

1200 East Colton Avenue, P.O. Box 3080, Redlands, CA 92373-0999. Admissions Phone: (909) 335-4074. Fax: (909) 335-4089. Email: admissions@redlands.edu. Website: redlands.edu. Costs (2002–03): Tuition and Fees: $22,750. Room & Board: $8,114. Payment Plan(s): installment plan. Institutional Aid (est. 2002–03): Institutional Aid, Need-Based: $16,585,895. Institutional Aid, Non-Need-Based: $1,927,837. FT Undergrads Receiving Aid: 71%. Avg. Amount per Student: $22,020. FT Undergrads Receiving Non-Need-Based Gift Aid: 6%. Avg. Amount per Student: $9,385. Of Those Receiving Any Aid: Receiving Need-Based Gift Aid: 98%. Avg. Award: $12,463. Receiving Need-Based Self-Help Aid: 96%. Avg. Award: $5,647. Upon Graduation, Avg. Loan Debt per Student: $18,956. Financial Aid Deadline: 3/2 (priority).

University of Richmond

28 Westhampton Way, University of Richmond, VA 23173. Admissions Phone: (804) 289-8640; (800) 700-1662. Fax: (804) 287-6003. Email: Admissions@richmond.edu. Website: richmond.edu. Costs (2003–04): Tuition and Fees: $24,940. Room & Board: $5,160. Payment Plan(s): installment plan, deferred payment plan. Institutional Aid (est. 2002–03): Institutional Aid, Need-Based: $9,905,656. Institutional Aid, Non-Need-Based: $4,566,526. FT Undergrads Receiving Aid:

30%. Avg. Amount per Student: $17,657. FT Undergrads Receiving Non-Need-Based Gift Aid: 28%. Avg. Amount per Student: $10,452. Of Those Receiving Any Aid: Receiving Need-Based Gift Aid: 100%. Avg. Award: $14,091. Receiving Need-Based Self-Help Aid: 72%. Avg. Award: $4,055. Upon Graduation, Avg. Loan Debt per Student: $16,115. Financial Aid Deadline: 2/25

University of Rochester*

Wallis Hall, P.O. Box 270251, Rochester, NY 14627-0251. Admissions Phone: (585) 275-3221; (888) 822-2256. Fax: (585) 461-4595. Email: admit@admissions.rochester.edu. Website: www.rochester.edu. Costs (2002–03): Tuition and Fees: $26,107. Room & Board: $8,504. Payment Plan(s): installment plan, pre-payment plan. Institutional Aid: FT Undergrads Receiving Aid: 60%. Avg. Amount per Student: $21,627. FT Undergrads Receiving Non-Need-Based Gift Aid: 37%. Avg. Amount per Student: $9,519. Of Those Receiving Any Aid: Receiving Need-Based Gift Aid: 99%. Avg. Award: $16,984. Receiving Need-Based Self-Help Aid: 83%. Avg. Award: $4,851. Upon Graduation, Avg. Loan Debt per Student: $20,998. Financial Aid Deadline: 2/1.

University of Scranton

University of Scranton, Scranton, PA 18510. Admissions Phone: (570) 941-7540; (888) 727-2686. Fax: (570) 941-5928. Email: admissions@scranton.edu. Website: scranton.edu. Application Website: www.scranton.edu/admission/fa_ao_apply online.asp. Costs (2002–03): Tuition and Fees: $20,448. Room & Board: $8,770. Institutional Aid (est. 2002–03): Institutional Aid, Need-Based: $22,375,856. Institutional Aid, Non-Need-Based: $2,952,603. FT Undergrads Receiving Aid: 65%. Avg. Amount per Student: $14,346. FT Undergrads Receiving Non-Need-Based Gift Aid: 7%. Avg. Amount per Student: $8,309. Of Those Receiving Any Aid: Receiving Need-Based Gift Aid: 93%. Avg. Award: $10,365. Receiving Need-Based Self-Help Aid: 81%. Avg. Award: $4,727. Upon Graduation, Avg. Loan Debt per Student: $15,000. Financial Aid Deadline: rolling; 2/15 (priority).

University of South Carolina—Columbia

University of South Carolina, Columbia, SC 29208. Admissions Phone: (803) 777-7700; (800) 868-5872. Fax: (803) 777-0101. Email:

admissions-ugrad@sc.edu. Website: www.sc.edu. Application Website: www.sc.edu/admissions. Costs (2002–03): Tuition and Fees, In-State: $4,984. Tuition and Fees, Out-of-State: $13,104. Room & Board: $5,064. Payment Plan(s): installment plan, deferred payment plan. Institutional Aid (est. 2002–03): Institutional Aid, Non-Need-Based: $8,005,262. FT Undergrads Receiving Aid: 44%. Avg. Amount per Student: $8,263. FT Undergrads Receiving Non-Need-Based Gift Aid: 36%. Avg. Amount per Student: $2,848. Of Those Receiving Any Aid: Receiving Need-Based Gift Aid: 53%. Avg. Award: $3,001. Receiving Need-Based Self-Help Aid: 81%. Avg. Award: $4,307. Upon Graduation, Avg. Loan Debt per Student: $15,260. Financial Aid Deadline: 4/15 (priority).

University of Southern California

SAS 208, Los Angeles, CA 90089-0911. Admissions Phone: (213) 740-1111. Fax: (213) 740-6364. Email: admitusc@usc.edu. Website: www.usc.edu. Application Website: www.usc.edu/students/admission. Costs (2002–03): Tuition and Fees: $26,954. Room & Board: $8,512. Payment Plan(s): installment plan, pre-payment plan. Institutional Aid (2001–02): Institutional Aid, Need-Based: $93,140,396. Institutional Aid, Non-Need-Based: $25,035,522. FT Undergrads Receiving Aid: 50%. Avg. Amount per Student: $24,941. FT Undergrads Receiving Non-Need-Based Gift Aid: 15%. Avg. Amount per Student: $12,042. Of Those Receiving Any Aid: Receiving Need-Based Gift Aid: 94%. Avg. Award: $18,699. Receiving Need-Based Self-Help Aid: 95%. Avg. Award: $6,768. Upon Graduation, Avg. Loan Debt per Student: $19,651. Financial Aid Deadline: 2/28, 1/21 (priority).

University of Tennessee

320 Student Services Building, Knoxville, TN 37996. Admissions Phone: (800) 221-8657; (865) 974-2184. Fax: (865) 974-6341. Email: admissions@utk.edu. Website: www.tennessee.edu. Application Website: http://admissions.utk.edu/undergraduate/ugadmissn.shtml. Costs (2002–03): Tuition and Fees, In-State: $4,056. Tuition and Fees, Out-of-State: $12,158. Out-of-state required fees are $830. Room & Board: $4,912.

University of Texas—Austin

P.O. Box 8058, Austin, TX 78713-8058. Admissions Phone: (512) 475-7440. Fax: (512) 475-7475. Website: http://www.utexas.edu. Application Website: http://utdirect.utexas.edu/adappw/apply.wb. Costs (2002–03): Tuition and Fees, In-State: $3,950. Tuition and Fees, Out-of-State: $10,490. Room & Board: $5,975. Payment Plan(s): installment plan. Institutional Aid (2001–02): Institutional Aid, Need-Based: $18,740,000. Institutional Aid, Non-Need-Based: $34,350,000. FT Undergrads Receiving Aid: 52%. Avg. Amount per Student: $7,470. FT Undergrads Receiving Non-Need-Based Gift Aid: 25%. Avg. Amount per Student: $4,810. Of Those Receiving Any Aid: Receiving Need-Based Gift Aid: 58%. Avg. Award: $5,280. Receiving Need-Based Self-Help Aid: 91%. Avg. Award: $4,300. Upon Graduation, Avg. Loan Debt per Student: $16,400. Financial Aid Deadline: rolling; 4/1 (priority).

University of the Pacific

3601 Pacific Avenue, Stockton, CA 95211. Admissions Phone: (209) 946-2211; (800) 959-2867. Fax: (209) 946-2413. Email: admissions@uop.edu. Website: uop.edu. Costs (est. 2003-04): Tuition and Fees: $22,555. Room & Board: $7,198. Payment Plan(s): installment plan. Institutional Aid (est. 2002–03): Institutional Aid, Need-Based: $20,490,212. Institutional Aid, Non-Need-Based: $2,340,381. FT Undergrads Receiving Aid: 68%. Avg. Amount per Student: $21,837. FT Undergrads Receiving Non-Need-Based Gift Aid: 9%. Avg. Amount per Student: $8,051. Of Those Receiving Any Aid: Receiving Need-Based Gift Aid: 98%. Avg. Award: $17,136. Receiving Need-Based Self-Help Aid: 91%. Avg. Award: $5,494. Financial Aid Deadline: rolling; 2/15 (priority).

University of the South

735 University Avenue, Sewanee, TN 37383-1000. Admissions Phone: (800) 522-2234; (931) 598-1238. Email: admiss@sewanee.edu. Website: www.sewanee.edu. Application Website: app.applyyourself.com/?id=uots-u. Costs (2003–04): Tuition and Fees: $24,135. Sewanee Education Access Loan (SEAL). Room & Board: $6,720. Payment Plan(s): installment plan. Institutional Aid (est. 2002–03): Institutional Aid, Need-Based: $6,451,958. Institutional Aid, Non-Need-

Based: $1,097,335. FT Undergrads Receiving Aid: 40%. Avg. Amount per Student: $21,067. FT Undergrads Receiving Non-Need-Based Gift Aid: 9%. Avg. Amount per Student: $6,165. Of Those Receiving Any Aid: Receiving Need-Based Gift Aid: 100%. Avg. Award: $15,289. Receiving Need-Based Self-Help Aid: 83%. Avg. Award: $4,028. Upon Graduation, Avg. Loan Debt per Student: $12,134. Financial Aid Deadline: 3/1 (priority).

University of Utah

201 South 1460 East Room 250 S, Salt Lake City, UT 84112-9057. Admissions Phone: (801) 581-7281. Fax: (801) 585-7864. Email: undergraduate@sa.utah.edu. Website: www.utah.edu. Application Website: www.acs.utah.edu/admissions/. Costs (est. 2003-04): Tuition and Fees, In-State: $3,650. Tuition and Fees, Out-of-State: $11,296. Room & Board: $5,036. Payment Plan(s): installment plan. Institutional Aid (est. 2002–03): Institutional Aid, Need-Based: $140,000. Institutional Aid, Non-Need-Based: $35,000. FT Undergrads Receiving Aid: 36%. Avg. Amount per Student: $6,310. FT Undergrads Receiving Non-Need-Based Gift Aid: 2%. Avg. Amount per Student: $2,562. Of Those Receiving Any Aid: Receiving Need-Based Gift Aid: 85%. Avg. Award: $3,714. Receiving Need-Based Self-Help Aid: 67%. Avg. Award: $4,687. Upon Graduation, Avg. Loan Debt per Student: $12,300. Financial Aid Deadline: rolling; 3/15 (priority).

University of Vermont

194 S. Prospect Street, Burlington, VT 05401. Admissions Phone: (802) 656-3370. Fax: (802) 656-8611. Email: admissions@uvm.edu. Website: www.uvm.edu. Costs (2002–03): Tuition and Fees, In-State: $8,994. Tuition and Fees, Out-of-State: $21,484. Room & Board: $6,378. Payment Plan(s): installment plan. Institutional Aid (2001–02): Institutional Aid, Need-Based: $22,641,721. Institutional Aid, Non-Need-Based: $1,956,447. FT Undergrads Receiving Aid: 50%. Avg. Amount per Student: $12,867. FT Undergrads Receiving Non-Need-Based Gift Aid: 11%. Avg. Amount per Student: $3,035. Of Those Receiving Any Aid: Receiving Need-Based Gift Aid: 91%. Avg. Award: $8,858. Receiving Need-Based Self-Help Aid: 84%. Avg. Award: $5,604. Upon Graduation,

Avg. Loan Debt per Student: $22,425.
Financial Aid Deadline: 3/15, 2/10
(priority).

University of Virginia

P.O. Box 400160, Charlottesville, VA 22904-4160. **Admissions Phone:** (434) 982-3200.
Fax: (434) 924-3587. **Email:**
undergradadmission@virginia.edu.
Website: www.Virginia.EDU. **Application
Website:** http://www.virginia.edu/
undergradadmission/. **Costs (2002–03):**
Tuition and Fees, In-State: $4,980. Tuition
and Fees, Out-of-State: $20,190. **Room &
Board:** $5,231. **Payment Plan(s):**
installment plan. **Institutional Aid (est.
2002–03):** Institutional Aid, Need-Based:
$11,553,813. Institutional Aid, Non-Need-
Based: $1,712,250. FT Undergrads
Receiving Aid: 21%. Avg. Amount per
Student: $11,462. FT Undergrads
Receiving Non-Need-Based Gift Aid: 18%.
Avg. Amount per Student: $5,383. Of
Those Receiving Any Aid: Receiving Need-
Based Gift Aid: 82%. Avg. Award: $9,374.
Receiving Need-Based Self-Help Aid: 73%.
Avg. Award: $3,903. **Upon Graduation,
Avg. Loan Debt per Student:** $13,536.
Financial Aid Deadline: 3/1 (priority).

University of Washington

1410 NE Campus Parkway, 320 Schmitz
Box 355840, Seattle, WA 98195. **Admissions
Phone:** (206) 543-9686. **Fax:** (206) 685-
3655. **Email:** askuwadm@u.washington.
edu. **Website:** www.washington.edu.
Application Website: www.applyweb.
com/aw. **Costs (2002–03):** Tuition and
Fees, In-State: $4,636. Tuition and Fees,
Out-of-State: $15,337. **Room & Board:**
$8,430. **Payment Plan(s):** installment plan,
deferred payment plan. **Institutional Aid
(est. 2002–03):** Institutional Aid, Need-
Based: $6,840,600. Institutional Aid, Non-
Need-Based: $3,476,000. FT Undergrads
Receiving Aid: 40%. Avg. Amount per
Student: $9,784. FT Undergrads Receiving
Non-Need-Based Gift Aid: 5%. Avg.
Amount per Student: $2,290. Of Those
Receiving Any Aid: Receiving Need-Based
Gift Aid: 67%. Avg. Award: $6,909.
Receiving Need-Based Self-Help Aid: 85%.
Avg. Award: $4,736. **Upon Graduation,
Avg. Loan Debt per Student:** $14,500.
Financial Aid Deadline: 2/28 (priority).

University of Wisconsin—Madison

Armory and Gymnasium, 716 Langdon
Street, Madison, WI 53706-1481.
Admissions Phone: (608) 262-3961. **Fax:**
(608) 262-7706. **Email:**
onwisconsin@admissions.wisc.edu.
Website: www.wisc.edu. **Application
Website:** www.apply.wisconsin.edu. **Costs
(est. 2003-04):** Tuition and Fees, In-State:
$4,840. Tuition and Fees, Out-of-State:
$20,240. **Room & Board:** $6,130.
Institutional Aid (2001–02): Institutional
Aid, Need-Based: $2,225,930. Institutional
Aid, Non-Need-Based: $5,753,461. FT
Undergrads Receiving Aid: 28%. Avg.
Amount per Student: $2,124. FT
Undergrads Receiving Non-Need-Based
Gift Aid: 15%. Avg. Amount per Student:
$2,472. Of Those Receiving Any Aid:
Receiving Need-Based Gift Aid: 40%. Avg.
Award: $5,549. Receiving Need-Based Self-
Help Aid: 85%. Avg. Award: $4,672. **Upon
Graduation, Avg. Loan Debt per Student:**
$15,904. **Financial Aid Deadline:** rolling.

University of Wisconsin—Stevens Point

Student Services Center, Stevens Point, WI
54481. **Admissions Phone:** (715) 346-2441.
Fax: (715) 346-3296. **Email:**
admiss@uwsp.edu. **Website:** uwsp.edu.
Application Website:
http://apply.wisconsin.edu. **Costs
(2002–03):** Tuition and Fees, In-State:
$3,631. Tuition and Fees, Out-of-State:
$13,677. Minnesota Reciprocity. **Room &
Board:** $3,816. **Payment Plan(s):**
installment plan. **Institutional Aid
(2001–02):** Institutional Aid, Need-Based:
$185,535. Institutional Aid, Non-Need-
Based: $601,783. FT Undergrads Receiving
Aid: 42%. Avg. Amount per Student:
$5,816. FT Undergrads Receiving Non-
Need-Based Gift Aid: 7%. Avg. Amount per
Student: $1,397. Of Those Receiving Any
Aid: Receiving Need-Based Gift Aid: 54%.
Avg. Award: $3,793. Receiving Need-Based
Self-Help Aid: 93%. Avg. Award: $4,048.
**Upon Graduation, Avg. Loan Debt per
Student:** $13,396. **Financial Aid Deadline:**
rolling; 3/15 (priority).

University of Wyoming

P.O. Box 3434, Laramie, WY 82071.
Admissions Phone: (307) 766-5160; (800)
342-5996. **Fax:** (307) 766-4042. **Email:**
Why-Wyo@uwyo.edu. **Website:**
www.uwyo.edu. **Application Website:**

http://siswww.uwyo.edu/adm/. **Costs
(2002–03):** Tuition and Fees, In-State:
$2,997. Tuition and Fees, Out-of-State:
$8,661. Regional or 'good neighbor' tuition
available. **Room & Board:** $5,120. **Payment
Plan(s):** installment plan. **Institutional Aid
(2001–02):** Institutional Aid, Need-Based:
$265,152. Institutional Aid, Non-Need-
Based: $2,386,364. FT Undergrads
Receiving Aid: 47%. Avg. Amount per
Student: $7,467. FT Undergrads Receiving
Non-Need-Based Gift Aid: 39%. Avg.
Amount per Student: $3,421. Of Those
Receiving Any Aid: Receiving Need-Based
Gift Aid: 39%. Avg. Award: $4,030.
Receiving Need-Based Self-Help Aid: 89%.
Avg. Award: $1,115. **Upon Graduation,
Avg. Loan Debt per Student:** $18,311.
Financial Aid Deadline: rolling; 2/1
(priority).

Ursinus College

P.O. Box 1000, Collegeville, PA 19426-1000.
Admissions Phone: (610) 409-3200. **Fax:**
(610) 489-3662. **Email:**
admissions@ursinus.edu. **Website:**
http://www.ursinus.edu. **Application
Website:** www.applyweb.com/ursinus.
Costs (2003–04): Tuition and Fees:
$27,500. **Room & Board:** $6,900. **Payment
Plan(s):** installment plan. **Institutional Aid
(est. 2002–03):** Institutional Aid, Need-
Based: $15,487,500. Institutional Aid, Non-
Need-Based: $2,012,500. FT Undergrads
Receiving Aid: 96%. Avg. Amount per
Student: $21,981. FT Undergrads
Receiving Non-Need-Based Gift Aid: 5%.
Avg. Amount per Student: $8,000. Of
Those Receiving Any Aid: Receiving Need-
Based Gift Aid: 90%. Avg. Award: $15,485.
Receiving Need-Based Self-Help Aid:
100%. Avg. Award: $6,496. **Upon
Graduation, Avg. Loan Debt per Student:**
$20,000. **Financial Aid Deadline:** 2/15.

Valparaiso University

Kretzmann Hall, 1700 Chapel Drive,
Valparaiso, IN 46383-6493. **Admissions
Phone:** (219) 464-5011; (888) 468-2576.
Fax: (219) 464-6898. **Email:**
undergrad.admissions@valpo.edu. **Website:**
www.valpo.edu. **Costs (2002–03):** Tuition
and Fees: $19,632 (soph., jr., and sr.
engineering students pay $640 fee). **Room
& Board:** $5,130. **Payment Plan(s):**
installment plan, deferred payment plan.
Institutional Aid (est. 2002–03):
Institutional Aid, Need-Based:
$13,768,000. Institutional Aid, Non-Need-
Based: $5,689,500. FT Undergrads
Receiving Aid: 64%. Avg. Amount per

Student: $16,448. FT Undergrads Receiving Non-Need-Based Gift Aid: 27%. Avg. Amount per Student: $8,024. Of Those Receiving Any Aid: Receiving Need-Based Gift Aid: 99%. Avg. Award: $12,100. Receiving Need-Based Self-Help Aid: 93%. Avg. Award: $4,700. Upon Graduation, Avg. Loan Debt per Student: $19,418. Financial Aid Deadline: 3/1 (priority).

Vanderbilt University

2305 West End Avenue, Nashville, TN 37203. Admissions Phone: (615) 322-2561; (800) 288-0432. Fax: (615) 343-7765. Email: admissions@vanderbilt.edu. Website: www.vanderbilt.edu. Application Website: www.vanderbilt.edu/Admissions/apply.html. Costs (2003–04): Tuition and Fees: $27,087. Room & Board: $9,060. Institutional Aid (est. 2002–03): Institutional Aid, Need-Based: $44,381,811. Institutional Aid, Non-Need-Based: $12,574,084. FT Undergrads Receiving Aid: 42%. Avg. Amount per Student: $27,981. FT Undergrads Receiving Non-Need-Based Gift Aid: 16%. Avg. Amount per Student: $15,798. Of Those Receiving Any Aid: Receiving Need-Based Gift Aid: 87%. Avg. Award: $17,876. Receiving Need-Based Self-Help Aid: 77%. Avg. Award: $8,159. Upon Graduation, Avg. Loan Debt per Student: $24,023. Financial Aid Deadline: 2/1 (priority).

Vassar College

Box 10, 124 Raymond Ave, Poughkeepsie, NY 12604. Admissions Phone: (914) 437-7300; (800) 827-7270. Fax: (914) 437-7063. Email: admissions@vassar.edu. Website: vassar.edu. Costs (2002–03): Tuition and Fees: $27,960. Room & Board: $7,340. Payment Plan(s): installment plan. Institutional Aid (2001–02): Institutional Aid, Need-Based: $20,787,098. FT Undergrads Receiving Aid: 53%. Avg. Amount per Student: $23,655. FT Undergrads Receiving Non-Need-Based Gift Aid: 1%. Avg. Amount per Student: $3,201. Of Those Receiving Any Aid: Receiving Need-Based Gift Aid: 98%. Avg. Award: $18,466. Receiving Need-Based Self-Help Aid: 100%. Avg. Award: $5,247. Upon Graduation, Avg. Loan Debt per Student: $17,170. Financial Aid Deadline: 2/1.

Villanova University

800 Lancaster Avenue, Villanova, PA 19085. Admissions Phone: (610) 519-4000. Fax: (610) 519-6450. Email: gotovu@villanova.edu. Website: www.villanova.edu. Application Website: www.admission.villanova.edu. Costs (2002–03): Tuition and Fees: $24,090. Room & Board: $8,330. (tuition, room and board vary). Payment Plan(s): installment plan. Institutional Aid (2001–02): Institutional Aid, Need-Based: $23,622,031. Institutional Aid, Non-Need-Based: $7,649,485. FT Undergrads Receiving Aid: 47%. Avg. Amount per Student: $17,641. FT Undergrads Receiving Non-Need-Based Gift Aid: 13%. Avg. Amount per Student: $7,399. Of Those Receiving Any Aid: Receiving Need-Based Gift Aid: 89%. Avg. Award: $23,719. Receiving Need-Based Self-Help Aid: 84%. Avg. Award: $5,591. Upon Graduation, Avg. Loan Debt per Student: $28,217. Financial Aid Deadline: 2/15.

Virginia Polytechnic Institute and State University

201 Burruss Hall, Blacksburg, VA 24061. Admissions Phone: (540) 231-6267. Fax: (540) 231-3242. Email: vtadmiss@vt.edu. Website: www.vt.edu. Application Website: www.admiss.vt.edu/apply.html. Costs (2002–03): Tuition and Fees, In-State: $4,736. Tuition and Fees, Out-of-State: $14,352. Room & Board: $4,070. Payment Plan(s): installment plan. Institutional Aid (est. 2001–02): Institutional Aid, Need-Based: $8,349,417. FT Undergrads Receiving Aid: 59%. Avg. Amount per Student: $7,124. FT Undergrads Receiving Non-Need-Based Gift Aid: 28%. Avg. Amount per Student: $4,244. Of Those Receiving Any Aid: Receiving Need-Based Gift Aid: 58%. Avg. Award: $4,606. Receiving Need-Based Self-Help Aid: 71%. Avg. Award: $4,422. Upon Graduation, Avg. Loan Debt per Student: $17,219. Financial Aid Deadline: 3/1, 2/25 (priority).

Wabash College

P.O. Box 352, Crawfordsville, IN 47933-0352. Admissions Phone: (800) 345-5385; (765) 361-6225. Fax: (765) 361-6437. Email: admissions@wabash.edu. Website: www.wabash.edu. Application Website: www.wabash.edu/admissions/apply/. Costs (2002–03): Tuition and Fees: $20,205. Room & Board: $6,397. Payment Plan(s): installment plan, deferred payment plan, pre-payment plan. Institutional Aid (est. 2002–03): Institutional Aid, Need-Based: $6,028,633. Institutional Aid, Non-Need-

Based: $3,152,777. FT Undergrads Receiving Aid: 68%. Avg. Amount per Student: $18,585. FT Undergrads Receiving Non-Need-Based Gift Aid: 28%. Avg. Amount per Student: $10,572. Of Those Receiving Any Aid: Receiving Need-Based Gift Aid: 99%. Avg. Award: $14,127. Receiving Need-Based Self-Help Aid: 83%. Avg. Award: $4,052. Upon Graduation, Avg. Loan Debt per Student: $14,969. Financial Aid Deadline: 3/1, 2/15 (priority).

Wagner College

One Campus Road, Staten Island, NY 10301. Admissions Phone: (718) 390-3411; (800) 221-1010 (out-of-state). Fax: (718) 390-3105. Email: admissions@wagner.edu. Website: www.wagner.edu. Costs (2003–04): Tuition and Fees: $22,600. Room & Board: $7,300. Payment Plan(s): installment plan. Institutional Aid (est. 2002–03): Institutional Aid, Need-Based: $6,932,805. Institutional Aid, Non-Need-Based: $3,246,673. FT Undergrads Receiving Aid: 60%. Avg. Amount per Student: $14,245. FT Undergrads Receiving Non-Need-Based Gift Aid: 23%. Avg. Amount per Student: $7,428. Of Those Receiving Any Aid: Receiving Need-Based Gift Aid: 99%. Avg. Award: $10,533. Receiving Need-Based Self-Help Aid: 96%. Avg. Award: $3,961. Upon Graduation, Avg. Loan Debt per Student: $23,994. Financial Aid Deadline: rolling, 2/15 (priority).

Wake Forest University

P.O. Box 7305 Reynolda Station, Winston-Salem, NC 27109-7305. Admissions Phone: (336) 758-5201. Fax: (336) 758-4324. Email: admissions@wfu.edu. Website: wfu.edu. Application Website: wfu.edu/admissions/online-app/introduction.html. Costs (2002–03): Tuition and Fees: $24,750. Room & Board: $7,190. Payment Plan(s): installment plan, pre-payment plan. Institutional Aid (2001–02): Institutional Aid, Need-Based: $11,604,439. Institutional Aid, Non-Need-Based: $5,140,363. FT Undergrads Receiving Aid: 32%. Avg. Amount per Student: $19,394. FT Undergrads Receiving Non-Need-Based Gift Aid: 32%. Avg. Amount per Student: $8,641. Of Those Receiving Any Aid: Receiving Need-Based Gift Aid: 94%. Avg. Award: $14,883. Receiving Need-Based Self-Help Aid: 82%. Avg. Award: $6,520. Upon Graduation, Avg. Loan Debt per Student: $24,769. Financial Aid Deadline: 2/1.

Warren Wilson College

P.O. Box 9000, Asheville, NC 28815-9000. Admissions Phone: (800) 934-3536. Fax: (828) 298-1440. Email: admit@warren-wilson.edu. Website: www.warren-wilson.edu. Costs (2003–04): Tuition and Fees: $16,674. Room & Board: $5,120. Payment Plan(s): installment plan. Institutional Aid (est. 2002–03): Institutional Aid, Need-Based: $2,041,920. Institutional Aid, Non-Need-Based: $326,150. FT Undergrads Receiving Aid: 54%. Avg. Amount per Student: $12,374. FT Undergrads Receiving Non-Need-Based Gift Aid: 20%. Avg. Amount per Student: $3,496. Of Those Receiving Any Aid: Receiving Need-Based Gift Aid: 90%. Avg. Award: $7,038. Receiving Need-Based Self-Help Aid: 100%. Avg. Award: $5,132. Upon Graduation, Avg. Loan Debt per Student: $16,142. Financial Aid Deadline: 4/1 (priority).

Washington and Lee University

Letcher Avenue, Lexington, VA 24450-0303. Admissions Phone: (540) 458-8710. Fax: (540) 458-8062. Email: admissions@wlu.edu. Website: www.wlu.edu. Application Website: www.commonapp.org. Costs (2002–03): Tuition and Fees: $21,175. Room & Board: $5,913. Payment Plan(s): deferred payment plan. Institutional Aid (2001–02): Institutional Aid, Need-Based: $5,331,854. Institutional Aid, Non-Need-Based: $3,175,651. FT Undergrads Receiving Aid: 27%. Avg. Amount per Student: $16,928. FT Undergrads Receiving Non-Need-Based Gift Aid: 22%. Avg. Amount per Student: $8,162. Of Those Receiving Any Aid: Receiving Need-Based Gift Aid: 72%. Avg. Award: $14,773. Receiving Need-Based Self-Help Aid: 45%. Avg. Award: $4,900. Upon Graduation, Avg. Loan Debt per Student: $15,634. Financial Aid Deadline: 2/1 (priority).

Washington University in St. Louis

Campus Box 1089, One Brookings Drive, St. Louis, MO 63130-4899. Admissions Phone: (800) 638-0700; (314) 935-6000. Fax: (314) 935-4290. Email: admissions@wustl.edu. Website: www.wustl.edu. Application Website: http://admissions.wustl.edu. Costs (2003–04): Tuition and Fees: $29,053. Room & Board: $9,240. Payment Plan(s):

installment plan, pre-payment plan. Institutional Aid (est. 2002–03): Institutional Aid, Need-Based: $40,826,054. Institutional Aid, Non-Need-Based: $6,694,252. FT Undergrads Receiving Aid: 45%. Avg. Amount per Student: $22,979. FT Undergrads Receiving Non-Need-Based Gift Aid: 15%. Avg. Amount per Student: $8,672. Of Those Receiving Any Aid: Receiving Need-Based Gift Aid: 98%. Avg. Award: $18,553. Receiving Need-Based Self-Help Aid: 78%. Avg. Award: $6,868. Financial Aid Deadline: 2/15.

Wellesley College

106 Central Street, Wellesley, MA 02481-8203. Admissions Phone: (781) 283-2270. Fax: (781) 283-3678. Email: admission@wellesley.edu. Website: www.wellesley.edu. Application Website: www.wellesly.edu/admission/application.html. Costs (2003–04): Tuition and Fees: $27,904. Room & Board: $8,612. Payment Plan(s): installment plan, pre-payment plan. Institutional Aid (est. 2002–03): Institutional Aid, Need-Based: $21,640,812. FT Undergrads Receiving Aid: 56%. Avg. Amount per Student: $22,614. FT Undergrads Receiving Non-Need-Based Gift Aid: 5%. Avg. Amount per Student: $4,500. Of Those Receiving Any Aid: Receiving Need-Based Gift Aid: 95%. Avg. Award: $19,893. Receiving Need-Based Self-Help Aid: 92%. Avg. Award: $4,180. Upon Graduation, Avg. Loan Debt per Student: $15,697

Wesleyan University

70 Wyllys Avenue, Middletown, CT 06459-0265. Admissions Phone: (860) 685-3000. Fax: (860) 685-3001. Website: http://www.wesleyan.edu. Application Website: http://www.admiss.wesleyan.edu/. Costs (2002–03): Tuition and Fees: $28,320. Room & Board: $7,610. Payment Plan(s): installment plan. Institutional Aid (est. 2002–03): Institutional Aid, Need-Based: $19,592,519. FT Undergrads Receiving Aid: 47%. Avg. Amount per Student: $24,532. Of Those Receiving Any Aid: Receiving Need-Based Gift Aid: 92%. Avg. Award: $17,726. Receiving Need-Based Self-Help Aid: 100%. Avg. Award: $6,806. Upon Graduation, Avg. Loan Debt per Student: $23,753. Financial Aid Deadline: 2/1.

West Virginia University

P.O. Box 6009, Morgantown, WV 26506-6009. Admissions Phone: (304) 293-2121; (800) 344-9881. Fax: (304) 293-3080. Email: wvuadmissions@arc.wvu.edu. Website: www.wvu.edu. Application Website: www.arc.wvu.edu/admissions/applications.html. Costs (2002–03): Tuition and Fees, In-State: $3,240. Tuition and Fees, Out-of-State: $9,710. Room & Board: $5,572. Institutional Aid (est. 2002–03): Institutional Aid, Need-Based: $2,113,859. Institutional Aid, Non-Need-Based: $3,925,737. FT Undergrads Receiving Aid: 46%. Avg. Amount per Student: $7,125. FT Undergrads Receiving Non-Need-Based Gift Aid: 37%. Avg. Amount per Student: $3,157. Of Those Receiving Any Aid: Receiving Need-Based Gift Aid: 68%. Avg. Award: $3,306. Receiving Need-Based Self-Help Aid: 91%. Avg. Award: $4,161. Upon Graduation, Avg. Loan Debt per Student: $19,186. Financial Aid Deadline: 3/1, 2/15 (priority).

Wheaton College

501 College Avenue, Wheaton, IL 60187-5593. Admissions Phone: (630) 752-5005; (800) 222-2419. Fax: (630) 752-5285. Email: admissions@wheaton.edu. Website: www.wheaton.edu. Costs (2003–04): Tuition and Fees: $18,500. Room & Board: $6,100. Payment Plan(s): installment plan. Institutional Aid (est. 2002–03): Institutional Aid, Need-Based: $8,384,750. Institutional Aid, Non-Need-Based: $978,913. FT Undergrads Receiving Aid: 46%. Avg. Amount per Student: $14,830. FT Undergrads Receiving Non-Need-Based Gift Aid: 20%. Avg. Amount per Student: $4,398. Of Those Receiving Any Aid: Receiving Need-Based Gift Aid: 83%. Avg. Award: $9,875. Receiving Need-Based Self-Help Aid: 89%. Avg. Award: $3,295. Upon Graduation, Avg. Loan Debt per Student: $15,864. Financial Aid Deadline: 2/15 (priority).

Wheaton College

26 East Main Street, Norton, MA 02766. Admissions Phone: (508) 286-8251; (800) 394-6003. Fax: (508) 286-8271. Email: admission@wheatoncollege.edu. Website: www.wheatoncollege.edu. Application Website: www.wheatoncollege.edu/admission/applying.html. Costs (2002–03): Tuition and Fees: $27,330. Room & Board: $7,260. Payment Plan(s): installment plan, pre-payment plan. Institutional Aid (est.

2002–03): Institutional Aid, Need-Based: $11,095,360. Institutional Aid, Non-Need-Based: $1,234,315. FT Undergrads Receiving Aid: 58%. Avg. Amount per Student: $20,390. FT Undergrads Receiving Non-Need-Based Gift Aid: 12%. Avg. Amount per Student: $7,053. Of Those Receiving Any Aid: Receiving Need-Based Gift Aid: 95%. Avg. Award: $15,098. Receiving Need-Based Self-Help Aid: 96%. Avg. Award: $6,243. Upon Graduation, Avg. Loan Debt per Student: $18,348. Financial Aid Deadline: 2/1.

Whitman College

515 Boyer Avenue, Walla Walla, WA 99362-2046. Admissions Phone: (509) 527-5176; (877) 462-9448. Fax: (509) 527-4967. Email: admission@whitman.edu. Website: www.whitman.edu. Costs (2002–03): Tuition and Fees: $24,274. Room & Board: $6,550. Payment Plan(s): installment plan, pre-payment plan. Institutional Aid (est. 2002–03): Institutional Aid, Need-Based: $6,880,000. Institutional Aid, Non-Need-Based: $4,560,000. FT Undergrads Receiving Aid: 43%. Avg. Amount per Student: $17,950. FT Undergrads Receiving Non-Need-Based Gift Aid: 43%. Avg. Amount per Student: $8,000. Of Those Receiving Any Aid: Receiving Need-Based Gift Aid: 100%. Avg. Award: $12,600. Receiving Need-Based Self-Help Aid: 82%. Avg. Award: $5,750. Upon Graduation, Avg. Loan Debt per Student: $15,000. Financial Aid Deadline: 2/1, 11/15 (priority).

Willamette University

900 State Street, Salem, OR 97301-3922. Admissions Phone: (503) 370-6303; (877) 542-2787. Fax: (503) 375-5363. Email: undergrad-admission@willamette.edu. Website: www.willamette.edu. Costs (2002–03): Tuition and Fees: $23,272 ($30 residence hall fee). Room & Board: $6,150. Payment Plan(s): installment plan, pre-payment plan. Institutional Aid (est. 2002–03): Institutional Aid, Need-Based: $13,910,405. Institutional Aid, Non-Need-Based: $5,186,966. FT Undergrads Receiving Aid: 65%. Avg. Amount per Student: $21,886. FT Undergrads Receiving Non-Need-Based Gift Aid: 30%. Avg. Amount per Student: $10,866. Of Those Receiving Any Aid: Receiving Need-Based Gift Aid: 100%. Avg. Award: $16,823. Receiving Need-Based Self-Help Aid: 89%. Avg. Award: $5,064. Upon Graduation, Avg. Loan Debt per Student: $17,660. Financial Aid Deadline: 2/1.

Williams College

P.O. Box 487, Williamstown, MA 01267. Admissions Phone: (413) 597-2211. Fax: (417) 597-4052. Email: admission@williams.edu. Website: www.williams.edu. Costs (2002–03): Tuition and Fees: $26,520. Room & Board: $7,230. Institutional Aid (est. 2002–03): Institutional Aid, Need-Based: $16,614,200. FT Undergrads Receiving Aid: 41%. Avg. Amount per Student: $24,390. FT Undergrads Receiving Non-Need-Based Gift Aid: 2%. Avg. Amount per Student: $3,299. Of Those Receiving Any Aid: Receiving Need-Based Gift Aid: 98%. Avg. Award: $21,813. Receiving Need-Based Self-Help Aid: 82%. Avg. Award: $3,665. Upon Graduation, Avg. Loan Debt per Student: $12,316. Financial Aid Deadline: 2/1.

Wittenberg University

Office of Admission, Springfield, OH 45504. Admissions Phone: (937) 327-6314; (800) 677-7558. Fax: (937) 327-6379. Email: admission@wittenberg.edu. Website: www.wittenberg.edu. Costs (2003–04): Tuition and Fees: $25,098. Room & Board: $6,368. Payment Plan(s): installment plan. Institutional Aid (est. 2002–03): Institutional Aid, Need-Based: $19,400,634. Institutional Aid, Non-Need-Based: $4,953,115. FT Undergrads Receiving Aid: 71%. Avg. Amount per Student: $21,286. FT Undergrads Receiving Non-Need-Based Gift Aid: 17%. Avg. Amount per Student: $8,276. Of Those Receiving Any Aid: Receiving Need-Based Gift Aid: 100%. Avg. Award: $15,646. Receiving Need-Based Self-Help Aid: 94%. Avg. Award: $3,551. Upon Graduation, Avg. Loan Debt per Student: $18,623. Financial Aid Deadline: 3/15 (priority).

Wofford College

429 North Church Street, Spartanburg, SC 29303-3663. Admissions Phone: (864) 597-4130. Fax: (864) 597-4147. Email: admissions@wofford.edu. Website: www.wofford.edu. Costs (2002–03): Tuition and Fees: $19,415. Room & Board: $5,780. Payment Plan(s): installment plan. Institutional Aid (est. 2002–03): Institutional Aid, Need-Based: $6,734,749. Institutional Aid, Non-Need-Based: $4,500,837. FT Undergrads Receiving Aid: 54%. Avg. Amount per Student: $15,796. FT Undergrads Receiving Non-Need-Based Gift Aid: 34%. Avg. Amount per Student: $10,905. Of Those Receiving Any Aid: Receiving Need-Based Gift Aid: 99%. Avg.

Award: $13,674. Receiving Need-Based Self-Help Aid: 54%. Avg. Award: $4,212. Upon Graduation, Avg. Loan Debt per Student: $12,470. Financial Aid Deadline: rolling; 3/15 (priority).

Xavier University

1 Drexel Drive, New Orleans, LA 70125-1098. Admissions Phone: (877) 928-4378; (504) 483-7388. Fax: (504) 485-7941. Email: apply@xula.edu. Website: www.xula.edu. Application Website: http://www.xula.edu/admissions.html. Costs (2002–03): Tuition and Fees: $10,900. Room & Board: $6,000. Payment Plan(s): installment plan, deferred payment plan, pre-payment plan. Institutional Aid (est. 2002–03): Institutional Aid, Non-Need-Based: $5,121,139. FT Undergrads Receiving Aid: 79%. Avg. Amount per Student: $9,091. FT Undergrads Receiving Non-Need-Based Gift Aid: 5%. Avg. Amount per Student: $5,106. Of Those Receiving Any Aid: Receiving Need-Based Gift Aid: 63%. Avg. Award: $3,722. Receiving Need-Based Self-Help Aid: 99%. Avg. Award: $4,089. Upon Graduation, Avg. Loan Debt per Student: $3,426. Financial Aid Deadline: 1/1 (priority).

Yale University*

38 Hillhouse Avenue, New Haven, CT 06520. Admissions Phone: (203) 432-9300. Fax: (203) 432-9392. Website: www.yale.edu. Costs (2002–03): Tuition and Fees: $27,130. Room & Board: $8,240. Institutional Aid: FT Undergrads Receiving Aid: 40%. Avg. Amount per Student: $23,480. Of Those Receiving Any Aid: Receiving Need-Based Gift Aid: 92%. Avg. Award: $17,430. Receiving Need-Based Self-Help Aid: 95%. Avg. Award: $6,326. Upon Graduation, Avg. Loan Debt per Student: $17,473. Financial Aid Deadline: 5\1.

Yeshiva University*

500 West 185th Street, New York, NY 10033-3201. Admissions Phone: (212) 960-5277. Fax: (212) 960-0086. Email: yuadmit@ymail.yu.edu. Website: www.yu.edu. Costs (2002–03): Tuition and Fees: $20,500. Room & Board: $6,550.

Index

How Did We Do? Grade Us.

Thank you for choosing a Kaplan book. Your comments and suggestions are very useful to us. Please answer the following questions to assist us in our continued development of high-quality resources to meet your needs.

The title of the Kaplan book I read was: _____

My name is: _____

My address is: _____

_____

My e-mail address is: _____

What overall grade would you give this book?   (A)   (B)   (C)   (D)   (F)

How relevant was the information to your goals?   (A)   (B)   (C)   (D)   (F)

How comprehensive was the information in this book?   (A)   (B)   (C)   (D)   (F)

How accurate was the information in this book?   (A)   (B)   (C)   (D)   (F)

How easy was the book to use?   (A)   (B)   (C)   (D)   (F)

How appealing was the book's design?   (A)   (B)   (C)   (D)   (F)

What were the book's strong points? _____

How could this book be improved? _____

Is there anything that we left out that you wanted to know more about?

Would you recommend this book to others?   ☐ YES   ☐ NO

Other comments: _____

_____

_____

Do we have permission to quote you?   ☐ YES   ☐ NO

Thank you for your help.
Please tear out this page and mail it to:

Managing Editor
Kaplan, Inc.
1440 Broadway, 8th floor
New York, NY 10018

KAPLAN®

Thanks!

Curious about what college is really like?

College students weigh in on:
- **Dorms and roommates**
- **The social scene**
- **Writing papers and studying for exams**
- **What professors and teacher's assistants really want**

Also available from Trent and Seppy:
- The Unofficial, Unbiased Guide to the 328 Most Interesting Colleges

Coming in December 2003:
- Broke! A College Student's Guide to Getting By on Less

Published by Simon & Schuster

Available wherever books are sold.

Want a High Score on the SAT?

We've got a guide for every student need.